blue
rider
press

THIS TOWN

THIS TOWN

Two Parties and a Funeral—Plus Plenty of
Valet Parking!—in America's Gilded Capital

MARK LEIBOVICH

BLUE RIDER PRESS
A MEMBER OF PENGUIN GROUP (USA) INC.
NEW YORK

blue
rider
press

Published by the Penguin Group
Penguin Group (USA) Inc., 375 Hudson Street,
New York, New York 10014, USA

USA · Canada · UK · Ireland · Australia
New Zealand · India · South Africa · China

Penguin Books Ltd, Registered Offices:
80 Strand, London WC2R 0RL, England
For more information about the Penguin Group visit penguin.com

Library of Congress Cataloging-in-Publication Data

Leibovich, Mark.
This town : two parties and a funeral—plus plenty of valet
parking!—in America's gilded capital / Mark Leibovich.
p.   cm.
ISBN 978-0-399-16130-8
1. Political culture—Washington (D.C.)   2. Politicians—United States.
3. United States—Politics and government.   I. Title.
JK1726.L45   2013   2013009796
306.209753—dc23

Printed in the United States of America
1   3   5   7   9   10   8   6   4   2

BOOK DESIGN BY AMANDA DEWEY
FRONTISPIECE © GLOBE TURNER / GETTY IMAGES

To my family

THIS TOWN

Prologue

June 2008

Tim Russert is dead. But the room was alive.

You can't work it too hard at a memorial service, obviously. It's the kind of thing people notice. But the big-ticket Washington departure rite can be such a great networking opportunity. You can almost feel the ardor behind the solemn faces: lucky stampedes of power mourners, about two thousand of them, wearing out the red-carpeted aisles of the Kennedy Center.

Before the service, people keep rushing down the left-hand aisle to get to Robert Gibbs, the journeyman campaign spokesman who struck gold with the right patron, Barack Obama, soon to be the first African-American nominee of a major party. If Obama gets elected, Gibbs is in line to be the White House press secretary. Gibbs is the son of librarians, two of the 10 percent of white Alabamans who will support Obama in November. "Bobby," as he was known back home, hated to read as a child and grew up to be a talker, now an increasingly hot one.

He keeps getting approached in airports and on the street for his autograph. He is a destination for a populace trained to view human interaction through the prism of "How can this person be helpful to me?" Gibbs has become potentially whoppingly helpful. People seek out and congratulate him for his success and that of his candidate, especially at tribal gatherings like this, a grand send-off for the host of *Meet the Press*.

Next to Gibbs presides another beneficial destination: David Axelrod, a Democratic media consultant and kibitzing walrus of a mensch who orchestrated Obama's run to the 2008 Democratic nomination. Known as "Axe," Axelrod is a sentimental RFK Democrat whose swoon over Obama is unrivaled even by Gibbs's. (Gibbs once called Axe "the guy who walks in front of Obama with rose petals.") Noting the big run on Gibbs and Axelrod, a columnist for Politico told me they were the new "it guys" at the service, and of course they were, in part for devising a communications strategy predicated on indifference to this very onrushing club of D.C.'s Leading Thinkers.

Joe Scarborough and Mika Brzezinski are mobbed as well; they can barely get to their seats: assaulted with kudos for the success of *Morning Joe*, their dawn roundtable on MSNBC and a popular artery in the bloodstream of the Leading Thinkers. People keep pressing business cards into the cohosts' palms, eager to get themselves booked, or their clients booked, or their books mentioned, just once, by Joe or Mika. "A new low, even for Washington tackiness," Mika will lament of the funereal hustle. But it's important to be part of the conversation, anyone would understand. You seize your moment when it comes.

Bill and Hillary Clinton walk stiffly down the left aisle. Heads lurch and the collective effects are unmistakable: that exotic D.C. tingle falls over the room, the kind that comes with proximity to Superpowers. Bill and Hill. They are given wide berth. It had been a tough stretch. Hillary has just conceded the Democratic nomination. It ended an epic primary saga in which Bill had disgraced himself, making unpresidential and maybe racially loaded remarks about Obama. Neither Clinton is in a particularly good "place" with Washington at the moment, or with the media, or with the Democratic Party—or, for that matter, maybe with each other.

Bill's top post–White House aide, Doug Band, is keeping a list on his BlackBerry of all the people who screwed over the Clintons in the campaign and who are now, as they say, "dead to us." Some of them dead are here at the Kennedy Center. There is a running joke inside Clinton World about all the bad things happening to the Clinton crossers. Ted Kennedy, who pivotally endorsed Obama in January, is now dying from a brain tumor. (After Kennedy's endorsement, which came months before the tumor was discovered, his colleague Lindsey Graham asked Kennedy if he could inherit his Senate hideaway office. Why? "Because the Clintons are gonna kill you," Graham joked.) John Edwards, who also endorsed Obama, was busted for cheating on his dying wife; his disgrace is now in full spiral. The state of Iowa, whose Democratic voters slapped a humiliating third-place finish on Hillary in January's caucuses, was devastated by biblical floods in the spring.

Now, true to her stoic and gritty precedent, Hillary is keeping her smile affixed like hardened gum and sending out powerful "Stay away from this vehicle" vibes. Ignoring the vibes, an eager producer for MSNBC's *Countdown* beelines toward her, introduces herself to the Almighty, and prepares to launch a Hail Mary "ask" about whether the senator might possibly want to come on *Countdown* that night.

"It is a *pleasure* to meet you," Clinton responds to the eager producer, while the smile stays tight and she keeps right on walking. Hillary has a memorial service to attend: the memorial service of a man she and her husband plainly despised and who they believed (rightly) despised them back.

But the Clintons are pros at death and sickness. They show up. They play their assigned roles. They send nice notes and lend comfort to the bereaved in that warm and open-faced Clinton way. They are here with empathetic eyes to pay respects, like heads of Mafia families do when a rival godfather falls. Washington memorial services have that quality when the various personality cults convene: Bill and Hillary walking a few feet away from Newt and Callista Gingrich and right past David Shuster, the MSNBC host who has just been suspended by the network for saying the Clinton campaign "pimped out" Chelsea by having her call superdelegates. (Shuster has been barely heard from since. To reiterate: Don't mess with the Clintons!) Bill and Hill, who appear not to have reserved seats, find two several rows back next to Madeleine Albright, the former secretary of state, and Condoleezza Rice, the current one.

Not far from the Gibbs and Axe receiving line, NBC's Andrea Mitchell walks in with her husband, the conservative monetary oracle and former Federal Reserve chairman Alan Greenspan. One of the most dogged reporters in the city, Andrea adores her work and her friends, but mostly adores Alan. He is a prime Washington Leading Thinker who even when being blamed by many for running the economy off a cliff can always be seen on Andrea's arm doing his courtly old dignitary thing at D.C. social events. If Washington was a comic book—and it sort of is—Greenspan would be in the background of every panel.

A few rows from Alan and Andrea sits Barbara Walters, the luminary TV interviewer and Chairman Greenspan's former girlfriend. Back when Alan and Andrea were first dating, during the George H. W. Bush administration, they attended a dinner to honor Queen Elizabeth at the British embassy. In the presidential receiving line, Bush introduced Andrea to the queen. "Your Majesty, this is one of our premier American journalists," the president said, then turned to Mitchell and said, "Hello, *Barbara*." Bush sent a personal note of apology to Andrea the next day.

At the memorial service, Barbara sat over near Ken Duberstein, a vintage Washington character in his own right, who did a brief stint as the White House chief of staff during the checked-out final months of Ronald Reagan's second term. Duberstein and Mitchell are old friends. Jews by religion and local royalty by acclamation, they once shared a memorable *erev* Yom Kippur—the holiest night on the Jewish calendar—at a most sacred of Official Washington shrines: the McLean, Virginia, mansion of Prince Bandar bin Sultan, Saudi Arabia's ambassador to the United States, and his wife, Haifa. Dick and Lynne Cheney were also there. It was such a coveted social function. Andrea and Ken felt pangs of Jewish guilt but ultimately could not say no to this most holy of obligations. "In the end, we both decided that the Lord and our parents would somehow understand," Andrea later explained in her book, *Talking Back*.

Now a lobbyist, Duberstein has been riding the D.C. carousel for years, his Rolodex flipping with billable connections. He is an archetypical "former." That is, a former officeholder who can easily score a seven-figure income as an out-of-office wise man, pundit, statesman, or, if you would be so crass (and a true statesman never would be), hired gun. "Formers" stick to Washington like melted cheese on a gold-plated toaster.

Duberstein is often referred to in these words: "It isn't exactly clear what Kenny does." You know you've made it in D.C. when someone says that—"It isn't clear what he does"—about you. Such people used to have an air of mystery about them. You assumed they did something exotic, like work for the CIA. Now you might assume the Kuwaiti government or someone is paying them a gusher to do something not terribly virtuous. They would prefer not to discuss their work, if you don't mind, and you have to respect their discretion. Ambiguity pays well here.

Duberstein is a regular at Ben Bradlee and Sally Quinn's and talks constantly on the phone to his close friend Colin Powell, and even more constantly to everyone else about what "Colin was just telling me." Like most formers, Duberstein sits on many boards and loves to read his name in print or pixel—except, God forbid, if someone identifies him as a mere "former Reagan administration official," not Reagan's "former chief of staff," in which case he will feel denied his full former bona fides and often complain. The standard line on Duberstein is that he spent six and a half months as Reagan's chief of staff and twenty-four years (and counting) dining out on it.

As John McCain was securing the Republican nomination, Duberstein made inquiries about running his theoretical transition team, according to several campaign aides. That would be a perfect assignment for someone of Duberstein's ilk, someone with an intuitive sense of who all the GOP usual suspects to populate an incoming administration will be. Duberstein denies ever lobbying for the transition job, but the McCain team was not interested in his services anyway, and eventually Duberstein wound up endorsing Obama, just after Colin did.

Duberstein keeps shaking hands and waving and looking mid-sentence over your glistening head to see who else is in the vicinity. He wears a big welcoming smile, which he relaxes, at the appropriate time, into an expression of grave distress over the loss of Timothy John Russert.

The ceremonies began this morning, June 18, first the funeral proper at the church in Georgetown, then the public memorial at the Kennedy Center. They are sweet, sober, and starstruck services that give Russert his full due and, more important, affirm everyone— by their presence—as worthy in the pecking order.

"All of the most important people in politics and media are in the same room," the columnist Anne Schroeder Mullins will later write in Politico, the emerging company-town organ for Political Washington, or "This Town," as people here refer to the place, with bemused faux disgust and a wry distance—a verbal tic as secret handshake. "And if you're there, too," Schroeder Mullins concludes, "you're a player among them." When you read that, it is impossible not to feel reassured at this precarious moment.

The showing today testifies to the man who died, Russert, the bold-faced impresario of the longest-running show on television and the most powerful unelected figure in the country's most powerful, prosperous, and disappointing city. A buoyant part of This Town was being put to rest today, an era interred with him at Rock Creek Cemetery after President George W. Bush and First Lady Laura spent forty-five minutes with the family at St. Albans for the wake.

And the gathering is itself testament to The Club, that spinning cabal of "people in politics and media" and the supporting sectors that never get voted out or term-limited or, God forbid, decide on their own that it is time to return home to the farm. The Club can be as potent in D.C. as Congress, its members harder to shed than ten-term incumbents. They are, in effect, the city fathers of This Town. They are not one-dimensional and are certainly not bad people. They come with varied backgrounds, intentions, and, in many cases—maybe most cases—for the right reasons. As they become entrenched, maybe their hearts get a bit muddled and their motives too. Not always: people are complicated, here as everywhere, and sometimes even conflicted (enough sometimes to see therapists, though we don't discuss that here, don't want to scare the vetters). But their membership in The Club becomes paramount and defining. They become part of a system that rewards, more than anything, self-perpetuation.

When seen together at tribal events like this one at the Kennedy Center, the members of The Club nourish the idea that the nation's main actors talk to the same twelve people every day. They can evoke a time-warped sense of a political herd that never dies or gets older, only jowlier, richer, and more heavily made-up. Real or posed, these insiders have always been here—either these people literally or as a broader "establishment." But they are more of a swarm now: bigger, shinier, online, and working it all that much harder.

While so much of the nation has despised Washington, a gold rush has enthralled the place. It has, in recent years, become a crucible of easy wealth, fame, forgiveness, and next acts. Punditry has replaced reporting as journalism's highest calling, accompanied by a mad dash of "self-branding," to borrow a term that had now fully infested the city: everyone now hell-bent on branding themselves in the marketplace, like Cheetos (Russert was the local Coca-Cola). They gather, all the brands, at these self-reverential festivals, like the April White House Correspondents' Association dinner, whose buffet of "pre-parties" and "after-parties" now numbers more than two dozen—because a single banquet, it is clear, cannot properly celebrate the full achievements of the People Who Run Your Country.

The insider swarm has been known by various names: "Permanent Washington." "The Political Class." "The Chattering Class." "The Usual Suspects." "The Beltway Establishment." "The Echo Chamber." "The Echo-System." "The Gang of 500." "The Gang of 600." "The Movable Mess." "The Club." "This Town."

This Town.

This is the story of This Town in a time of alleged correction. "Change elections" keep convulsing the local order, the pundits say. There was one in 2006; there would be another in 2008 and another in 2010, and probably more in the coming decades. The nation's leaders keep throwing out the word "Washington" as a vulgar abstraction. Nothing new here: the anti-Washington reflex in American politics has been honed for centuries, often by candidates who deride the capital as a swamp, only to settle into the place as if it were a soothing whirlpool bath once they get elected. The city exists to be condemned.

The city has also always enjoyed pockets of wealth, usually of the old-money variety: bankers, railroad barons, and aristocrats from other parts of the United States serving in administrations (and in foreign capitals as ambassadors). Being the seat of the federal government, which isn't moving anywhere, has usually ensured a baseline of economic stability. But in recent years Washington has defied the national economic slump and become the richest metropolitan area in the country. Getting rich has become the great bipartisan ideal: "No Democrats and Republicans in Washington anymore, only millionaires," goes the maxim. The ultimate Green party. You still hear the term "public service" thrown around, but often with irony and full knowledge that "self-service" is now the real insider play.

Likewise, from the late 1990s, This Town was riveted by bigger–than–*West Wing* mega-news: Monica, the 2000 recount, 9/11, and the wars that followed. Politics and Washington became *the* game, perhaps the dominant story of the young century. George W. Bush's Washington was held out as the polestar of the nation's safety and the world's democracy. That cost money, much of it spent here, and they were also fattening up social programs like Medicare while at it. Suddenly it had never been so easy to "monetize" taxpayer-subsidized government service. Then, in 2008, a for-the-ages presidential campaign culminated in a historic election and coincided with a fiscal calamity, at which point This Town was entrusted with saving the nation's economy too. In both administrations, Washington appeared deeply divided by politics, but the fights were sufficiently huge and loud to affirm everyone's hyper-relevance—the reason they pay you (the cable outfits, the corporations, the foreign governments) to explain "how Washington really works." Because *you* are part of This Town, and that in itself is a value proposition, central to the brand.

With the rise of Obama, the more immediate question became, once again: Could Washington really change? Because, rest assured, This Town as we knew it would have no friend in the Democratic nominee. No more lobbyists in the White House, or "politics as usual," or tending to the needy oracles of Beltway groupthink that foster consensus views like Hillary being "inevitable" or America not being ready to elect a black president. What would become of The Club in a Wild West of disjointed megaphones, charismatic insurgents, hope, and resignation?

No matter how disappointed people are in their capital, even the most tuned-in consumers have no idea what the modern cinematic version of This Town really looks like. They might know the boilerplate about "people who have been in Washington too long," how the city is not bipartisan enough and filled with too many creatures of the Beltway. But that misses the running existential contradictions of D.C., a place where "authenticity and fantasy are close companions," as the *Washington Post*'s Henry Allen once wrote. It misses that the city, far from being hopelessly divided, is in fact hopelessly interconnected. It misses the degree to which New Media has democratized the political conversation while accentuating Washington's insular, myopic, and self-loving tendencies. It misses, most of all, a full examination of how Washington may not serve the country well but has in fact worked splendidly for Washington itself—a city of beautifully busy people constantly writing the story of their own lives.

What is my story?

People ask me a lot if I am a member of The Club. I started getting that question, in so many words, when I began writing this book. Yes, I'm guilty. I write about national politics at a big media outlet. I've been in This Town sixteen years, nine spent working for the *Washington Post* and the last seven for the *New York Times*. I have a title, an affiliation, and a business card that seem to impress. People appear to believe I am worth knowing (and I must be, because sometimes I get to go on *Morning Joe*!). I have lots of Washington friends and also some real ones.

People then ask, legitimately, would it be possible to write honestly about The Club from the inside? "Who discovered water?" goes the old Yiddish riddle. "I don't know, but it wasn't a fish." I am a fish. I have chosen to live, work, and raise my family in the murk. This might well be an easier pursuit for a citizen on solid land. But I have no plans to leave. People ask me about that too. Why? It's not like I'm making lobbyist or TV money. I plead reality: my wife and I have built a good life here.

I also plead optimism: If Washington, D.C., is a civic lab rat of the Nation Exaggerated—all good and petty tendencies concentrated into a few monument-bedecked square miles—then we want to believe that what goes on here can be a flattering microcosm, right? It might not be at a given moment or decade, and surveys show an overwhelming majority of Americans judge Washington to be a mortifying perversion of national ideals. But as Barack Obama proved in 2008, hope can be a powerful force, if not necessarily sustainable (as Obama also proved).

And while living in D.C. can encourage cynicism, it can also breed daily wonder. When I drop my daughter off at kindergarten, I watch her and her friends stare out the window at the vice president's motorcade as it sirens past en route to the White House. In the day-to-day, we can all be those kids with noses pressed against the glass. That's how Tom Brokaw described Tim Russert when he first came to Washington from Buffalo as a young aide to Senator Daniel Patrick Moynihan. They are a local archetype, the starstruck operators, arriving new to revivify the city with fresh waves of scared energy and the desire to make it in This Town.

Washington is one of the two or three most popular destinations in the country (along with New York and possibly Los Angeles) for those seeking self-creation, reinvention, and public purpose on a grand and national scale. People work obscenely hard, and they do it despite/because of the baggage they bring. And they do it, in many cases, with a desperation that, to me, is the most compelling part of the Washington story, whether now or before: it is a spinning stew of human need.

I make no claims of immunity. Or—Lord knows!—superiority. I am part of this culture and under no illusion that it cannot reinforce my worst tendencies at times: vanity, opportunism, pettiness— it's all there on the psychic résumé. I struggle with all of it and more. But this is my home and my experience and I write from it willingly.

It is also, of course, a position of privilege. My job allows not only for a prime spot against the glass but also forays behind it to see the momentous and ridiculous up close. I have profiled hundreds of political figures over the years and have spent considerable time in their presence (and who knows why they continue to allow this?). They will often play to caricature—their own and the city's—but they are also human beings who are usually engaged in important work. The entertainment value here can be great but ultimately incidental. Washington is not Hollywood (or "Showbiz for Ugly People" as the dumb cliché goes). The stakes are real and higher.

In the words of Republican senator Tom Coburn of Oklahoma, today's Washington has become a "permanent feudal class," a massive, self-sustaining entity that sucks people in, nurtures addiction to its spoils, and imposes a peculiar psychology on big fish and minnows alike. It can turn complex, gifted, and often damaged individuals into hollowed-out Kabuki players acting in the maintenance of their fragile brands. I have seen this up close, too, often in the most fateful environments, like this, Tim's send-off, the biggest tribal pageant This Town had seen in some time.

You know someone big has died when they play "Amazing Grace" on the bagpipes and interrupt the president with news of the passing: George W. Bush was told of Russert's death while dining in France with President Sarkozy. They have metal detectors at the funeral entrance, because so many high-value targets have come. And many men in the crowd are glowing with Queen Elizabeth levels of Pan-Cake makeup as they are coming straight from their TV stand-ups, or "hits."

"I feel almost like we did when somebody—when Jack Kennedy or even Katharine Graham died," blogged Sally Quinn, a former *Washington Post* reporter who is a Georgetown hostess and the wife of the *Washington Post*'s illustrious former editor, Benjamin Crowninshield Bradlee.

Sally is shattered. But looks fantastic, at almost seventy. So does Ben, even better (nearing ninety). Will the silver-haired BFF to JFK get a send-off like this? Lord knows he will deserve one, but it will hopefully not happen for the longest of whiles. Ben was the Washington alpha journo of his day, with a presidential scalp to end any discussion. He also played the transactional local game as well as anyone. "Did he use me? Of course he used me," Bradlee said of his late friend John F. Kennedy in a 1975 interview. "Did I use him? Of course I used him. Are these the ground rules down here in Washington? Hell, yes." Ben Bradlee is the Man. He is The Club.

Tim Russert was the mayor of it. He was a superb journalist—

not so much in the sense that he wrote or produced stories or un-earthed wrongdoings, but in the sense that he was a guy on TV whom everyone knew, who asked the "tough but fairs" of important newsmakers and did so in a way that was distinctive and combative and made for good TV. If you were a politician of serious ambition, an invitation to his set was your rite of passage and your proving ground. "It was like you were being knighted," Bradlee said of get-ting on the show. "All of a sudden you went up a couple of ranks in their class." And then, when the program was done, everyone would rate your performance.

Russert became more famous than most of the people he inter-viewed. After a while in Washington, the fame itself becomes the paramount commonality between the parties. You are a com-modity, Someone on TV, with an agent and a chief of staff. (Even Chelsea Clinton has a chief of staff now!) You start using "impact" as a verb.

After a while, the distinctions between the clans all run together—the journalists, the Democrats, the Republicans, the su-perlawyers, the superlobbyists, the superstaffers, the supercommit-tees, the David Gergens, the Donna Braziles, and the loser on Facebook who says he'll be on *Headline News* at 2:20 p.m. They run together like the black-tie dinners, or the caricature drawings of no-table Washingtonians on the wall at the Palm on Nineteenth Street. If you're lucky and you stay long enough, you can get your picture taken with some really notable Washingtonians and then show off the photos on your office "Me Wall."

Yes, Russert was the mayor of This Town. To be sure, the "real" city of Washington has an actual elected mayor: black guy, deals with our city problems. But that's just the D.C. where people live, some of them (18.7 percent) even below the poverty line, who drag down the per capita income to a mere $71,011—still higher than any American state but much less than what most anyone at the Russert funeral is pulling down. Yes, Washington is a "real city," but This Town is a state of belonging, a status and a commodity.

Russert was such an intensely present figure, his face filling the whole screen like he was right there in front of you. People would approach him at Reagan National or after one of his paid speeches, where he would tell the same jokes and stories over and over, like a politician does. Non–*Meet the Press*–worthy lawmakers chased him into the men's room, trying to make a charismatically folksy impression. Strangers told him all about their cousins from Buffalo and commended Tim for "holding our leaders accountable" and for being so real, because somebody in Washington had to be *real*. That was Tim's job. Fans would ask him to deliver a message to the president, as if everyone in This Town lived together in the same high-rent group house and bickered over the rent and shared Bob Dole's peanut butter.*

Tim possessed all of the city's coveted big-dog virtues: He was not to be fucked with. He seemed happy and excited and completely confident at all times, and why not? His killer persona combined a Guy's Guy exuberance with gravitas. Tim had a great table at the Palm and drank Rolling Rock from a bottle and ate good, manly food that wasn't drizzled with anything. He testified at the Scooter Libby trial. He had great seats for the Washington Nationals and people asked him to sign their tickets between innings, and maybe Greenspan had signed the ticket before, and James Carville, too, and also Bob Schieffer, all of them together on the same ticket—like a D.C. version of a '52 Mantle baseball card.

Russert, of course, had many friends, which he worked at with a politician's attention to gesture. He would handwrite sympathy and thank-you cards and send baby pillows embroidered with the name of your newborn. He went to spring training every year and

---

* Semi-obscure *Saturday Night Live* reference to Bob Dole's peanut butter.

brought back a Jason Giambi autograph for E. J. Dionne's son. Tim was classy that way. When the former Senate leader Tom Daschle's father died, Tim sent his widow an ensemble of T-shirts, hats, and a jacket bearing the *Meet the Press* logo. Mrs. Daschle could be seen for years wearing the jacket around Aberdeen, South Dakota.

I probably had about a half-dozen conversations with Russert over the years, usually about sports or politics. Our last in-person encounter was in February of that year, 2008, at a Democratic presidential debate in Cleveland, which he was moderating. He had just finished a workout in the gym of the Ritz-Carlton and was walking through the lobby in a sweaty sweatshirt, long shorts, black loafers, and tube socks. A network spokesman tried to declare the mayor's outfit "off the record," which I of course made a point of mentioning (gratuitously) in a future story in the *New York Times Magazine*.

Before I did, I called Russert to give him a heads-up about this, because nothing is more important in Washington than giving or getting a "heads-up," the better to avoid the intolerable humiliation of being surprised or blindsided by some piece of information. One could argue that an entire boom industry, lobbying, is predicated less on influencing the government than on giving heads-ups to big-paying clients about something that is going to happen whether or not they paid a lobbyist a $50,000-a-month retainer.

Anyway, so I called the mayor to give him a heads-up about how I would not be honoring the flack's off-the-record outfit request. He laughed so hard I had to move the phone away from my ear. "Just do me one favor," he said. "Say they were rubber-soled shoes, will you?"

He laughed again, and we talked briefly on the topic of how so many people in This Town are obsessed with where they rank in the great pecking order. Concern over one's place is hardly original to these times in Washington. But the orgy of new media, news-about-news, and the rolling carnival of political moneymaking and celebrity has only exacerbated This Town's default vanity.

"You can drive yourself crazy if you worry too much about that stuff," the mayor said, with the self-assurance of a man solidly atop the pig pile and comfortable in his shoes.

Then, three months later: "Did you hear about Tim Russert?"

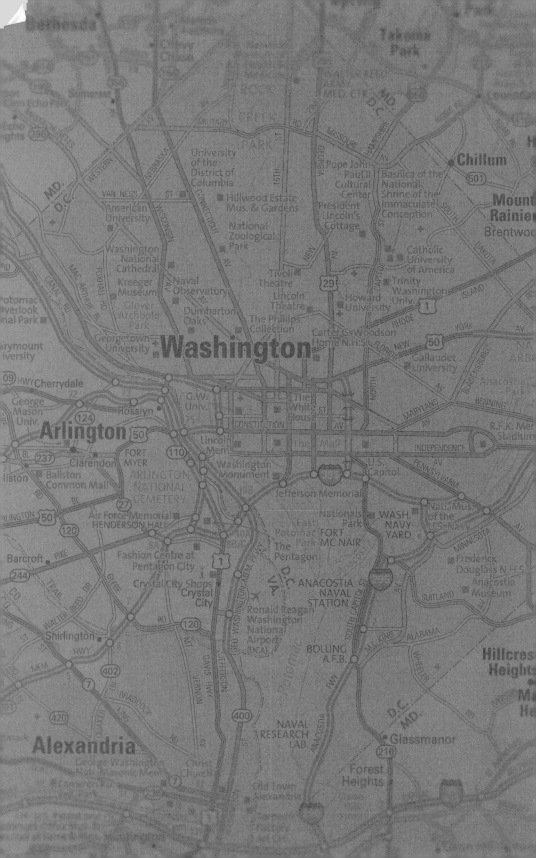

Heaven's Green Room

Apparently cholesterol plaque ruptured one of Russert's arteries. It caused a sudden coronary thrombosis. He was in an audio-tracking booth at NBC's Washington bureau recording voice-overs for that Sunday's show when he collapsed. The EMTs defibrillated but could not resuscitate. He was pronounced dead at Sibley Memorial Hospital.

Russert had just returned from Italy. He had been celebrating his son Luke's college graduation and had recently placed his eighty-four-year-old father into an assisted-living home in Buffalo. Tim had struggled with his weight and was looking tired, and his many pals had been worrying about the stress he was under. He had suffered from asymptomatic coronary artery disease, which he treated with medication and exercise. He did well on a stress test seven weeks earlier, on April 29. Tom Brokaw promised him a Chuck Berry album if he lost ten pounds by that summer's political conventions. "What's happening?" were Russert's last words, a greeting to the person on the other end of the audio feed. The autopsy showed an enlarged heart. Flags were ordered at half-staff by the mayor of Buffalo.

"He will be missed as he was loved, greatly," said Brokaw, announcing the death live on NBC.

Russert—"Tim"—reached the top of the pecking order while shrouding a cutthroat ambition in his slovenly nonchalance. While a focused and surgical ambition is vital to success in D.C., the ability to be appropriately sheepish about it is more so. Russert had a nice, easy populism about him—just a guy out of Buffalo who cherished his country, loved his dad and his son and his Bills and his T-shirts and all that. "Rumpled" is always good for the brand here, and Tim had that nailed.

He was also acutely status-conscious. Known primarily as a TV star, he preferred to identify himself by his more hierarchical title, "Washington bureau chief." (Russert told a *Washington Post* reporter in 1991 that he wanted to be president of NBC News.) Brokaw once asked if he ever considered entering the priesthood. Yes, he said.

"Cardinal?" Brokaw asked.

No, Russert said. "Pope."

That was a joke but Tim had just seen the pope a few days earlier, when in Rome. He sat up front for the weekly prayer service, and then His Holiness (the pope, that is) had to leave.

Tim liked his seat in the corporate boardroom and his large home in Nantucket, "The House That Jack Built," as the sign outside identified the Nantucket house—Jack being Jack Welch, the longtime CEO of NBC's corporate parent, General Electric. Russert and Brokaw attended Ronald Reagan's funeral as guests, and then walked outside the Washington National Cathedral to anchor the news coverage for NBC.

Tim lived in the sweet spot of the big, lucrative revolving door between money, media, and politics. He also died there. Every wannabe, is, and has-been in Washington was issuing statements. "We will never see his likes again," "He touched so many lives," etc. Big distinctions were bestowed—"the preeminent political journalist of his generation," John McCain said. "One of the finest men I knew," Obama said. Small kindnesses were recalled. "When my mom died, he sent two dozen roses," said Ann Klenk, a producer at MSNBC. "I adored him."

He was indeed adored—in that unmistakable vintage of Washington "adored" that incorporated fear and need and sucking up. You needed to be on *Meet the Press* to be bestowed with a top-line standing in what Joan Didion called "that handful of insiders who invent, year in and year out, the narrative of public life." You needed to be friends with Tim, the closer the better, as so many people advertised with deft turns of posthumous networking. People on TV jockeyed to outgrieve one another. Network and cable channels paid tribute with their favorite homage: overkill. This was particularly true on NBC, and doubly particularly true on its little cable sister, MSNBC, which Russert—in life—was always wary of spending too much time on, for fear of slumming away his mayoral status in the high-numbered channels.

"He called me 'Mitch,'" NBC's Andrea Mitchell said on MSNBC. Same thing her father called her. "Go get 'em, K.O.," Tim used to say to MSNBC's Kelly O'Donnell. Keith Olbermann said Tim had said the exact same thing to him ("Go get 'em, K.O.").

"'Pal, go get 'em,'" Matt Lauer said, choking up as he relayed what Tim used to tell him before he conducted big interviews. Lauer went on to assure viewers that Russert was now sitting up in "heaven's green room." And really, who would doubt for a second that God's place of eternal reward did not precisely mimic the layout of a network television studio?

. . .

No one was bigger than Tim within the celebrity-industrial complex that had exploded at the nexus of politics and media in the late twentieth and early twenty-first centuries. Russert was a product of both: a star aide to Daniel Patrick Moynihan, the late senator from New York, and later to former New York governor Mario Cuomo. He went into television and quickly shot to the top there too. There have always been Famous for Washington types, a term that captures both the distinction of being a big deal in the capital and the provincialism that makes Famous for Washington such a lame compliment. Russert was not so much Famous for Washington or even a "talent." He was a full-on "principal," the D.C. usage for elected behemoths and cabinet secretaries—the Main Bitch. The Mother Eagle.

No one was better attuned than Russert to the cultural erogenous zones of powerful men. He spoke endlessly and nostalgically about dads and sons and sports and Springsteen. He gave on-air shout-outs to Joe DiMaggio, who never missed a *Meet the Press*. He was expert at the male bonding rituals that lubricate so many chummy capital relations. George W. Bush quizzed him in the Oval Office on the starting lineup of the '61 Yankees, while Al Gore won a dinner of Buffalo wings from him in a football bet. Like Dubya, Tim addressed people with thrown-off locker room nicknames ("Tommy B" Brokaw, "Matty" Lauer). He brought a contagious enthusiasm for the politics-as-football sensibility that defined the modern boy's game. The ethos conveyed to and evolved with the next generation of boys. It has been embodied by Politico, the testosteroned website that aims to gorge political junkies like ESPN does sports fans.

Tim had become so entrenched in the electronic political scenery that it was slightly jarring to actually see his face in front of you, in person. Ted Kennedy had the same effect. When you saw him around town, it was like seeing a guy wearing a Ted Kennedy mask. Or maybe a Ted Kennedy float in the Macy's Thanksgiving Day parade, the pageant that D.C. can resemble in certain settings. Everyone is their own float, their own inflated balloon, some bigger than others, some leading the parade, others trailing.

Chris Matthews, whose verbal filtering deficiency makes him a refreshing oddity in this overfiltered environment, was particularly fragile about his place in the parade, especially in relation to Russert. In an interview with *Playboy* years earlier, Matthews volunteered that he had made the list of the top fifty journalists in D.C. in *Washingtonian* magazine. "I'm like 36th, and Tim Russert is No. 1," Matthews said. "I would argue for a higher position for myself." That spring, Matthews had received his twenty-second honorary degree from an institution of higher learning—that's compared with forty-eight for Tim at the time of his death, in case someone (like Chris) was keeping track.

But today in Washington is for Tim, the leading balloon lost, leaving everyone so ostentatiously deflated. He is given great due: Barack Obama and John McCain sitting together at the request of the Russert family, who want the event to provide a spectacle of unity. It is a time to pause and tolerate one last bipartisan moment, or pose, before the presumptive nominees embark on their big general election adventures, each vowing to shake things up, like they always do. It is a moment to honor a great man and a great country, to stand jointly and upright and to partake of a comforting tribal event for permanent Washington. Obama and McCain share a hug at the end.

David Axelrod met Mark Salter, his counterpart on the McCain campaign, for the first time at the service. "The two of us are going to have our moments," Axelrod said to Salter, McCain's longtime chief of staff and most passionate defender. "But I love my guy and you love your guy and I respect that." Salter proffered an earnest wish that the upcoming campaign would be worthy of the country, and of Tim.

Russert would have loved the outpouring from the power mourners. And he also would have understood better than everyone that all of the speeches and tributes and telegenic choke-ups were never, not for a second, about him. They were about people left behind to scrape their way up the pecking order in his absence.

The morning begins at Holy Trinity Catholic Church in Georgetown in a procession of Town Cars and shapely haircuts and somber airs. One after another, the holy trinity of pols, People on TV, and permanent Washington types arrives. Obama is missing a meeting with the national intelligence director. Sally Quinn, an avowed atheist for much of her life, takes Communion, which "made me feel closer to him," she will later blog. Liz Moynihan, Daniel Patrick's widow, declines Communion, on the other hand, saying she is "angry at God."

"Senator Kennedy on the left!" the excited soundman calls out. "Oh . . . no," he corrects himself, "it's Al Hunt." The actual Vicki Kennedy is here. The wife of Ted, who is battling cancer. She is amazing and courageous. People wish her the best, tell her they've been thinking of her and assure Vicki that "Teddy is a fighter and will beat this thing." The Kennedys loved Tim and vice versa. After Teddy was diagnosed, Russert sent Vicki a set of rosary beads, blessed specially by the pope. "These have gotten me through some very tough times," Tim wrote, and after Tim died, the Kennedys sent the beads back to the Russert family, who placed them in Tim's casket.

"John McCain, pulling up," the soundman says. The soon-to-be GOP nominee pops out of a limo. He is in a period of transition from disruptive figure (beloved within This Town as a balm to the everyday bullshit) to a more cautious and smartly saluting standard-bearer of the party he once tormented. I last saw McCain on his campaign plane a few months earlier, just before he was fitted with his nominee's straitjacket. He volunteered to me that Brooke Buchanan, his spokeswoman seated nearby, "has a lot of her money hidden in the Cayman Islands" and that she earned it by "dealing drugs." She was also "Pat Buchanan's illegitimate daughter," "bipolar," "a drunk," "someone with a lot of boyfriends" and who was "just out of Betty Ford." Everyone misses this man.

For the likes of McCain, the ritual of watching *Meet the Press* on Sunday was like attending Mass—and actually going on the show was like a First Communion. But now the high priest was gone and there was no heir apparent.

McCain greets a few well-barbered and golf-tanned colleagues and makes his way to his seat next to Obama. He waves in the general direction of Mitchell and Greenspan; McCain proposed the latter as an overseer of a panel that would simplify the tax code. "If he's dead or alive, it doesn't matter," McCain said of the then eighty-one-year-old Greenspan. "Prop him up and put some dark glasses on him, like *Weekend at Bernie's*." Senator Charles Schumer, the New York Democrat, walks slowly into the church and adheres to the distinctive code of posture at the fancy-pants funeral: head bowed, conspicuously biting his lips, squinting extra hard for the full telegenic grief effect. People carry themselves in a certain way when they know they are being watched, or think they are being watched, or sure hope they are being watched. But funerals, in Washington, offer a particular theater for projection. "Legacies" are a preoccupation here with people of a certain stature. "We're all obituaries waiting to happen," Henry Allen, my former *Post* colleague, once wrote. "At the same time, the city of Washington feels like a conspiracy we're all in together, and nobody else in America quite understands, even though they pay for it."

Schumer nods over at a bank of cameras outside Holy Trinity. He is so lens-happy, even by senatorial standards, that Jon Corzine, a former senator and governor of New Jersey, once compared the futility of sharing a media market with Schumer to sharing a banana with a monkey. "Take a little bite of it and he will throw his own feces at you," Corzine lamented in a speech at the National Press Club—thankfully not a dinner speech.

Schumer is joined in an extended cluster at the entrance by his senate colleagues, Christopher Dodd and Joe Biden, both of whom ran unsuccessfully for president earlier in the year and are carrying rosary beads into the church. Biden, who was scheduled to be a guest on *Meet the Press* on the Sunday after Russert died, will eventually win the lottery and be picked by Obama as his running mate. As he enters Holy Trinity, Biden offers a thumbs-ups to the celebrity-watchers who have assembled to watch This Town bid their humble host a premium farewell.

You couldn't miss the Italian shoes and tailored suits in the audience, the glitter handbags, antique cuff-links, and three-figure haircuts on the men in makeup. Luke Russert looks around the church from the podium as he reads his father's favorite biblical passage: "To whom much is given, much is expected," Luke says, then flashes a wry smile and continues. "And after seeing the make of some of the suits and dresses in the room, a lot is expected from this crowd."

Saadalla Mohamed Aly, the longtime green room "attendant" at *Meet the Press*, is devastated by Tim's death. He could not make the funeral because he is traveling in Egypt at the time, but of course he sends his respects.

For many years, "Mr. Aly" served up a gourmet smorgasbord of eggs, salmon, fresh fruits, juices, and breakfast meats to the elite class that passed through the *Meet* green room. He is "family" at the show, the "perennially tuxedoed butler," as the *Washington Post* later describes him. Tom Friedman speaks Arabic to him.

"In a Washington way," James Carville will say in the *Post* after Aly's death in early 2011, "he was kind of a friend."

In a Washington way. Kind of a friend. Everyone party-chatting in the same feedback loop and telling the same green room stories and reading the same morning e-mail tip sheet in Politico, Mike Allen's Playbook.

Russert had a favorite joke about growing up in South Buffalo, where everyone knew one another and one another's relatives. "How many South Buffalonians does it take to change a lightbulb?" the joke went. "I don't know exactly, but my neighbor's cousin's girlfriend's priest knows a guy who will help you out."

He could have been talking about his own invitation-only "public" memorial service: the Kennedy Center concert hall becomes a palatial ant colony. At first glance, it might seem a random mass of busy critters, but a closer gaze reveals distinct patterns, people jitterbugging toward strategic destinations, working.

I watch Duberstein move through the Kennedy Center waving, shaking hands with everyone. He then greets the attractive blonde seated next to me: Susanna Quinn, the third and much younger wife of Democratic lobbyist Jack Quinn. Jack Quinn, who in 2000 founded the bipartisan lobbying powerhouse Quinn Gillespie & Associates with Republican Ed Gillespie, was the general counsel to President Clinton in the pre-Monica years. Russert had always been a sweetheart to Jack, especially after Quinn spent serious time "in the barrel," as Quinn says, referring to a period of disgrace he endured after successfully petitioning his former boss President Clinton to issue a last-minute pardon for his client, the fugitive financier Marc Rich. Jack was ostracized in the press and shunned by his former Clinton friends and hauled before Congress; as a result, he retreated into "a very dark place personally," he says. Quinn battled depression and alcoholism. His lobbying partner, Gillespie, stood by him. He reassured him that after a few months all anyone would remember about Jack Quinn's little scandal was that he "got something big done." And it would be good for business. He would always have lunch in This Town again.

Sure enough, Quinn Gillespie boomed with the rest of the lobbying sector and Jack and Ed cashed out in 2004 for a sum that eventually reached $40 million. Few people remember Marc Rich, let alone who his attorney was, or what Jack Quinn was even in the barrel for. Only that he's a rich lobbyist who has nice fund-raisers at his house in Northwest D.C. and sweet parties and a decent golf game that merited a Politico video feature. And that he is married to the lovely Susanna, an emerging socialite, granddaughter of a Democratic senator from Oklahoma, and an old family friend of Duberstein's, who helped get her into his alma mater, Franklin & Marshall. And she looks phenomenal in a bikini, by the way, as everyone knows from her Facebook page.

As Duberstein greeted Jack at the Kennedy Center, in bounded Terry McAuliffe, the former Democratic National Committee chairman, known as "the Macker." McAuliffe loved the back-and-forth with Tim on camera and off. He would invoke Tim's expertly branded dad, "Big Russ," a retired sanitation worker in Buffalo and the hero of Tim's bestselling book, *Big Russ and Me*, one of two sentimental volumes Tim devoted to the glories of uncomplicated fifties-era dads. McAuliffe made several appearances on *Meet the Press*. Like many guests, he tried to ingratiate himself to the host by mentioning Big Russ on the air. Once, he imagined Big Russ to be "up in heaven" and "probably having a Scotch, looking down." Russert gently pointed out to him that Big Russ was in fact still alive, up in Buffalo, probably watching the show at that very moment from his Barcalounger.

McAuliffe made his mark as one of the most irrepressible money men in American political history, or better. "The greatest fund-raiser in the history of the universe," Al Gore dubbed him. You can be the most detestable person in the world—and the Macker is not, for the record—but you would still be assured of having thousands of elegant friends by being a good fund-raiser. So committed is the Macker to his art that he even stopped off at a fund-raiser on the way home from the hospital with his wife, Dorothy, after she gave birth to their newborn son, Peter. Dorothy stayed in the car, crying, while the baby slept and the Macker did his thing. "I felt bad for Dorothy," he would later write. "But it was a million bucks for the Democratic Party."

If McAuliffe's signature is fund-raising, his principal identity is as a professional best friend to Bill Clinton. The title of McAuliffe's memoir *What a Party!* might as well be *Let Me Tell You Another Story About Me and Bill Clinton.* (One such story involved South Korean intelligence agents thinking McAuliffe and Clinton were *more than just friends.*) To deprive McAuliffe of the words "Bill Clinton" would be like depriving a mathematician of numbers. If he is not dropping the name of the forty-second president, he is telling you that he just got off the phone with him, or that President Clinton is actually calling now, and can you please excuse him just for a second? ("Hello, Mr. President!") And if Mr. President is not on the phone, there is a good chance he is somewhere close by.

Sure enough, as McAuliffe makes his way down the left-hand aisle, Bill and Hillary are a few yards away. Russert was a longtime Clinton nemesis dating to Russert's former patron, Daniel Patrick Moynihan, who had been chairman of the Senate Finance Committee during the Clinton years. Moynihan felt slighted that the Clintons did not seek his collaboration on their ill-fated health-care bill in 1993. The Clintons always believed Russert was much tougher on Hillary than on her opponents. They are convinced Russert disliked them and were not wrong. He thought the Clintons were "phonies," he told many people privately. And the Monica thing—in the OVAL OFFICE!!! Jesus, don't get him started.

Tim's crowning smack against them, the Clintons believed, occurred on the May evening that Obama defeated Hillary in the North Carolina primary and came close in Indiana. "We now know who the Democratic nominee will be," declared Russert of Obama on the air, definitively, with the kind of live-TV authority that few possessed. The Macker paid Tim a visit at the office soon after. They went back and forth, agreed to disagree, and laughed quite a bit, like they always did.

The Kennedy Center memorial service is broadcast live on MSNBC, complete with pregame and postgame. Luminary speakers, polished remarks, Brokaw hoisting a Rolling Rock at the lectern, and Bruce Springsteen materializing via satellite from Germany. Brian Williams, the NBC News anchor, is given a prime place in the Murderers' Row of celebrity eulogists. The Russert family is, uh, surprised about this, since Williams was never really one of Tim's guys. Nor is the family happy about the presence at the funeral of former NBC president Andrew Lack, whom Tim despised, or the degree to which NBC has hijacked the Kennedy Center time as a network branding opp. But such a dance is part of living and dying as public property. They understand that, as Tim must have understood it, and the Russert family will benefit, none more than Luke, who already has his own sports talk show on XM satellite radio with his and Tim's buddy James Carville. Luke's amazing eulogy will effectively launch his television career. He will be hired by NBC soon after—just like McCain's kid, and W's kid, and, eventually, Bill and Hillary's kid. At some point NBC became a full-employment agency for famous political offspring.

But Luke is a special prince, and will eventually be assigned the Capitol Hill beat for MSNBC, where he will become our congressional sage before his twenty-sixth birthday and be auctioned off for charity ("tour of the Capitol and lunch with Luke: current bid $1,050"). He will grow nicely into the family business. But today's service is a star turn for Luke: funny, sentimental, and poised to a point where you could almost hear all of Bethesda and Chevy Chase hissing at their inert teenage/college-age sons, "WHY CAN'T YOU BE MORE LIKE LUKE RUSSERT?"

Tim spoke with bottomless pride about Luke, his only child. They talked every day. For pioneering the joys of fatherhood, Tim was rightly recognized: among other accolades, the National Father's Day Council named him "Father of the Year" in 1995 and *Parents* magazine honored him as "Dream Dad" for 1998.

Washington eats up the dad conceit. Unusually high proportions of ambitious men—and potential male book buyers—love to self-mythologize through their fathers. John Edwards was "the son of a mill worker," John Boehner "the son of a barkeeper," etc. The prevailing social dynamic in Washington—a city of patrons—mimics the quest for paternal love. "Who do you work for?" is typically the first thing people ask here.

Russert, who described Moynihan as his "intellectual father," died just before Father's Day, at the dawn of a general election campaign that featured two presumptive nominees, Obama and McCain, whose sagas were steeped in fraught paternal legacies. Obama's memoir was titled *Dreams from My Father*, while McCain's was *Faith of My Fathers*. "A man's either trying to make up for his father's mistakes or live up to his expectations," Obama told *Newsweek*'s Jon Meacham that summer.

"My dad was my best friend," eulogizes Luke, twenty-two. "To explain my bond with my father is utterly impossible to put into words."

And then the white screen rolls down and Springsteen enters via satellite. Like Bruce, Tim deftly made himself a spokesman for America. He was "the Boss" of the nostalgic male playgrounds he presided over in the nation's capital. "Luke, this is for your pop," Springsteen says, leading into an acoustic version of "Thunder Road."

As I walk out, I get a big hug from Tammy Haddad, a veteran cable producer who repurposed herself in recent years as a professional party host, event organizer, and full-service convener of the Washington A-list. Haddad, a towering in-your-face presence with black hair bisected by a white streak, is a human ladle in the local self-celebration buffet. She tells you how great you are, how you really need to meet the author, or cohost, or honoree, or whoever, and that by the way, *she just talked to Justice Breyer!* "Over the Rainbow" plays as Tammy and I and the rest of The Club schmooze our way up to the Kennedy Center roof for an actual cocktail party.

And there, glowing over the Potomac and the monuments: a double rainbow, surely a message from heaven's green room to the power mourners, now sipping Heinekens and white wine. Everyone says so. "Is anyone still an atheist now?" Luke asks, according to Tammy, who will write a blog post later about the "Russert Miracles."

Or: an opposing viewpoint on the rainbow from the since-departed atheist Christopher Hitchens, writing in Slate: "No benign deity plucks television news show hosts from their desks in the prime of life and then hastily compensates their friends and family by displays of irradiated droplets in the sky."

God could not be reached for comment. But let us at least agree that He is quite obviously attuned to the doings of politics and media. That is why so many would-be leaders say they are being "called upon" to run for president, and why eulogists lean so heavily on the trope that God runs an HR department that recruits people like Sunday hosts and yachtsmen into heaven. When Andy Rooney died a few years later, the CBS anchor Scott Pelley compared Rooney to Cicero and Dickens and certified that "apparently, God needed a writer." (Apparently CBS did not, because Rooney had been pushed out a month earlier.)

And God just loves Washington; of that we are certain. His presence is indeed potent at the Kennedy Center, although everyone keeps looking around for someone more important to talk to.

Tammy can't stop talking about the Russert rainbow. It makes for an enthralling, powerful, and stagnant spectacle—that same wonderland feel that can make Washington's monuments seem like a stage set. Is it real or papier-mâché? Or maybe God meant the rainbow to resemble an NBC peacock—a celestial branding play. Whatever, it all fits the "narrative" of a momentous time. It is no longer enough just to follow the unsexy business of governance in the seat of power. No more boring and stodgy in This Town. Vintage square rooms have given way to light-headed news cycles and public servants have graduated into killer personal franchises. The Washington story has become something more momentous, befitting a "narrative": a pumped-up word in a pumped-up place where everything is changing, maybe more than in any city in the country, in line with the hopeful imperative of the next president.

Or maybe nothing is changing at all, and the only certainty is that the city fathers of This Town will endure like perennials in a well-tended cemetery.

2

•••••••••••••••

Suck-up City

The founding fathers, whose infinite wisdom gave
us a Constitution and form of government well nigh
perfect, located the seat of that government in a
stinking, steaming swamp.

JACK LAIT AND LEE MORTIMER,
Washington Confidential

September 2008–January 2009

t was a time of hope and rebirth, except that the economy was cratering. That was a problem, and for the media too. I ran into Andrea Mitchell at the October 2008 debate in St. Louis between opposing running mates Joe Biden and Sarah Palin. Andrea was in the midst of a rough moment because a lot of people were blaming her husband, Alan Greenspan, for the financial collapse. His free-market, Ayn Rand–influenced policies while running the Federal Reserve were not looking good now. His image had been "tarnished," said the *Wall Street Journal*. Not only that, but some of those uptight media-ethics types, at places like the *Columbia Journalism Review*, were "raising fundamental questions" about how Mitchell could possibly cover the major story of the day for NBC without running up against questions of Greenspan's culpability and legacy.

Mitchell says she has always been a stickler for avoiding conflicts of interest. But in Alan and Andrea's rarefied and interconnected realm, that was like an owl trying to avoid trees. She was a model citizen of This Town. A Club officer. The administrations and campaigns that Mitchell covered overlapped considerably with her social and personal habitat. In her 2005 memoir, Andrea described her 1997 wedding to Alan, officiated by Justice Ruth Bader Ginsburg at the Inn at Little Washington. "Our friend Oscar de la Renta designed my dress," Andrea said. There was no honeymoon because she and Alan both had to work, and besides, they had a state dinner to attend two nights later, "our first as a married couple," Andrea pointed out. "Although the dinner was in honor of the prime minister of Canada, it felt as though we were still celebrating our marriage."

Once, as part of the White House press pool, Mitchell encountered Bill Clinton's Treasury secretary, Lloyd Bentsen, outside the Oval Office—and was embarrassed when Bentsen thanked her and Alan for hosting him and his wife for dinner the night before ("Oh, Andrea, I was gonna write you a note, we had such a good time last night," Bentsen said). There were weekend getaways to the home of George Shultz, others with Gerald and Betty Ford, and another to visit Liz and Pat Moynihan. There was the memorable dinner in Virginia with Al and Tipper Gore, back when they were still married, and that great surprise fiftieth-birthday bash for Condi Rice at the home of the British ambassador.

Mitchell's main coverage area has been national security and foreign affairs. This generally kept her clear from the monetary and economic policies over which her husband held enormous sway for decades. But not always, and of course, the politics and politicians of

Washington are never so neatly compartmentalized. Mitchell also hosted a midday show on MSNBC, which focused broadly on the politics and, obviously, the captivating campaign in progress. Citizens of This Town—including many inside NBC—had wondered for years how Mitchell could possibly navigate the big Washington gray areas between the demands of friendship and journalism, and what constituted a social and professional setting. "She knows where to draw the line," NBC News head Steve Capus told the *New York Times* in response to "questions being raised."

Still, the financial crisis was a special case. It would be like Laura Bush covering the federal government's reaction to Katrina, the *Columbia Journalism Review* wrote. "There is an excessively large elephant in the [NBC] control room," the magazine added. "Its name is Alan Greenspan."

Speaking of elephants, the Andrea–Alan union called to mind a dictum coined by former *New York Times* editor A. M. Rosenthal: "I don't care if you fuck an elephant," he said, "just so long as you don't cover the circus."

No one covered the circus like Andrea, a fierce, smart, and tenacious journalist and pioneer among women broadcasters in a male-dominated realm. She was also a real-deal reporter in a sector—TV news—that had been increasingly given over to bimbos and blowhards. Girls tell her they want to grow up to be "news anchors," not "journalists." Andrea is a journalist, and no one works harder.

But given the calamity at hand, and the campaign, special accommodations were in order. Mitchell would not be allowed to talk on-air about the causes of the crisis. Only the politics of it. "We see a distinction between pure analysis of the bailout—such as the conditions that led to the crisis, which we've decided to keep her away from—and coverage of the politics related to it," NBC Washington bureau chief Mark Whitaker said at the time. Andrea was not pleased about the arrangement, she told colleagues, and did not think it was fair. She had always been confident about her ability to draw lines. When there were doubts, she could always hash it out with Tim Russert, and he had always protected her from such nonsense.

Washingtonians love the "So-and-so is spinning in his grave" cliché. Someone is always speculating about how some great dead American would be scandalized over some crime against How It Used to Be. The Founding Fathers are always spinning in their graves over something, as is Ronald Reagan, or FDR. Edward R. Murrow is a perennial grave spinner in the news business (though in fact, Murrow was cremated).

It would be a mark of his impact and legacy that Tim Russert was declared to be spinning in his grave from almost the moment of his interment. Such were the prevalent offenses being visited upon the changing world of the media and politics and in the pecking order he presided over.

When David Gregory was named as Russert's full-time replacement as the host of *Meet the Press*, many people at NBC guessed that Tim would have been displeased given the internal belief that Gregory was overly ambitious, excessively full of himself, and unworthy of "the chair." While the TV news business is rife with jealousy and backbiting, Gregory was a target of particular distrust. After a Democratic debate in Ohio a few months earlier, a lot of national media types were boarding a D.C.-bound flight that included several NBC talking heads—Chris Matthews, Russert, and Mitchell. When someone noted that if the plane crashed, it would devastate the network's talent pool, Matthews quipped that Gregory was at that moment sabotaging the engine. Gregory's true ambition was to host the *Today* show, it was assumed inside the network—assumed widely enough for Matt Lauer, the current host, to joke to an NBC colleague, "If I end up floating dead in the Hudson River, there will be two suspects: my wife and David Gregory."

. . .

Notwithstanding the economy being in the sewer and Tim being in the ground, Barack Obama provided a shot of adrenaline and ignited the hottest local media swoon since Camelot. His critique of Washington—the silliness and smallness of its politics—was powerful for both its eloquence and timeliness. It also incorporated the broader ethic of his campaign, a promise that the Chicago-based enterprise operated on a plane above the cynical sensibilities and petty vanities of the capital. Obama's top lieutenants were extravagant in detailing their contempt for the city, even though many of them had lived in D.C. for decades and were living out of suitcases in Chicago. They boasted that their opponents in the race, first Hillary Clinton and then John McCain, were susceptible to making tactical decisions based on some encounter with a Washington insider they had seen at the market, at a dinner, or on cable. "In part because we were in Chicago and in part because of our approach, we did not do 'cocktail party' interviews," said Dan Pfeiffer, the campaign's communications director, who would hold the same job at the White House. "These are interviews that you agree to because you were always bumping into the reporter at cocktail parties, and they keep asking for the candidate's time. We would laugh every time our opponents would do them."

Staff members were encouraged to ignore new websites like the Page, written by *Time*'s Mark Halperin, and Politico, both of which were widely read by the Washington insider set. "If Politico and Halperin say we're winning, we're losing," Obama's campaign manager, David Plouffe, would repeat around headquarters. His least favorite words in the English language, he said, were "I saw someone on cable say this. . . ."

Obama himself vowed that his administration would steer clear of other corroding Beltway forces, summarized as "the people who've been in Washington too long." This worked, more or less, as a proxy for the kind of usual suspects who would support his opponents. It also carried the implication that Obama's administration would not be susceptible to the capital's Fat City seductions. They would resist the cults of celebrity and personality that affix themselves to the incoming kings of the pecking order. They would operate at a distance from the money culture that could entice them to "monetize their government service," as the clinical term went. Ed Rogers, a former aide to Reagan and the first President Bush who went on to be a top lobbyist, said he tells many prospective hires to go "back to school and get a postgraduate degree." By this he means they should spend a few years working on Capitol Hill or in an executive branch agency to bolster their résumés and earning potential. Left unsaid is that people in high-level positions, including elected officials, will be maintaining their K Street contacts throughout their time in "graduate school."

In a sense, the leaders of the Obama campaign—which included Gibbs, Pfeiffer, and Plouffe—railed against the useful rhetorical meme of Washington rather than the pleasant home and workplace of it. Their campaign was a force for "a politics of unity, hope, and common purpose," said Plouffe, who in particular reserved special disdain for Beltway doomsayers as "bed-wetters," press hordes as "jackals," and the political noise machine as "the cluster-fuck." You could detect in all of the Obamaphiles a smirking grievance of underdogs who had been doubted and who had proved the haters wrong.

But there was a deeper resonance to the critique: a notion that the D.C. models they were running against were governed chiefly by the capital commandments of self-interest, self-importance, self-enrichment, and self-perpetuation. It was, implicitly, a character attack on the kinds of people who engage in the behavior necessary to get ahead in This Town. Obama himself said that politicians came in two types: those who are in the game to make money, and those who are the true public servants. People who worked on the Obama transition staff received a "no ego, no glory" document reminding them that they were volunteers working for the good of the country and should not expect anything (i.e., a job) in return.

"We believe this isn't about us," Gibbs said a few weeks before Obama's inauguration. "It's about something bigger."

From the moment Obama secured the Democratic nomination, he and his staff were subjected to a frantic frenzy of flattery. Serial sucking up is common to any hot political enterprise, but it reached comic levels of desperation in this case. Bill Richardson, who was then the governor of New Mexico and had run unsuccessfully for president earlier in 2008, pulled aside Joe Biden before a campaign event in Mesilla, New Mexico, in October. "Joe, you got to make me secretary of state," Richardson pleaded in an exchange that surprised nearby campaign staffers for how naked—and public—it was.

Obama himself possessed a post-ironic detachment from politics that was true to his personality. Whenever he lapsed into shtick, a behavioral category that incorporated much of what politicians do in public, it was with an implicit nod to the game transpiring. He was playacting, in other words, and he wanted you to know that he knew it.

In early 2005, shortly after his election to the U.S. Senate, I interviewed Obama in his temporary office in the basement of a Senate office building. He and Gibbs were sprawled in identical postures like frat brothers watching football. They were pushing the message that Obama was no prima donna. Obama, they kept reminding me, had already sat through countless town meetings in Illinois and committee hearings on Capitol Hill. *What a trouper he was!* The article I wrote poked gentle fun at Obama for his and Gibbs's zealous efforts to show how unzealous Obama was about climbing the ladder. "Jeez, was it really that obvious?" Obama said to me when I ran into him and Gibbs on Capitol Hill a few weeks later. "Nice going there, Gibbs," Obama said, pretending to smirk.

As I just demonstrated, a favorite flaunt among political insider types is to advertise how far they go back with Obama—maybe to Springfield, Illinois, or (if you're supercool) some Indonesian sandbox. It's a form of currency, or status marker, in the same way that people in Silicon Valley love to talk about how they used to hang out with Sergey Brin back in his Stanford days, before he cofounded Google.

Here is my less-than-awesome offering about when I first met my old pal Barry:

It was when he was a U.S. Senate candidate at the 2004 Democratic Convention in Boston, on the eve of the keynote address that would propel his stardom. Obama's flight had arrived from Springfield at four a.m. and he was awake at six to do *Meet the Press*, then *Face the Nation*, then CNN's *Late Edition*. And now he was being forced to endure a reception hosted by the Congressional Black Caucus on a cruise ship docked in Boston Harbor. People kept coming up to the young state senator, saying how excited they were to hear his speech, how they had donated to his campaign, and whatnot; and Obama, as a mantra, kept telling everyone that he just needed a nap. It was the opposite of those politicians—Bill Clinton—who drew energy from crowds.

Like any deft officeholder/seeker, Obama can nod his head and knit his eyebrows and look interested in almost anything. He can glide from conversation to conversation, room to room, but he will sometimes sigh too audibly and tighten his face in a manner that betrays the look of a man too eagerly en route to forty winks. "I can stagger through receptions with the best of them," he boasted to me before mentioning again that he needed a nap.

Obama appears immune to the neediness that afflicts so many politicians. Any attempt to win his favor through praise was futile, or counterproductive. This air of above-it-all confidence was also evident among Obama's top advisers. They were a cohesive and devoted group who often evinced the temperament of loners. Like Obama, they possessed a quiet sense that the prevailing social lubricants of politics—the sycophancy, the gossip, and the cloying salesmanship—were not just distasteful but pathetic.

In a deeper sense, there was an implicit belief among the Obama people that Washingtonians constituted one of the most insincere collectives in the world. To them, members of The Club were like playactors performing weird pantomimes of the sort no one in, say, Chicago would engage in. The Obama people declared themselves consistently above the "insider Washington" game.

But "insider Washington" is much larger than it used to be, to a point where it becomes inescapable. The elite dinner party salons of Georgetown used to include a revolving class of a few hundred power brokers, wealthy socialites, and current and former members of Congress, cabinets, and White House staffs, along with a smattering of ambassadors and big-shot journalists. Today's insider Washington has become a sprawling "conversation" in which tens of thousands partake by tweet, blog, or whatever. Jail break in the peanut gallery. Standards of local "celebrity" have dropped through the floor. The birthdays of junior Hill staffers are generally given equal weight to the president's in Mike Allen's Playbook. In other words, Washington is a much bigger swirl of mashed potatoes than it ever used to be—and it has never seemed smaller.

In the local literary tradition, such as it is, Washington is said to mimic high school. Meg Greenfield, the longtime editorial page editor of the *Washington Post*, loved and nurtured the notion, as did the *New York Times* columnist Russell Baker and a clique of others. The cliché is apt, to a point. There are plenty of bullies and nerds here. Familiar tableaus, like the floor of the Senate and the White House briefing room, are set up like classrooms. Congress goes out on "recess." It also provides a useful frame for some inescapably high schoolish characters. "No one who has ever passed through American public high school could have watched William Jefferson Clinton running for office in 1992 and failed to recognize the familiar predatory sexuality of the provincial adolescent," Joan Didion wrote in her book of political essays, *Political Fictions*. In a *Rolling Stone* profile of John McCain set during the 2000 presidential campaign, David Foster Wallace described the then maverick Republican as a "varsity jock and a hell-raiser whose talents for partying and getting laid are still spoken of with awe by former classmates." McCain's actual nickname in high school was "Punk."

Eager-to-please crossing-guard types are certainly drawn to Washington in large proportions. Lone wolves don't do as well here as in, say, the market-gaming Wild West of Wall Street or misfit genius labs of Silicon Valley. "Loners may be able to sell themselves electorally at home," Greenfield wrote in her civic memoir, *Washington*. "But they cannot win in Washington, no matter how bad or good they are. Winning here means winning people over—sometimes by argument, sometimes by craft, sometimes by obsequiousness and favors, sometimes by pressure and sometimes by a chest-thumping, ape-type show of strength that makes it seem prudent to get with the ape's program."

But the high school comparison breaks down in the modern version of This Town. For one thing, Washington—like high school—used to be a transient culture. People would expect to graduate eventually or drop out. But almost no one leaves here anymore. Better to stay and monetize a Washington identity in the humming self-perpetuation machine, where people not nearly as good as Tim Russert or the Obama dynamos can make Washington "work for them."

Quaint is the notion of a citizen-politician humbly returning to his farm, store, or medical practice back home after his time in public office is complete. "One thing our founding fathers could not foresee was a nation governed by professional politicians who had a vested interest in getting reelected," Ronald Reagan said in 1973. "They probably envisioned a fellow serving a couple of hitches and then looking forward to getting back to the farm."

Obama often told friends that, like Ronald Reagan, it was important for him to convey a message of a candidate who did not *need* the job of president. He wanted it known that he derived none of the psychic gratification that so many others seek in public life. When he was in the Senate, Obama once instructed a colleague to "shoot me" if he ever wound up staying in Washington after he left office.

One friend of Obama's says that the president despises the "derivative culture of D.C.," meaning that people become defined by their proximity to other people and institutions. The presidency is a popular target for those seeking derivative status. People glom on to it in some way, emphasizing their own connection as if that makes them, too, a bit presidential. The Las Vegas wedding of Ed Henry, who covered the White House for CNN and later Fox News, featured a cake that was a seventy-pound replica of the White House.

Over time, people achieve a psychic fusion to their public personas and their professional networks. The essence of self becomes lost, subsumed in a flurry of Playbook mentions and high-level name-drops. Self becomes fused with brands, and brands with other brands.

I first heard the term "Suck-up City" from a top Obama adviser during the 2008 campaign. He was describing the Beltway culture that Obama was running against—and then, after he won, that his White House vowed to change. "Suck-up City" holds multiple meanings, the most obvious being the sycophantic: you suck up to someone you want to please and, more to the point, when you want something from them. You could make the case that sucking up is the mother's milk of politics itself, or politicking. It is also central to Obama's disdain for the usual process. Back in the 2008 primary campaign, his New Hampshire political guy, Mike Cuzzi, set up a dinner for Obama in the town of Rye with a bunch of self-important local activists (a redundancy in New Hampshire, given the top-level attention lavished on them every four years). Obama stayed for hours, told stories, talked about the campaign, asked everyone about their lives, concerns, etc. They all had a splendid time, by every indication. But not a single one of them committed, recalled Reid Cherlin, an aide to Obama in New Hampshire. "What do I have to do," Obama asked Cuzzi as they were leaving, "wash their cars?"

Sucking up is as basic to Washington as humidity. There is a financial component. It has never been easier for "strategists" and "consultants" and "agents" of all stripes to affix themselves like barnacles to the local money barge, sucking in green nutrients.

There is no better connected operator in Washington than Robert Barnett, the superlawyer/dealmaker who can legitimize a person's earning power just by representing him or her. This service to his country includes a strenuous ability to promote his clients in the media and an equally strenuous ability to remind people of those deals in the interest of promoting himself. This makes him a "superlawyer." The degree to which so many elite D.C. players stream to a single superlawyer cash redemption center is striking even by the parochial standards of the ant colony. Barnett has all the antique cuff-links he could ever collect and all the money he could ever need. But he still loves the thrill of being at all the big parties and dinners and funerals, and also reading his name in Mike Allen's Playbook.

Bob loves Playbook. He touts Mike hard and is always good about giving him a heads-up on deals set to be announced. Playbook, in turn, mentions Barnett all the time, even if it's quoting some boilerplate praise from a lesser-known politician in the acknowledgments section of a book Barnett arranged.

And it tickles Bob when Mike mentions his birthday and that of his wife, Rita Braver, and daughter, Meredith, and baby grandson, Teddy. Speaking of Teddy, it was Mike Allen who broke the news of his birth in Playbook in 2010. I ran into Barnett a few days later and he told me he had received "probably four thousand e-mails" of congratulations after that Playbook mention; Bob was clearly over the moon with his new grandson.

To Barnett, Allen—with his mentions, his birthday wishes— helps Washington keep its priorities straight and encourages a sense of community. "In a world in which we all tend to pay not enough attention to people around us and their real lives, that's a real public service," Barnett affirmed in reference to Allen and Playbook in an interview with the *Washington Post*. In a bylined piece for Politico that ran on the eve of the 2008 election, Allen even included the name "Washington Superlawyer Robert Barnett" on a short list of potential Obama appointments to the Supreme Court (Barnett led the list, ahead of Sonia Sotomayor and Elena Kagan).

A native of Waukegan, Illinois, Barnett retains a sharp midwestern accent but is unabashed in his love of Washington. By attaching himself to the owners of the most rarefied job titles in town—presidents and first ladies on down—Barnett has created a boutique industry that he fully dominates.

While public officials profiting after leaving office is an evergreen custom here, Barnett has operated in a market that barely existed thirty years ago. With the exception of a few outliers (Barnett got Reagan's budget director, David Stockman, a reported $2.4 million advance in 1985), the money was not here then, the electronic circus was not in place, and political operatives like Karl Rove did not possess the celebrity appeal that has allowed them to leverage their "brands" into big multiplatform media deals. The rise of cable news gave everyone a face.

On the same night I encountered Andrea Mitchell at the Biden–Palin debate in St. Louis, I ran into Barnett. He had been hanging out in the media filing center—the kind of center-of-the-action place he loved. Enthusiastic as ever, Bob was always talking about his latest big deals and updating acquaintances on his roster of premium clients. One of his bigger parlays back then was the mega book, speaking, Fox News, *Newsweek*, and *Wall Street Journal* package he had negotiated for Rove after he left the White House. Rove had just been in Philadelphia for a "debate" with former Senator Max Cleland, the Democrat who lost an arm and two legs in Vietnam, and also his Senate seat in Georgia (in 2002) after his Republican opponent ran an ad featuring likenesses of Osama bin Laden and Saddam Hussein, while attacking Cleland for not supporting President Bush's Homeland Security bill. Cleland mostly blamed Rove for this. Debating Rove was like "going up against the devil himself," he said. "It's a source of income for me," Cleland told me of the joint appearance, which was sponsored by an insurance trade group. Cleland, whose own book deal was also negotiated by Barnett, was paid $15,000 for his night's work in Philadelphia; Rove made $40,000.

Barnett is the prototype of a person who made Washington work for him. He has also been the recipient of some of the most sustained and positive press coverage in the city, often benefiting from the hyperbolic testimony of his clients (or their surrogates). Hillary Clinton is always game to pay public testimony to Barnett, who negotiated an $8 million advance for her memoir, *Living History*, and more than $10 million for her husband's memoir, *My Life*—and even brokered a deal for Hillary to anthologize a bunch of kids' letters to the first pets, Socks the cat and Buddy the dog. Hillary's spokesman Philippe Reines once told the *Baltimore Sun*, "If God were writing the Bible again, he would surely call Bob Barnett."

While Bob is effective at his job, he has also made a lot of money for many of the top journalists at outlets where a lot of this good press appears. "To list Barnett as a signifier of Washington connectedness is like calling the sun a symbol of heat," hyperbolized David Montgomery of the *Washington Post* in a 2010 profile. The piece appeared under the leadership of then editor Marcus Brauchli, for whom Barnett had negotiated a $3.4 million package on the way out the door of his previous job at the *Wall Street Journal*. There is no indication that Brauchli steered Montgomery to write in any particular direction. Still, it's never rare for journalists—of which Barnett estimates he represents 375—to find themselves too close to the Barnett sun.

Barnett is also a signifier of Washington's special tolerance for conflict of interest, if not by the legal/ethical definition, then certainly by the "raises fundamental questions" definition. The term comes up a lot around Barnett, even from his clients and friends. It's often said with some measure of a shrug ("Only in Washington") and in fact admiration—as if to say, "Well, Bob's the big game in town for this, so of course he'll have a connection to both sides— and he has made me a lot of money, so it's all good." I've had many political figures and news colleagues over the years who have said they were, at the very least, uncomfortable that Barnett had been negotiating on their behalf with people (or counsel thereof) he also had represented. Also, when Barnett helps orchestrate, say, a book rollout for one of his well-known clients, is he playing favorites with the media hosts or outlets that he also represents?

Barnett says he discloses every possible conflict to his clients beforehand in writing, and they are free to go elsewhere, or fire him. Most of them do not. "He is a walking conflict of interest," says one longtime client, a well-known television journalist. The journalist also expressed great appreciation for Barnett, and added she has every intention of using him to negotiate her next deal.

Barnett prides himself on discretion and humility. It has been pointed out in the press that his office at the D.C. law firm Williams and Connolly does not include a "Me Wall" that displays photos of him posing with President X or foreign leader Y. But what Barnett lacks in Me Walls, he will make up for in his conversational skill at the cocktail parties he frequents, telling you that "Hillary" (or George W. Bush, or whoever) just e-mailed. He loves going out, seeing people, being seen, working, working; he might be the hardest-working person in Showbiz for Ugly People. He enlists his famous clients to get him invited to exclusive dinners, like the annual Alfalfa Club banquet, that are packed with political-media elites. He prefers Nantucket to Martha's Vineyard, he once told me, because the Vineyard is too sprawling and lacks a central square like the one Nantucket has. Plus, he loves shopping.

To certain key members of Obama's inner circle during the campaign, Barnett epitomized the Suck-up City operator who plays all sides, is tireless in his self-promotion, and is mercenary in his alliances. He was also a fierce supporter of Hillary Clinton's campaign during the Democratic primaries, owing to his longtime friendship with the former first lady and her husband that predates the book deals he arranged for them.

While Barnett takes great pride in his legal and deal-making ability, he craves standing as a principal. He hates being called an "agent," with its hired-gun connotations. He fashions himself as an all-purpose friend, editor, fixer, confidant, and promoter. Barnett is bipartisan in his business, having represented the last three presidents, first ladies, and vice presidents of both parties. But he is an avowed Democrat who takes great pride in his work preparing the party's nominees for their debates during general election campaigns. The only photos of Barnett with famous clients in his office are of him standing with candidates on a podium during the practice sessions.

After Obama secured the Democratic nomination in June 2008, Barnett wanted badly to be part of the team that trained the nominee for his debates against McCain. He had an in with Obama in that he negotiated the then senator's deal to write his bestselling 2006 book, *The Audacity of Hope*.

But some of Obama's top aides were insistent that Barnett was precisely the kind of Washington insider their campaign should avoid. He also had a reputation for oversharing with the press, a constituency he was especially attentive to (and married to: his wife, Rita Braver, is a correspondent for CBS News). Hillary Clinton was also fully aware of this, and had often warned her aides not to tell Barnett too much because he talked too much in general.

But Clinton deputized Barnett to be one of her liaisons to the Obama campaign after her exit from the race in June. He lobbied the Obama people for some debate role through the summer. After one brief conversation at the campaign's Chicago headquarters, Plouffe told colleagues he was struck by how obsequious Barnett was.

Finally, the campaign gave Barnett a small position on the team that negotiated debate parameters with the McCain campaign and the debate organizers: the sizes of the lecterns, the temperature in the room, and whatnot. He traveled to the sites of the three presidential debates as well as the vice presidential debate in St. Louis between Joe Biden and his Republican counterpart, Sarah Palin. Barnett spent much of his evening in the media filing center and postdebate "spin room" at Washington University. The only person Barnett appeared to be spinning for was himself. He seemed very much in his political-media see-and-be-seen element. At one point he even chatted up Palin's communications aide Nicolle Wallace—who was with her husband, Mark, also a top McCain–Palin official.

Barnett ended up securing Palin's business after the election, winning her well into eight figures in book, speaking, and TV deals. "Few public figures not in office have leveraged the nexus between media and political positioning as Sarah Palin has," Barnett later said of his new friend from Alaska.

Even better, while there was no bigger detractor of Barnett on the Obama campaign than Plouffe, the campaign manager, Plouffe's aversion stopped when it came to his own livelihood: he hired Barnett to negotiate a reported seven-figure advance for his book about the 2008 campaign, *The Audacity to Win*. This was revealed a few weeks after the election, in Playbook: "Robert Barnett, who also represents the president-elect, the secretary of state-designate, the commerce secretary-designate, the soon-to-be health and human services secretary-designate, and the national economic adviser-designate, among others, will handle the project for Plouffe."

In the book, Plouffe denigrated Republicans as "a party led by people who foment anger and controversy to make a name for themselves and to make a buck." Plouffe made more than that. Barnett set him up at the Washington Speakers Bureau, a popular outfit in the thriving local pontificate-for-pay sector. Plouffe earned $1.5 million in 2010, according to White House disclosure statements, which included a portion of his book advance, proceeds from his management consulting work for Boeing and General Electric, and close to $500,000 for paid speaking gigs around the world, including $100,000 from MTN Nigeria, an African telecommunications firm.

No one in Obama World would ever deny Barnett's effectiveness when it came to getting "public-to-private" deals for them after work on campaigns or in the White House was finished. Typically there was not even a second choice. Barnett was once described as "the doorman to the revolving door"; he has been known to quote that line in speeches, in a self-deprecating way, of course.

"You make a certain deal with a devil when you reach a certain level of visibility," one longtime Obama confidant and aide told me. "Everyone here knows what Bob is about. But the reality is, if you don't hire him, you're probably leaving money on the table, and ninety-five percent of people here aren't willing to do that."

Still, Barnett's client relationships at the highest levels of Obama World could create conflicts in the day-to-day of the White House. Early in the Obama presidency, national security speechwriter Ben Rhodes received a call from an aide to Nelson Mandela asking if the president would write a foreword to Mandela's autobiography. Rhodes, an idealistic former novelist, entered politics after seeing the plane strikes on the Twin Towers. He took the Mandela request to the president, who readily agreed to do it. Soon after, Barnett became involved in his role as the president's lawyer on book matters. He expressed the view that the White House should have taken into account the unique issues that arise when a president contributes to a published work—something he dealt with during Bill Clinton's presidency. E-mails were exchanged, and eventually Rhodes became annoyed, pointing out that something so cut-and-dried as the president's writing a short foreword for one of his heroes should not be this complicated. Ben, whose brother, David Rhodes, would become president of CBS News, told colleagues that he later wrote an indignant e-mail to a number of Obama associates, including Barnett. He acknowledged it was probably a mistake to send it, but in any case, the issue played out with lawyers, and Obama eventually wrote the foreword for Mandela's book.

When I asked Ben Rhodes about the episode, he confirmed that it had occurred, but declined further comment, citing the fact that Barnett represented his brother.

. . .

Obama's victory in November 2008 opened a love spigot. Before his victory speech in Chicago's Grant Park, many of his campaign aides and top supporters walked in a procession past the press pen to hear the president-elect's speech. I watched many of the Obama people sharing prolonged hugs with reporters, reinforcing the notion (advanced by the Clinton and McCain campaigns, among others) that the media had fallen into the thrall of Obama—a thrall immortalized by Chris Matthews, who declared on the air that he "felt this thrill going up my leg" upon hearing Obama speak. Media reporter Howard Kurtz, then of the *Washington Post*, initiated an "Obama Adulation Watch" that noted postelection comparisons of Obama to Franklin Roosevelt and Abraham Lincoln. Several reporters would wind up joining the administration in high-profile communications jobs. This often happens, especially in Democratic administrations, but not to the degree it did in the Obama presidency, which became a full-employment service for former journalists; a reported nineteen would join the administration through its first term.

It is also common for hot new administrations to be widely celebrated, flattered, and generally paid great attention. Particular darlings are alumni of winning Democratic campaigns who move into plum White House jobs. Hamilton Jordan and Jody Powell, top aides to Jimmy Carter, appeared on the cover of *Rolling Stone* magazine shortly after Carter was elected. In 1992 the *New Republic* initiated a "Clinton Suck-Up Watch."

But the extreme hype that attended the Obama invasion went well beyond even the historic impact of his election. It bordered, at times, on out-and-out panting. "As Barack Obama stacks his staff with studs whose looks are as outstanding as their credentials, it's clear that the nation's 44th president won't be the only man on the hill who can rock a suit—bespoke or bathing," the New York *Daily News* reported just before the inauguration. The story was accompanied by a photo spread on "Hotties of the Obama Cabinet."

Opulent welcoming parties surged through the city as the rest of the country spiraled into a financial crisis. On a Thursday night in early December 2008, Gibbs and his wife were feted at a Capitol Hill tavern by many of the same people who were there to pay tribute to Russert (and Gibbs) that day in June. The invitation urged guests to "honor Robert and Mary Catherine Gibbs with drinks, laughs, some humiliating deference, respect and sucking up." That month alone, incoming Obama people were "honored" at fourteen such galas.

But the Obama followers were determined to resist being sucked up by the seductions of Suck-up City. They offered themselves as incorruptible canaries that would fly above the filthy flattery mines of D.C. In a system that had degenerated into a big and unctuous game, they would refuse to play. They would stay humble and focused on their work.

The week before his inauguration, the president-elect was invited to a dinner party at the Chevy Chase, Maryland, home of the conservative columnist George F. Will. The dinner, ostensibly, would welcome the new president back to town and acquaint him with some of the media's top conservatives: the columnists David Brooks of the *New York Times*, Peggy Noonan of the *Wall Street Journal*, and William Kristol of the *Weekly Standard*, among others. The dinner was originally planned for during the campaign. Axelrod had pushed for it but Plouffe nixed the idea. Plouffe believed that to attend such an insider Washington salon would be a waste of time, while Axelrod argued that it could be a useful olive branch, consistent with the president-elect's promise to unite the country. Plouffe prevailed at the time, and the invitation was tabled until after the campaign. Obama ate portobello mushroom salad and lamb chops and declared the two-and-a-half-hour confab "fun" upon departure.

Later that week, Obama met with the editorial board of the *Washington Post*, a constituency he had proudly blown off during the campaign. After the meeting, Obama worked the *Post*'s fifth-floor newsroom to a flurry of cell phone cameras. "I want to talk about the Redskins and the Nationals," Obama declared, playing the new neighbor eager to fit in.

As discrete events, Obama's visits to Will's home and the *Post* meant little. They signaled a natural shifting of the constituencies that presidents speak to when they are outside Washington (running for president) to when they are in Washington (being president). Politics often boils down to an exercise of knowing your priorities and constituencies, neither of which are static. "It's sort of an ac-cepted rite of passage that a presidential candidate can talk bad about Washington without anyone in Washington accusing him of being a hypocrite afterwards," said Marlin Fitzwater, the press sec-retary to Presidents Reagan and George H. W. Bush. Sooner or later, the key constituencies of Washington "all know that he will come to them," said Fitzwater, listing these constituencies as lobby-ists, lawmakers, and the ephemerally dreaded "special interests."

Even so, Obama and his entourage held themselves out as an unusually pure brigade. Their furious assault on lobbyists during the campaign and their vow to keep them out of the White House upon arrival made for heated disagreements. A debate broke out between Obama aides over whether to make exceptions to their no-lobbying rule, especially in the case of people who worked on behalf of do-gooder causes (like, say, cancer research). Axelrod, a hard-liner, ar-gued that Americans did not distinguish between "good lobbyists" and "bad lobbyists" and there was a greater principle at stake. "It's not who we are," or "It's not in our DNA," was a common refrain among the hard-liners, which also included Plouffe and Gibbs. A less rigid position within the White House held that these guide-lines were arbitrary. By signing an executive order to keep lobbyists out of the administration, Obama would be constricting his hiring pool or tempting embarrassment if he made exceptions—as he did when a former Raytheon lobbyist, Bill Lynn, was granted a waiver to serve as deputy secretary of defense.

One of the stubborn truths of Obama-era Washington is that everyone is now, in effect, a special interest, a free agent, performing any number of services, in any number of settings. It goes well beyond the technical classification of "registered lobbyists." Self-pimping has become the prevailing social and business imperative. "The firstnamelastname-dot-com syndrome" is how a Republican media consultant, Kevin Madden, described the phenomenon. Or, as the *Onion* once described it, it's like being "the CEO of the company called 'Me.'"

What's more, as everyone was their own "special interest," or brand, it was impossible to know who was carrying what water for whom. It was certainly not as easy as going down a list of "registered lobbyists" and excluding them from White House employment or dealings. Lobbying was just one segment on the revolving door. Cozy areas of overlap abounded—perhaps even "deeply troubling" ones. For instance, Michael Froman, chief of staff to Clinton Trea-sury secretary Robert Rubin, was a managing director at Citigroup while serving on Obama's transition team. Another Rubin protégé, then New York Fed president Tim Geithner, helped engineer a tax-payer bailout of Citigroup a few weeks after Obama's election. Fro-man later received a $2.2 million bonus from Citigroup after being hired by the administration. (He ultimately gave it to charity.)

Still: "Resist the gold rush," went the mantra inside the new White House. The rising unemployment numbers and collapsing banks should make it easy to remain humble. Or not. Washington was fat and the love was abundant for the refreshed White House, home to what the new social secretary Desirée Rogers called "the best brand on earth: the Obama brand" in the *Wall Street Journal*. "Our possibilities are endless."

The new administration made dozens of White House staffers available to the *New York Times Magazine* for a shiny photo essay on "Obama's People." It placed the staffers very much on-limits as extensions of the Obama brand. Rogers and Valerie Jarrett, a top presidential adviser and a close first family confidante, posed for a glamorous cover shoot in an exclusive "White House Insiders" edition of the thick-paged *Capitol File* magazine. It was a terrific play for Brand Valerie and Brand Desirée. But top aides to Obama were appalled that staffers would partake of such an ostentatious display, especially in such a frighteningly bad economy. (Jarrett told me later, "If I had it to do again, I wouldn't have done that.")

In a broader sense, the spectacle triggered suspicion that certain "White House insiders" were enjoying their newfound celebrity a bit too much and that Team Obama would be just the latest enterprise to campaign against Washington, only to quickly succumb to post-election charms. "Everyone here has been warm and welcoming and inclusive," Jarrett told *Capitol File*. "There hasn't been a person I've met who hasn't said 'Welcome to Washington,' and you get the feeling they actually mean it."

Whether they did mean it or not, Washington sucked up every crumb of "insight" on the Obama brand. The appetite was insatiable, evidenced by the items the new-media faucet kept spewing forth.

- Within the first weeks of the new presidency, Politico "broke" the story that the president's aides sang "Happy Birthday" to the assistant press secretary, Nick Shapiro!

- And surprised him with a chocolate cake!

- And also that deputy White House press secretary Jen Psaki "was in her pajamas" when her boyfriend made dinner for her and proposed marriage!

- The *Washington Examiner* reported that White House chief of staff Rahm Emanuel was spotted "getting money at the SunTrust Bank in the Safeway on the corner [of] 17th St. and Corcoran St. NW"!

- Reggie Love, Obama's personal aide, was declared the winner of the Huffington Post's "Who's the White House's hottest employee?" contest (not to be confused with the "Hottest Obama Hottie" contest that ran on Gawker.com in January, in which Mr. Emanuel triumphed)!

- The *Wall Street Journal* scooped the nugget that the White House Office of Management and Budget chief, Peter Orszag, enjoys Diet Coke!

In other news, the country still faced two wars and an economic crisis.

"It started as sort of a joke to treat official Washington as a celebrity culture," said Ana Marie Cox, who helped create the genre online by starting the website Wonkette in 2004. "Now it seems that a lot of the irony has been lost and the joke has turned real."

White House officials were quite eager to share with me how ambivalent they all were about their quasi-celebrity. Some acknowledged a tension between living up to the administration's stated goal of being "transparent" and "open" while also following the Obama staff ethic of being understated, cool, and modest. "We have a culture here that abhors all of that," Dan Pfeiffer said. When I told Pfeiffer I was contemplating a story for the *Times* about "all of that," he suggested it might "get bumped off the front page by a story about the first lady's hair." He was referring to a front-page article in the *Times* the previous week about how the new president's hair was going gray.

Arianna Huffington hosted the signature D.C. party on the eve of Obama's inauguration. It was held at the Newseum, a place cherished by Tim Russert, whose idea it was to inscribe the first forty-five words of the First Amendment on the building's façade overlooking Pennsylvania Avenue and the National Mall.

The rise and reinvention of Huffington, impresario of the fast-growing website, the Huffington Post, had been a source of great annoyance to Russert. In 1994, when Huffington's former husband, Michael Huffington, was a Republican senatorial candidate from California and Arianna was an outspoken conservative who was orchestrating his campaign, Russert's wife, Maureen Orth, wrote a withering profile of Arianna that characterized the Greek-born spouse as a despotic boss, a New Age flake, and the "Sir Edmund Hillary of Social Climbers." Resentment between the parties simmered for years and boiled anew when Huffington started her website and initiated something called Russert Watch. The feature ridiculed *Meet the Press* as a hothouse of conventional wisdom, reflexive partisanship, and Beltway gamesmanship. Huffington told me later that media criticism had always been a big part of the website's mission, and she started Russert Watch to chronicle how the host's "kid-gloves-handling of the D.C. establishment allowed the conventional wisdom to survive unchallenged." It had nothing to do with any personal history with Russert or Orth, she said.

Regardless, Russert, who despite his top-of-the-class station could be quite thin-skinned—and quite Irish in holding grudges—

complained bitterly about Huffington's Russert Watch. Arianna was conspicuously lukewarm (or silent) about Russert during the canonization that followed his death. She did not attend the funeral. Luke Russert says he will always refuse to shake Arianna's hand.

Huffington's resurrection into a new-media queen was completed three years later when AOL paid $315 million for the right to merge with the Huffington Post. The arrangement put her in charge of the whole moussaka. When the then CEO of NBC Universal, Jeff Zucker, later revealed that the network had itself pursued an acquisition of Huff-Po, it also no doubt set Russert spinning in his you-know-what. On the morning the AOL news broke, Sally Quinn, who in recent years has become fascinated with religion and now runs the "On Faith" website on WashingtonPost.com, forwarded the announcement to her old pal Orth, a devout Catholic.

"How could God let this happen?" Sally asked.

"It must be part of God's divine plan," Tim's widow said.

Huffington's red carpet on Inauguration eve was dense with Demi Moores, Ashton Kutchers, Stings, David Axelrods, and Valerie Jarretts. Arianna addressed the reveling mob from a fourth-floor balcony. She wore a black gown with a long tail and looked every bit a re-reinvented queen of a changing universe. (Disclosure: my sister Lori works for Arianna at the Huffington Post, so this could get slightly awkward.)

In the mad dash to get in with the hot young White House, Arianna, at fifty-eight, appeared to be a frontrunner. The White House press shop paid close and solicitous attention. Obama himself was dropping Arianna's name—only her first name necessary—into interviews with the *New York Times*. He volunteered that Arianna disapproved of his redecoration of the Oval Office. Valerie Jarrett called Huffington an "icon" and a "phenomenon" at a party Tammy Haddad threw for Huffington to celebrate her new book on the American underclass, *Third World America*. (And who knew there would be valet parking in Third World America? Or specially embroidered *Third World America* pillows!)

Outside the Newseum, the magnificent Tammy—Tim called her "the Tamster" and now so did I—was trolling the sidewalk. She was surveying the long, snaking queue of people waiting to get into the bash and kept pulling worthies out of line, declaring her D.C. Chosens in real time. Okay, I admit I was one of them. I felt like a jackass, walking ahead of everyone. But it was really cold, and Arianna had also promised "live tweeting stations" at her party, so yay for her, yay for me, and yay for the Tamster.

You gotta love the Tamster. Actually you don't, and some don't, though not in any deep or greatly malicious way, at least in most cases. Tammy is a contradiction in that she is also one of those people of whom it is often wondered: What exactly does she do? But she also gets points for transparency (in whatever it is she does). Or at least ubiquity. She eschews the high-minded pretense that this is anything but a festival of vanities and gossip and a variation on the Miss America Pageant that she herself has judged and still sits on the board of. She has blasted a place for herself in the city: impossible to miss, if not resist—six feet and not shy about invading your personal space and telling you about how she knows everyone (and how wonderful YOU are too) and putting you on camera. Her signature accoutrement is a little video camera she carries around, called the "Tam Cam." With it, she walks up to people she knows—and who, by extension, *matter*—and initiates quick little ambush interviews, which she will often put online. The interviews are generally quick and painless, if somewhat intrusive, "like a light enema," in the words of one friend/victim.

"My job is to be around the most successful people, the most up-and-coming people, and the people who have impact," Tammy told me. She kowtows to them, or those who think they are "them," or want to be. This group has always existed in the ornate playground of social climbing that is This Town. Only now it is big enough to contain an entire subeconomy, and a business for Tammy Haddad.

Haddad grew up in Pittsburgh, the granddaughter of Syrian immigrants and the daughter of a gas station owner. Her father, Edward David Haddad, eventually started a truck rental company above his Amoco station that grew into a large operation known as Haddad's Trucks (the "Can-Do People"), which specializes in renting to the makers of feature films—the first being *Flashdance*, filmed in Pittsburgh in 1983. Haddad's now operates up and down the East Coast with a particularly large and intrusive presence in New York City. The behemoth loads will often insinuate themselves into the city's crowded streets and take up lots of space—an association that seems particularly apt for the Tamster. "Your brother's trucks are blocking my street," Mayor Michael Bloomberg once complained to her.

Tammy graduated from the University of Pittsburgh, where she was head of the student programming council and played the flute and the piccolo in the school's marching, jazz, and concert bands.

She went on to become an accomplished cable TV producer. That's what she did for *Larry King Live*, a show she helped create and produce for many years. Given King's cachet and reputation for friendly interviews, Haddad was immediately exposed to a veritable parade of fame. In other words, there were worse places to build a network of "people who matter." She did a series of other jobs in TV, eventually landing with Chris Matthews as a producer of *Hardball*. That marriage ended in 2007, with some of Matthews's friends worrying that if it continued, Matthews would have a nervous breakdown (in fairness, many of Tammy's friends worried that the same would happen to her). Regardless, after leaving *Hardball*, Haddad went into full Force of Nature and reinvention mode. She became a perfect flower of an emerging Washington moment.

Part of the producer's job is to make the talent feel comfortable and confident. That makes it easier for them to go on the air and project comfort and confidence, no matter what their ratings or what the critics say. That's what she does, or tries to do, for fancypants Washington—those who are invited! "Hi, doll!" she will boom, and, "You just have to meet the supertalented author. Come with me." Next thing you know, you're across the room, part of a scrum waiting to meet the supertalented author. As you wait, Tammy holds court, going on about how Austan Goolsbee, Obama's economic adviser, is such a total sweetheart, and how you have to meet him, too, and how Cate Edwards, John and Elizabeth's oldest daughter, is engaged, and how Arianna was just telling her something or other. And here comes the big cake that Tammy arranged, and the presents, and maybe a special toast for the honored guest, or even a skit. She plants herself right in the nation's courtyard and enables This Town's perpetual adolescence.

Tammy loved Tim, and Tim thought Tammy was a trip and maybe a little much at times, but he appreciated her because he liked Washington originals, and that's what the Tamster was and is. Perhaps a bit of a cartoon. And we could leave it at that, except that Tammy has made herself "necessary" and deftly ensconced herself into an Obama World that had also vowed to avoid precisely her ilk of Washington socialite.

Shortly before the first Obama inauguration, the *New York Times* published a story on what Washington hosts were doing to attract the new president and first lady to their parties. The first step is to reach out to the people who have influence with the Obamas, Tammy was quoted as saying. "The social question is,

Who are the closest people to the Obamas personally?" she said. "Who is the hottest property inside their small circle?"

Haddad knew exactly who the hottest Obama properties were. And she got right up in their faces like that towering Great Dane from the old *Marmaduke* comic strip. Resistance was futile. They became her *really good friends*. She hosted parties "honoring" them. She welcomed them to town and celebrated their new jobs. She helped organize parties at which the featured guest was Valerie Jarrett, the Obama BFF and White House senior adviser; she organized a dinner for Dan Pfeiffer as he was ascending to White House communications director. She helped arrange events and throw parties for people, whether they wanted to be feted or not ("party rape," one close friend of a reluctant honoree called the phenomenon).

Tammy also worked to raise money and awareness for epilepsy research, even though she had no personal connection to the disease. But her new friends David and Susan Axelrod did, and they welcomed her help, as any parents would. Clearly, David Axelrod's elevated status in Washington was helpful to their cause, and no one was more helpful than Tammy. She became a tireless promoter and fund-raiser for CURE (Citizens United for Research in Epilepsy), which raised $1.6 million from private sources in 2009, according to financial statements—three times as much as it had raised the previous year, before David was in the White House. None of these donors have been disclosed, nor are they required to be. But donating generously to CURE could at least carry an appearance of trying to curry favor with the new White House. Tammy learned about the Axelrod family saga after reading a cover story about it in *Parade* and then seeing Susan Axelrod interviewed on the next day's *Today* show. Tammy was moved by the story and also saw great possibility in Susan.

Other than possibly the Tam Cam, Tammy is best known for

the A-list brunch she throws on the day of the White House Correspondents' Association dinner. The event has become a massive spectacle that attracts swarms of Hollywood, Washington, and New York celebrities, in addition to plenty of media attention. Part of the game is to have big-ticket "sponsors" for the event and also to attach it to "good causes" that will attract attention and coat the sweaty affair in a virtuous glaze. Tammy wrote a letter to Susan Axelrod, whom she had never met. She knew David a little (but not well), in part because, as she likes to say, she "covered" the 2008 campaign with the Tam Cam for *Newsweek* and the *Washington Post*. She turned up a fair amount at political events, debates, conventions, and big scenes like that. Indeed, Tammy exists in a murky space between being a journalist, a businessperson, a philanthropist, a producer, a party host, and a full-service gatherer of friends of different persuasions unified by the fact that they in some way "matter." Susan Axelrod not only mattered, but also was a good and compelling and committed soul whose daughter had suffered tragically. And it also didn't hurt that her husband was the new president's closest adviser. When Tammy finally got through, she told Susan that if she served as a cohost of that year's brunch (with NBC's Ann Curry), Tammy would devote the following year to helping her campaign to promote awareness about epilepsy.

In October 2009, Tammy helped organize a luminary gathering at a Georgetown mansion to watch David and Susan discuss their parental ordeal with Katie Couric on *60 Minutes*. Several top administration officials showed up at the watch party, including Vice President Biden and Rahm Emanuel. "There's nothing worse than having your child cognizant enough to know what's going on, and know what's happening, and begging you to help," Susan Axelrod said. The Couric interview was another tremendous boon to CURE. The following year, Tammy was honored with the annual Friend of CURE award at a party at the Newseum. David Axelrod says that Haddad has never asked for any favors relating to his official role, and Haddad says she has been careful not to do so.

Tammy would make herself many close friends in the Obama White House. She was pals with Goolsbee, a top economic adviser to the new president; and she cohosted a party for Michelle Obama's chief of staff's son, the "supertalented author" who had written a novel, and one for David Axelrod's assistant, who was headed off to law school, and another for Rahm Emanuel's longtime senior adviser, who had taken a new job at Bloomberg News, one of the many media companies that Tammy's media company, Haddad Media, did work for. Haddad helped with video producing. She organized special events and did various odd jobs to create "buzz" for herself and for her clients and for her thousands of superstar friends. She brings boldface names together.

Along the way, Haddad acquired a coveted mantle of her own: someone who had "connections" to the Obama White House. She won access to key quadrants of Obama World, even as the administration was taking great pride in refusing access to traditional influence peddlers, like lobbyists. One top White House aide described Tammy to me as an "access peddler." Her business has thrived.

Tammy is not a Washington social convener type in the tradition of Georgetown hostesses like Sally Quinn, Katharine Graham, and Pamela Harriman, all of whom were married or linked to wealthy and powerful men or institutions. Their social efforts might have carried some business impetus (Quinn and Graham on behalf of their newspaper, Harriman for her work as a political activist and eventual diplomat). But none of them were working on behalf of paying clients like Haddad often does. She was doing consulting work for media outlets such as Politico, Bloomberg, *National Journal*, *Newsweek*, the *Washington Post*, Condé Nast, and HBO. Her work seemed to include video production, event planning, and some promotional components. She is also helpful in using her connections to gain journalistic access for her clients. When Politico did a ten-week series of videotaped interviews with administration officials, Haddad arranged the bookings with high-level administration officials. In addition, Tammy signed on to be a consultant to *Newsweek* through her friend Jon Meacham, who was then the magazine's top editor. She worked on special video projects, did Tam Cam interviews, and performed assorted odd jobs.

The struggling newsweekly had been trying for months to land an interview with the president. Haddad "worked her contacts"—her friends in the White House, the hottest of properties inside the Obama's small circle. She helped deliver the *Newsweek* interview as well as one with the first lady.

On the website of "Haddad Media," there is a photo of Tammy aboard *Air Force One*, towering over Meacham—"a poet-historian," she called him—as he interviewed President Obama. She includes, on the website, a description of her experience riding on "the Bird," as insiders (like Tammy) call the presidential jet. Obama mentioned that he'd heard she'd had a great party the previous weekend. Tammy was thrilled by such high-level acknowledgment, naturally, and also by the "Cadillac-quality leather toilet seat cover" in the bathroom, "as wide as any Sumo wrestler could want."

She also gushed over how generally roomy the *Air Force One* bathrooms seemed. "I could have comfortably brought a friend in," she said.

Comfortably! This is what makes us great.

Alas, Tammy did not take any video of the *Air Force One* visit or the Meacham interview for *Newsweek*. In other words, it was not immediately clear what Tammy was doing there. Only that she was there, and that it mattered, and how could This Town not be impressed?

Three Senators for Our Times

*A man never stands taller than when he is down on
all fours kissing somebody's ass.*

Rahm Emanuel

ntrusted with a Senate supermajority and endowed with all the
magnetism of a dried snail, Harry Reid owned the beleaguered
face of change in 2009.

But the opening scene, at least mine—because I was in the
room!—played out a few years before, on Election Night of 2006,
the night Democrats regained control of the House and Senate for
the first time since 1994.

Reid, then the Senate minority leader, and Chuck Schumer,
who had run the Democrats' Senate campaign committee, were
watching returns in a suite at the Hyatt Regency Washington on
Capitol Hill. The Felix-and-Oscar pair—Reid a hush-voiced Mormon from Searchlight, Nevada, and Schumer a bombastic Jew from
Brooklyn—was becoming more and more silly as the night wore on.
At one point Schumer, whose chin was smeared with mustard in
two distinct splotches, exploded off the couch. CNN was calling the
close Missouri Senate race for Democrat Claire McCaskill.

"Yeah," Schumer grunted out through his food, holding two fists over his head.

Reid, a man of thoroughgoing cynicism, is nonetheless capable of a boyish hullabaloo at times like this. So what did Harry Reid do to mark this key step in his ascent to Senate majority leader? He rose from the couch and he kissed the TV—tenderly, caressing the screen. And then he sat back down to receive from Schumer something between a pat on the head and a noogie.

Reid then started placing congratulatory calls to the Democrats who had won. None of the calls exceeded thirty seconds, and each was punctuated by a variant of "I love you." Reid professed his love to Senator Kent Conrad, who was reelected in North Dakota ("Love you, man"), Sherrod Brown in Ohio, and Hillary Clinton in New York, who told Reid she loved him back.

I was standing a few feet away from the couch, sanctioned that night by Reid and Schumer to be a "fly on the wall," a journalistic practice that is both a cliché and a misnomer: no one notices an actual fly on the wall while everyone is fully mindful of the maggot reporter taking notes. But these moments can be revealing, especially in the midst of such punch-drunk victories. Reid must have detected my amusement at the "I love yous," which he explained to me matter-of-factly. "They need to hear that," he said.

"They" are political people. And Reid, their leader, a former Nevada gaming commissioner, parcels out love like casino chips. Whether it is real love or pseudo love doesn't quite matter. Love is gold currency in the rolling transaction of politics, a game played by the nation's most ambitious and insecure class. In his stooped and unassuming and easy-to-miss way, no one understands this better than Harry Reid.

A few months later, Reid showed up on the Senate floor to hear John Kerry announce that he would not run for president again in

2008. It was a difficult moment for Kerry, the 2004 Democratic nominee who was now shedding an ambition he appeared to have held since kindergarten. Just before the 2006 midterms, Kerry had acquired a nasty case of political cooties after attempting a laugh line about the war in Iraq—never a good idea—which many construed as a knock against U.S. soldiers. Now Kerry was making this heavy announcement to a near-empty chamber that included only Reid and Kerry's fellow Massachusetts senator, Ted Kennedy. After Kerry finished, Reid, who was standing next to him, gave Kerry a hug and said a few words for the record.

"He is one of those people who meant so much to me," Reid said of Kerry, belying the scorn he had expressed to others for the lanky Bay Stater over many years. Reid had observed privately to colleagues that Kerry had no friends. No matter: Reid was John Kerry's friend today, publicly, and it felt nothing but sincere.

"So I say to John Kerry," Reid concluded, "I love you, John Kerry."
Kerry nodded slowly and appeared to choke back tears.

Bespectacled and slight, Reid is frequently described in terms of something else ("He looks like a civics teacher"). It is similar to how, say, the size of hail is never described on its own merits, only in terms of other things—marble-size, golf-ball-size. Reid could also pass for an oddball taxidermist who keeps a closet full of stuffed pigeons, or maybe the harried proprietor of the pet store that has just been robbed for the third time this month (or, in his case, hit up by Ben Nelson of Nebraska for some provincial goodie in the stimulus bill). What Reid does not look like is the amateur boxer and habitual street-fighter he was in his youth—or, more to the point, one of the most potent, odd, and overlooked phenomena of This Town.

. . .

Reid once invited me to his home in the desert smudge of Searchlight, Nevada, population 539—a town of twelve brothels and not a single church during his childhood of unspeakable poverty. It was just after he had become the minority leader of the Senate in 2005. This was not an invitation that Reid would typically extend a reporter on his own. But he had been catching heat for having made a series of inelegant comments—calling, among other things, President Bush a "loser" and a "liar," Alan Greenspan a "political hack," and Clarence Thomas "an embarrassment"—and his image guardians feared the remarks might "negatively impact his brand."

Reid welcomed me into his kitchen with an overly self-conscious—or self-consciously self-conscious—string of solicitations.

"Hey, you want a drink or something? Water?"

No, thanks, I said.

"They said I'm supposed to offer you a drink, so that's what I'm doing. If anyone asks, just tell them I offered you a drink." In other words, this charming mannerly recipe that Reid was following came from someone else ("them").

"I don't go to dinner. I don't do any of the social things," Reid said later. By contrast, he said, Tom Daschle, the top Senate Democrat before him, went to dinner every night. "I have beady eyes," Reid points out, and "lousy posture." And he doesn't "speak well." He is always reciting the litany of reasons why he is so unfit for his big-deal Washington job. He is an anti-prototype of This Town, which makes him an unlikely king of the place. The needy actors can have their love, just as long as Harry Reid gets to be in charge. "There are people who could be majority leader who could probably be better than I am," Reid told me years later in his office. "They're smarter, they're better-looking, they speak better. But they don't have the job. I have the job."

Reid's movie would be in black-and-white, and maybe slightly pink to account for his facial coloring. Known as "Pinky" growing up, Harry Mason Reid is slight and tiny-eyed and looks about his age (seventy-three) but could also pass for someone born in the 1800s. He sees all of "that Hollywood stuff" as a great market inefficiency of Washington. Like how Billy Beane, the protagonist of Michael Lewis's *Moneyball*, strips away all the intangibles of evaluating baseball talent: emotional attachments to players, their "makeup," and ephemeral notions such as "clutch hitting" and "baseball tradition." The only thing that matters to Beane is creating better methodologies and blocking out the traditional metrics. To Reid, the obsession in Washington to the show-horse aspects of the game (getting credit, being "seen") is misspent energy that brings clouded thinking. What matters is maximum efficiency and, ultimately, survival.

"I can get in and out of a fund-raiser in five minutes," Reid boasted to me. He was once leaving the Capitol in the back of his chauffeured SUV when he spotted my *New York Times* colleague Carl Hulse, a longtime congressional reporter, walking through the parking lot and wearing a tuxedo. "Where are you going, Carl?" Reid asked through an open window. Carl said he was headed to the annual Congressional Dinner, a big to-do for Hill types being held that year at the Ritz-Carlton, where Reid lives when he is in Washington. Reid offered Carl a ride over. When they arrived, Carl told Reid it would have been convenient for him if he were going to the dinner. "Carl," Reid assured him as he headed up to his condo, "I wouldn't go to this thing if it were in my living room."

In Tim Russert's final months, Reid's spokesman at the time, Jim Manley, dragged the majority leader to the sixtieth-anniversary party for *Meet the Press*. It was held at the Newseum, and partygoers who appeared as guests of *Meet the Press* were delineated by special blue ribbons on their lapels—a kind of varsity letter. Reid hurried in, not bothering with his ribbon. He walked to the front of the long receiving line, congratulated Tim, and was, by Manley's guess, in and out in eight minutes.

Reid loves being alone, either with his thoughts or with his wife, Landra, to whom he has been married fifty-three years. He also has a great eye for political loners and bringing them into his fold. He recognized immediately that Barack Obama was an outlier when he came to the Senate in 2005. Obama was a charming and persuasive "natural" of a performer but unreachable in basic ways and not well suited to the chamber. It was Reid who in 2006 encouraged Obama to run for president. This came as a shock to Obama at the time and to the Hillary Clinton camp when this conversation was revealed. Reid, who had repeatedly stated his neutrality in the 2008 presidential race, believed that Obama would never have the patience to hang around the Senate long enough to achieve the impact he craved. It also appealed to Reid, on a level somewhere between mischievous and Darwinian, to watch the two celebrity members of his caucus, Obama and Clinton, kill each other.

As Obama's presidency unfolded, Reid appealed to a side of him that was fiercely pragmatic and transactional. "Harry has the toughest job in Washington," Obama said of Reid. "He just grinds it out." Obama, whose favorite movie is *The Godfather* and who has something of a Mob fetish, has always been drawn to loyal fixer types like Reid who quietly take care of business. He once drew a favorable parallel between his press secretary, Robert Gibbs, and the consigliere role played by Robert Duvall in *The Godfather*.

As Democrats had gained a supermajority of sixty votes in the

Senate, Obama's chief of staff, Rahm Emanuel, spoke of "putting points on the board"—an early mantra of the new White House that meant doing what was necessary to pass bills. This suited Reid, who became Obama's key legislative partner, wrenching the administration's prime accomplishments through a scared Senate: a $787 billion economic stimulus bill in early 2009 and the health-care bill a year later.

Reid and Emanuel became close allies. (As an aside, Emanuel is an observant Jew, and Reid loves Jews. Reid's wife, Landra, was Jewish before she met "Hank," as she calls him, and they became Mormons. A mezuzah still hangs in the doorway of the Reid home in Searchlight.) Reid and Emanuel spoke often by phone, usually for a bare minimum of seconds, just long enough to transact.

Both could be crass, especially Rahm. Shortly after Obama took office, he and Emanuel were meeting with Nancy Pelosi, when the chief of staff started cracking his knuckles. When Obama turned and expressed annoyance with the habit, Emanuel held the offending knuckle up to Obama's left ear and snapped off a few special cracks for his presidential benefit.

Both Emanuel and Reid could be vindictive, especially Reid. Back when Nevada's other senator was the exuberant Democrat Richard Bryan, a running joke had it that Bryan woke up every morning wondering how many hands he could shake, while Reid woke up wondering how many enemies he needed to screw.

Reid rarely wastes his powers of persuasion on policy arguments or charm offensives. "He goes straight to 'What do you want?'" said Senator Susan Collins, a moderate Republican who supported the stimulus bill. Again, despite the pugilistic tendencies of Reid and Emanuel, their philosophy of managing Democratic lawmakers usually came down to accommodation.

Harry Reid understands his customers' needs: which senators need to be home, if possible, to put their kids to bed, or whose father is ill, or who might need special praise for their forgettable floor speeches. If they are going to Vegas, Reid will help them get dinner reservations or show tickets. He is adept at recognizing people who might feel overlooked. For instance, Susanna Quinn, Jack Quinn's wife, can sometimes feel like an appendage to her lobbyist husband—like when a cartoon rendering of Susanna with Jack on the wall of the Palm identified her merely as "Mrs. Quinn" (the restaurant later added her full name). "Susanna is really a charmer," Reid said in a special toast to her at a fund-raiser the Quinns hosted for the senator at their home. "I know I tell everyone that I love them but I REALLY love Susanna," Reid continued. "Jack has been such a good friend to me, but Susanna makes all of us feel so good about ourselves." This made Susanna feel good about herself.

It turns out that Susanna Quinn's grandfather, a Democratic senator from Oklahoma, used to sit at the desk on the floor that now belongs to Reid. Susanna's then eight-year-old daughter Jocelyn wrote a letter to Reid, and Reid in turn sent her a signed copy of a book he wrote about Searchlight and a kid's book written by Ted Kennedy in the voice of his dog, Splash. (Reid signed that one too.)

Reid caters with supreme efficiency, no wasted motion. To keep phone calls streamlined, Reid often skips saying good-bye. The other party might keep talking to a dead line for several seconds without realizing it.

I first met Reid in 2005, not long after he had become the Democratic leader. When Jim Manley walked me into his office and introduced me, Reid barely looked up and said to Manley, "Is this the sleazeball you told me about?" He had me at "sleazeball."

Reid randomly called my desk a few years later to wish me a "happy Jewish holiday." I don't remember what Jewish holiday it was, or if I even knew it was a Jewish holiday. Reid then bragged to me that he was a "hero" to the then nine Jews in the Senate because he had adjourned the chamber in time for them to get home for whatever Jewish holiday it was. He reeled off the names of all the Senate Jews: Lieberman, Schumer, Barbara Boxer and Dianne Feinstein of California, etc. He concluded with Ron Wyden of Oregon, and when I expressed surprise that Wyden was Jewish—and mock surprise they even had Jews in Oregon—Reid deadpanned, "Yes, there are two of them in Oregon, and we have one of them." And he hung up without saying good-bye, or shalom.

When wandering alone, Reid will sometimes break into a slight grin, as if he has just told himself a joke. Reid reminds me sometimes of a child—a peculiar child who has an imaginary friend who he speaks to unfiltered when he is alone, or not alone. Reid was once being wired up for a television interview in Las Vegas and was overcome by the need to tell the technician fastening his microphone that he had "terrible breath." When an aide asked Reid later why he would possibly say such a thing, Reid calmly explained that it was true.

He has a heightened sense of smell. He once complained about the body odor of summer tourists trekking through the Capitol, taking the occasion of a dedication ceremony for a new Capitol visitor center to make his annoyance public. "In the summertime," he said, "because of the high humidity and how hot it gets here, you could literally smell the tourists coming into the Capitol."

He is also surprisingly food- and body-obsessed, more evocative of a teenage girl than an earthy old boxer. He will occasionally partake of yoga (in black Lycra stretch pants) with Landra in their Ritz-Carlton apartment. He can be harshly judgmental of fat people and other ill-conditioned creatures. When George W. Bush invited Reid to the Oval Office for coffee as a gesture of goodwill at the end of his presidency, Reid promptly insulted the president's dog, Barney, who had trotted into their meeting. "Your dog is fat," Reid told the president.

. . .

Reid often invokes the desert blotch of Searchlight to explain his unfiltered style. He talks interminably about his hometown, even for a member of Congress. Washington politicians love talking about their hometowns, especially when running for reelection. They swoon over how the storied villages embody all that is great about America and how Washington could learn much from the town's good values. (This is usually around the time their spouse gets an even bigger lobbying job and they buy a new mansion in McLean, Virginia, where they will live out their days.) The hometown can be an especially useful prop if it provides a tableau of personal adversity to overcome. Bonus points if the town name is an evocative noun, like Hope, Arkansas, or Plains, Georgia, or Searchlight.

But Searchlight is especially rich in this regard. Gold was discovered there in 1897, and there have been few highlights since. "The boom peaked in 1907 and quickly faded along with the town," it says on a plaque in front of the Harry Reid Elementary School. Reid says he plans to be buried in a Searchlight graveyard, next to Landra.

Reid is a master of "that practiced, pale-faced-bumpkin-from-Searchlight act," says Las Vegas political guru Jon Ralston. This masks a savvy, rough-hewn politician whom Ralston describes as "ruthless" and "Machiavellian." Still, Reid clearly loves Searchlight, and his hard-bitten story is legitimate. The third of four brothers, Reid grew up in a wooden shack with no hot water or indoor toilet or trees. Only rocks. He tells of leafing through the Sears catalogue, just to browse the items they could never afford at Christmas, and then ripping out pages to deploy later as toilet paper in the outhouse.

"I look at these pictures, I cannot believe how I lived," Reid told me. He compares the Searchlight of his boyhood to "that place in

West Virginia." There's a word he's looking for. Hmm. "You know, where things are so bad? Poor?"

"Appalachia?" I said.

"Yes, Appalachia," Reid said, and then broke into a curiously big laugh.

Harry Sr. was a hard-rock miner who suffered chronic pain from on-the-job injuries. He battled alcoholism and depression, and spent time in jail. He killed himself in 1972, at fifty-eight. The senator's mother, Inez Reid, was a redhead with few and eventually no teeth. As a teenager, Harry took a job at a gas station and bought her a false set. "It changed her," Reid says of his mother's new teeth. "I mean, you can imagine how good she felt with teeth after all those years."

When I asked him if it's ever painful to recall his own youth, Reid shrugs. "The only thing I don't like is to watch movies about suicide and stuff like that," Reid says, as close as he comes to publicly contemplating his inner life. But he is capable of pointed moments of empathy. Once, a young communications adviser, Rebecca Kirszner, who had just started working in Reid's Senate office, kept misreading a phone number that Reid had been trying to dial for a radio interview. In his straight-to-the-point manner, Reid asked her, "Do you have a learning disability?" Embarrassed, she quietly said yes. Reid looked Kirszner in the eye and said, "You must have worked twice as hard to have gotten where you are." No one had ever said this before to Kirszner, who was taken aback, and moved. "I did," she whispered.

Reid's sense of Washington psychology is grounded heavily in seeing—and, in certain cases, exploiting—the past humiliations of others. As with many politicians who grew up in poverty and endured family turmoil and other adversities, Washington has also been a powerful reinvention canvas for Reid. The city is filled with proving grounds that double as sanctuaries, like the Senate floor.

. . .

Sometimes during intense legislative debate and machinations, I sit up in the gallery and watch the floor. No words from below can be deciphered, only the low rumble and occasional laugh echoing up, and a pageant of body language. Senators are constantly engaged in physical contact, particularly the men shaking hands, squeezing shoulders, and bro hugging. It is the ritual power dance of faux fellowship, Capitol version. Michael Maccoby, a Washington psychoanalyst and author of the management and business book *Narcissistic Leaders: Who Succeeds and Who Fails*, says he is struck by the "homoeroticism of politics." Not homosexuality per se, but just an abiding sense of love on the Capitol floor, even among adversaries. "There is a sense of people cherishing being together, even at a time when camaraderie supposedly no longer exists," Maccoby says.

Maccoby speaks of a "pseudo love" that people in politics can derive from the approval of their patrons, the loyalty of their staffs and supporters, and the reflective glory of their marquee friends. Multibillion-dollar industries have been born to foster pseudo love through image-buffing public relations, lobbying, advertising, or political campaigns.

"Washington is both a secretive and intensely scrutinized place and it can breed paranoia," Maccoby says. It relies on a form of total loyalty that is at once widely available and fleeting in D.C. It self-selects a personality type that gravitates to the high-wire act of the public affirmation game. The floors of Congress provide case studies.

Harry Reid is always careening across the Senate floor. "I always feel like I'm missing something if I'm not there," Reid says. In his memoir, *The Good Fight: Hard Lessons from Searchlight to Washington*, Reid writes about how his father was never as happy as when he was down in his workplace, the gold mines. It didn't matter that the work was sporadic and backbreaking and that the pay was awful. "I truly believe that it was one of the few places he was comfortable in this world," Reid wrote.

Harry Reid feels similarly about mining votes on the Senate floor. The early Obama years were a bitch. Reid faced a tough re-election race in 2010 in a state where he was hardly loved to begin with. And this was before he engineered passage of an unpopular health-care bill and Republicans had made him their fattest electoral bull's-eye in the country. Reid's unfavorable rating in Nevada had risen to 52 percent by the end of 2009. "Reid fatigue," diagnosed Ralston, the Nevada political couch doctor.

Reid stopped sleeping during the health-care debates of 2009 and early 2010. His caucus was getting harassed at town meetings by a newfangled phenomenon called the Tea Party. The White House kept wanting to know why the deliberations were taking so long. It was becoming clear that Reid was going to have to keep sixty Democratic senators in line to pass a bill; many of them were unreliable, some of them were double-dealers, and two of them were on death's door. When then ninety-two-year-old Robert Byrd of West Virginia was hospitalized, Reid spoke to the state's Democratic governor, Joe Manchin III, about replacing Byrd quickly "in the event that he could not carry out his duties." Before Ted Kennedy died in August, Reid made calls to Massachusetts's Democratic governor Deval Patrick and state lawmakers urging them to change a state law mandating that the seat stay vacant until a special election was held a few months later; this could cost Democrats a decisive vote. The law was changed and Patrick named Paul G. Kirk Jr. as interim senator.

Until that special election, Reid had become preoccupied with the most basic of political duties: survival—literally, in the case of Byrd, the longest-tenured senator in history. Could the nonagenarian West Virginian hang on long enough—and remain ambulatory enough—to vote for the bill? Byrd's looming expiration date became an ever-present subtext. It was too delicate to reference in public, except when Republican Tom Coburn declared in a floor speech that "what the American people ought to pray for is that somebody can't make the vote." Coburn said he was referring to a snowstorm that had been predicted for D.C., but many people assumed he was talking about Byrd.

Coburn later clarified through a spokesman that he does not wish misfortune on anyone, but you wonder if he might not wish just a little on Harry Reid.

He hung up on me again," Coburn was saying, dumbstruck, to an aide after Reid curtly ended another phone call. It's not clear what this particular call was about, only that Coburn had initiated it and Reid had ended it.

Coburn, a Republican from Oklahoma, might have been calling to complain that Reid's office had issued a statement accusing Coburn of not caring about kids eating lethally unsafe food. Or maybe this call was about how Reid might have accused Coburn of being a racist because Coburn wanted to offset funding for the Justice Department to investigate hate crimes. Whatever: he did not take kindly to Reid saying whatever he said, so he called Reid to say so, and Reid hung up, and this cycle tends to repeat periodically between the two men.

For what it's worth, Reid says he is trying to get better about ending his phone calls with the proper sign-off but allows that it might be futile. ("I can't do it," he says, "because I have nothing more to say.")

Also, for what it's worth, Coburn does not care what Reid or anyone else thinks of him. Known as "Dr. No," Coburn, a family practice physician, has built a Washington reputation on displeasing the constituencies politicians spend most of their time trying to please: special-interest groups, local entities looking for funding, party leaders, Republican activists, and often his colleagues, or the ones who call him arrogant and sanctimonious and "Dr. I Know Better." Coburn doesn't care. "Caring" is a Coburn market inefficiency.

Coburn looks like he has a headache. He has intense squinty eyes under small wire-rimmed glasses and a face cast in a slight grimace. The front of his white-gray hair bristles up like a porcupine's quills. Like Reid, with whom he is oddly of a piece, Coburn is content to let the noise and fury of modern politics roll off him, or at least he pretends to be oblivious.

Coburn's "disappointment" with his colleagues is palpable. He insists they're "wonderful people," albeit clueless and cowardly. He has prescribed a "spinal transplant" for 70 percent of the chamber. Or, moving down the body, he has diagnosed his colleagues as having "reproductive organs the size of BBs" and to be generally lacking in "gonads."

But Coburn's bond with Reid—"my friend from Nevada," as they say in the formal bullshit of the Senate—is special. In keeping with the gentleman's-club protocol of The Club, Coburn and Reid have described their relationship as "cordial"—"cordial" being the bare minimum salute and Washington dog whistle for obvious hatred.

(Here is an example of how two senators with a "cordial" relationship deal with each other: In 2005, when Rick Santorum was still in the Senate, I wrote a profile of the brash Pennsylvania Republican, who had managed to claw his way into his party's leadership despite being disliked by many of his colleagues. Santorum's unpopularity was common knowledge on Capitol Hill. As a reporter, however, getting a senator to disparage a colleague on the record can be next to impossible, given protocol against even the mildest slander of fellow members. I tried. And I turned up the predictably limp platitudes from senators who plainly could not stand Santorum—which is "Latin for asshole," as Democrat Bob Kerrey of Nebraska once helpfully translated. Finally, I encountered Democrat Mary Landrieu, of Louisiana, just off the Senate floor. As she walked by, I asked her, "What do you think of Rick Santorum?" To which Landrieu grimaced and replied, "You couldn't quote what I'd have to say about him." That was good enough for me. I quoted Landrieu saying that. And sure enough, next time they were on the floor together, Santorum made a beeline for Landrieu, saying in so many words that his feelings were hurt. In turn, Landrieu did what most self-respecting lawmakers do when cornered about saying something objectionable: she blamed her staff; specifically, she blamed her communications director, Adam Sharp, who by any reading of the situation had nothing to do with it. But Landrieu reamed him out anyway and demanded he craft a letter of apology to Santorum. He did; Landrieu reviewed it and then refused to sign it herself, apparently not wishing to authenticate this travesty with her pristine signature. The office autopen had to suffice.)

Between fistfuls of Hot Tamales in his Senate office, Coburn paralleled for me the two places where Reid has lived and thrived, the exotically American cities of D.C. and Las Vegas. Both D.C. and Vegas feed on human weakness, Coburn said. They are addictive cultures—to gambling in Vegas and to power in D.C. Both places reward hustlers. "You think you can get something for nothing," Coburn says. "You think you can really go to Las Vegas and win? If you could, then we'd all go to Las Vegas and then Las Vegas would not be there anymore. Both Washington and Las Vegas are something-for-nothing cultures."

As a physician who has treated drug addicts, Coburn compares the craving for power to dependence on morphine. Like morphine, power "dulls the senses, impairs judgment," and leads politicians to make choices destructive to their characters and our democracy.

Like Las Vegas, Washington is a city that leads people to behave in exaggerated versions of who they really are, Coburn included, which he would characterize this way: "I'm sort of a grumpy old grapefruit," he says.

Another favorite Coburn invocation is what C. S. Lewis called the "Inner Ring." In his essay of that name, the Irish-born writer describes the human craving to be part of an elite circle, or Inner Ring. Coburn applies the notion to Washington. Politicians become obsessed with the Inner Ring, the place where decisions are made, where one is privy to the information that allows them to be "in the know." Some are inside the ring, others are outside. "The sensation of stepping inside the Inner Ring of Congress is exhilarating," Coburn wrote in *Breach of Trust: How Washington Turns Outsiders into Insiders* (coauthored by John Hart). Washington today affords a broadened and democratized Inner Ring. One needn't be an elected official, or hotshot lobbyist, or TV pundit to be, or feel, "in the know," to achieve do-it-from-home insider status.

In an interview in his office, I asked Reid what he really thought of Tom Coburn. He paused for several seconds, and I imagined a little self-editing gerbil inside his skull hurling itself in the unimpeded pathway that typically connects his brain directly to his mouth. A look of slight agony fell over Reid's sober countenance, the look of someone whose self-editing gerbil is not well-trained.

"Here's what I think of Tom Coburn," Reid said finally, and then there was another long pause. "I am going to have to go off the record for this, otherwise you won't get a good idea of what I think of him." This was Reid being cordial to Tom Coburn.

A few weeks later, Reid and Coburn had another cordial exchange, this one over FAA funding legislation. Coburn wanted to block an attached bill that would have provided funds for squirrel sanctuaries. Reid in turn called Coburn a "dictator" in a floor speech. (In an irresistible postscript, a bipartisan group of Senate aides were discussing the "dictator" remark the next day, when they were overheard by Senator Orrin Hatch of Utah, a devout Mormon and one of Washington's kings of unintentional comedy. "Wait a minute, he called Tom a dickhead?" said Hatch. "That is outrageous.")

Coburn is as devout a fiscal conservative and small-government hawk as there is in the Senate. But he would more readily identify with "antiestablishment" than "antigovernment," the government being just part of what he calls the city's pervasive illness, or "permanent feudal class." Coburn was viscerally anti-Washington before that sentiment coalesced into the Tea Party. He might in fact be the "spiritual godfather" of the movement (*Newsweek* declared him as much). Reid, for his part, referred to members of the Tea Party as "evil-mongers."

Coburn was a blister on the leadership of both chambers, or sometimes something more dangerous. (In the House, he participated in two coups against Newt Gingrich, the second one successful.)

After Trent Lott became Senate majority leader in 1996, Coburn recalls talking to Lott about a government reform initiative; Lott shot him down by saying that there would be plenty of time for "good government" after Election Day. "I'm an order kind of guy," Coburn quotes Lott. "Trent was essentially saying that staying in office was more important to him than anything else. It was amazing to me that he would actually say that."

Trent Lott was born in a rural hospital in north-central Mississippi, the only child from a miserable union of financially stressed parents. "My daddy liked whiskey and women, and that was very traumatic for me," Lott told me in 2009, shortly after Obama took over, the economy had cratered, and Lott was ensconced in his lavish lobbying office on M Street.

Like many political figures, Lott honed his powers of charm and persuasion in dicey childhood circumstances. "When I was Senate leader and Bill Clinton was president and Newt Gingrich was speaker," he pointed out to me, "we were three southern boys that come from dysfunctional families." Lott is a stickler for neatness and order, loath to allow the different foods on his plate to touch. Every surface of his life is arranged just so, beginning with his luscious helmet of senatorial hair. He is a devout creature of routine, waking just after six, drinking three cups of Maxwell House, reading in his pajamas, and spraying his hair into perfect form. Upon arriving back home after work, Lott must—within seconds of walking through the front door—take off his clothes and put on his pajamas.

In 2008, Lott started a boutique lobbying firm with a former Senate colleague, John Breaux, a Louisiana Democrat who as a member of the House once memorably declared that his vote could not be bought but "could be rented." After a member of the House leadership called him a "cheap whore," Breaux protested, saying he was "not cheap."

If Reid is the inside orchestrator of the Senate and Coburn the Tea Party godfather, Trent Lott is another This Town archetype of the age—a "former." His career path had surprised no one. Nearly all of the most recent Senate leaders (Lott, Daschle, Bob Dole, George Mitchell) have stayed in or close to town after they left office, as have most former Speakers of the House and majority leaders (Gingrich, Dennis Hastert, Richard Gephardt, Tom DeLay, Dick Armey). Daschle and Lott identify each other as among their closest post-Senate friends. They appear on the Sunday shows together, "advise" clients, sit on boards, and dine with their wives at the Four Seasons in Georgetown. I had a phone conversation with Lott shortly after he left the Senate. I had called him for a story I was writing about his ailing former colleague Ted Kennedy—"Tiddy

Kennedy," Lott called him. Lott kept gushing over the sanity of his new life.

His tone shifted when I mentioned that Kennedy had kept a letter from Lott hanging in his Senate conference room. It was a thank-you note Lott had sent to Kennedy after Kennedy had purchased a painting for Lott on Cape Cod. "Really?" Lott said quietly. "Did Tiddy really keep that hanging up? I had no idea." There was a pause on the line, and it occurred to me that Lott was choking up.

Ted Kennedy died, expectedly, in August 2009. Large swaths of This Town, including about half the Senate, convened for the funeral at the Basilica of Our Lady of Perpetual Help in Boston. This was one of those This Town field trips where the most usual of suspects convene in a satellite sanctuary—Chuck Schumer, Walter Isaacson, Tom Brokaw, the Clintons, et al. Even John Edwards showed up, on furlough from his perpetual doghouse and trailing several feet behind his cancer-stricken and cuckolded wife, Elizabeth. It was Edwards's first emergence in a while. He drew numerous "What's that asshole doing here?" stares and planted himself in a prime spot near the center aisle. (In a stroke of justice, a seat in front of Edwards was taken, at the last second, by Bill Russell, the six-foot-nine-inch Boston Celtics great.)

Lott couldn't make the trip, but he sent regards. He assured me, in an interview a few weeks later, that he would never forget Tiddy Kennedy.

Sitting in his swank lobbying office, Lott seemed well satisfied that he himself had not been forgotten. He mentioned to me that Senator Tom Carper, Democrat of Delaware, calls him on his birthday every year. "October the ninth, phone rings, like clockwork, it's Tom Carper," Lott says. "Why would he bother? I'm gone, I'm retired. I can't do anything for him—nothing. But he calls. It's nice."

Lott collects these expressions like snow globes. "The gestures really do matter to Trent," said Daschle, whom Lott—in a nice gesture of his own—called after Daschle was forced to withdraw his nomination as Obama's secretary of health and human services over his failure to pay taxes on a personal driver and another income. "There is so much artificiality in politics, so much phoniness," Daschle says. "On the surface, you can say these phone calls and notes are bull, politicians acting like politicians. But many political figures are very insecure people." Part of this, Daschle says, is that Washington is such a delicate place that anything lending the illusion of a permanent bond can be meaningful. "Even the most powerful people need to hear those attaboys," Daschle says. "They need to know that they're not forgotten."

Lott told me he had recently received a phone call from Herb Kohl, the Democratic senator from Wisconsin, who served for many years with Lott. But Kohl, an enigmatic outlier, had almost no relationship with Lott. Yet there was Kohl on the phone, just to tell Lott that he missed him. "That's so nice of you, Herb," said Lott. He said it was one of the nicest gestures anyone's made to him in a long time, and he has told the Herb Kohl story several times.

Lott represents a wedge between distinct Washington models waging battle in the Obama era. Detractors, like Coburn, view Lott as an emblematic former, an entrenched and well-heeled installation of the "permanent feudal class." Harry Reid loves Lott: he views him as just the deal-maker pragmatist today's Senate craves. "I miss Trent Lott," Reid is always saying, which for Reid also doubles as a backhanded whack at Lott's Republican leadership successors (Bill Frist and Mitch McConnell) but which Lott still appreciates, of course.

Lott is a neo–Washington celebrity. His presence is desired at parties, on boards, and on annual duck-hunting trips on the Eastern Shore of Maryland with a bipartisan boy's brigade that can include Terry McAuliffe and Dick Cheney and the Democratic mega-lobbyist Tommy Boggs and the journalist Tucker Carlson (until recently, they convened at a place owned by Boggs called Tobacco Stick Lodge).

Lott reads about himself in Politico, hears that someone saw him shopping for ties at Brooks Brothers, and tweeted about it, whatever "tweet" means. He gets invited onto the Sunday shows and hosts fund-raisers. His brand has proven durable. He is regularly seen eating lunch in the cafeteria of the Dirksen Senate Office Building.

He always has lunch. He is making seven figures a year, easy. He is, once again, a big man in This Town.

In October 2009, as the health-care bill was heading to the Senate floor, I visited Coburn at his home in Muskogee, Oklahoma, about an hour southeast of Tulsa. Armadillos keep trying to tear up his lawn. He keeps pulling fat water moccasins out of his swimming pool. "I kill them," Coburn said with relish, "by slicing their heads off with the sharp edge of a shovel."

He planned to do the same to the health-care bill. Enacting the legislation would be catastrophic, Coburn said, and he was determined to gum up the process. "My mission is to frame this health-care debate in terms of the fiscal ruin of this country," said Coburn, who had a few days earlier railed on the Senate floor that the federal debt was "waterboarding" his five grandchildren.

As he stood in the driveway of his seven-acre estate, Coburn kept looking back on the ground behind him, distracted. One of his two dogs, the skinnier one, Beau, had a terrible case of eczema on his belly. Beau kept rolling onto his back, exposing a raw, hairless patch of the afflicted area. He kept whimpering, begging for scratches, until Coburn finally obliged. The dog squeaked with delight and the senator wheeled around with a point to make.

"See, that's like what the average politician's like. They all need to have their bellies scratched. It's all about the strokes."

Before I left Coburn's house, the senator described for me the Zen state he could achieve when mowing his lawn. Coburn then invited me to take a spin on his prized John Deere tractor, which I did, and it did not end well—that's to say, in a collision with the side of the senator's barn. (There is obviously a larger lesson to draw here about city Jews not being meant for tractors, but that would be stereotyping, which we should never do.)

Back in his Senate office, Coburn became most animated on the subject of political psychology. His next book, he says, will be on the power of "anxiety, worry, and fear" in Washington. These emotions lead politicians to cling to the safest, most conventional methods of staying in power. In contemporary Washington, he says, the easiest way to remain in office is to embrace rigid partisanship. This, he says, "usually signals a deeper faith in careerism than in conservatism or liberalism."

Coburn's Senate career has evolved in a more mainstream direction in recent years. He is no less of a pest, or nemesis, to Harry Reid, but much less of an outlier in a Republican caucus that now includes many of the younger Tea Party bomb-throwers who viewed him as an iconoclastic role model. Coburn's iconoclasm today is often defined by his willingness to compromise and work with Democrats. He was hailed in a 2012 *60 Minutes* piece as "one of the most influential and conservative members of the Senate," and one of the few members of either party willing to work with the other side. Reid loyalists hated this story, which elicited this tweet from Jim

Manley: "Reporters out there that take Coburn seriously (I am talking about you steve kroft/60 minutes) are morons." Tom Coburn's biggest crime against Republican fealty is his friendship with Obama. They hit it off at an orientation for new senators in 2005, and so did Michelle Obama and Coburn's wife, Carolyn, a former Miss Oklahoma. When Obama moved into the White House, Coburn sent him weekly scripture passages; he visits the president periodically and describes him as a wonderful man. He calls the White House to buck up Obama during rough times, or with congratulations when the president is triumphant—a genuine gesture, Coburn says, as opposed to the false ones that This Town runs on.

"He always hugs me after we have our meetings," Coburn says of Obama, sounding a little more enriched by such a gesture than I would have expected.

I asked Coburn if he knew Tim Russert, who I suggested had been the leader of The Club, or Washington's Inner Ring. Not well, Coburn said. But he said he liked Tim. "I always got the sense that Tim opened the window and let you see Tim Russert. No false guile. It's a lot more fun dealing with someone when you don't feel you're being gamed."

Coburn never made it to Russert's funeral. He doesn't go to those kinds of things. "Sounded like a scene," he said. Coburn compares Washington to a "parasitism."

"It is one parasite feeding off another parasite feeding off another parasite," he says. "The reason you attach yourself to someone else is so you can gain something yourself. Parasites don't attack our intestines because they like the environment. That's just the milieu in which they advance their livelihood. That might sound a little harsh. But in Washington if you can't be connected, you can't gain anything."

4

The Entourage

Every great cause begins as a movement, becomes a
business, and eventually degenerates into a racket.

ERIC HOFFER
The Temper of Our Time

n February 2010, just as Obama's health-care bill was about to
pass, Washington's divisions appeared irreparable as ever, and the
unemployment rate was approaching 10 percent, it was time for
another party.

Tammy Haddad and a cast of admirers that included David
Gregory and Jon Meacham threw a fortieth-birthday party for Betsy
Fischer, the New Orleans–bred and well-loved executive producer of
Meet the Press.

The Tamster was going to host a Mardi Gras–themed party
at the home of a neighbor and close friend, the Democratic media
consultant/former lobbyist/CNN pundit Hilary Rosen, in the Pali-
sades neighborhood of Northwest D.C. But a snowstorm would
have made things hard for the valet parkers on her dead-end street.
Instead the bash was held at the Northwest home of the Democratic
lobbyist Jack Quinn and his wife, Susanna. No one really worried

about "the appearances" of this—what it might look like for a prominent lobbyist (who represented an array of health-care interests) to host an event for the executive producer of the beyond-reproach public affairs program—a party that several members of the anti-lobbyist Obama White House would attend. Oh, maybe a few people worried: a few NBC types and Obama invitees told me they felt funny about the thing and stayed away. But the bottom line was that Betsy deserved to be celebrated, and it was a great chance for everyone to enjoy Bourbon Street decor, jambalaya, and the warm stew of one another's company.

Maybe Tammy was also a little worried about "appearances," because a few hours before the party she sent out an e-mail to the guest list declaring the festivities "off the record," which everyone either laughed at or ignored. But really: the gathering was intended as "a private party among friends," an NBC flack explained. Tammy insisted later that the off-the-record provision was to keep away a nettlesome reporter for the local media website FishbowlDC, who she feared would crash the party and write snarky things about it.

Whatever, the turnout was a swell testament to Betsy and the multilateral interests who admire her: there were members of Congress, People on TV, and White House officials, all here together. I saw many people I knew, including a woman who used to be on TV but then went to the White House and then became a "strategic consultant" for someone, I forget who, and she asked me to follow her on Twitter, the new thing that everyone was suddenly talking about, which is like one giant Larry King/*USA Today* column, everyone "tweeting" random notions back and forth all day.

Everyone at the party seemed to be congratulating someone on a recent story, book deal, job, show, speech, or haircut. A photographer for *Washington Life* magazine immortalized the doings. Fox News's Greta Van Susteren was chatting up David Axelrod next to a tower of cupcakes. In the basement, a bipartisan conga line was coursing through the room to a loud hip-hop song. Upstairs, Gregory took the floor and—along with Meacham—gave nice speeches about Betsy. Over by the jambalaya, Alan Greenspan picked up some Mardi Gras beads and placed them around the neck of his wife, Andrea Mitchell, who bristled and quickly removed them.

On the second floor, two "video journalists" from Politico were pulling Notables aside and inviting them to hum the *Meet the Press* theme song to honor Betsy and the franchise she represented. One of the video journalists, Politico's Patrick Gavin, asked some of the performers whether the turnout at the party was in fact a testament to Betsy or, more to the point, to the importance of getting invited back onto *Meet the Press*. Silly question, so cynical ("It's because they love Betsy," Hilary Rosen assured). When invited to hum the theme song, Bob Barnett looked into the camera and demurred, saying that it would be wrong for him to "endorse" one public affairs program over the others. So instead Bob sang his college fight song, "On, Wisconsin!" which was adorable.

Terry McAuliffe was there, too, even though he has had some issues with Jack Quinn over the years. Specifically, the Macker did not like how the former White House counselor had lobbied his former boss Bill Clinton to pardon Quinn's client Marc Rich, a massive embarrassment to Clinton, who—did McAuliffe mention?—is also Terry's best friend. The Macker arrived just as the former Republican National Committee chairman Ed Gillespie, Jack Quinn's former lobbying partner, was skipping out.

Terry and Eddie have become outstanding friends too. Everyone is outstanding friends, yes, but especially these two. They forged a "green room marriage" after years of doing televised talking-point tangling when they were party chairmen. They eventually became partners on the paid speaker's circuit—top dog Democrat and Republican, going at it for entertainment's sake and fifty grand a pop. Washington coming together, disagreeing without being disagreeable! "I love Terry," says Gillespie, explaining his love-hate relationship with McAuliffe at the beginning of their dog-and-pony show, "and I hate myself for it."

Gillespie, who began his career on Capitol Hill as a parking lot attendant, is always telling people that he has come to despise the Washington "scene" and the whole cult of celebrity that has grown up here in recent years. But he was here at Betsy's party because he had been on *Meet the Press* many times and also out of loyalty to Jack Quinn, his dear friend and former business partner, whom he also met in a green room.

It was the late nineties, before a joint appearance on Fox News hosted by Bush's future press secretary Tony Snow. Both Quinn and Gillespie came from working-class Irish Catholic backgrounds in New York (Quinn) and New Jersey (Gillespie) and were lured to Washington for their love of politics and for college (Quinn to Georgetown, Gillespie to Catholic University). They were both pugnacious but generally respectful on camera, congenial and knowing off-camera. A friendship developed. Eventually, so did a lobbying partnership: Quinn Gillespie & Associates, founded in 2000, was considered perhaps the first major bipartisan "one-stop-shopping" firm that was equally adept at lobbying well-placed members of both parties.

As a class, lobbyists are not beloved. The Obama campaign and subsequently the White House have done much to vilify them, which Quinn says he does not appreciate and somewhat resents. "We have families too," he says. In Quinn's case, six children (from three wives) and six grandchildren, who hear all these bad things being said about what Dad/Grandpa does for a living. It's not fair, Quinn says: the perception that they are all as scuzzy as Jack Abramoff, the notorious Republican lobbyist who at the time was doing forty-three months for fraud and conspiracy.

"That was not the world I knew," Quinn says of Abramoff's high-rolling "Casino Jack" playground.

Quinn worked hard, for many years. He tried to restore his good name after Marc Rich. The Rich aftermath was brutal. Quinn wondered if people were looking at him when he walked into restaurants, what they were saying. Friends abandoned him. ("Washington is a place where no one takes friendship too personally," Tony Snow used to say.) Once, during a really low moment at the height of the Rich crisis, Quinn drove off to the Eastern Shore of Maryland, just to get away. His phone rang. It was Connecticut senator Chris Dodd, a dear friend, whom he had come to know during his time as White House counsel. He was just calling to say he was thinking of Jack, who raised a lot of money for Dodd, as he does for a lot of other senators and congressmen. A parade of them wished Jack well in a birthday video that Susanna Quinn made when Jack turned sixty in 2009.

Jack has big red cheeks and a serene chuckle and sighs a lot. He started out in politics as a true-believing lefty for Eugene McCarthy and George McGovern. He now conveys an aura of someone whose main objective is to not be hassled. He does not enjoy lobbying. He would prefer to write, or read, or play golf, or spend time at the ski lodge in Steamboat Springs, Colorado. He has taken on side projects, which seem to excite him far more than discussing his core business: he joined the board of Blackwater Worldwide, the private military contractor whose hired-gun security forces kept killing civilians in Iraq, which created a bit of a branding headache for the firm. Blackwater eventually changed its name, twice, first to Xe, then to Academi, though most people still referred to it with some variation on "the company that used to be Blackwater before it changed its name, for obvious reasons."

But Jack's primary occupation remains as the head of Quinn

Gillespie's offices in Washington. He needs the money, he says—a lot of it—to support his six kids and two ex-wives and current wife, Susanna, with her specialists and the personal makeup artist who comes over before big parties and dinners. ("It's the same makeup artist that does Michelle Obama," Susanna mentions.)

So yes, Jack is still a lobbyist, and despite the terrible national economy and the lingering stench of Abramoff and the hostile new president, 2009 was the most profitable year ever for the profession: special interests collectively spent $3.47 billion lobbying the federal government in 2009, compared with $3.3 billion the previous year.

Obama's aggressive change initiatives were in fact a boon to lobbyists. Whenever there is complicated new legislation, there will be plenty of business for lobbyists. "Complication and uncertainty is good for us," said the Democratic mega-lobbyist Tony Podesta, who speaks with a bug-eyed intensity leavened by frequent giggles at the ends of his sentences.

"This agenda has been great for OUR economy," a Republican lobbyist told the Huffington Post. "We get paid to get Republicans pissed off at Democrats, which they rightfully are. It's the easiest thing in the world. It's like getting paid to get you to love your mother."

Quinn pointed out that Obama's antilobbyist rap has merely driven a lot of the business underground, or at least into thin disguise. "There are a lot of people who have been registered to lobby for years who are now calling themselves 'public affairs consultants' or 'strategic advisers,'" Quinn says. At the same time, Washington is now crawling with people who are not registered to lobby but who nonetheless get paid to advocate full-time for some business, organization, or industry agenda (either directly to a powerful official or via some PR work). In other words, they are engaged in lobbying even if their work does not meet the legal standard requiring them to register as lobbyists. This ilk is known around town as "unregistered lobbyists."

In recent years, Quinn Gillespie had been trying, with limited success, to rebrand itself as "QGA Public Affairs," in part to deemphasize its lobbying work. Another reason is that Gillespie hasn't been involved with the firm for several years. He is closely associated with high-profile campaigns, as he was with the Romney campaign in 2012, and would perhaps launch his own campaign for governor of Virginia one day; having your name stuck on a lobbying firm these days isn't exactly a great voter turn-on.

Even so, Jack and Ed talk all the time and remain the closest of friends. I once asked Quinn what appealed to him about Gillespie when they first started bonding in the bipartisan DMZ of the green room. "Ed got the joke," explained Quinn. It was not immediately clear what he meant by "the joke." What was the joke? Who was it on? Did it refer to the conceit that much of the Washington economy—lobbying, political consulting, and cable news—is predicated on the perpetuation of conflict, not the resolution of problems? Did "the joke" refer to the fact that all of the shouting partisanship that we see on television is just winking performance art? And in reality, off-air, everyone in Washington is joined in a multilateral conga line of potential business partners? What was "the joke"? I asked Quinn. "Ed and I both appreciate that everyone involved in the world in which we operate," Quinn said, "is a patriot."

ere, I will step back and proffer a brief tutorial on the recent history of the Washington entourage:

The biggest shift in Washington over the last forty or so years has been the arrival of Big Money and politics as an industry. The old Washington was certainly saturated with politics, but it was smaller and more disjointed. There were small and self-contained political consultancies that worked on campaigns or raised money for elected officials or contracted a service (i.e., direct mail). PR people tried to promote a client's interests in the media, while lobbyists did the same by engaging directly with government actors. But that "sector," such as it was, typically comprised mom-and-pop operations. It looked outward with some level of fear and humility. It generated some wealth but not enough to make a discernible impact on the city, its culture, and its sensibilities.

Now those subindustries not only have exploded but have been folded under a colossal umbrella of "consulting" or "government affairs." "No single development has altered the workings of American democracy in the last century so much as political consulting," Jill Lepore wrote in the *New Yorker*. "In the middle decades of the twentieth century, political consultants replaced party bosses as the wielders of political power gained not by votes but by money."

Over the last dozen years, corporate America (much of it Wall Street) has tripled the amount of money it has spent on lobbying and public affairs consulting in D.C. Relatively new businesses such as the Glover Park Group—founded by three former Clinton and Gore advisers—provide "integrated services" that include lobbying, public relations, and corporate and campaign consulting. "Politics" has become a full-grown and dynamic industry, a self-sustaining weather system all its own. And so much of its energy is directed inward.

Whenever there is an aura of money and power, an entourage grows up, and that is what's happened in D.C. For much of the last century, the notion of a permanent D.C. was a handful of power brokers embodied by Clark Clifford. Clifford, an adviser to four presidents, was the town's original Beltway superlawyer and wise eminence—at least until he was indicted for bank fraud. They also included a few "celebrity journalists" like James "Scotty" Reston of the *New York Times* and Jack Nelson of the *Los Angeles Times*. But the political entourage was not an industry on a par with Hollywood or Wall Street. Nor were they packaged like celebrities, with pictures splashed on blogs, stories blasted out on Twitter, and agents working multiplatform deals.

In that era, a former campaign official or White House staffer—a 1960s version of, say, Republican TV pundit Mary Matalin—might have hung around and accepted a political appointment if her candidate won. But she never would have joined a mega-industry inside The Club. "Those inside the process had congealed into a permanent political class, the defining characteristic of which was its readiness to abandon those not inside the process," Joan Didion wrote in *Political Fictions*.

Perhaps more than anything, Watergate—and *All the President's Men*—made journalists a celebrated class in This Town unlike in any other. The triumphs of Woodward and Bernstein and the killer persona of Ben Bradlee defined a sector of Washington at its romantic best, even while the city, during Watergate, exhibited her disgraceful worst. Bradlee partook fully of that. "We became folk heroes," he said, while knowing that the postgame high of Watergate would never last. After the *Post* won the Pulitzer in 1973 for its Watergate reporting, Bradlee wrote a letter in anticipation of that day when "this wild self-congratulatory ski-jump" would end and they would all "hit solid ground again." It would happen soon enough, with a meteor crash in 1981, when the *Post* was forced to give back a Pulitzer Prize won by a young *Post* reporter who fabricated a story about an eight-year-old heroin addict. Yet the celebrity aura of the news business in This Town never really abated.

The cable news boom of the 1990s—the Clinton years—accelerated this exponentially. It created a high-profile blur of People on TV whose brands overtook their professional identities. They were not journalists or strategists of pols per se, but citizens of the green room. Former political operatives sought print outlets, not so much because they wanted to write, but because it would help get them on TV. After leaving Tip O'Neill's office, for example, Chris Matthews got himself a column for the *San Francisco Examiner*. He was even named the *Examiner*'s Washington bureau chief, though he was the only one in Washington for the *Examiner* and it had no footprint beyond being the Bay Area's sleepy afternoon newspaper. But the affiliation and title helped Matthews get on TV. He begged himself onto political shout fests like *The McLaughlin Group*. *Hardball* had its debut in 1997, on CNBC, and was catapulted by the Clinton–Lewinsky scandal. In his book about the media's conduct during the Monica saga, Bill Kovach, the founding chairman of the Committee of Concerned Journalists, anointed Matthews as part of a "new class of chatterers who emerged in this scandal . . . a group of loosely credentialed, self-interested performers whose primary job is remaining on TV."

Now the likes of Matthews are full-throttle personalities commanding five figures a pop on the speaking circuit, big book advances, and—in Matthews's case, at least for a while—a $5 million-a-year contract at MSNBC. Fame and celebrity feed on themselves, to a point where people outgrow their first public identities—say, in Mary Matalin's case, as a Republican strategist. A few years back, Matalin signed a deal as a celebrity voice to present the safety instructions before takeoff on Independence Air. She is brand-oriented.

Washington's exportable sex appeal has continued to grow even as the modern political game has grown so repellent to so many Americans. It is hard to pinpoint exactly when this started, but it seemed to again coincide with the arrival of Bill Clinton. As big money is an inherently sexy lure, Clinton's hiring of a Wall Street mega-titan, Robert Rubin, to be his Treasury secretary created an aura of wealth creation in the city that hadn't existed under George H. W. Bush (who presided over a bad economy) and Ronald Reagan (under whom the lobbying culture certainly thrived, but nowhere near to the degree it does now). The Clinton years also brought a new generation of staffers to routinely parlay their "service" positions into lucrative financial services jobs. Few of them had MBAs or banking experience, but the mystique of having served at high levels of politics—particularly in the White House—had become instantly bankable. Rahm Emanuel, for instance, resigned his job in the Clinton White House in 1998 to join the investment banking firm of Wasserstein Perella. Emanuel was not a "numbers guy," he admitted, but more of a "relationship banker." Relationship banking paid well. By the time he left to run for Congress in 2002, Emanuel had amassed more than $18 million in two and a half years and was then free to return to his life of "public service."

Clinton also represented a killer hybrid of pop culture cachet. He was telegenic, young, and willing to discuss his underwear on MTV—and, of course, had a titillating penchant for Big Trouble in his personal life. All this lent Clinton a box-office allure. Hollywood types started showing up at the annual White House Correspondents' Association dinner, which had previously been a musty spring affair and the highlight of the local social calendar by default. The dinner has sold out every table since 1993 at a price, in recent years, of about $2,500 per, and the spectacle has festered into a glitzy cold sore of pre-parties, after-parties, and live television coverage from the red carpet.

Bill Clinton's winning presidential campaign of 1992 also spawned the Rise of the Celebrity Operative. While there have always been famous or infamous political aides (Ted Sorensen for JFK, Lee Atwater for Reagan and Bush 41), the Clinton campaign ushered in a fascination with "entourage" characters such as James Carville and George Stephanopoulos, among others, who themselves became stand-alone brands. Carville, for instance, was a journeyman political gym rat who had never advised a winning national campaign until Clinton's in 1992 and has not played a major role in advising a domestic one since. Yet with his direct and homespun drawl, urchinlike appearance, and bipartisan romance to a well-known Republican pundit—Matalin—Carville has become a marquee imprint whose five-figure speaking fees, TV pundit deals, and book projects have made him and Matalin exceedingly wealthy.

The Carville–Matalin merger was not so much a joining of two warring tribes as it was the sanctification within the political class. Carville quotes Walter Shapiro, the veteran political reporter for *Time* and other publications, who marveled that anyone would treat the Carville–Matalin union as some kind of exotic mixed marriage. "If either of them had been in love with a tree surgeon from Idaho," Shapiro said, "that really would have been something." His larger point is that Political Washington is an inbred company town where party differences are easily subsumed by membership in The Club. Policy argument can often devolve into the trivial slap fights of televised debate: everyone playing a role, putting on a show, and then introducing a plot twist—in this case, "Hey, these people yelling at each other on TV are actually a couple and they're getting married."

The joint venture of Matalin–Carville—"Brand Mataville"— itself became a potent commercial force. The couple wrote a book about their relationship, *All's Fair: Love, War, and Running for President*, which enjoyed a solid run on the bestseller list and expanded the Mataville imprint beyond the ghetto of political junkies. One of the notable aspects of the book's success was that it was marketed less as a political book or feel-good tale of political tolerance as it was a showbiz merger. While Carville and Matalin both packed solid middle-American appeal—Carville as a liberal bayou populist, Matalin as a smart-aunt conservative—neither was positioned in the marketplace as "average Americans." These were political pros whose status as celebrity operatives was unquestioned and solidified by their joining forces. Casual observers of politics not inclined to buy books by celebrity operatives could instantly wonder, *How do these people stand each other?* as if mixed-political marriages did not exist in every suburban neighborhood in America. Still, the fact that these were celebrity partisans who promoted their views on behalf of presidential clients, and argued them on television, made the marriage appear man-bites-doggish. It infused Mataville with a crossover appeal.

They endorsed products, like Maker's Mark, the Kentucky-made bourbon, which paid them to make a series of videos on behalf of the distillery. Carville is an old friend of Maker's Mark magnate Bill Samuels, who first met Carville in the 1980s when the latter ran the winning gubernatorial campaign of Kentucky Democrat Wallace G. Wilkinson. Samuels thought James and Mary would make perfect spokespeople for a marketing campaign they were doing that urged everyone to resist mainstream political parties in favor of a single, unifying platform: bourbon. It was known within Maker's Mark as its "Cocktail Party" promotion.

James and Mary decamped to a glorious old home in New Orleans in 2008, right as the death of Tim Russert had left them both devastated. But certainly the capital of Mataville remained Washington, D.C. One veteran Washington media consultant remembers attending a wedding party for Carville and Matalin at the White House in November of 1993. The guests included dozens of establishment Democrats and Republicans, and the party occurred on the same night that Al Gore and Ross Perot were debating the North American Free Trade Agreement on CNN's *Larry King Live*. She recalls watching the debate and then the postgame commentary from pundits of both parties—many of whom had attended the White House reception earlier. There was broad agreement in support of Gore, whose position on NAFTA was consistent with the Clinton administration's and that of most Republicans in Congress. Perot, the third-party insurgent who opposed NAFTA, was portrayed as a yahoo and a crank. Which might have been true, by the way; but the consultant, a Democrat, was struck by the juxtaposition of the White House bash attended by elites of both parties, followed by the debate and the piling on against the irritant nonmember of The Club by these same bipartisan elites. "You had a sense [that] the members of the establishment, who had literally been at the same party at the White House earlier, were now closing ranks against the party-crasher," she said. "Perot had this contempt for Washington and had this belief that changing the place went far beyond partisan politics. And in retrospect that night proved him to be absolutely correct."

Theodore H. White discovered the mass appeal of behind-the-scenes political drama with his "Making of the President" series, beginning in 1961. The debut book—about the previous year's Kennedy–Nixon showdown—treated the backroom operatives and image makers as marquee players and stayed on the bestseller list for a year. But the Clinton years ushered in a latter-day fascination with the modern political ensemble in popular culture. *The War Room*, a documentary about the rapid-response operation of the Clinton campaign headquarters in Little Rock, became a cult classic and helped solidify Carville and Stephanopoulos as sellable media imprints. *Primary Colors*, the anonymously written political bestseller by (it was later revealed) journalist Joe Klein, was based on the Clinton experience. Late in the Clinton years, the hit NBC show *The West Wing* romanticized the fast-paced, high-stakes action of the modern White House.

These successes also complemented the exhaustive reach of political television coverage. Members of Congress say their body changed dramatically when C-SPAN began live coverage of their proceedings in 1979 (with a speech by an upstart Democrat from

Tennessee, Al Gore). Same with the White House press corps after Clinton press secretary Michael McCurry began allowing live coverage of the daily media briefing in 1995. The environment fostered a play-to-the-cameras feel in so many environments that were previously more businesslike, anonymous, and, God forbid, kind of boring.

These true-to-life fictional tableaus coincided with a sustained growth in the political news media. Its master form—and fattest market—was debate, the hotter and more partisan the better. Suddenly it appeared anyone without facial warts could call themselves a "strategist" and get on TV. Or start an e-mail newsletter, website, or, later, blog, Facebook page, or Twitter following—in other words, become Famous for Washington.

Never before has the so-called permanent establishment of Washington included so many people in the media. They are, by and large, a cohort that is predominantly white and male and much younger than in the bygone days of pay-your-dues-on-the-city-desk-for-ten-years veterans for whom the elite political jobs were once reserved. They are aggressive, technology-savvy, and preoccupied by the quick bottom lines (Who's winning? Who's losing? Who gaffed?). Such shorthand is necessitated by their short deadlines, nervous editors, limited space, constrained reader attention spans, intense competition, and the fact that they are writing for wannabe (or actual) insiders like themselves.

Today's Washington media has also never been more obsessed with another topic that has long obsessed the Washington media: the Washington media.

In 2002, ABC launched something called the Note, a widely read tip sheet of morning and overnight political news that catered to what it called "the Gang of 500." Coined by the Note's founder, the

ABC News political director at the time, Mark Halperin, "the Gang of 500" was a simultaneously self-deprecating and self-congratulatory term that described the expanding world of Washington political operatives, journalists, lobbyists, and self-styled insiders. The Note, which was disseminated on the Internet and via e-mail, took a horse-racy approach to covering politics and presented the day's events in a lively and knowing way. It turned marginally known political reporters and mid-level campaign operatives into familiar names within the Gang. It was, arguably, the first online forum that leveraged "Famous for Washington" as a business model.

The late 2000s brought an explosion of Washington's celebrity culture and the expanded entourage. Obama was a historic candidate who defeated another one, Hillary Clinton, in the most captivating primary campaign of recent memory. The 2008 race was also the most exhaustively followed, and the first campaign that took place fully in the infinite hyperspace of New Media. New entities such as Politico and the Huffington Post devoted full-on coverage, and TV viewers tuned in in record numbers to emerging cable colossi such as Fox News. The Gang of 500 of the mid-decade had grown into a vast and self-sustaining industry. A marker of this has been the rise of Politico, the caffeinated trade site founded in 2007 by two *Washington Post* alumni.

The liaison between sex appeal and Washington has always been stout but clunky. This Town is a place where for many years Henry Kissinger was considered a sex god. Now entire publications and cable shows are predicated on the day-to-day drama and personalities of the Gang. It is not so much the right or wrong or results of politics, the doing good or making a difference. Rather, it is the politics themselves. They are supposedly sexy, packed with high drama ("narrative") and the jockeying for power, which, as Kissinger famously said, is "the ultimate aphrodisiac."

The formula has imposed an often absurd level of breathless

attention on the prosaic grind of Washington reality. It was suddenly news in the capital when (actual items) former House speaker Dennis Hastert had his gallbladder removed, Representative William Lacy Clay of Missouri got his braces taken off, Karl Rove was spotted at a Kennedy Center performance of *Who's Afraid of Virginia Woolf?*, and Paul Wolfowitz was busted in a photograph that revealed holes in his socks. Never has the national political story been so awash in the burps, warts, and appendectomies of the People Who Run Your Country. (Full disclosure: I authored a story on the proliferation of flies in the White House that appeared on June 17, 2009, in the *New York Times*.)

Politico often gets blamed for defining down and amping up political news today. The "haters," as Politico's editors call their critics, are often the same Washington insiders whom the publication reports on—and who read the thing religiously. "I've been in Washington about thirty years," Mark Salter, a former chief of staff and top campaign aide to John McCain, says. "And here's the surprising reality: on any given day, not much happens. It's just the way it is." Not so in the world of Politico, he says, where meetings in which senators act like themselves (maybe sarcastic or like asses) become "tension-filled" affairs. "They have taken every worst trend in reporting, every single one of them, and put them on rocket fuel," Salter says of Politico. "It's the shortening of the news cycle. It's the trivialization of news. It's the gossipy nature of news. It's the self-promotion."

Politico's mission is to "drive" conversation in the capital— "drive" being a higher-velocity version than the stodgier verb "influence." If, say, David S. Broder and R. W. Apple Jr. were said to "influence the political discourse" through the *Washington Post* and the *New York Times* in the last decades of the twentieth century, Politico wanted to "drive the conversation" in the new-media landscape of the twenty-first. The target audience is the "insiders" and "opinion makers" with no pretense of being representative of the population at large.

Politico's chief franchise is Playbook, an online tip sheet delivered mostly via e-mail that has become a more influential morning document than the Note was in the early to middle 2000s. Written and sent out 365 days a year by the hyperactive and nocturnal Eagle Scout Mike Allen, Playbook is an insider's dog's breakfast of overnight news, press release previews, random sightings around town, and birthday greetings to people you've never heard of. These are "data points," as Allen calls his dawn offering—the business of the nation in the form and voice of a summer camp newsletter. It reaches a target audience of what Politico calls "influentials": elected officials, political operatives, lobbyists, journalists, and other political-media functionaries. This is the expanded Club or entourage of contemporary Washington—"the Playbook community," in the words of Allen, who, around early 2009, many White House officials, members of Congress, staffers, and journalists began describing as the most influential journalist working in Washington today.

Politico is an organization of healthy self-regard. Company higher-ups tout Allen as not just its franchise player but something greater. Fred Ryan, a former Reagan administration official who is Politico's CEO, told me that Allen will go down as a momentous figure in the annals of American journalism. "In the same way that Murrow was with one era and Walter Cronkite was with another era," Ryan said, "I think Mike Allen is going to be viewed as one of the defining journalists of this period."

Playbook's success is emblematic of modern life in a time-starved place in which the power-and-information hierarchy has been upended. It also offers daily fodder for those who deride Washington as a clubby little town in which usual suspects talk to the same usual suspects all day.

A big part of Allen's appeal, I'm convinced, is the volume of names he mentions. He will sometimes list more than a dozen birthdays alone on a given morning, which he will cull from Facebook, news sources, and his enormous word-of-mouth/e-mail network. He parcels out simple recognitions, fossil fuel to the Washington ego.

At any given time, the city is filled with formers and has-beens whom we might charitably describe as "still kicking around town." Allen, with his mentions, gives a warm tingle of notice. The acknowledgment section of Terry McAuliffe's memoir runs six single-spaced pages and includes the names of every member of the Democratic National Committee during his time as the party's chairman. The index runs several more pages, making it a perfect vehicle for "the Washington read," defined as the practice of "reading" books by scouring the index and acknowledgments for the Holy Grail, aka your name. (*New York Times* columnist David Brooks has an alternative definition of "Washington read": the act of telling someone, "I didn't read your book but did praise it on TV.")

"There is no sweeter word in Washington than your own name," said Marshall Wittmann, then a top aide to Senator Joe Lieberman and one of the great career vagabonds, ideological contortionists, and political pontificators ever to inflict himself on a city full of them. Wittmann is a Trotskyite turned Zionist turned Reaganite turned bipartisan irritant turned pretty much everything in between—including chief lobbyist for the Christian Coalition, the only Jew who has ever held that position. After leaving Lieberman's office upon the senator's announced retirement in 2012, Marshall became the top flack for the American Israel Public Affairs Committee (AIPAC).

Marshall was raised in Waco, Texas, worked for Cesar Chavez in the 1970s, Linda Chavez (a Republican Senate candidate from Maryland) in the 1980s, Ralph Reed of the Christian Coalition in the 1990s, and Bruce Reed of the centrist Democratic Leadership Council in the 2000s. Above all, Wittmann reveres his many political heroes. They include Teddy Roosevelt, Kinky Friedman, and his two most recent patrons, Lieberman and John McCain.

Washington, Marshall says, is all about having a shtick and a role and an ability to hone them in a way that builds a brand. Seeing and hearing your name is an important part of this. It conjures a split second of mindshare. Mike Allen is the local king of mindshare. He doles out morsels of proof that your brand is ticking, that your name is out there, that you're alive in This Town.

Embedding

I n early 2010, I set out reluctantly on a *New York Times Magazine* story about Mike Allen.

I was reluctant for a few reasons. One, the story was an exercise in meta-journalism—journalism about journalism—that would reinforce the (largely true) notion that the media is overly self-involved. My own association with Allen would have to be a data point. I have known Mike—whom many people call "Mikey"—for more than a decade. We worked together at the *Washington Post*, where I also came to know Politico's cofounders, Jim VandeHei and John Harris. We all have the same friends and run into each other a fair amount. In other words, I would write this from within the tangled web of Allen's "Playbook community."

My reluctance to write about Allen dissipated, as it was clear that Playbook had become an inescapable catalyst for the day-to-day Washington conversation. Allen's selections of which stories to highlight or disregard were pivotal in "driving" coverage throughout the day. "The people in this community, they all want to read the same ten stories," Allen told me. "And to find all of those, you have to read one thousand stories. And we do that for you."

As with much in today's political world, media is a derivative operation. Mikey, who draws heavily (or "aggregates") from the work of others, has become a de facto assignment editor for many of the time-starved (or lazy) journalists who stare at screens all day under intense pressure from similarly screen-fixated and Playbook-devouring bosses.

At eight a.m. on a campaign bus, there's a good chance that at least half of the passengers are reading Playbook. Or they are reading a story linked from Playbook, or are e-mailing with nervous editors about chasing a story flagged in Playbook. "Washington narratives and impressions are no longer shaped by the grand pronouncements of big news organizations," says Allen, a former reporter for three of them: the *Washington Post*, the *New York Times*, and *Time* magazine.

Allen's bearing combines the rumpledness of an old-school print reporter with the sheen of a new-school "cross-platform brand" who has become accustomed to performing on camera. Every time Allen starts to speak—in person or on the air—his eyes bulge for an instant as if he has just seen a light go on. His mannerisms resemble an almost childlike mimicry of a politician—the incessant thanking, the deference, the greetings, the smiles with teeth clenched, and the ability to project belief in the purity of his own voice and motivations. He speaks in quick and certain cadences, on message, in sound bites, karate-chopping the table for emphasis. In different settings, Allen will often repeat full paragraphs almost to the word.

As Tim Russert did, Allen has an intuitive sense of Washington as a small town and interlocking power structure—Lake Wobegon with power. Allen is an unabashed Washington exceptionalist. He marvels about the "amazing times" he is living through here and all the "amazing friends" who inhabit This Town.

Allen's "Playbook community" is an electronic corollary to the media-cluster phenomenon portrayed in *The Boys on the Bus*, Tim Crouse's travelogue and critique of the elite political operatives and journalists on the 1972 presidential campaign. Crouse popularized the concept of "pack journalism," which referred to the groupthink and implied self-censorship rules that govern the "freakish, insular existence of the press bus." Subversion was frowned on. Even the most independent scribe could not "completely escape the pressures of the pack," Crouse wrote.

The path from *The Boys on the Bus* to Playbook is not a straight line. The evolution must obviously account for the anarchic environment of the Internet, the perpetual nature of today's news cycle, and the rise of ideological journalism, all of which Allen incorporates into his daily e-mail. The "pack" still exists, in other words; it's just bigger and more diverse.

But the one-world notion of the "pack" remains unchanged. Whether journalists are gathered on a physical bus or reading a virtual document, it is a shared space. They are encountering the same names and characters and, after a while, acquiring a shared language and sensibility. "If there was a consensus," Crouse wrote, "it was simply because all the national political reporters lived in Washington, saw the same people, used the same sources, belonged to the same background groups, and swore by the same omens. They arrived at their answers just as independently as a class of honest seventh-graders using the same geometry text—they did not have to cheat off each other to come up with the same answer."

The troublemakers of the bus are stigmatized just as today's version, Playbook, generally avoids trouble. Mikey is more of a pleaser, a delighter, and, perhaps, an enabler.

If Mikey has a bias, it is in favor of Washington—the village, the mind-set, and the big, heady dream of it all. Since Washingtonians tend to engage oppressively in inside baseball, his focus tends toward the game itself—a morning romp through the city's thriving vanity sectors: elites listening to elites, trading sound bites, and going into business together. In the post-Russert era, Mikey was, in his own eccentric and online way, a new mayoral figure. The great presider.

Allen spent his childhood in Seal Beach, California, in Orange County, the oldest of four—two boys, two girls. He told me he had an apolitical upbringing but wanted to attend college near Washington. He enrolled at Washington and Lee University in Lexington, Virginia, which he said seemed close to D.C. on a map but was in fact a five-hour Greyhound ride away.

Sometime in his teenage years, Allen became fascinated with the doings of the Capitol. He arrived in Washington as he remains now: wide-eyed, reverent, and in constant motion. Allen darts in and out of parties, at once manic and serene, chronically toting gifts, cards, and flower arrangements that seem to consume much of an annual income that is believed to exceed $250,000. He kisses women's hands and thanks you so much for coming, even though the party is never at his home, which not even his closest friends have seen. It is as if Mikey is the host of *one big party*, and by showing up anywhere in Washington, you have served the Playbook community and are deserving of the impresario's thanks (or "hat tip" in Playbookese).

Playbook has become the political-media equivalent of those food pills that futurists envision will replace meals. He offers a twist—if not a rebuttal—to the notion that the Internet promotes democratization of the news and diminishes the returns on clubby access. But Allen "wins the morning" (in the lingo of Politico) in part because of his extreme clubby access. It's just that the political and news establishment—The Club—is so much bigger now, and includes so many wannabe insiders that it lends a more democratic feel. They love Mikey. The feeling is mutual and transactional.

They use him and vice versa ("love" and "use" being mutually non-exclusive in Washington). He seems to know everyone and works at it. "I consider him a very good friend," said Peter Watkins, a former press aide to President George W. Bush who now runs a small communications shop in Salt Lake City. "Of course, there are about fifteen thousand people in Washington that consider him to be their best friend."

If such qualities can coexist, Mikey can be perceived as both a decent and solid friend, and also an exemplar of the D.C. operator. He is always touting Playbook, cultivating his brand as the city's ultimate "entrepreneurial journalist," another one of those fashionable news business terms.

"The most successful journalists have their own unique brand and circle of friends," VandeHei, Politico's executive editor, said. "This is the Facebook-ization of politics and D.C. The more friends or acquaintances you have, the more time you spend interacting with them via e-mail and I.M., the more information you get, move, and market." VandeHei's conceit equates Allen's circle of friends to a commodity—exactly the kind of mutual back-scratching undercurrent that gives "friendship" in Washington its quotation marks. "Playbook is D.C.'s Facebook," VandeHei concluded. "And Mike's the most popular friend." Allen's closest friend is probably Vande-Hei, who is protective of Allen and posits him as a rare island of goodness in a racket of frauds and two-faced operators. "Mike is unique in our world," VandeHei says. "He has authentic power while being authentically gracious, honest, and selfless. He's the real deal— and it drives the haters mad."

Not long ago, I received an e-mail that read: "Craig likes Craig Crawford on Facebook and suggests you like him too."

Who is Craig Crawford and why does he like himself?

Craig is a classic poli-media specimen who has worked for places like the Hotline and Congressional Quarterly and written a few books and shows up serviceably on cable. I run into him at the occasional book party or spin room. He is jolly and friendly, mid-fifties-ish, giggles a lot, southern accent, slicked hair, fancy glasses, stylish suits. I wouldn't say he is a "friend," except maybe in the Facebook sense, although apparently that window is now closed with him, according to this auto-generated Facebook message. "Craig says, 'I've reached my friend limit!'" he relayed in the deflating e-mail. "Please join me on my new Facebook fan page.—Craig"

It was nice of him to ask, but I decided I didn't know Craig well enough to be a "fan." It would be something for us to work toward.

Parallels between Facebook and D.C. come up a lot. Both are spaces to collect people, show off our shiny hordes, and leverage our "connections." The Washington friendship is best kept public. What's the use of a high-level bond with "my good friend from (state name)" if the world doesn't know about it? It is not uncommon for senators and congressmen to have encyclopedic recall of all the colleagues who supported them publicly in leadership elections, or screwed them by endorsing someone else. But everyone is a "friend." Protocol demands it.

Like D.C., Facebook is a vast and growing network, evolving and under some assault, but secure in its permanence as an empire. It is no surprise that a pipeline of Washington political talent has joined Facebook in recent years—most prominently Joe Lockhart, the Monica-era press secretary in the Clinton White House who was for a time the company's head of corporate communications.

Washington, the most socially networked city in the United States, is a perfect incubator of a latter-day "network effect." Commonly invoked in Silicon Valley, the term "network effect" refers to products gaining value through the size of the network they serve. Mikey is of course on Facebook. But his true network is the Playbook community. As of April 2013, that had included the roughly one hundred thousand who have signed up to receive it.

The Playbook community puzzles some over Allen. People wonder whether he actually lives somewhere besides the briefing rooms, newsrooms, campaign hotels, and going-away dinners for Senator So-and-so's press secretary that seem to be his perpetual regimen. And they wonder, "Does Mikey ever sleep?"

The query tires him. He claims he tries to sleep six hours a night, which seems unrealistic for someone who says he tries to wake at two or three a.m. to start Playbook after evenings that can include multiple stops and virtual trails of midnight-stamped e-mail. He speaks all over the country and makes constant TV and radio appearances. I asked Allen if he slept during the day and he said no.

Allen has been spotted dozing in public—on campaign planes, at parties—clutching his BlackBerry with two hands against his chest like a teddy bear. He has also been seen asleep over his laptop, only to snap awake into a full and desperate type, as if momentary slumber were just a blip in the 24/7 political story Mikey is writing.

No shortage of friends will testify to Mikey's thoughtful gestures, some in the extreme. They involve showing up at a friend's son's baseball game (in South Carolina) or driving from Richmond to New York to visit a fraternity brother and heading back the same night. He attends a nondenominational Protestant church and a Bible study group. "He is one of the most thoughtful people I have ever met," Josh Deckard, a former White House press aide, says. "Philippians 2:3 said, 'In humility, consider others better than yourselves,' and I think Mike exemplifies that better than anyone."

Yet even Allen's supposed confidants say that there is a part of Mikey they will never know or ask about. He is obsessively private. I asked three of Allen's close friends if they knew what his father did. One said "teacher," another said "football coach," and the third said "newspaper columnist." A 2000 profile of Allen in the *Columbia Journalism Review* described his late father as an "investor."

When sharing a cab, Allen is said to insist that the other party be dropped off first. One friend describes driving Allen home and having him get out at a corner; in the rearview mirror, the friend saw him hail a cab and set off in another direction. I've heard more than one instance of people who sent holiday cards to Allen's presumed address, only to have them returned undeliverable.

Allen is a serious hoarder and pack rat. When I worked with him at the *Post*, enormous piles of yellowing papers, clothes, bags, and detritus leaned ominously above his cubicle. It got so bad at *Time*, where Allen was given his own office, that it became difficult to even open the door. (Note: Allen is hardly the only journalist with a slovenly workspace. When the *Washington Post*'s David Broder died in 2011, Nixon-era sandwiches were reportedly still being excavated.)

Allen has achieved a seamless merging of life and work, family and Playbook. He is deeply committed to his mother, younger brother, two younger sisters, and eight nieces and nephews scattered on both coasts. They make Playbook cameos. A former editor at the *Post* told me that Allen today has taken refuge in his status as a public entity. He deploys Playbook as a protective alter ego. It reminded me of something former Senator Tom Daschle told me once: that a lot of politicians are shy, private people and that they enter the business because it allows them to remain shy and private behind a public cut-and-paste persona—to hide in plain sight.

My first meeting with Allen for the *New York Times Magazine* story was a casual get-together in February 2010 over appetizers at the Bombay Club, an Indian restaurant near the White House. Mikey had "spotted" me the day before in Playbook (eating lunch at that same restaurant) and mentioned me again for something the next day. The first thing he asked when we sat down was when my daughters' birthdays were so he could list them in future Playbooks. (I didn't have the heart to tell him that the girls, then three, six, and nine, were not yet reading Playbook.)

Over a twenty-five-year newspaper career, Allen has been known as an unfailingly fair, fast, and prolific reporter with an insatiable need to be in the newspaper. "The worst thing you could say to Mike Allen was 'We don't have space for that story,'" says Maralee Schwartz, the longtime political editor at the *Post*. "It was like telling a child he couldn't have his candy."

Jim VandeHei, who is forty-two, is contemptuous of Washington's "It used to be better" reflex as it relates to news. "Those institutions and reporters," he says, referring to traditional ones, "were never as good as their reputations. And they limited, in consequential ways, the information flowing to people who cared about politics. It was largely—and this was true for decades—a small group of middle-aged, left-of-center, overweight men who decided how all of us should see politics and governance."

VandeHei distills today's "New World Order" to a few journalistic premiums: speed, information, gossip, and buzz, all of which Allen excels in. "He has built the most successful brand in journalism, Mikey, Inc.," VandeHei says, "and its subsidiary, Playbook."

Nowhere is Washington's ambivalence over Politico more evident than in the Obama White House. They consider the publication a bastion of "snowflake news," a term coined by Ron Brownstein of *National Journal* that refers to small, buzzy stories that are evanescent for a second but then dissolve on contact.

The Obama and Politico enterprises have had parallel ascendancies to an extent. They both fashioned themselves as tech-savvy upstarts bent on changing the established order—of politics (Obama) and of how it is covered (Politico). They started around the same time, early 2007, and their clashing agendas were apparent early. On the day that Politico published its first print edition, Obama's campaign manager, David Plouffe, identified it as just the kind of inside-the-Beltway masturbation that might distract the campaign. He walked into the campaign's offices and slammed a copy of the new publication on Dan Pfeiffer's keyboard. "This," Plouffe declared, "is going to be a problem." Generally speaking, the Obama brigade viewed itself as a cleansing force for all that was self-centered, shallow, and divisive about Washington—whereas they believed Politico was in fact perpetuating and profiting from all of it.

White House aides have bitched interminably about what they consider Politico's trivial attentions to Washington's lame celebrity doings, namely their own. When a citizen paparazzo posted on the Web a photo of speechwriter Jon Favreau and press aide Tommy Vietor playing bare-chested beer pong at a Georgetown bar one Sunday, Politico ran a prominent story wondering if the Obama White House had become overexposed, suggesting that a designated "grown-up" needed to be brought on staff and declaring that some Obama "personalities" have "not disguised their pleasure at the fast-lane opportunities opened up by their new status in Washington." The story equated the beer pong photo to reports, in 1979, that White House chief of staff Hamilton Jordan had snorted coke during a visit to Studio 54 (a special counsel's investigation resulted in no charges).

Favreau sent an e-mail to Politico editor in chief John Harris complaining that this was "another example of Politico extrapolating some larger cultural meaning or political lesson from absolutely nothing." Harris in turn said that after the pectoral-bearing beer pong picture was published, he had been "hearing a lot of conversation about this as a minor Washington cultural moment," thus the story was justified.

White House officials said it was an indictment of the "Washington mentality" that the city was sustaining Politico. In early March 2010, David Axelrod was sitting in his West Wing office, complaining to me about the "palace-intrigue pathology" of Washington. "I prefer living in a place where people don't discuss Politico over dinner," he said.

Yet most of the president's top aides are steeped in this culture and work hard to manipulate it. "What's notable about this administration is how ostentatiously its people proclaim to be uninterested in things they are plainly interested in," observed Harris. Likewise, Politico's saturation coverage of the Obama entourage has raised considerably the profiles of people like Plouffe and Axelrod, allowing them to better "monetize" their service with book, speaking, and TV deals. New-media entities such as Politico have clearly transformed not just the Washington conversation but also the city's information economy. The six-year-old publication has taken a significant bite from the *Washington Post*'s "political paper of record" franchise and threatened other specialized information sources such as *National Journal*.

Politico—particularly Allen—is prone to trafficking suggestive notions in the spirit of "driving the conversation." The conversation then gets picked up on cable and blogs ("I'm hearing talk about . . ."), and then Politico will report on "something that is getting a lot of buzz" to a point that merits coverage as a viable possibility, something that's "out there."

"Good Saturday morning," Mikey wrote in April 2010 as President Obama was looking for a Supreme Court justice to replace the retiring John Paul Stevens. "For brunch convo: Why isn't Secretary Clinton on the media short lists for the Court?" By Monday, the convo had moved from the brunch table to MSNBC's *Morning Joe* (where the host, Joe Scarborough, advocated for Clinton) and *Today* (where the Republican senator Orrin Hatch mentioned her too). Later that day, Ben Smith, then writing for Politico, quoted a State Department spokesman who "threw some coolish water on the Clinton-for-Scotus buzz in an e-mail." By then the cable, blog, and Twitter chatter was fully blown. The White House issued an unusual statement that Secretary Clinton would not be nominated. Politico then sent out a "breaking news" alert, and Smith reported that the White House had "hurriedly punctured the trial balloon." End of convo.

For what it's worth, Philippe Reines, a Clinton adviser, says that he told another Politico reporter the previous Friday that the chances of his boss's being nominated were "less than none" and added, "Something being a sexy media story shouldn't be confused with truth."

But, of course, it is categorically confused all the time in today's D.C. Fact and speculation swirl in the same blizzard. As long as something is circulating "out there"—getting page views, generating buzz, driving convo—it can have impact, ephemeral or otherwise. The thrown-off nature of Twitter has turned phrases like "Hearing that," "Word on the street is," and "I get the feeling that" into acceptable attribution units.

Bob Woodward, the best-known investigative reporter in history, suggested in a pundit capacity on CNN that Obama might dump Biden for Hillary on the 2012 ticket ("It's on the table"). Conservative oracle William Kristol wrote a column suggesting the same thing. *New York* magazine's John Heilemann, coauthor of *Game Change: Obama and the Clintons, McCain and Palin, and the Race of a Lifetime*, wrote an October 2010 cover story on "President Palin" ("How Sarah Barracuda Becomes President"), which set in motion the Playbook community as well as the televised breakfast nook of *Morning Joe*, where Heilemann is a regular talker, along with Woodward and Allen.

Morning Joe innkeeper Joe Scarborough, a former Republican congressman from the Florida Panhandle, has himself become a key impresario of the conversation. He is also a topic.

Scarborough was "discussed" as a possible candidate for president in 2012, or maybe a vice presidential candidate on an independent ticket led by New York mayor Michael Bloomberg. Whether either one was ever an actual possibility is beside the point—because it was *out there*, thus meriting journalistic notice, generating "buzz." Howard Fineman, a former *Newsweek* writer and veteran cable pundit who joined HuffPost in October 2010, heard about "the discussion." And got a great ride out of a story he wrote about a Bloomberg–Scarborough ticket, or "the Independent Odd Couple," as Huff-Po played it big on its website.

Scarborough confirmed speculation that discussion about the speculation had taken place, or so he speculated in a discussion with Fineman about the speculation.

"We haven't discussed it directly," Scarborough told Fineman, adding, "Have people discussed it in his sphere and in my sphere? I think so."

Mikey then quoted this in Playbook, igniting more discussion in the Playbook community, which overlaps considerably with Scarborough's and Bloomberg's "spheres."

When I later asked Fineman about his "Independent Odd Couple" story and the blather that ensued, he maintained that Scarborough was and is serious about the possibility of an independent candidacy. He also acknowledged that the whole episode was "probably the ultimate example of the political-media complex flying up its own asshole."

One of my last meetings with Mike Allen was over breakfast at D.C.'s Mayflower Renaissance Hotel. Like many reporters, Allen would much rather ask the questions than answer them. He led off with one: "What's the most surprising thing you learned about me?"

It was what I learned about his father, I told him. Gary Allen was an icon of the far right in the 1960s and 1970s. He was affiliated with the John Birch Society and railed against the "big lies" that led to the United States' involvement in World Wars I and II. He denounced the evils of the Trilateral Commission and "Red" teachers. Rock 'n' roll was a "Pavlovian Communist mind-control plot." He wrote speeches for George Wallace, the segregationist governor of Alabama and presidential candidate. He wrote mail-order books and pamphlets distributed through a John Birch mailing list.

None of Mike Allen's friends knew any of this about his father (or they were diverting me with other monikers, like "football coach," which he indeed was; Gary Allen coached a Pop Warner team that included Mike, who played center—badly). In an earlier phone interview, Allen said his dad was a "writer" and "speaker." After I mentioned his father at breakfast, Allen flashed a smile that remained frozen as I spoke. He had described his upbringing to me as nonpolitical. He said he never read anything his father wrote.

I did not want to overreach for a Rosebud. "Life isn't binary," Allen said a few times at breakfast. But I could not help being struck by the contrast between father and son.

Gary Allen's writings conveyed great distrust of the established order. He saw conspiracies in both parties, despising Richard Nixon and Henry Kissinger for their internationalism and the "establishment media" for enabling the "communist conspiracy." Mike Allen traverses politics with a boyish and almost starstruck quality toward the assumed order. He is diligent in addressing leaders by proper titles, ranks, "Madam Speaker," and "Mr. President." Friends said he seemed particularly enthralled to be covering the White House during the Bush years and was spotted at all hours around the briefing room and press area.

When Allen was preparing to leave a job at the metro section of the *New York Times* to cover the White House for the *Washington Post*, his boss, Jonathan Landman, tried to convince him to stay. "I gave him the usual reasons," Landman recalled, which included the standard New York metro editor's take on the White House beat (herd journalism, etc.). Allen had an unforgettable comeback: "I want to be present at great moments in history," he said.

And at the end of our discussion about his father, Mikey made a point of ending on a sweet and orderly data point. After Gary Allen died, at fifty, many of his former Pop Warner players filled the church in tribute. Allen said he recalled no talk of his father's political work at the memorial, but he will never forget one detail: a giant blue and gold floral arrangement in the shape of a football was placed onstage, a gift from the kids on Gary Allen's team, the Phantoms.

As I was finishing the story about Allen, I was meeting with Politico's John Harris in his office, when Mikey himself walked in. He welcomed me, thanked me for coming, and returned to his desk. I visited his cubicle later but Allen was gone. To the left of his desktop was a picture of Allen standing upright and asking President Obama a question at a White House news conference. His work area was notable for its lack of clutter: there were a few small stacks of magazines and newspapers and a tray of mint Girl Scout cookies on the top of his terminal.

In the days leading up to a photo shoot for the article, Allen's work area became spotless, surfaces shining. I kept asking Politico's then executive vice president, Kim Kingsley, "Who cleaned up Mikey's room?" but neither she nor Allen would say. All great questions come from small questions. And some just hang there until they vanish.

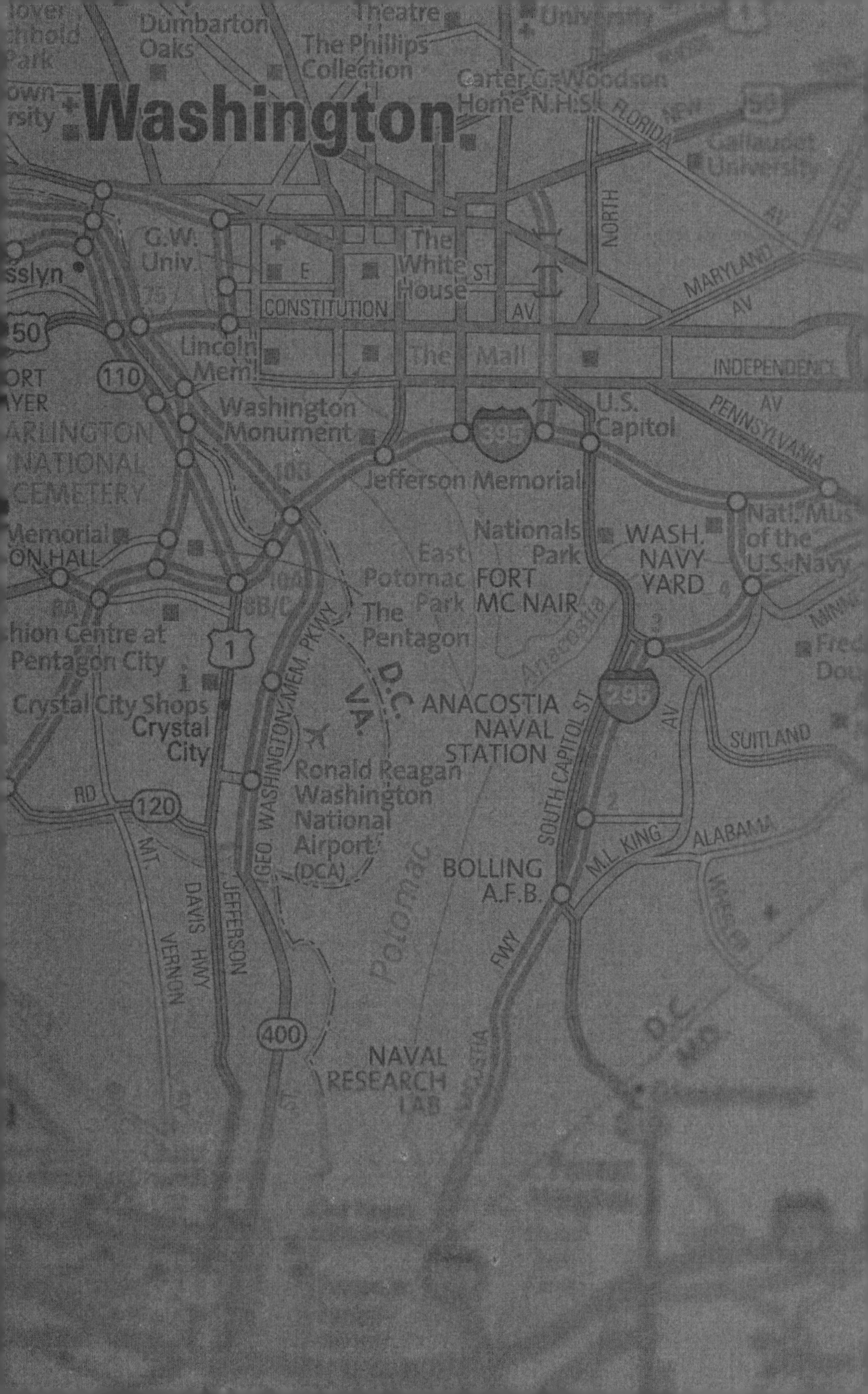

Dumbarton Oaks
The Phillips Collection
Carter G. Woodson Home N.H.S.
Washington
FLORIDA
G.W. Univ.
The White House
E
ST
CONSTITUTION
AV
NORTH
MARYLAND
AV
50
Lincoln Mem.
The Mall
INDEPENDENCE
110
Washington Monument
395
U.S. Capitol
PENNSYLVANIA
AV
Jefferson Memorial
Nationals Park
WASH. NAVY YARD
East Potomac Park
FORT MC NAIR
The Pentagon
Anacostia
1
D.C.
VA.
ANACOSTIA NAVAL STATION
295
Crystal City Shops
Crystal City
GEO. WASHINGTON MEM. PKWY
Ronald Reagan Washington National Airport (DCA)
SOUTH CAPITOL ST
AV
SUITLAND
RD
120
M.L. KING
ALABAMA
BOLLING A.F.B.
Potomac
MT. VERNON
DAVIS HWY
JEFFERSON
FWY
400
NAVAL RESEARCH LAB

·················

"Thank You for Your Service"

The most consequential political story of 2010—maybe all of Obama's first term—was written by a troublemaker, Michael Hastings of *Rolling Stone*. His June profile of General Stanley McChrystal, "The Runaway General," included a host of unflattering statements from the general's staff about civilian government officials such as Vice President Biden, National Security Adviser James L. Jones, and ambassador to Afghanistan Karl W. Eikenberry, among others. McChrystal apologized as soon as the story was posted, and was summoned to Washington by the commander in chief. His staff (and, by implication, McChrystal himself) had clearly spoken out of school, or "off message"—or candidly. Gaffe! The idea that speaking the truth as you see it should be a virtue is nothing but a Pollyannaish and naive notion within the great unfurling process story of life.

Bottom line: McChrystal and his aides were "ill-advised" and showed "bad judgment" by participating in the *Rolling Stone* profile. So went the logic of the almighty narrative. The substance and merit of the remarks were beside the point. Because McChrystal was play-ing the game wrong. He made a dumb PR move. He was not cau-tious. He forgot that, in the words of media writer Michael Wolff, everyone in government must behave like "a thwarted, deracinated, ever-second guessing him- or her-self, mutated individual." He for-got what Robert Gibbs forgot that summer when he was pilloried (by Nancy Pelosi, among others) for admitting on *Meet the Press* that Republicans might win back Congress that November—*the possibil-ity really existed, imagine that!*

Within minutes of the *Rolling Stone* story's publication, the con-versation was completely given over to a classic Washington "Will he or won't he?" cliff-hanger. As in: Will McChrystal keep his job or won't he? Anticipation built over his fateful White House meet-ing with Obama. This Town loves a deathwatch.

McChrystal was swiftly fired. But in the finest D.C. tradition of failing upward, technically Obama accepted McChrystal's resig-nation "with extreme regret," and the general then set off to launch "The McChrystal Group," the requisite lucrative postgovernment consultancy offering "leadership solutions for complex problems." Bob Barnett hooked him up with a nice book deal, JetBlue and Navistar brought McChrystal onto their boards of directors, and he was hired to teach a graduate seminar in modern leadership at Yale. He was getting $60,000 a pop for speaking gigs.

And The Club turned its attention to the troublemaker. After Hastings's story was published in *Rolling Stone*, the writer was ac-cused of violating an implied agreement not to reveal the general's unguarded comments. Also, the military officials had apparently been drinking—the implication being that maybe Hastings should have cut them some slack. And there were rumblings within the military and among journalists that Hastings had violated an off-the-record understanding with McChrystal and company. Some members of McChrystal's staff said as much in *Army Times* and the *Washington Post*. But the charges, made anonymously, received little traction, McChrystal made a fulsome apology, and Hastings denied violating any ground rules.

The military's biggest mistake was to let Hastings in to begin with, Mikey pointed out, under the cautionary headline of "Failure to Google."

"A quick search would have showed McChrystal that caution was warranted around the irreverent reporter," Allen wrote in Playbook. He pointed out that Hastings, a former Iraq correspondent who had previously worked for *Newsweek*, had written an article for *GQ* in 2008 titled "Hack: Confessions of a Presidential Campaign Reporter": "There was no small amount of hypocrisy when it came to journalists discussing the sex lives of the people they cover, since fidelity wasn't exactly a prized virtue among reporters on the campaign trail," Hastings wrote. "For my part, I watched a lot of porn. . . . It occurred to me . . . [that enjoying pornography] in a hotel room was not unlike the larger experience of campaign reporting."

In other words, "troublemaker" should have been tattooed on the "irreverent reporter's" forehead.

Hastings was quizzed on CNN's *Reliable Sources*, the Sunday-morning show about the media hosted by longtime *Washington Post* media reporter Howard Kurtz. Kurtz, known within the pack as "Howie," mentioned that "it's been widely commented upon that there was some drinking going on." To which Hastings replied, "Yes. There was drinking going on."

David Brooks wrote in the *New York Times* that McChrystal had been victimized by the "culture of exposure" that has prevailed in journalism since the Vietnam War. He called out Hastings— a "product of the culture of exposure"—for making McChrystal's "kvetching" the centerpiece of his story, though certainly the comments would have caused a storm whether Hastings had made them the centerpiece or not.

But the harshest criticism came from inside the pack. CBS's chief foreign affairs correspondent Lara Logan was brutal, saying that Hastings had violated an "unspoken agreement" between reporters and military officials. It is understood, she said, that journalists should not embarrass troops "by reporting insults and banter." She implied that Hastings had disingenuously gained the trust of his subjects and even that Hastings made up the offending material—or at the very least burned the military leaders on an off-the-record agreement. "I know these people," Logan told Kurtz on *Reliable Sources*. "They never let their guard down like that. To me, something doesn't add up here." She went on to say that there are many good beat reporters in the field. "And to be fair to the military, if they believe that a piece is balanced, they will let you back," she said. It went without saying that Hastings would not be "let back."

The criticism of Hastings from the pack had a circling-the-wagons quality. Even though his was the most talked-about story in Washington for several days and led to the ouster of a decorated war commander, Hastings was treated as a suspicious interloper. He had few defenders. His most passionate was *Rolling Stone* colleague Matt Taibbi, a wicked screed artist and one of the few legitimate heirs to Hunter S. Thompson in a blog-inspired generation of gonzo wannabes. "If there's a lower form of life on the planet earth than a 'reputable' journalist protecting his territory, I haven't seen it," Taibbi wrote in a blog post titled "Lara Logan, You Suck." "If I'm hearing Logan correctly, what Hastings is supposed to have done in that situation is interrupt these drunken assholes and say, 'Excuse me, fellas, I know we're all having fun and all, but you're saying things that may not be in your best interest!'"

Taibbi's broader point is that everyone is obsessed with being "reputable" and desperate to be "part of The Club so so badly." By "Club" he meant it not like Tim Crouse would delineate between the "pack" and the "nonpack," "troublemakers" or "non-troublemakers." Rather, "reputable" in terms of being a made man in the "Club" that allows for a TV deal and a Bob Barnett imprimatur and an invite to Tammy's garden party. Someone properly in The Club who would never say—as Hastings did to Kurtz—that he used his charm and friendliness to build a rapport with his subjects so that they felt comfortable saying things to him. This is what journalists do but are not supposed to say—what Janet Malcolm wrote so famously/infamously of in the opening of "The Journalist and the Murderer": "Every journalist who is not too stupid or too full of himself to notice what is going on knows that what he does is morally indefensible."

The bigger point in this case concerns the place of the "reputable journalist" in the Washington Club—or lifetime banishment from it. Hastings trashed The Club. He was a skunk at the garden party. He made the other guests look bad. "Most of these reporters just want to be inside the ropeline so badly," Taibbi concluded.

"God forbid some important person think you're not playing for the right team!"

The McChrystal story provided a useful context for what had become a defining characteristic of life "inside" in the new century. Starting in Iraq, reporters began doing something known as "embedding" with U.S. combat units. While embedding brings an increased risk of a reporter's losing independence and perspective, the practice certainly carries a practical benefit on the battlefield—to say nothing of a safety benefit. To some degree, embedding was a formalized version of the bunker relationships that arose organically in previous wars like Vietnam: journalists and soldiers enjoying a mutual reliance.

But around 2004, the notion of embedding had spread beyond war zones and into far less hazardous environs of domestic reporting, like presidential campaigns. Networks began designating reporters to embed with campaigns. Their charge was to provide minute-to-minute coverage of what was happening "inside" it, or at least inside the campaign bubble, which was markedly different from looking inside the actual substance of the campaign. Regardless, embedding promised readers a real-time sense of what it was like "inside" the campaigns, even if it came at the expense of the whimsy and creative and less filtered impressions a nonembedded reporter could provide away from the bubble. "The chroniclers of political and cultural debates increasingly move in a caravan with one side or another," David Ignatius wrote in a May 2, 2010, *Washington Post* column on the dangers of "embedded journalism."

Certainly the *Boys on the Bus* bubble of 1972 represented an earlier form of journalistic embedding from a small rank of elite, group-thinkish reporters. But the practice existed largely in the service of giving readers a single day's roundup of what the candidate did and said. It was not so much giving them a constant sense of what life was like inside their campaign bubble—the breaking news, say, about what Mitt Romney ordered at Chipotle (a pork burrito bowl) before the big debate; or several photos tweeted instantly by reporters of Ann Romney serving muffins to other reporters on the campaign charter.

Being an "insider" has always been a coveted status in This Town. But it is now both an ethic and easily available snack food. Playbook blasts out a daily charge of Beltway knowingness (Ignatius calls Mike Allen "the town crier for a niche community of Washington insiders"). Tammy Haddad's website is called WHC Insider—WHC standing for "White House Correspondents," though it has little to do with the White House or its correspondents and has everything to do with the word that is actually spelled out, "insider." Everyone can come inside, click on, and be embedded here together in this thrilling cocoon.

McChrystal's saga played out shortly after the White House Correspondents' Association dinner, the late-April affair that has grown into a multiday symbol of the city's self-intoxication. Held at the Washington Hilton, the dinner began in 1920 and had traditionally been a sleepy social affair in which news organizations bought tables rounded out by employees, sources, and special guests—maybe a White House official or senator. In 1987, however, journalist Michael Kelly, then of the *Baltimore Sun*, invited along Fawn Hall, the mysterious and glamorous secretary for Lieutenant Colonel Oliver North during the Iran-Contra scandal. This set off an arms race among news organizations to attract celebrity guests to future dinners. Over the years, an increasingly huge showbiz contingent has invaded, as well as a posse of New York and Silicon Valley finance and media sweeties and pop culture finger foods like Ozzy, Paris, and the Donald.

Tammy's Saturday mob-scene brunch is always a highlight of the festival, and the towering hostess has deftly seized upon the Correspondents' Association dinner as her trademark occasion. The event, she says, is about being in the room. That's Tammy's thing. She is casual and transparent about it. When asked by Politico to explain the enduring appeal of the Correspondents' Association dinner, Tammy distilled it to its star-fucker essence: "Who doesn't want to be in the room?" she asked. "You're in the room with powerful people and anything can happen."

She explained that she began hosting her brunch because "it was the only time everyone I knew from all over the country was in

Washington." In other words, all the people who come to town for the Correspondents' Association dinner—celebrities—are people that she knows.

People snicker and complain that the brunch has gotten out of hand. Yet they show up and embed. Actor Tim Daly—the guy from the TV show *Wings*—once made the mistake of complaining in Politico that the brunch has become too crowded and is now populated by "too many d-bags." Never wise to say this publicly. And Daly was compelled to bring flowers to Tammy. She was thrilled with the authenticating amends, and the picture of the flower presentation ran in Politico. All was good among the d-bags.

You could do worse to explain the disconnect between Washington and the rest of the country than to assemble a highlight reel from the Correspondents' Association weekend's events juxtaposed with scenes of economic despair, a simple military death toll, or montage of poor oil-soaked pelicans in the Gulf Coast, which had suffered the worst spill in history a few days before the 2010 dinner.

Just as the nation does not share in Washington's self-love, it is not joining in the media's Era of Good Feelings about itself. Poll respondents kept expressing overwhelming disapproval of its performance. Bureaus were closing, reporters were being laid off, and revenues were down sharply at several traditional and new media outlets. The Washington Post Company would announce that week that it was selling its venerable news magazine, *Newsweek*, which had been losing tens of millions dollars a year.

But as the White House Correspondents' Association festivities proved, the city operates in a reality distortion field. The non-self-awareness is doubly astonishing for a place so preoccupied with how things "play." It all unfolds in a champagne fog. Is that all actually happening? Or is it some rhetorical trope that unimaginative populists concocted to reflect Washington fat cats and insiders, a celebrating gang of d-bags?

My mind leaps to a *Daily Show* parody that played during a weeklong visit to D.C. that year by the cast of the Comedy Central show. The correspondent Wyatt Cenac played a hungry reporter who comes to Washington vowing that "it will be my life's purpose" to tell the real story of how corrupt Washington really is. "Hey, is that a Town Car?" Cenac says, interrupting himself, and notes how cool it is that the Town Car in fact has his name in the window. In the next scene, Cenac excitedly reports that he has moved on to a cocktail party in Georgetown at the home of "a wealthy senator's ex-wife" in which (over by the braised duck) he sees the chairman of the House Armed Services Committee, "who's talking to a college roommate who happens to be an ABC News reporter and his girlfriend who's a lobbyist." Cenac again vows to "nail these bastards" but by now has drifted into a drunken bliss, sipping from a martini ("as dry as Harriet Tubman's vagina!") before moving on to a "post-cocktail jammy jam" hosted by the defense contractor Lockheed Martin. When Jon Stewart expresses concern that Cenac should not be partying so much with the bastards he is promising to nail, Cenac promises to check himself—right after he uses the free tickets he scored from a lobbyist to the Washington Wizards home opener!

Clever locals refer to the Correspondents' Association dinner as "Nerd Prom." This is one of those self-congratulatory Beltway terms masked as self-deprecation. "Nerd" implies that everyone would of course much rather be immersed in the deep wiring of some issue, something of weight and substance—they are "nerds," after all—rather than this obligatory fizz. They could be curled up at home with a Brookings Institution white paper if not for this distraction from the serious work they do.

But they are obliged to make the dinner, because it is big. The Club swells for the night into the ultimate bubble world, the evening's pinnacle moment coming when the three thousand tux-and-gowners rise as one in the ballroom of the "Hinckley Hilton" and offer a solemn toast "to the President of the United States." It is an instant when the bicoastal cast reminds itself that everyone here—not just the commander in chief at the head table, but everyone—wishes the best for the team; that the nexus of politics, media, and celebrity resides at the most garish heights of patriotism.

It is of paramount importance that the president show up to receive his toast and confirm the great seriousness of it all (the First Amendment, leaders being held accountable, being "fair" and fact-based and tenacious and things like that). And they show up without fail, fifteen presidents in total, going back to Calvin Coolidge in 1924. If you think about it, a president blowing off the Correspondents' Association dinner might be a political boon in this anti-Washington day and age, a nod to the "average Americans." Indeed, to the outside world, the dinner and its collateral goings-on present an image of Washington as one big game and costume party, everyone bathed in the same frothy mix of fame and fun and flattery and (most of all) *belonging*. It all looks terrible.

But for a president to miss this dinner would also send a terrible message to This Town. And a president—especially a Democratic president—is never advised to offend it too badly, because (let's be honest) This Town leans left and assumes like-mindedness, so it tends to be especially tough on its own if respect is not paid. Jimmy Carter annoyed This Town by acting all too pure for the permanents (you can run against Washington, fine, but don't make it personal). The Clintons got off to a rotten start when the *Washington Post*'s Sally Quinn invited Hillary to a welcome-to-Washington luncheon in 1993 and the first lady declined. Bad feelings ensued. "There's just something about her that pisses people off," Quinn later told the *New Yorker*. Some years later, when Bill Clinton was preparing to nominate Quinn's husband, Ben Bradlee, for a Presidential Medal of Freedom, the president quipped thus to his aides: "Anyone who sleeps with that bitch deserves a medal!"

After Monica, Quinn penned a memorable piece in the *Post*'s Style section about how Bill Clinton had not only betrayed his wife, his oath, and his country but also his duty to his hosts, the Washington "establishment." The establishment was "outraged by the president's behavior," Quinn declared while acknowledging that "the polls show that a majority of Americans do not share that outrage." She went on to quote a string of aggrieved establishment types saying things like "This is *our* town" (Senator Joe Lieberman), "This is a demoralized little village" (Reagan's social secretary), "You don't foul the nest" (politically versatile talking head David Gergen), "We all know people who have been terribly damaged personally by this" (NBC's Andrea Mitchell), and, perhaps most pointedly, Clinton "came in here and he trashed the place, and it's not his place" (the *Washington Post*'s David Broder).

The "trashed the place" quote from Broder received a great deal of attention. "Not his place" was read as an assertion that Washington—"This Town"—does not belong to Clinton or the people who elected him but to a presiding class of city fathers. With such status comes a heightened sense of moral duty and authority. Outsiders could never fully appreciate their sense of custodianship. "Every time I went into the Oval Office I put on a coat and tie," said the supreme former, Ken Duberstein, reassuring a grateful nation.

Even in the late Clinton era, the Correspondents' dinner was still smallish compared with what it has since become—a moneyed and multiday Mardi Gras that resembles a national political convention except that it occurs annually. Like a convention, the festivities are covered top to bottom by the media but typically produce no news besides the marathon roundups of boldface names and a rehash of whatever the best lines were in the president's comedy routine.

On the day of the 2010 Correspondents' Association dinner, Obama delivered a commencement address at the University of Michigan in which he bemoaned the "24/7 echo-chamber" of cable news and tendency of pundits to make "their arguments as outrageous and as incendiary as possible."

Obama viewed his Correspondents' Association dinner duties as something of a chore but also enjoyed a good comedy routine and delivered it deftly. He also viewed his act as a humorous outlet to say how he really felt, and one of his favorite peeves—on this and other occasions—was the idiocy of the media. In his speech at the 2010 dinner, the president played a clip of CNN anchor Rick Sanchez discussing a volcano in Iceland whose eruption wreaked havoc on transatlantic flight schedules. Sanchez laughed while expressing surprise that Iceland was not "too cold to have a volcano." After the video played and Obama remained silent through the crowd's laughter, he added dryly of CNN: "I guess that's why they're the most trusted name in news."

The president was especially harsh on Politico, deadpanning that it is unfair to say Politico puts new focus on "trivial issues, political fodder [and] gossip" because in fact they have been doing it for centuries. He described a faux historic Politico headline, "Japan Surrenders—Where's the Bounce?"

The president's attentions were flattering to Politico, authenticating its ascendance at an event that the publication treats as its Super Bowl. It produces dozens of stories about the event leading up to it, a commemorative insert, and a newly established day-after brunch at the publisher's mansion at which crowds of gawkers assemble outside, hoping for a glimpse of the Jonas Brothers, or Dennis Kucinich.

There can be upward of twenty-five parties planned around the event, a long and rolling heave of martinis and Miller Lites and "Good Causes." It is The Club's version of the High Holidays, without the fasting or spiritual nourishment (unless you count those who pray for an invite to Tammy's).

In recent years, the Correspondents' Association dinner kickoff party has taken place a full five days before the actual dinner, on *Tuesday*. It has been hosted by Jack Quinn's lobbying shop, Quinn Gillespie. "We know that the dinner itself is not actually a celebration of the White House press corps but instead a celebration of politicians and celebrities," Quinn explained to the *Washington Post*. "To us, journalists are celebrities. White House correspondents are the rock stars of Washington for the political class."

This was gracious of Jack to say, although it was not always the case. For many decades, journalists were considered the freezer-burned broccoli of the D.C. buffet spread, compared with the caviar politicians, diplomats, and lawyers of influence. When the *New York Herald Tribune* columnist Joseph Alsop arrived in town in 1935, Arthur Krock, the D.C. bureau chief of the *New York Times*, warned, "You know, Alsop, the first thing you have to realize is that in Washington newspapermen have no place at the table."

Now they have standing places at multiple tables. They do all year, but it becomes an orgy around the Correspondents' Association dinner: a blurry romp of lobster tails and truffles and Andrea Mitchell getting her heel stuck in the cobblestone driveway of the St. Regis hotel outside the *Time/People* party. The latter episode, by the way, was witnessed by Reid Cherlin, an assistant White House press secretary at the time, who gallantly came to Mitchell's aid and helped keep her massive *Time/People* gift bag from spilling. "She thanked me graciously," Cherlin recalled.

All the while, nasty news kept spewing out in the American elsewhere. A massive explosion destroyed the Deepwater Horizon oil rig in the Gulf of Mexico, which was being leased by

BP. An underwater camera showed a rush of crude into the Gulf, which made a tidy visual for an out-of-control problem and, as the ever-literary media pointed out, a metaphor for a *suddenly helpless presidency*. It also symbolized the free flow of cash from British Petroleum into Washington to "manage" the crisis. BP was moving to secure every Republican and Democratic flack and lobbyist they could soak up for help with their "positioning" problem.

Washington becomes a determinedly bipartisan team when there is money to be made—sorry, I mean a hopeful exemplar of *Americans pulling together in a time of crisis*. BP's Beltway dream team included Republican whales like Ken Duberstein and the Democratic superlobbyist Tony Podesta; a top spokeswoman for Vice President Cheney, Anne Womack-Kolton; a longtime spokesman for Republican speaker Dennis Hastert, John Feehery; and a well-known Democratic media mastermind, Steve McMahon, also a regular on *Hardball*. It boasted McMahon's business partner, the Republican media guru Alex Castellanos; their firm, Purple Strategies, spearheaded a $50 million television campaign on the company's behalf, according to a report on CNN (where Castellanos is a contributor). "Purple" was brought into the fold by Hilary Rosen, a devout Democrat and tireless advocate for same-sex marriage who was then running the Washington office of Brunswick Group, a London-based PR firm that was also working for BP. A CNN pundit herself, Rosen was also an unpaid contributor to the Huffington Post—until the BP thing became a potential "optics" problem, and a temporary breakup ensued.

The human toll of BP's spill was great and far-reaching. Chief among the tragedies in This Town was that it meant Governor Haley Barbour of Mississippi had to stay home to monitor the crisis and could not attend the Correspondents' Association dinner.

It's always good to see Haley at the dinner. He is an old stalwart in This Town and was thinking seriously about running for president in 2012. Barbour was scheduled to travel to Washington the night before the dinner to speak at a party for the CNBC host Maria Bartiromo—aka "the Money Honey"—who had just published a book called *The 10 Laws of Enduring Success*. Everyone in The Club was happy for Maria, a fierce and vivacious presence who had made a nice brand for herself. Ed Rogers, a founder of Barbour's old lobbying firm, was the party's host.

Prudishly speaking, a journalist's agreeing to be celebrated at a party hosted by a lobbyist and headlined by two newsmakers might be seen as compromising—especially when one of the newsmakers (Barbour) was thinking seriously at that point about running for president and when the honoree (Bartiromo) wound up moderating a Republican debate the following year.

But you could nitpick a few "troubling appearances" involving journalists and lobbyists and politicians every week in Washington if you wanted to. "It is what it is," as everyone says here all the time.

The Money Honey reception was held in an elegant function room off the lobby of the W Hotel. Guests could conveniently stop by to congratulate Maria and then head upstairs to another preparty hosted by the *New Yorker* on the roof, or several others within a few blocks. Ed Rogers always does a tasteful job with these things, and the wine on this Correspondents' Association dinner eve was particularly excellent. Haley loves a good glass of wine, or six, another reason it was such a shame he could not be here. Few politicians are as fun as the former Republican National Committee chairman, political director in the Reagan White House, and legendary tobacco lobbyist. Barbour is a throwback to a time when politicians would tell dirty jokes, boast of all the cigars they smoked, and refer to their friends—on the record—as "drinking buddies." He speaks in a mud-mouthed Mississippi drawl and looks like a grown version of Spanky from the Little Rascals.

Barbour's favorite political memento is a framed sequence of photos of himself trading off-color jokes with his former boss, Reagan. In the first photo, the young White House aide is seen telling the president a joke, "the one about the three couples joining the church," Barbour says. The punch line features one of the couples doing something enormously inappropriate in the frozen-food section at Kroger.

In the next picture, Reagan is saying, "Haley, have I ever told you the one about the two Episcopal preachers?"

"No, sir, Mr. President."

"One of the preachers said to the other, 'Times have really changed, haven't they? I never had sex with my wife before we were married, did you?'

"And the other Episcopal priest said, 'I don't know, what is your wife's maiden name?'"

Barbour doesn't even try to play the "I'm an outsider, I'm not a politician" game. He is just the perfect specimen of a fat-cat Republican that liberal Hollywood screenwriters would concoct to conjure the perfect specimen of a fat-cat Republican (southern, cigar-smoking, rich, fat; actor John Goodman would play him as he did a similar caricature on *The West Wing*).

Columnist Michael Kinsley noted how so many veteran reporters were longing for Haley to run for president. Why? Barbour, Kinsley wrote, "plays on the social insecurity among journalists." He "doesn't literally wink as he spins, but he manages to send the message: This is all a big game—a big wonderful game—and you have the privilege of playing it with me."

In his love of the game and popularity in This Town, Barbour reminds me of another former party chairman, Democrat Terry McAuliffe—a Haley "drinking buddy," not shockingly. They are good-time guys and "Washington fixtures" even though Barbour set off to seek the Mississippi governor's mansion in 2003 and McAuliffe wants to shed the "Washington fixture" label and become the next governor of Virginia. He ran and lost in 2009 and will run again in 2013. Haley and Terry also met in that most Washington of love incubators, the green room. They argued on TV in the 1990s, did the Right versus Left thing, and were soon doing business together. In late 1999, Barbour and Democratic lobbyist Tommy Boggs were planning to open a downtown restaurant called the Caucus Room, which the *Washington Post* described as a "red-meat emporium" that "will serve up power, influence, loopholes, money and all the other ingredients that make American Democracy great." Seeking investors, Barbour called McAuliffe and asked for $100,000, which he sent over immediately. A while later, Barbour called back, said they were oversubscribed, and sent McAuliffe back a check for $50,000. "So I figure I made fifty in the deal," said McAuliffe, who never saw a penny more.

It was around this time that Bill Clinton asked the Macker what ambassadorship he wanted for all the service he'd performed on his behalf. McAuliffe had just put together a fund-raiser at Washington's MCI Center that sucked in more than $26 million for the DNC. ("The biggest event in the history of mankind," McAuliffe told me. "As you know.") He told Clinton that he wanted to be the ambassador to the Court of St. James's, or Britain. But McAuliffe figured his appointment was no sure thing, given that it required Senate confirmation and that Republicans, who held a majority at the time, had little incentive to help a president they had just impeached. McAuliffe enlisted his friend Barbour and asked him to lobby his friend and fellow Mississippian Trent Lott, the Senate majority leader, on his behalf.

The next day, Barbour called back and said the conversation went well. When I asked Barbour about the transaction, he seemed mildly annoyed at the suggestion that Republicans in the late 1990s would punish a buddy of Bill Clinton's, or, alternatively, that McAuliffe would receive any special treatment because he was Haley Barbour's friend. McAuliffe, he said, was qualified and effective and would represent the nation with distinction. "It would be awful if just because he was effective for the other side, we punished him," Barbour said. "We need more of those guys, who understand that this is not personal, just because we disagree. This business should not be vengeful."

But it would be wrong to assume that Barbour and Lott were acting out of pure nonpartisan motives. McAuliffe later learned from Lott, his occasional hunting buddy, that when Barbour called him about the appointment, his first thought was how convenient it would be to get the best political fund-raiser in the Democratic Party out of the country in time for the 2000 elections. "Tell the son of a bitch I'll walk him to the airplane," Lott told Barbour, according to McAuliffe.

As it turned out, the 2000 Democratic National Convention in Los Angeles was in serious financial trouble, and McAuliffe wound up taking it over at the urging (begging) of the nominee-to-be, Al Gore. After the election, McAuliffe became chairman of the DNC during George W. Bush's first term.

Even after Barbour became governor of Mississippi he retained strong links to the capital. "Washington has been very nice to me," he said. "I have a lot of Democratic friends. I have a lot of liberal friends. I even have friends in the news media."

In Barbour's absence, McAuliffe stepped in as a featured toaster at the Bartiromo book bash. As Washington book parties went, it was a . . . Washington book party.

Chairman Greenspan was there with Andrea, Betsy Fischer was with her new boyfriend, Politico's Jonathan Martin, along with a bunch of other People on TV and lobbyists and random Hollywood types, like the seventy-two-year-old film producer Jerry

Weintraub, whom Ed Rogers introduced as "legendary" and who volunteered that his secret to longevity was that "I still make love."

Politico's Patrick Gavin was videotaping everybody for a brief video clip of the action that would run the next day. He is precisely the kind of "entrepreneurial" journalist who would have, in another age, honed his craft by writing several stories a week on things like city council meetings in places like Ames, Iowa. If he worked hard and carpet-bombed midsize papers like the *Philadelphia Inquirer* and the *Dallas Morning News* with clips, maybe they would hire him someday. And maybe, if he was really lucky, he would get to Washington to cover something big-time for the *Inquirer* or the *Morning News*, or cover something on Capitol Hill for a place like *Roll Call*. Now the Patrick Gavins can come straight to D.C. and, in short order, get a job that includes the privilege of videotaping other journalists at parties. Gavin belongs to a Washington speakers' bureau ("Leading Authorities"), which theoretically could land him speaking gigs across the country to supplement his Politico salary. (In reality, demand for Gavin's speaking services has been limited or nonexistent.) "Gavin explains how Washington works in untraditional ways," touts the Leading Authorities website. He "focuses more on the players—especially those behind-the-scenes people you do not normally hear about—than the issues. Gavin also appears frequently as a television commentator on nearly all major networks." And of course—being a notable Washingtonian—Gavin merits his own caricature drawing at the Palm on Nineteenth.

In the corner sipping wine stood the once eminent financial reporter Jeffrey Birnbaum. Birnbaum's coverage of the burgeoning lobbying sector for the *Wall Street Journal* and the *Washington Post*, and his classic book, *Showdown at Gucci Gulch: Lawmakers, Lobbyists, and the Unlikely Triumph of Tax Reform* (written with Alan Murray), made Birnbaum the best-known lobbying journalist in Washington. That is, until Birnbaum left journalism to join

Barbour, Griffith & Rogers to head the firm's public relations division. People move within The Club all the time, especially in these lucrative Washington days in which the so-called revolving door has been so lavishly greased. Journalists become People on TV or go into public relations or lobbying; politicians and staffers become lobbyists or consultants or commentators; lobbyists (like Haley) run for office or go back into the government to "refresh their credentials," or earning power, before taking their rightful place back in the retainer class.

But Birnbaum joining a lobbying firm was an extraordinary passage, akin to Bob Woodward joining a White House staff. Lobbyists joke about the big-game "purists" whom they can lure to their side. They speak of the naive but powerful suckers who have left money on the table by staying in their lower-paying journalism or elected or government staff jobs. Back in his lobbying heyday, Haley received large retainers from firms just to keep him from working for the other side. He told one friend that his main goal was to get paid by as many people as possible for doing as little work as possible. He had amassed an eight-figure fortune by the time he set out to run for governor. After deciding not to run for president, Barbour returned to BGR and undertook a healthy regimen of paid speeches.

K Street people often boast of the purists on the Hill, in the White House, and increasingly in the journalism ranks whom they have corrupted or deflowered. Or "co-opted," as the former Senate-majority-leader-turned-lobbyist Trent Lott vowed to do with the incoming group of Tea Party–propelled House members a few months later. Rogers hailed Birnbaum to me as "one of the highest-ranking people ever to switch teams."

Implied here was not only that Birnbaum was a big catch but that people "switch teams" here as a matter of routine, which they do. Even so, the overriding message of the Correspondents' Association dinner weekend is that everyone, ultimately, is playing for the same team.

Working the Maria Bartiromo bash, the Macker was his usual red-faced and excitable self. He delivered a frenzied elevator speech to me about the electric car company he was starting, Green-Tech Automotive, a company he promised would "reinvent the automobile." Left unsaid was that he also hoped it would reinvent Terry McAuliffe as he approached another run for governor of Virginia. GreenTech could be a vehicle for him to escape his pigeonhole as a political money man and carnival barker and reposition himself as a more serious "Democratic businessman fighting for Democratic Causes and Creating Jobs," as his website says. It hardly mattered that a lot of these jobs would be in Mississippi, not Virginia, because Terry was able to secure a package of tax and price incentives from Haley in order to build a 400,000-square-foot facility in the northern Mississippi town of Horn Lake. GreenTech's story is a monument to the power of a politically connected company. The company raised more than $100 million in capital, much of it deriving from McAuliffe's network of political connections. Its board includes a former governor of Louisiana and a former IRS commissioner. Bill Clinton showed up at the grand opening of GreenTech's plant in Mississippi.

Around the time of the party, I visited McAuliffe at his office in the northern Virginia town of Tyson's Corner. The office was vast and mostly uninhabited and adorned with monuments to the Macker's friendship with Bill Clinton: lots of photos of Terry and Bill playing golf, and even some Clinton-era relics tucked away in the side offices—including Hillary's actual brother, Hugh Rodham, holed up behind a desk. ("Look, a Real-life Clinton *Family Member*, everybody. He *walks*! He *talks*!") I imagined Terry walking into Hugh's office periodically and just gazing at the Real-life Clinton, like a kid fixating on a panda at the National Zoo. Hugh Rodham has some role in the financing of the operation, by the way.

McAuliffe was now determined to refashion himself as a Washington outsider type. This was laughable for anyone who knew him but a smart political strategy in this day and age. "I am an entrepreneur, baby," he said to me. "Don't forget that, I'm an entrepreneur." Okay, he's an entrepreneur, not a "Washington insider," albeit one whose wedding party included Richard Gephardt; who has been a regular at ABC's Sam Donaldson's annual holiday party; who runs into his neighbor Dick Cheney at his daughter's (and Cheney's granddaughter's) soccer games; and who initially put up the money for Bill and Hillary Clinton's postpresidential home in Chappaqua, New York.

As Terry worked the room at the Bartiromo book party, he popped into a back room for a minute to take a call from U.S. commerce secretary Gary Locke (or "MR. SECRETARY!" as he boomed into the phone). It concerned a trade mission to Hong Kong they would soon be taking together. After finishing his phone call, McAuliffe came back to where I was standing and, wouldn't you know it, the conversation moved to the off-message topic of how unpleasant it is for Terry to receive his prostate exam. "I once said to the doctor, 'Doc, I may be the chairman of the Democratic Party,'" he shared, "'but I still hate having a finger stuck up my ass.'"

And with that, it was time for hors d'oeuvres.

And brief remarks about the Money Honey. McAuliffe exalted Bartiromo as "the greatest economist, the greatest woman ever to be involved in dictating how world economic policy is done." Andrea Mitchell went on likewise about her colleague Maria. But first she paid tribute to the fun-loving trio of McAuliffe, Barbour, and Rogers, singling Barbour out for special citation for his efforts in the gulf. "Haley Barbour is really a hero to a lot of people," declared Mitchell, who has known Barbour since he worked in the Reagan White House, which she covered for NBC.

Soon after, everyone raised a glass—to the Money Honey, to the Macker, to Barbour, to the whole team.

The pub crawl continued up on the roof at the *New Yorker* party: sushi bar, butterscotch milkshakes, and bottomless drinks served on napkins imprinted with politically oriented *New Yorker* cartoons. On one, a sinner is pleading to Saint Peter at the Pearly Gates: "Wait, those weren't lies," the sinner says. "That was spin!"

Afterward, my wife and I were riding down on an elevator with Ed Henry, then the White House reporter for CNN, and his future wife, Shirley. Ed is a very genuine and earnest person. I know this because when he was hired to do the same job at Fox, he was asked in an interview with *Adweek* to describe his on-air style. Ed replied that Roger Ailes and others at his new network were drawn to him by his "sincerity." And not just any kind of sincerity! "One of the reasons they wanted to hire me," Henry explained, "was I have a sincerity that you can't make up."

Another man on our elevator introduced himself to Ed as an aide to the French ambassador. As soon as the words "French ambassador" escaped the guy's mouth, Henry genuflected—an obvious play to gain access to the Bloomberg/*Vanity Fair* after-party to be held at the French ambassador's mansion the following evening. Ed and the French guy's conversation continued in the lobby. At the end of it, the French guy took down Ed's information and Ed kept thanking him, sincerely.

A s guests filed into the Correspondents' Association dinner the following night, a would-be terrorist was attempting to blow up Times Square. The dinner and pre-parties went on as planned. It lent the festivities a "while Rome burns" feel—or, in this case, while an explosive-laden Nissan Pathfinder burns in the middle of America's busiest crossroads. The car was discovered by a street vendor at around 6:30 p.m., just as the Washington nobility was peacocking down the red carpets of the Hilton with the Biebers and Kardashians and Peter Orszags of the galaxy. C-SPAN covered the arrivals live and the cable news networks blanketed the dinner with an occasional break-in to update viewers on the off-message Nissan. MSNBC didn't bother to mention the near bombing until almost eleven p.m., after Jay Leno—the dinner's featured "entertainment"— was done imploding at the Washington Hilton.

By then, many of the network's top executives and personalities had repaired to a massive MSNBC after-bash for sushi, hot dogs, and the privilege of watching Morgan Freeman dance to Kool & the Gang under a massive poster of Ed Schultz. But the marquee after-dinner happening was put on as expected by Bloomberg and *Vanity Fair* at the French ambassador's residence in Kalorama. It offers one of Washington's truly hypnagogic environments. OMG! "Hey, isn't that . . . ?" Someone from *Glee*, *Melrose Place*, Colin Powell! Goofy stuff happens, things you remember: some actress running up to David Axelrod and saying, "Um, why can't you just turn off the oil? From the leak?" And Axelrod has no idea who she was and turns to his assistant, Eric Lesser, and asks "Who the hell was that?" and Lesser doesn't know either.

Some years earlier, before the Bloomberg and *Vanity Fair* parties were merged like Exxon and Mobil, my *New York Times* colleague Mark Mazzetti rushed up to the bad-girl actress Shannen Doherty, late of *Beverly Hills, 90210*, and somewhat ironically proclaimed himself a "big fan." She asked him what he did. And when Mark told her he was a reporter, she replied simply, "Oh, I love current events."

There is a peculiar genius to that, the elementary school terminology of "current events." Hollywood also loves "current events." And they love meeting the people they see on Sunday morning television "not quite denying" things and "not ruling out" things and "not closing the door" on things. It proves our friends from Hollywood are also smart and serious and cause-oriented. It is partly why they have descended to the level of This Town for the weekend—to walk among the Gods of Current Events.

Orange and purple sorbet–toned lights illuminated the trees over the French ambassador's back patio in a neighborhood of mansions and wrought-iron fences overlooking Rock Creek Park. Low-flying helicopters circled overhead and a light mist machine completed the aura of the bubble world. News of the Times Square situation seeped in, mostly via Twitter. Mayor Bloomberg resisted his namesake party to jet back to New York. Otherwise, Times Square interfered not at all with anyone's good time.

Guests were milling around, sipping flutes of champagne, serially affirming each other. That US Airways pilot, Sully, was a particular hot spot. He's the one who landed the plane in the Hudson River the year before. He accepted serial thanks for his service. There are always a lot of drunken losers at these things stumbling up to anyone in a uniform and saying "Thank you for your service." Many military guys I've spoken to find this hilarious. And if the salute comes from a woman, they will sometimes receive it as an opener for getting "patriotic" with them.

The next morning *Meet the Press* made its first broadcast ever from a new high-definition studio at the network's Washington bureau. The innovation had been in the works for some time and was promoted as an old-media institution adapting to the state-of-the-art norms of modern broadcasting. NBC's top executives— NBC News head Steve Capus and CEO Jeff Zucker—traveled to the Nebraska Avenue studio for a special brunch reception following the show. David Gregory, who had been moderating *Meet the Press* for seventeen months, cast a more telegenic and HD-ready figure than did Tim Russert. Unlike Russert, Gregory did not come up as a political operative but went directly into TV. It's all he wanted to do.

Gregory was a familiar Washington trademark who covered the Bush White House for NBC and gained a reputation for asking combative questions in televised briefings. He did an excellent Bush impersonation on the press bus. Colleagues and Bush officials at times accused him of showboating in the briefing room, a polished and more urbane version of ABC's Sam Donaldson, who made his name in the 1980s shouting questions at President Reagan. President Bush, who called Gregory "Stretch"—that seemed to be W's unclever default nickname for tall people—ridiculed Gregory once for asking a question in French of Jacques Chirac, then president of France, at a joint press conference. "The guy memorizes four words and he plays like he's intercontinental," Bush quipped.

In late 2008, the Intercontinental Man prevailed in a beauty contest to succeed Mr. Buffalo. It was an intense competition that was in evidence even at Tim's memorial service at the Kennedy Center. MC Tom Brokaw welcomed friends of Tim's, family members, and the largest contingent in the hall, "those who think they should be his successor on *Meet the Press*." Gregory was in solid standing within The Club. His tendency to project prima donna airs was leavened (some) by a playful and self-deprecating sense of humor. He once participated in a skit with Karl Rove at the Radio and Television Correspondents' Association dinner. He was a regular on the city's dinner-and-cocktail circuit and a participant in a Torah study group with other well-known D.C. political and media figures. He tweeted about giving his young daughter five dollars after she lost her first tooth.

Gregory had struggled in trying to fill Russert's chair on *Meet the Press*. He acknowledged as much in a short speech at the unveiling for the new HD set. "This has not been an easy transition," Gregory said, choking up while invoking the legacy of Tim and raising a glass of orange juice, or maybe it was a screwdriver. "A new era of NBC News," Capus called it.

It was a new era all around. While the *Meet the Press* ceremony wrapped up, a maiden Sunday brunch tradition was kicking off at the $24 million Georgetown home of Politico's founding publisher, Robert Allbritton, an emerging goofball of a media magnate who was clearly moving up in the pecking order. As testament to Allbritton, his brunch generated much heat, especially in Politico. The *New Republic* credited Allbritton with "reshaping the way we follow politics." When I was writing about Mike Allen earlier that year, Allbritton told me that he viewed his stewardship of Politico in terms of a vital community service.

"I don't have to be doing this," said Allbritton, the heir to a Washington banking and media fortune. "I can go find myself a coconut drink and go hang out in the islands for the rest of my life if I want to. But a lot of this now is about contributing something back."

Something back: in this case, a crepe station; Maine lobster poached in court bouillon and served warm in a white Chinese spoon napped with a grapefruit beurre blanc; citrus salmon toasts; baby prime-beef burgers drizzled with truffle oil; and mini eggs Benedict, among other goodies (hat tip: Playbook). Paparazzi gathered outside the gated mansion, along with a few gawkers, someone shouting questions at Alan Greenspan, and a would-be party crasher intent on seeing the Jonas Brothers and trying to pass herself off as *PBS NewsHour* correspondent Gwen Ifill (who is black, unlike the would-be party crasher).

"I can't imagine anyplace I'd rather be," said Jack Quinn, the

Democratic superlobbyist who started it all with a party five days earlier. Reports on the brunch were stellar, of course, a lavish gathering of the same Tammys and Mikeys and Axes you see on TV, read about in Playbook, and run into again and again on a special week like this.

Gregory stopped by the brunch after *Meet the Press*, one of six Sunday shows that Homeland Security secretary Janet Napolitano would appear on that morning. Meanwhile, the president headed to the Gulf Coast to inspect the oily residue there.

The Roach Motel
of Power

Summer 2010

Aleftover from the French ambassador's house, well after midnight, maybe around two. There, in the grand entrance, Morgan Freeman was giving a foot massage to his date, Katie Couric. I will leave that snapshot as is, except to observe that both seemed to be having a lovely time at the party, especially Freeman. He moved graciously through the grand rooms, solicitous of the perky anchor on his arm. He was "Driving Miss Katie."

Freeman fielded kudos for his work, particularly in *The Shawshank Redemption*. That was the paramount prison film in which Freeman's character, Red Redding, grew dependent upon the self-sustaining regimen behind bars. Red muses on the odd seductions of the sealed-off culture. Inmates arrive as outsiders, become accepted, and before they knew it, they are, as Red says, "institutionalized."

Washington's cushy institution is ideologically diverse. They take their constitutionals together in the courtyard: members of Congress and D.C. journos in awkward jogging outfits walking laps around the mall, led by Mika and Joe, in a continuous walk-and-talk. (From Playbook: "LIVE FROM THE NATIONAL MALL at 8 a.m. on MSNBC—The 'Morning Joe' Bipartisan Health Challenge, a 3K challenge to promote healthy living," hosted live by Joe Scarborough, Mika Brzezinski, and Willie Geist, with the Capitol dome behind them. "Participants include friends of the show Valerie Jarrett; Sens. Gillibrand, Collins and Thune; Reps. Shadegg, Ryan, Cantor and McCarthy . . .")

Chatting away a few feet from Freeman and Couric was a thoroughly institutionalized Washington character, Christopher Dodd, Democrat of Connecticut. He is the five-term senator whose father held the same job years before. He worked as a Senate page at sixteen and was elected to the Senate at thirty-six after three terms in the House. He was first elected to Congress in 1974 as part of a Watergate-era groundswell of new liberal members who were hailed as a "breath of fresh air." By 2010, many of Dodd's constituents viewed him as the exemplar of why Washington was again in need of fumigation.

It did not matter that, legislatively speaking, Dodd was in the midst of a sweet last hurrah. He played key roles in the health-care overhaul that Obama signed a few months earlier and a major banking bill later in the year. Nor did it matter that colleagues of both parties loved Chris Dodd, an inimitable fellow of the chamber who looks and sounds like a senatorial cartoon. He has a silvery helmet of hair, stentorian voice, and backslapping manner, as if delivered straight from preschool to cloakroom.

Electorally speaking, this was a bad time to be such an archetype. Dodd exemplified the rule that the more Washington-fortified a politician was in 2010, the less popular he was outside. Dodd's poll numbers back home were deep in the cesspool. He drew scorn for receiving a special rate on a mortgage from a firm, Countrywide, that he would later try to assist as chairman of the Senate Committee on Banking, Housing and Urban Affairs after the collapse of the housing market. He was perceived as someone who had been in Washington too long, who had grown too cozy with Wall Street, and whose self-indulgence was evidenced by his quixotic campaign for president in 2008. Dodd raised a good portion of his money for that race from the banking and financial services sector. His fundraisers touted him as either the next president or, failing that, still the powerful chairman of the banking committee. Dodd moved with his family to Iowa for several weeks before the state's caucuses as the banking crisis was worsening into what would become a full meltdown. He won a pittance of the vote in Iowa and dropped out that night.

Dodd was coming off a dreadful year in which he was diagnosed with prostate cancer, his sister died, and, a few weeks later, so did his closest friend in the Senate, Ted Kennedy. He had recently announced that he would not be seeking a sixth term, citing that he was in "the worst political shape of my life." He was, on the other hand, excited by the prospect of doing something different. I interviewed him around this time. When he spoke of his next chapter, eating a chilled lobster salad in the Senate dining room, Dodd's eyes widened. Or maybe it was wistfulness for something he knew he could not escape, an awareness that any life "outside" for him was not feasible.

Regardless, Dodd was bandying options and seeming to enjoy the fantasies. Maybe he could just rip the whole thing up and sever the umbilical bond of his fully gestated Washington career. No looking back. His name had come up as the next president of the University of Connecticut. He mused about possibly rejoining the Peace Corps, repeating a youthful tour in the Dominican Republic. Perhaps, Dodd said, he might try joining a start-up company in

Silicon Valley or a nonprofit. He was excited about getting off "the same old treadmill," he told me.

When I saw Dodd squeezing arms at the French ambassador's house and taking thanks for his service, I asked him if we would see him again the following year at the Correspondents' Association dinner parties. He was obliged to flash a practiced smirk—good-bye to all this, this compulsory Washington schmoozing that had sucked up so much of his six decades on the planet. "Doubtful," he said, laughing.

This was a slight hedge compared with what Dodd promised when I asked him if he would ever consider becoming a lobbyist. "That I can take off the table right now," said Dodd, one of many published occasions in which he reiterated his "no lobbying" vow.

No surprise how this story ends. A few months after Dodd finished up his service in the U.S. Senate, he was named head of the Motion Picture Association of America, a $1.2 million position in which he would lead Hollywood's foremost lobbying group. Former Democratic senator Bob Kerrey, who nearly took the MPAA job himself before Dodd did, described Dodd's new job as "just being an overpaid lobbyist." Still, he was tempted to take the gig himself, he told me—"Damn right I was," said Kerrey, who had been president of the New School in New York. He does not particularly like Washington, Kerrey says, one reason he did not take the job. Nor does he care about issues important to the MPAA, like piracy. "I don't give a fuck about piracy," Kerrey told me. "But for that money, I have to admit, I started getting a little interested in piracy."

When I last talked to Kerrey, in January 2012, he was thinking about running for his old Senate seat in Nebraska. Ben Nelson, the Democratic incumbent, was retiring, and Kerrey was getting pressure from top Democrats to get back in. He might do it, he said, though he didn't sound excited. "The problem is, the second your hand comes off the Bible, you become an asshole." Nonetheless, Kerrey wound up running, and lost.

Dodd, for what it's worth, is no asshole. No one who engaged in a doughnut-throwing fight with former congressman Harold Ford Sr. could be that bad. It was also fun watching Dodd stump for president in 2007 and seeing the joy on Dodd's face even as it belied the obvious fate in store for his doomed-from-the-start campaign. "Tip O'Neill once came down here and asked for a grit," Mr. Dodd said, belly-laughing his way through a diner in South Carolina. "That was Tip's way of connecting with the local folks: by asking for a grit." Later, Dodd talked about how he had recently been speaking at a firehouse in Pahrump, Nevada. He looked out a window, and there it was: a billboard advertising the Brothel Art Museum. "You wouldn't see this kind of thing in Fairfield County," Dodd noted.

So Dodd lied about never lobbying. Or maybe his thinking just "evolved." He made this no-lobbying promise, Dodd explained, "before this opportunity was on the radar screen." Also, he pointed out, the MPAA job involved more than lobbying.

Indeed, Dodd was involved in far more than just lobbying: just a few months into his new job, Dodd hosted a big dinner and cocktail reception the night before the White House Correspondents' Association dinner.

Relationships are to Washington what computer chips are to Silicon Valley (or casino chips are to Vegas). Unlike computer chips, relationships are not grounded in exact science. But that does not stop people from trying, or paying a lot, to create and nurture them. Corporations have figured out that despite the exorbitant costs of hiring lobbyists, the ability to shape or tweak or kill even the tiniest legislative loophole can be worth tens of millions of dollars.

Harry Reid tells a favorite story about his friendship with the late Forrest Mars, the billionaire candy magnate who kept a home in Nevada and struck up a friendship with Reid. Reid liked Mars because he was an odd character, and he likes odd characters. He never gave Reid any money, but Reid kept visiting him because he liked talking to Mars. Finally, Mars wrote Reid a check for $1,000. "I'm doing this because I like you, not because I think it will do me any good," Mars told Reid. "I learned a long time ago, if you give your money to lobbyists, they will do a lot more good for you." His reasoning is that the lobbyists, rather than individual donors, are far more likely to get meaningful access to the elected official.

Lobbyists were present in the Capitol even before the Capitol was in Washington. When the first session of Congress gathered in New York in 1789, business representatives showed up bent on thwarting a tariff bill. The American tradition of lobbying the government dates back four centuries to the Virginia colony, according to the former *Washington Post* managing editor Bob Kaiser in his book on the modern lobbying culture, *So Much Damn Money: The Triumph of Lobbying and the Corrosion of American Government*. But until recently these "lobbyists"—supposedly named for the area of the buildings in which they congregated—did not constitute the critical mass they do now. In the sixties, businesses often avoided and even ignored the city altogether, believing it was not relevant or was counterproductive to their fortunes.

Now, nearly every major corporation, trade association, and union either employs their own lobbyist or army of lobbyists, or pays handsome retainers—often in the neighborhood of $50,000 a month, regardless of what work they actually do—to a lobbying practice. Corporations will routinely pay large sums to D.C.-based trade associations and also hire their own lobbying teams to hedge their bets in case the trade association is not effective.

Lobbying is a thriving example of Washington's middleman economy in which a third party (the lobbyist) facilitates a relationship or some illusion thereof between a client and a government official. Even those who do not formally register to lobby the government can market lucrative services via a "strategic communications" or "strategic public affairs" practice (everyone here has a "practice" now, as if they're doctors performing surgery). One way or another, almost every engine of new wealth in the region has derived from the federal government, or at least the desire to be close to it.

Calculations vary on how many former members of Congress have joined the influence-peddling set. By the middle of 2011, at least 160 former lawmakers were working as lobbyists in Washington, according to First Street, a website that tracks lobbying trends in D.C., in April 2013. The Center for Responsive Politics listed 412 former members who are influence peddling, 305 of whom are registered as federal lobbyists. Hundreds more were reaping huge, often six- and seven-figure salaries as consultants or "senior advisers," those being among the noms de choice for avoiding the scarlet L.

In addition, tens of thousands of Hill and administration staff people move seamlessly into lobbying jobs. In a memoir by disgraced Republican lobbyist Jack Abramoff, the felon wrote that the best way for lobbyists to influence people on the Hill is to casually suggest they join their firm after they complete their public service. "Now, the moment I said that to them or any of our staff said that to them, that was it, we owned them," said Abramoff, who spent forty-three months in the federal slammer after being convicted on fraud and conspiracy charges. "And what does that mean?" Abramoff continued. "Every request from our office, every request of our clients, everything that we want, they're gonna do. And not only that, they're gonna think of things we can't think of to do."

Lobbyists can offer, in other words, an implicit preemptive payoff to powerful government officials. It happens not only on the Hill but in the boastfully antilobbyist, anti-revolving-door Obama White House. Scores of administration officials had by 2010 left the administration for K Street jobs without anyone so much as pointing out that they were defying a central tenet of the Obama political enterprise. If it was noted at all, the news was treated as a natural turn within the revolving door. After five legislative affairs staffers left the White House in the first part of 2011—three of whom went to K Street—Politico reporter Amie Parnes presented the trend as a natural by-product of administration staffers working hard for a period of time and then getting rewarded. "There are good jobs waiting at the end of the tunnel," Parnes quoted Stephen Hess, an oft-cited "governance studies" expert at the Brookings Institution. Parnes made no mention of Obama's public antipathy to K Street and his vow to slow the city's revolving door. Still, the work can be a grind, Parnes wrote sympathetically, with the plum lobbying gigs awaiting them as just rewards. "There's a payoff," Hess concluded, using the word "payoff" with no apparent wryness.

As Dodd was finishing up his financial regulatory bill in the summer of 2010, I spoke about him with outgoing senator Robert Bennett, a Republican of Utah who had been defeated in his reelection bid by a Tea Party favorite, Mike Lee. Bennett said he was surprised by how personally the voters of Connecticut had felt betrayed by Dodd. "They seemed to think Chris was actually corrupt," Bennett said, adding that this was not fair and that he certainly did not believe this about Dodd. He said the people of Utah were more pleasant to him when they tossed him aside than the cranky voters of Connecticut were to poor Dodd.

Bennett and another retiring senator, Byron Dorgan, Democrat of North Dakota, announced on the same day they would be joining Arent Fox, a major downtown law firm that includes a large lobbying component. Both Bennett and Dorgan had served on the Senate Committee on Appropriations, which gave them vast knowledge of how Congress allocates cash. It also made them coveted recruits for K Street.

Technically, former senators are forbidden from lobbying their old colleagues by a two-year "cooling-off period," so Bennett and Dorgan joined Arent Fox as "senior policy advisers" in the government relations department. There is little practical difference between what a former officeholder who lobbies does and what a former officeholder who "senior advises" does. For instance, someone like Dorgan could correctly say he has not formally registered to lobby even though he also owns the title of co-chair of the firm's government relations practice. In other words, he essentially oversees a staff of lobbyists. He talks all the time to his former lawmaking colleagues, and he can also use his specialized knowledge and access to call on old colleagues, friends, and fund-raisers to advance his clients' interests in bending a law or provision to their favor. He knows not only whom to call but also the phone number and who hired the staffer and precisely what to say to make things "happen."

While in the Senate, Dorgan was often quick to get all contemptuously righteous about people on the Hill cashing in their public service. When Jack Abramoff testified before the Senate Committee on Indian Affairs, Dorgan beat him up over the "cesspool of greed" that surrounded Abramoff's lobbying practice. In his subsequent memoir, Abramoff wrote of Dorgan, "I guess it wasn't a cesspool when he had his hand out to take over $75,000 in campaign contributions from our team and clients." (The *Washington Post* reported in 2005 that Dorgan said he would return $67,000 in donations from Indian tribes that Abramoff represented.)

When asked if his career change could be classified as "cashing in," Robert Bennett replied, "Is there anything in the Constitution that forbids me from earning a living?"

Representative David Obey, the cantankerous liberal appropriator from Wisconsin, retired in 2010 and—to the shock of many—joined the lobbying shop run by former colleague Richard Gephardt, the former Democratic majority leader whose willingness to reverse long-held positions in the service of paying clients was egregious even by D.C.'s standards of hired-gun opportunism. Examples abound in the case of Gephardt, a Teamster's son who represented a working-class district in eastern Missouri for twenty-eight years and was known as one of Congress's great champions of organized labor. But that was when he was in Congress and twice ran for president, in 1988 and 2004, with the substantial backing of labor. He would don a union windbreaker and blow out Teamsters' halls. "I'm fighting for *yoouuu*," he would boom over raucous crowds, and he was always convincing. His dad drove a milk truck, even.

Gephardt was praised by AFL-CIO head John Sweeney as "a real friend of working people and a powerful voice for working families on issue after issue." But after leaving Congress in 2005, Gephardt became a powerful force for Dick Gephardt on issue after issue. He joined the Washington offices of DLA Piper as a "senior counsel" before starting his own lobbying shop in 2007. By 2010, Gephardt Government Affairs was listing his annual billings at $6.59 million, up from a pittance of $625,000 in 2007. In addition to having a top-drawer roster of corporate clients that included Goldman Sachs ($200,000 in 2010), the Boeing Company ($440,000), and Visa Inc. ($200,000), Gephardt became a "labor consultant" for Spirit AeroSystems, where he oversaw a tough antiunion campaign; also while in Congress, he supported a House resolution condemning the Armenian genocide of 1915, only to oppose the resolution as a lobbyist who was being paid about $70,000 a month by the Turkish government, according to the *Washington Post*. Genocide goes down a little easier at those rates.

Some Einstein in the White House decided to christen these sticky months of July and August 2010 in Washington the "Recovery Summer." It was a sweet turn of branding indeed, given the still-sputtering economy. The phrase was meant to highlight the "surge in Recovery Act infrastructure projects" and all of the "jobs they'll create well into the fall and through the end of the year," according to the White House website. As it turned out, the economy wasn't recovering much at all, though the D.C. economy, which was humming right along, had nothing to recover from. And the sector of lame-duck lawmakers was recovering quite nicely from the collective dings and indignities they had suffered as Washington officeholders circa 2010.

Evan Bayh, for instance, was in dire need of a Recovery Summer. He was worn down and burned out. In announcing his retirement from the Senate earlier in 2010, the Indiana Democrat was extravagant in his grief over what Washington had become. Like Dodd and Bennett, Bayh was a senator's son: daddy Birch Bayh served from 1963 to 1981. Evan was savaged in the most personal ways during the debate over health care. His wife, Susan, sat on numerous corporate boards, making more than $1 million a year since leaving as first lady of Indiana, from numerous corporate interests. (The Fort Wayne *Journal Gazette* described Susan Bayh as a "professional board member," having been a director of fourteen corporations since 1994, eight since 2006.)

Evan's insistence that his wife's deep financial stake in the industry would have no bearing on his role in overhauling it was met with open derision. Salon's Glenn Greenwald called Bayh the "perfectly representative face for the rotted Washington establishment," while Matt Yglesias, writing for ThinkProgress, said Bayh was "acting to entrench the culture of narcissism and hypocrisy that's killing the United States Congress."

On the way out, Evan Bayh wrote a much-discussed op-ed in the *New York Times* cataloguing his many frustrations with politics and how the overall spirit of Washington was "certainly better in my father's time." He complained about the "unyielding ideology" of the Senate. He took the critique several steps further when he declared, "I want to be engaged in an honorable line of work," a remark that predictably rankled many of his former colleagues. Bayh also elicited eye rolls from senators who wondered where this man had been for the last twelve years—or eye rolls because they could predict precisely what was coming next.

But Bayh didn't stop there, soothing his deep despair over institutional conditions in Washington with dreams of "giving back" on the outside. He talked about joining a foundation. He waxed nostalgic for a previous chapter of his life in which he taught business students at the University of Indiana. He yearned to once again feel that tangible end-of-the-day satisfaction in his work. He fantasized lavishly to the *Washington Post*'s Ezra Klein about coming home to his wife after a long day of work and saying, "Dear, do you know what we got done today? I've got this really bright kid in my class, and do you know what he asked me, and here's what I told him, and I think I saw a little epiphany moment go off in his mind."

Bayh's valedictory lament and corollary yearnings might have been the most memorable statements he made in an otherwise ordinary two terms in the Senate. And if he had followed through on trying to fix the ills he had described on his way out ("the corrosive system of campaign financing," "the strident partisanship"), Bayh's post-Senate life could have made a greater impact than his time in office did. He might have made a tiny dent in how politicians in Washington are perceived by the general public, which he characterized this way: "They look at us like we're worse than used-car salesmen."

He then showed just the shameless opportunism that would repel any used-car buyer ("Make Crazy Evan an offer!").

After decrying "strident partisanship" and "unyielding ideology," Bayh joined Fox News as a commentator. The man who called upon members of Congress and their constituents to engage in "a new spirit of devotion to the national welfare beyond party or self-interest" signed on as a highly paid "senior adviser" to a large private equity firm (Apollo Global Management) and to a massive law and lobbying firm (McGuireWoods). Bayh, who was a finalist to be Barack Obama's running mate in 2008, vacuumed up as many sweet gigs as he could fit into his Club-issued trick-or-treat bag. He would eventually join the most potent business lobby in Washington, the U.S. Chamber of Commerce—arguably the most fervent opponent of the Obama administration's agenda. Bayh and Andrew Card, the former White House chief of staff under George W. Bush, embarked on a summer "road show" on behalf of the chamber's interest in stopping certain regulations on business. Think *Thelma & Louise* without the headscarves. Or think, as Steve Benen wrote in the *Washington Monthly*, a former senator who is "practically a caricature of what a sell-out looks like."

Trent Lott never saw the use in hiding his intentions: the whole "I will never lobby" meme. Why bother? He was the leader of the Senate, after all, and he had earned his reward.

Two thousand ten was a year for formers to dream, and dream big. News of the latest former deals kept breaking, tantalizing: like when congressman-turned-lobbyist Billy Tauzin became the Alex Rodriguez of the revolving door, setting a new benchmark for formers by making $11.6 million in 2010 to run the chief lobbying arm of the pharmaceutical industry (the Pharmaceutical Research and Manufacturers of America).

So why not Trent? He grew up mud poor and did his time.

Actually, Lott was a little shifty when he abruptly quit the Senate, not long after his Republican colleagues made him their whip. Everyone speculated that Lott was bolting because of a new law about to go into effect that would forbid lawmakers from lobbying their former colleagues for two years after they left office. Lott announced his resignation on November 26, 2007, just a few weeks before the new law would be enacted. By the old rules, Lott had to wait only one year out of office to lobby.

In the news conference in which Lott announced his resignation, he said the new law had no bearing whatsoever on his move. He officially left his office on December 18, 2007—and, three weeks later, announced that he and his former colleague, Democrat John Breaux of Louisiana, would start their own lobbying firm with offices just down the street from the White House. Their company would bring in $11 million in lobbying revenue in 2009, up 34 percent from 2008; it was acquired the following year by the behemoth lobbying shop, Patton Boggs, run by Tommy Boggs, son of the late House majority leader Hale Boggs.

Even at his Senate apex, or scandal low point, you could have carved "future lobbyist" into Lott's pillowy hair. "I lived on a fixed income for thirty-nine years," Lott told me, referring to the top tax-bracket salaries he earned over four decades in the House and Senate. He had big staffs and many perks and two homes (until Katrina wrecked the one in Mississippi). But he was never rich, he boasted, a self-testament to his up-from-nothing triumph.

Now he is, fresh millions pouring in every year. "How much is Trent clearing?" one former Republican House colleague asked me out of the blue when I mentioned Lott's name to him. It's something of a parlor game for many Hill alumni, trying to guess what the other formers are making. "About three or four million, maybe, for Lott?" the congressman-turned-lobbyist, a Republican, speculated. "That's what a former leader can command." The former congressman sheepishly rates a little more than a million a year himself, he said.

Naturally, Lott says he hates Washington. Why does he stay? The former senator/lobbyist squinted, assessing my sanity. Two reasons: "One, Washington is where all the problems are," he said. He can still make a difference and continue to be involved with the proverbial issues he was "passionate about."

"Washington is where the money is," Trent Lott said. "That's generally what keeps people here."

The dynamic fairly glared with the outgoing Senate and House classes of 2010. Big numbers of them were announcing their retirements, saying they were worn down by the city and the gridlock and the bushels of resentment they were getting from the voters and shouting demagogues on cable and talk radio. One after another, lawmakers would grieve over the state of things and gallantly announce that they were stepping away, washing their hands of all the affectation and hypocrisy and invective and blame. It had all become so personal. All those Tea Partyers, they rued, or the "professional left," as Robert Gibbs dismissed impatient liberal activists. The haters were all being so unfair and indiscriminate in lumping all of Washington together as a cache of smooth-talking sellouts.

And then, with light-headed speed, so many of the departing officeholders would settle into the retainer class. Even if they really hated Washington—in their bones, not just their sound bites—they can't leave, because they are institutionalized, and the reality of it shines upon them soon enough: that maybe it's not so bad in Washington after all. In fact, maybe it's the greatest city in the world.

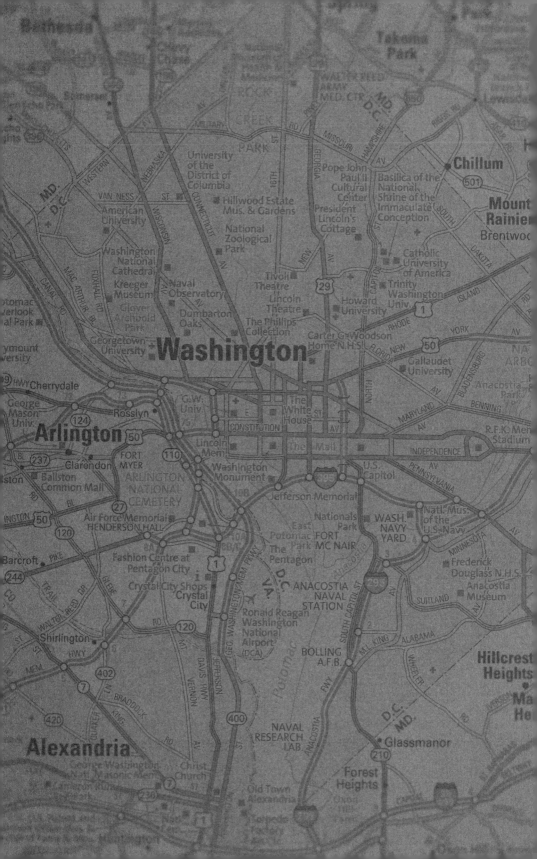

....

How It Works

"Who the hell is Kurt Bardella?"

That was my first thought—and first sentence—about the ankle-biting young flack for Representative Darrell Issa, Republican of California. I had mentioned to a colleague possibly writing a story about Issa. The colleague warned that doing so would mean dealing with Bardella, whom he called the most self-inflated press aide on Capitol Hill, maybe even more so than most actual members of Congress.

Bardella was also, the colleague added, probably the Hill's most effective press secretary. As proof: the unrivaled volume of press heaped on Issa before the November 2010 midterms.

I first met Bardella in May 2010, when he was really starting to make a name for himself, along with his boss. If Republicans won the majority in November, Issa was in line to become chairman of the powerful House Oversight and Government Reform committee. Good for Darrell and, by the first law of Washington career gravity, good for Kurt: nothing elevates a staff person faster than being stapled to a rising boss. If you're an aide lucky to be so positioned, it is vital to earn status as a "super-staffer." Super-staffers are an advantaged subspecies of aides adept at getting noticed, either because the boss pays special attention to them or because they are believed powerful or because they have achieved good recognition outside the office. Kurt was thriving in all super-staffer categories.

The first surprise to meeting Bardella is his appearance. His Italian name, terse e-mails, and blustery phone comportment suggest a big, aggressive presence. In fact, he is a rail-thin Asian-American who looks much younger than his twenty-seven years—closer to a teenager. His pin-striped suit and matching hanky in breast pocket conjure a kid dressing up like a grown-up.

Bardella is not the classic guy you can root for. He activates your radar and not in a good way. He laughs too much and too loud. He hangs out in cigar bars. You suspect you are being worked.

I liked him instantly.

By that I mean Kurt gave me a headache but I admired that he flouted the norms of being a smooth Washington operator: that even the most rabid striving must be cloaked in a sense of ease.

Kurt never pulled this off or even tried. He was not shy about sharing—on his Facebook page—his ultimate ambition: to become the White House press secretary. He was not reticent in acknowledging a danger of his brash style: "I'm never that far away from blowing myself up completely," he told me once. "It's all part and parcel to my inferiority complex. I struggle with things. But generally I'm pretty good at channeling this in a way that serves Darrell Issa."

Kurt evinced a frantic vulnerability and desperation to do well by his boss. It might make him more honest than people in Washington typically are. Or maybe "transparent" is a better word than "honest," since Kurt in fact lies a lot, certainly to me. So maybe that's all a bit of a contradiction, or a whopper of one, but one that can exist in This Town. Whatever, Kurt had begun to see himself as a truth-teller/whistle-blower, a particularly dangerous breed in Washington.

Something about Kurt cried out for mothering, or fathering, which I suspected might be true regardless of whether three of his fathers (one birth, one adopted, one step-) had not abandoned or alienated him on the way up. There was also a certain terror to Bardella. He said the displacement of his youth, lack of a college degree, and entry into the political workforce at a very young age (eighteen) engendered in him a profound fear that he had no business running with these bulls. It did not help, either, that Bardella had been fired from two different grown-up jobs while most of his high school peers were still in college: at nineteen, he was terminated from a job as a district rep for a California state senator ("I was just too young and immature and rubbed people the wrong way"); at twenty-one, he was sacked from the office of a San Diego city councilman (the chief of staff was easily threatened, he said, especially by him). So he was a jittery wreck, working long into the night. He needed to please Issa, or else.

"Darrell cares about me," Kurt says. "He fills a certain void."

Kurt stuck out among Hill deputies, but there was also something quintessentially D.C. about him. The city was his big proving ground. Capitol Hill, a self-contained village within a village, was a place for kids trying to stick at the grown-up table. That was perfect for a guy like Kurt. Like a lot of people in the city, he says he was an adult in spirit well before he became one in age.

He used to wear a coat and tie in high school and he carried a cell phone at age fifteen; this was the late 1990s, before most people were walking around with cell phones at all, let alone teenagers. Once Kurt's phone rang in the middle of class; instead of being embarrassed, Kurt picked it up. It could be important, maybe even the mayor. "Just take it outside," his teacher told him.

Bardella seemed very much to be measuring up and making a nice little brand for himself in Washington. He turned up quite a bit in Politico and Playbook. He loved his boss and the boss loved him back, to a point that others in the office could resent Kurt at times. But it was the right kind of resentment, the kind he would never draw if he weren't getting traction.

Another vivid Bardella trait was that he believed he was a total fraud. It hardly made him unique here: the impostor syndrome is the psychological common cold of D.C. (disproportionate numbers of residents lie about reading the *Economist*). But Kurt had a particularly dreadful case. He comes to it honestly in that he really was unwanted, at least by his birth parents, who abandoned him in his cradle at the front door of a church in Seoul, South Korea. He was placed in an orphanage, where the shunned baby hated to be set down in his crib. He craved human contact and made constant noise, as if he was fighting to talk well before he knew how.

The unnamed Korean baby was adopted at three months by a childless young couple in Rochester, New York. His new mom, Diane Bardella, was pursuing a degree in literature at the University of Rochester while her husband, Alfred Bardella, worked as a security guard. They named the baby "Kurt" and divorced when the little chatterbox was three.

Kurt lived with his mother and spent every other weekend with his father. He was enrolled in a Catholic school and often strayed off message with the nuns, questioning the all-knowing powers of God, among other disruptions. He was bullied and teased because he "looked Chinese." The bullies called him "chink," whatever that meant, he had no idea. Kurt was also named "Mr. Personality" of his kindergarten class, although Kurt suspects he was a sympathy choice.

Diane Bardella remarried; her new husband was Jim Nesser, an aspiring psychologist. They had two natural sons. Kurt would taunt his new brothers by telling them, "You were had, I was chosen." When Kurt was ten, his stepfather was accepted into a Ph.D. program in San Diego and the family moved west, separating Kurt from his adoptive father, Alfred Bardella.

After graduating from high school in 2001, Bardella took a summer internship with a Republican state legislator, who eventually offered him a full-time job. He jumped at the chance, envisioning a political life as presented in the speedy chess game of NBC's *The West Wing*, which obsessed him. The lure was enough for Kurt to blow off a planned enrollment at the University of California at Davis. Instead, Bardella spent two years answering phones and attending community outreach events for his boss. He eventually left to take a job as an assignment editor for the CBS affiliate, kicking off a brief ping-pong between local TV and politics. He jumped back into politics in 2005 to work for the San Diego mayoral campaign of Republican businessman Steve Francis. Francis lost, but Kurt's late-night hours—especially compared with the relative sleepwalk of his nine-to-five colleagues—caught the notice of Steve Danon, a public relations and political consultant who had worked for Francis. Danon noted the insecurity behind Bardella's drive, the eagerness to defy his lack of college training and prove he was adequate, or better. In Danon's estimation, Bardella had super-staffer potential.

Bardella's Washington stars first aligned in 2005 when the San Diego–area congressman, Republican Randy "Duke" Cunningham— best known in D.C. for flipping off his constituents, referring to gays as "homos" on the House floor, and suggesting the Democratic leadership "be lined up and shot"—got hit with a sack full of white-collar criminal goodies (bribery, conspiracy, mail fraud, wire fraud, tax evasions). The Duke headed off to jail and Kurt headed back into politics.

Danon's firm was hired by Brian Bilbray, one of fourteen Republican candidates in a special election to fill Cunningham's seat. Bilbray, who had served in Congress from 1995 to 2001 before leaving to become a lobbyist, will never be confused with a titan of the House. But he managed to eke by in the special election.

Bilbray's win in 2006 was Kurt's own passport to Washington, which might have well been a lottery ticket. Danon, who would become Bilbray's chief of staff, hired Bardella to run the press operation in D.C. There are idealists among the fresh waves of young people who come here: civic-minded kids who come to the nation's capital to make the axiomatic "difference." But this was not Kurt, the whole "make a difference" deal. When I first met him, he admitted to me that he was not much of a true believer in any particular direction, at least politically. The Republicans simply found him first back when he was a teenager. But he was not so much an R or a D as he was an O—"an opportunist," he told me. It's crass to actually come out and speak like this, but Kurt couldn't help himself. What Kurt believed in most deeply was the Hollywood version of Washington, the city at its most titillating and televised. Kurt was of the generation of neo-political junkies whose passions were ignited not by an inspirational candidate or officeholder like Barack Obama, John F. Kennedy, or Ronald Reagan but by operatives on TV, fictional (Josh Lyman) or real (James Carville). They were the players in a thrilling screen game. He wanted in.

"When I first came here," Kurt told me, "I was standing on the street corner with my suitcase, thinking, 'There's no way I belong here. This is crazy. I'm going to get eaten alive.'"

But most important, he was here. He had made it, to the real-life set of Washington, D.C, compensating for his abject unfitness by working conspicuously hard and being effective and solicitous in the service of the right people.

. . .

When Kurt first got to town, he immediately noticed the people on the inside, or the people who seemed to have that air of *being someone.* "You can tell that there were certain people that everyone kind of gravitated to," Bardella said. "They walked in, and people just knew who they were. I remember thinking, I wonder what it would be like to be one of those people. The cool kids."

One cool kid was Kevin Madden, a handsome-devil press secretary for John Boehner, the Republican leader of the House. Every Monday when the House was in session, Madden presided over a meeting of Republican press secretaries on the Hill. Bardella, then working for Bilbray, always made a point of showing up early. He sat near the front of the room, nodded a lot, and asked questions. He was eager to learn and improve, and was conspicuous in a room that otherwise had the ambience of a bored college class. More important, Bardella was eager to *show* he was eager to learn and improve— which is itself a wonderful impression to convey.

Madden, whose resemblance to Mitt Romney's sons disguises his Yonkers-cut edges, was amused by Kurt's obsequiousness. He also appreciated Kurt's hyper-earnest efforts. He, too, had been an impatient, eager-to-show press aide not long before, working the low press rungs of the Bush–Cheney reelect in 2004. He recognized what Kurt was doing; it wasn't hard to miss. And more power to the kid. Few of the House press secretaries ever made themselves known in these meetings, if they even stayed awake or showed up. Bardella would stay after class. He would introduce himself to featured speakers and approach Madden, asking (sheepishly) whether he could steal five minutes from Kevin's busy schedule.

He would then urge Madden to tell him if there was something he could do to improve, *anything at all*, because he wanted to learn and get better. He was also dangling himself before Madden in a bald effort to win his ownership as a mentor. This could bring them closer and maybe turn Kevin into an advocate for Kurt, someone who would look out for him.

As a teen political addict, Bardella read the memoir of the celebrated Clinton aide George Stephanopoulos, *All Too Human: A Political Education*. He enjoyed the book thoroughly and followed Stephanopoulos's career after he left the White House and joined ABC, first as a political commentator, then as the host of *This Week* and eventually *Good Morning America*. What struck Bardella was Stephanopoulos's description of being an altar boy in the Greek Orthodox sanctuary of his childhood in Cleveland. Being an altar boy, Stephanopoulos wrote, exposed him to the inner workings of the church in ways he had never experienced. It excited him to be within the sanctum, a privileged club, which he compared with the similar thrill he would feel as a political operative who penetrated the "inner" ring where decisions are made. This resonated with Kurt, who had been an altar boy in his Catholic church in Rochester.

"There is that place to get in Washington that everybody is striving for," Kurt told me in one of our first conversations. We were eating sushi near his Capitol office. As he made his points, Kurt tended to bob his head up and down, as if his words were being set to music. When reaching his sentence crescendos, Kurt's head went from a bob to more of a sway. "Once you get to that place, that inside place, you kind of just know it," he says. "It's exciting. I felt it when I was an altar boy. And there are times when you feel it here. But you're never sure if that feeling is going to last, or if other people are seeing you as someone on the inside. It puts you on edge, constantly."

All you know is, once you've experienced being on the inside, you don't want to lose that feeling, he added.

Getting "inside," to that place, into The Club, is a consuming pursuit in D.C. The divide between haves and have-nots is not so much economic here; House congressional aides hardly live large, but they're not have-nots either. Rather, the divide is between people who are "inside" and not—a highly subjective and fast-changing judgment.

As a twenty-two-year-old flack for Bilbray, Bardella sent Stephanopoulos a fan note. He wrote about how much he had enjoyed *All Too Human* and how much he had admired Stephanopoulos. No downside to writing a note like that, right? And wouldn't you know it: Stephanopoulos wrote back and invited Kurt to drop by next time he was in the neighborhood of ABC's Washington bureau near Dupont Circle.

Bardella made a point of being in that neighborhood soon after. He sought career advice, which is always an effective networking Vaseline. Kurt had been thinking about taking a job in the Senate office of Republican Olympia Snowe of Maine. He asked George what he thought, a query that also carried an unspoken message that Kurt was being *sought after*, that he was "in play." George offered the advice that, given Snowe's exotic position as one of the last moderate Republicans on the Hill, she would be an object of press attention—and thus a visible place for a press aide to land. Stephanopoulos signed a copy of *All Too Human* for Kurt, inscribing it, "Good luck with your political education."

Months later, Bardella was surprised to receive a call from his new friend at ABC. Stephanopoulos was working. He wanted to know if a certain immigration bill was going to pass the Republican conference in the House. Bardella believed the House measure would pass the GOP conference, which he told Stephanopoulos—

and which, a few hours later, Stephanopoulos passed on to viewers of *World News Tonight*. He cited "congressional sources." Kurt was a "congressional source"! He described the experience as his "first time playing with live ammunition."

A few months later, in December 2007, Kurt jumped to the office of Senator Snowe. He spoke of being around the "much higher caliber of people" in the Senate.

But Bardella lasted less than a year with Snowe. He found the Senate boring, plodding—too gentlemanly, not his thing. He returned to the lower-chart primates in Bilbray's office and identified his next big game: Darrell Issa.

Issa was a savvy and ambitious member who did not need the job or the money. He was already the wealthiest man in Congress, thanks to his magnificently successful car alarm company. Kurt liked that. He also admired Issa's confidence. While Congress lacked no shortage of members who believed they were the smartest guy in the room, Issa might have had a legitimate claim, at least to the top tier. He had sixteen patents under his name from his manufacturing heyday. Like Kurt, Issa was not shy about inflicting all he knew. Or, in Issa's case, showing it (the patents are framed on a wall of his office).

Bardella would camp out in Issa's office, which was next door to Bilbray's in the Cannon House Office Building. He befriended Issa's staff and pestered them until they hired him to be Issa's press secretary.

What Issa needed in Congress was to make a name for himself, to be more famous in The Club. This mattered to him, and was an obsession with Kurt. "I am completely focused on making Darrell a household name," Bardella told me in the summer of 2010.

"If, say, Chuck Todd is talking about something that happened that day, I want him to think of what Darrell might think."

I was struck that Bardella and Issa were focused on the approval of the Washington insider types—the ones who were anathema to the populist Tea Party uprising that would sweep Republicans (and Issa) into the majority. Before long, Issa was getting noticed inside The Club. He was living in green rooms. He owed much of this to Kurt, who was getting noticed himself—too much. Kurt had a dangerous (for a staffer) knack for getting his name in print, and an even more dangerous knack (for a staffer) for craving more.

"There is an expression here on Capitol Hill," Issa told me. "'Don't ever get between a member and a camera.'" That can be particularly harrowing in the case of Issa, who had purchased a T-shirt for Bardella that said: "It's all about me."

Kurt's self-promotional bent violated a basic Capitol Hill rule that aides should stay in the background—and, ideally, out of the press.

Yet Bardella's public imprint kept growing. It brought smirks. He was particularly eager to show off how plugged in he was at all times, an ever-churning operator. Kurt volunteered his testimony to an October 2009 Politico story that explored whether excessive BlackBerry use could be a drag on a staffer's dating life.

And when Bardella stopped using his BlackBerry during a vacation, it was a newsworthy event in Politico. "I haven't sent a press release, statement or ICYMI in about six days," Bardella was quoted as saying, adding that his boss had e-mailed him during his Black-Berry silence, wondering if he was still alive.

Politico was gold for the likes of Kurt Bardella. It provided an accelerated chronicle of his amped-up life and a willing outlet to "place" stories helpful to Issa. Politico was also generous in bestowing fame (of a sort) on the traditionally innocuous staffer.

The workaholic regimen of the politically spellbound was a recurring theme in Politico. These are the aspiring Ari Golds or Josh Lymans whose stressed countenances have been copied and exaggerated as a D.C. pose. They are direct, often crude, and fully steeped in the cutting, sardonic, and somewhat snarky tones characteristic of many of the essential-to-the-operation twentysomethings around town. Politico wrote a trend piece about this ("Bring on the Snark") in which Kurt declared that Washington "is a city that has been built on false premises and false pretenses." Availing oneself of a sarcastic or sardonic tone can come across as more authentic, he added.

Kurt was always happy to volunteer his example as someone who was working extremely hard, day and night. "It is only 11:30 a.m. but Kurt Bardella is on his third Red Bull, and he's got a fourth on deck," Politico wrote of Bardella in a profile that accompanied his being named one of "50 Politicos to Watch" in 2009.

"I don't ever stop," Bardella was quoted on January 15, 2010, in another Politico treatment, this one posing the question "Could my job be killing me?" The story was pegged to the sudden death of then Minority Leader John Boehner's chief of staff. But it was also about Kurt, like everything.

"It rubbed a lot of folks the wrong way that he would use that opportunity to remind everyone how hard he works," one Republican communications aide told *Washingtonian* in a profile of Bardella that came a year later, when he had become really notorious.

Kurt couldn't help himself. He had found love. Politics and Issa, sure, but also the whole thrall of the political-media experience circa 2010. There was little slog to it, as there is in so much of political office: the policy debates, the town meetings, the committee hearings, the constituent visits. Screw that. Press is immediate gratification. It's where most politicians truly live, the realm of how others see and judge them, the hour-to-hour score sheet of their massively external definition. "Nothing is more powerful than shaping public perception on public policy," Bardella asserted in a 2007 profile in *The Hill*. As such, the press and communications lieutenants on the Hill, as opposed to the policy advisers or legislative aides, are often the staffers who become closest to the principals.

As the 2010 midterms approached, it was looking more and more like the GOP would reclaim the majority for the first time since 2006, the year Kurt first arrived in Washington. These were fast and expectant times for Republicans on the Hill, and Kurt himself was feeling every bit ascendant in This Town. He would send talking points over to "Newt" (at his personal e-mail!) in case a particular topic came up on the former speaker's appearance on *Fox News Sunday*—and Newt was writing back, thanking him. He could be seen backslapping his way through the Capitol Hill Club, preferred hangout of Hill Republicans. Kurt also did a lot of public interacting with the sexy somebodies in the media. He kept a huge whiteboard behind his cubicle that listed in boldface all the media names he was warding off at that particular crowded moment (Jessica Yellin at CNN, David Gregory at *Meet the Press*, "Greta" at Fox). They all wanted time with "Darrell"; Kurt would do his best to make it happen ("Greta has always been fair"), no guarantees. But first he has a call on the other line, and two hundred e-mails from bookers to deal with, and the boss calling him on the cell—*Good God, does it ever stop??!!*

As he graduated from starstruck to name-dropper, Kurt had no desire to hide in plain sight.

- He posted Facebook updates about how he was in a meeting with "Darrell and Chairman Bernanke."

- "At the Senate barber with the Boss and Ralph Nader."

- "At CNN with the Boss who is about to go on Sit Room with Wolf at 5:28 p.m."

Bardella was always diligent about sending out Playbook-inspired birthday messages. He would reel off the "We've never met before but" notes and the fan mail that fortified his fattening collection of contacts around town. That's how I first encountered Bardella.

Kurt sent me fan e-mail in the spring of 2010 after I had written the story about Mike Allen for the *New York Times Magazine*. This was very nice of him. In his e-mail, Bardella said the Allen story captured the crazy acceleration of the modern D.C. news cycle.

Politics now operates in "cycles"—news cycles, election cycles—and it is one of those words that came into vogue in recent years. There's now even a political show on MSNBC called *The Cycle* (which, as the *Washington Post*'s Karen Tumulty pointed out, was obviously not named by a woman). "Cycle" connoted the perfectly circular existence of today's exercise—perpetual motion, winding up in the same place.

"The Cycle" was a full-toned topic for Bardella, as it was very much the Washington carnival he inhabited and excelled in. Politics was his ticket to the inside. And it gave him a competitive charge like his favorite sport, basketball, did; he played with the abandon of his favorite player, Kobe Bryant, whose initials he was proud to share.

In his e-mail to me, Bardella suggested that the article on Allen could be the basis of a book or a movie about how Washington works today. Bardella saw the world before him as a bracing struggle between man and news cycle—a cubicle drama that Mike Allen narrated for This Town every morning. Kurt spun in the middle of it all. He would be eager to demonstrate for me how it worked.

When Kurt e-mailed me to introduce himself and pay the compliment, I had only the shallowest associations with Darrell Issa. I knew him as one of those super-rich California business types who had tried and failed to spend his way into statewide office. (California has had quite a few of these over the years.)

Issa had run unsuccessfully for the state's GOP Senate nomination in 1998 despite spending $9 million of his own money. Issa was first elected to something in 2000—Congress, from a conservative district near San Diego. He was known as a smart, capable, and hard-driving member who rubbed quite a few colleagues the wrong way with his excessive bent for self-promotion, even by congressional standards. He ran twice for leadership posts, losing both times. He wanted to replace California governor Gray Davis in the state's recall campaign of 2003. Issa helped fund that election, to the gratitude of state Republicans, who thanked him very much by rallying to the eventual winner, Arnold Schwarzenegger. But Issa's profile rose considerably in the first two years of the Obama administration. Representative Tom Davis of Virginia, the chairman of the House Oversight and Government Reform Committee, had not run for re-election in 2008. This opened the ranking Republican slot to Issa, making him a key figure in a panel charged with the broad watchdog mandate over the White House.

Every Congress produces a paramount pest, adept at drawing attention to nuisance issues (and his nuisance self) while making trouble for the other party when it controls the White House. Democrat Henry Waxman of California played that role during the Bush years, while Republican Dan Burton of Indiana tormented Bill Clinton during his scandal-stinking presidency.

Next came Issa, who was drawing much notice by shouting forth on matters both high-profile (the Obama administration's response to the BP oil spill) and obscure (a possible conflict involving a member of the National Labor Relations Board). He was a tireless publicity seeker with the smile of a game-show host and a Bluetooth affixed to his ear. His ink-black congressional hair was brilliantly in place. The boom in cable and online media had created a bottomless need for the spew of news releases Bardella kept issuing, day and night, on Issa's behalf. He was perfectly in tune with the second-to-second pressures that media people were under. "The appetite for the stuff we throw up there is immediate and constant," Bardella told me in the summer of 2010. Even if a few reporters correctly questioned whether many of Bardella's releases and pitches were significant, there were always media outlets happy to grab them. It was partly laziness that made them do that, Bardella said. But mostly pressure and demand. They needed to be first with the little snowflakes that Issa/Bardella was blowing at them nonstop. It gave them the modern news-cycle version of a scoop, and kept their editors happy.

I first considered writing about Issa in the summer of 2010. He was showing up a lot in the press, the stories always saying that Issa could become an even bigger nuisance to Obama if House Republicans won the majority in November.

If that came to pass, as was appearing likely, Issa would gain the right to call investigations and issue subpoenas and do whatever he wanted to distract, embarrass, and essentially mess with the Obama undertaking. Issa called himself a Reagan Republican, but his true compass in 2010 seemed to be whatever most got under the administration's skin and himself on television.

As the summer progressed and lawmakers hit the campaign trail, Democrats began focusing more and more on the prospect of a subpoena-packing Issa taking over the House Committee on Oversight and Government Reform. At least two Democratic political enterprises—the White House and the Democratic Congressional Campaign Committee—were circulating fat opposition files on Issa. "Opposition files," or "oppo," is the political term of art for a cache of unflattering material on the designated "opponent." Oppo about Issa always begins with a *Los Angeles Times* exposé that was published during his unsuccessful campaign for the Senate in 1998.

The story details Issa's checkered history during what he describes as "a colorful youth"—a period that apparently stretched well into his twenties. He pleaded guilty to a misdemeanor gun charge in 1972 (he was carrying an unlicensed pistol) and, with his brother William, was indicted on felony charges related to car thefts in 1972 and 1980. The charges were never pursued for lack of evidence. Issa calls himself a victim of guilt by association and blames his brother. The *Los Angeles Times* piece also includes, among other things, harrowing accounts of Issa allegedly threatening a business associate with a gun and a detailed description of a very suspicious fire in an Issa-owned factory.

Through his political career, Issa has always shrugged off his history as having been a "rotten young kid." He also held an obsessive grudge against the author of the *LA Times* story, Eric Lichtblau, now of the *New York Times*. Issa has described Lichtblau as being a "notorious hatchet man" and a "scoundrel." (Lichtblau, for what it's worth, now sits one cubicle away from me in the Washington bureau of the *New York Times*—and is a pretty good guy for a hatchet-wielding scoundrel.)

But I had no idea about any of Issa's blotchy history until I got a call one summer afternoon from the White House, peddling oppo.

Bill Burton, the deputy press secretary at the White House, called me at my desk one afternoon. Burton, an able cable surrogate for Obama during the 2008 campaign, has a breezy demeanor that can obscure a pit-bullish approach to the political skirmish. He was a top lieutenant to then congressman Rahm Emanuel in 2006 when Emanuel ran the Democratic Congressional Campaign Committee and his party wrenched control of the House after twelve years.

In his phone call, Burton wanted to tell me about Darrell Issa.

As oppo calls went, this one was pretty tame. Burton asked me what I knew about Issa. Not much, I said. He urged me to spend some time "getting to know him." As an hors d'oeuvre, Burton mentioned Issa's auto thefts. Interesting. And kind of funny, since Issa made his nine-figure fortune selling car alarms. Not only that, but Issa's car alarm product, the Viper, is the one that features a man's deep voice warning would-be burglars to "please step away from this car." I thought that was funny. It was summer, and I needed a story. Issa was timely, so I pursued it.

All went smoothly, although at one point my antique tape re-corder jammed and Issa—a gadget geek and the former head of the Consumer Electronics Association—was kind enough to intervene. Issa was a smooth and engaging interview, though he twice launched into tangential assaults against Lichtblau, which went on and on. After I made an innocuous fact-checking inquiry with Bardella the next day about the old auto-theft charge, Issa called very agitated minutes later, suggesting that I have "that hatchet man Lichtblau" write the story for me, just to save time. Not necessary. I wrote the piece fairly straightforwardly: I introduced Issa to readers not famil-iar with him, and talked about how he was harassing the White House and positioned to become an even greater nuisance after No-vember. There were a few cursory paragraphs about Issa's criminal history.

To me, the most memorable part of this Issa excursion was meeting Kurt Bardella and seeing the Mini-Me factor at work. His adoring rapport with "boss" or "Darrell" (rather than the customary "Congressman" or "sir") was unusual in its deference approaching worship. As Issa spoke, unleashing his practiced lines about holding the White House accountable, Kurt kept gazing up adoringly at his man. Kurt and Darrell even shared verbal tics, filling their sentences with distinctive "y'dohs," a variant of "you know."

You hear the formulations "He's like a father to me" and "He's like a son to me" quite a bit in Washington. It follows naturally in a place—a city of patrons—where so many career arcs turn on the uncertain axis of mentors and protégés, professional associations mirroring familial ones. These people spend so much time together and become so dependent that it's only natural that some lineal bond forms. Tim Russert started talking like and mimicking the mannerisms of his guy, Senator Daniel Patrick Moynihan: "my intellectual father," Tim called him. Russert developed such a killer impression of Moynihan's urbane inflections and academic affect that he sometimes placed calls on his boss's behalf without the other person's (or Moynihan's) knowing it was him. Once, Moynihan—the real one—placed a call to Ted Kennedy, and Kennedy abruptly said, "Fuck you, Russert," and hung up. After Moynihan called back and Kennedy apologized, Moynihan admonished his impersonator with a simple refresher: "Me Moynihan, you Russert."

Kurt went heavy into the Issa-as-father theme. He treated it as a genuine conceit, not some pat Washington cliché. Shortly after he arrived in Washington, Kurt had become estranged from Jim Nesser, the man he considered to be his father after he stopped hearing from his first adoptive father, Al Bardella. Nesser and Kurt's mother had split up, his mother was struggling financially. She had her health insurance canceled and wound up taking a job as a hotel maid. "I had just gotten to Washington, trying to get my head around everything," Kurt was telling me, "and my mother breaks down one night bawling in my arms, saying she has no idea how she's going to make it. That kind of changes everything. I had to do everything I could to keep things together for her. I've been told I have a bit of a hero complex."

Bardella and Issa bonded during a trip to New York in 2009, shortly after he joined the congressman's staff. The new flack had engineered an appearance for Issa on Sean Hannity's show on Fox News. For a Republican congressman, scoring a Hannity spot is like winning a trip to Disney World—and big props to Kurt for making this happen. They couldn't get a train or a flight, so Issa just drove. The round trip allowed for ten hours of captive car time for Kurt with the boss. That was the first time Kurt talked to Issa about his messy family circumstances. "Darrell was a good listener," Kurt says, adding that Issa himself could identify with Bardella's jagged line to D.C.

In November 2010, the Daily Beast's Howard Kurtz conducted a phone interview with Issa, or so he thought. He quoted the congressman accordingly—except that it was Bardella talking on the phone to Kurtz, not Issa. On the list of embarrassing reporter errors, this was a whopper, especially for someone like Howie, a longtime media reporter for the *Washington Post* who had spent much of his career covering the failings of his colleagues. It was made even worse because Kurtz pointed out in his story that Issa liked referring to himself in the third person.

But the Kurtz lapse also belonged safely in the "There but for the grace of God go I" category. It was the kind of boneheaded thing an overworked reporter might conceivably do, especially on deadline. After Kurtz's story was published, Bardella sent him an e-mail informing him of his mistake.

Hey Howard—

Saw your piece ran this weekend, and I think there's a little confusion. It wasn't the Congressman you spoke with, it was me speaking in capacity as his spokesman—that's probably why the "speaks in the third-person" reference you made was out there since it was me and not him. Not sure how we got our wires crossed but I thought you should know.

kb

Kurtz did not respond to Bardella's e-mail and did not correct the record. This moved Kurtz's error from the "understandable whopper" category to the "reporter possibly withholding information to save self from humiliation" category. Several weeks passed without anyone's learning of the mishap. Kurtz would have avoided detection if Bardella had not mentioned the episode to reporter Ryan Lizza, who was profiling Issa for the *New Yorker*. It was only after a *New Yorker* fact-checker called Kurtz and asked him about the error—six weeks after the original story appeared—that Kurtz acknowledged it. Kurtz blamed laziness for his long delay. He also claimed he addressed the other speaker as "Congressman" during the conversation but Bardella never corrected him. Kurt denied this to Lizza.

"I think anyone who knows me well enough knows I'm far too fond of myself to abdicate my own identity in favor of someone else's," Bardella said.

On Election Night, as had been expected, Republicans regained control of the U.S. Congress after a romp that netted the GOP sixty-three seats—a shellacking for Democrats, President Obama called it. While the political wise guys dubbed this to be another "change election," Election Nights in Washington tend to follow numbingly similar rhythms in repeating venues. People will drink heavily on both sides, regardless of how the voting goes; like the Tea Party guy I met—who had obviously been drinking more than tea—stumbling out of the Republican bash at the Hyatt Regency Washington on Capitol Hill wearing a "Don't Tread on Me" hat. Not two seconds after he handed me his business card, he proceeded to vomit magnificently all over the hood of a waiting cab. ("Don't Puke on Me," I thought.)

Bardella spent the big night working at Issa's Election Night victory party at the Westgate Hotel in San Diego. As the new chairman of the House Committee on Oversight and Government Reform, Issa was now unquestionably one of the most visible and powerful Republicans in Washington.

Bardella now legitimately viewed *himself*—not just his boss—as a news driver. Reporters would be coming to him, not the other way around. If Bardella decided, for instance, to give the story of Issa's first subpoena to Jake Sherman at Politico rather than Alan Fram at the Associated Press, Sherman could boast of a nice little scoop for himself, while Fram might suffer an unpleasant "Why we no have?" from his editor. The whole cycle might reverse itself two hours later when Kurt was ready to parcel out his next nugget.

He was beginning to feel ever more powerful, and was being loved accordingly in the form of flattering e-mails from reporters and television bookers eager to win his favor. "Is anyone on the Hill as good at his job than you?" one CNN booker asked Kurt in an e-mail. Sucking up to gatekeepers is reflexive practice among journalists. Barbara Walters herself, the queen of the "get," has elevated it to an art form. After landing an exclusive interview in late 2011 with the savage Syrian dictator Bashar al-Assad, Walters tried to help Assad's young press assistant get an internship at CNN and admission to Columbia University, according to e-mails that were made public by a Syrian opposition group. Walters referred to the twenty-two-year-old aide in her e-mails as "dear girl" and signed them "Hugs, Barbara." The aide, Sheherazad Jaafari, replied that Walters "can never be a better mom to your adopted child (me)." She signed off, "I love you so much and thanks again." Walters later apologized for her conduct.

Kurt's higher perch empowered him to go beyond his usual portfolio. He took on little projects to sow mischief for the opposition. In the weeks after Election Day, Democrats on the Committee on Oversight and Government Reform were in some dispute over who would be their ranking member now that they were in the minority again. It was assumed that the job would go to Edolphus Towns of New York, who had been the chairman of the committee in the last Congress. But several key Democrats in Congress and the White House viewed Towns as an ineffectual chairman who was easily steamrolled by Issa. They wanted to jettison him for Elijah Cummings of Maryland, who was viewed as a much more formidable figure—something Issa/Bardella also believed, which led Bardella to talk as much as possible about how marvelous Towns was: "Just a terrific human being," Kurt said, smiling, "someone who did an outstanding job as chairman. We just love Ed Towns."

In the middle of November, a liberal Democrat on the Committee on Oversight and Government Reform, Dennis Kucinich, went on Ed Schultz's show on MSNBC and started criticizing Issa for making false claims about the White House. Seeing this, Kurt immediately called some Hill reporters and wondered if they had heard anything about Kucinich running for the ranking membership position. This was Kurt's way of putting the notion into "the bloodstream." He believed Democrats would never place Kucinich, a two-time fringe candidate for president, into such a visible and strategically important job. His candidacy would bolster Towns by turning him into a more reasonable alternative. It would create uncertainty among Democrats, which would in turn benefit Issa. Mostly, it was just fun for Kurt to feel he was manipulating the doings of Congress.

On his show the next day, Ed Schultz endorsed Kucinich to be the committee's ranking member. At which point Bardella decided to call over to Towns's office to give his counterpart in the communications office a "heads-up" about Ed Schultz's endorsement. "It looks like Kucinich is trying to make a move on you guys," Bardella helpfully told his counterpart. This was Kurt's way of nurturing doubt in his opposition in the guise of being supportive. "If there is anything I can do to assist, please let me know," Bardella said. Towns's people were grateful for his offer. "We're all on the same team," Kurt assured them.

Towns then issued a "Dear Colleague" letter to Democrats on the committee to say he was running again to be their ranking member. Within a few days Kucinich put out a similar letter. Kurt believed he had something to do with this by talking up Kucinich's candidacy and making it "self-fulfilling." This all might have happened anyway, but at the very least Kurt believed he had made the principals "show their cards before they were ready to." The drama created a distraction for Democrats that was "politically advantageous for Darrell." In the end, the White House and Democratic leadership intervened and installed Elijah Cummings as the ranking member.

Not long after Election Day, I visited Kurt on Capitol Hill. We escaped the crowded cubicle environs of Issa's office and headed to a vacant hearing room that was in the midst of a noisy renovation. Over the summer, I had mentioned to Kurt that if Republicans won the majority, I might be interested in depicting Issa as a character for this book. That was a nonstarter, Kurt said. And just as well, I figured, because I was really more interested in Kurt, an emblematic super-staffer who was making Washington work for him and trying to move up in The Club. He was a kind of will-to-power orphan who was feverishly devising his persona on the fly. I loved the sheer unabashedness, even jubilance, of Kurt's networking and ladder climbing and determination to make it in The Club.

Clearly enamored of his own narrative, Kurt was intrigued by my proposition. Actually, if I was reading his face correctly, he had already been thinking about who would play him in the TV treatment. But Kurt said he also believed his was an important story to tell. He could be an instructive vehicle for showing how Washington works in the twenty-first-century information carnival.

He also saw a higher purpose to his story. Kurt viewed himself as the truth-teller type, which is of course a dangerous breed in On-Messageville. The notion carries an inherent vanity—*that my story is important*—that staff-level aides are trained to subvert from day one.

Kurt said he needed to check with his bosses. They approved, provided that Kurt's involvement did not hurt Issa or interfere with the work of the committee. Kurt assured them it would not.

I told Bardella that I would visit with him periodically in the ensuing months and encouraged him to send along random thoughts and observations by e-mail. Even better, he would copy me on occasional e-mail correspondence that was, he believed, reflective of how he was spending his days and how he interacted with The Club. I don't remember whose idea this was, mine or his, but Bardella thought the notion made sense. "My e-mails can basically be read as a diary of how I do my job in this crazy world," he told me. It was a perfect virtual window into "how Washington works." True enough. And of course, for my purposes, e-mail is the kind of documentary source material to help tell a story in real time. For his part, Kurt did not appear to think twice about sharing correspondence from people who did not know their e-mails were being shared—a group that sometimes included actual members of Congress who e-mailed him directly (since he was kind of a big deal). In his view, e-mail was not significantly different from digital media tools such as a Facebook page or Twitter account. The e-mails were mostly innocuous, he felt, and most people know better than to share anything truly sensitive in an e-mail.

For instance, Kurt did not think Congressman Jason Chaffetz

would mind him sharing a pissed-off e-mail about an article in Yahoo! News that the congressman had stumbled upon. Chaffetz, who was the chairman of the Subcommittee on National Security, Homeland Defense and Foreign Operations, was not pleased that he was not informed about the story, which dealt with his area of jurisdiction:

> *I would appreciate a review of how the Committee and the Sub-Committee are going to work with our office. Did I ever get a heads up on this? I don't think so, but perhaps I am wrong. I believe I am the Chairman of the Sub-Committee with jurisdiction on this matter. Some how, some way we are going to have to be better coordinated on this stuff. I find it unacceptable and potentially embarrassing for all involved. Also, why is this not even on the list of potential items given to me by the Sub-Committee staff?*

At the end of my discussion with Kurt about him forwarding e-mails to me, I recall mentioning that this was a bit unusual—that it was something maybe he should think about. He reassured me that he did not think it would be a problem.

Kurt concluded this conversation with a favorite phrase among hard-charging Washington types who glory in pushing boundaries: "I've always thought it was easier to ask forgiveness than permission," he said.

Bardella would be asking forgiveness soon enough. But the year started well. Congressman Issa spent the first Sunday of the year, January 3, appearing on three Sunday interview shows—an impressive showing and another sign of Issa's surging property value. (In local slang, three Sunday show appearances on a single morning was known as a "triple Ginsburg," an exploit named for Monica Lewinsky's personal lawyer, William H. Ginsburg, who on the Sunday of February 1, 1998, haunted all five shows in what became known as a "full Ginsburg.")

Meet the Press wanted Issa for the following Sunday. He would be appearing after Senate Leader Harry Reid, who was already booked on the same show. Kurt turned *Meet* down because Issa was planning to spend time with his wife in California after a stop at the annual Consumer Electronics Show in Las Vegas.

"*Meet the Press* is not what it once was," Bardella observed to me after mentioning that David Gregory himself had called and appealed to him to put Darrell on. Sorry, not possible, Bardella said to Gregory—or "David," as he called him.

"Maybe," Bardella joked to me, "I should have just said, 'I would do it if Tim was still here.'"

Republicans formally took over the House that Wednesday, January 5. Outgoing speaker Nancy Pelosi relinquished the gavel to her Republican successor, John Boehner, who pounded the 112th Congress into session. Such benchmark days in the institution mix a sense of slight renewal with a hammering sameness. Former members and sparkling lobbyists and musty perennials wander the wide halls past lost newcomers. Voters might have turned out the old and the entrenched in the wave election of 2010. But one of the palpable messages of a day like this is that Club membership is for life.

In a single hallway, I saw the former Pennsylvania senator Rick Santorum (voted out in 2006), former New Hampshire senator John Sununu (sent home in 2008), and former vice president Dan Quayle (beaten in 1992). And who knew that the hearts of former House Republican leader Bob Michel and long-ago Nevada senator Paul Laxalt still beat? Both are still here, too, chugging along, slapping shoulders. There, on Independence Ave., strode the superlobbyist and former senator John Breaux, his eyes fixed on his BlackBerry as he entered a premium cab, hitting his head on the edge of the roof on the way in.

Bardella spent much of that afternoon moving into his new big office. His stately digs compared roughly to the size of a hotel room—a major expansion from the crowded cubicle bullpen Kurt inhabited in the minority days. He placed on the shelf a photo of himself between former boss Brian Bilbray and former speaker Dennis Hastert, and another of himself sandwiched by Bilbray and Newt Gingrich.

News that Robert Gibbs would be stepping down as White House press secretary was breaking on all three televisions. This is Kurt's dream job, as we know from his Facebook page. I asked him, absurdly, what he would say if Obama called asking the young mouthpiece to replace Gibbs—to be *his* Mini-Me. Bardella actually seemed to consider the question for a second. "If the president calls, I would have to take it seriously," he said solemnly before catching himself. "But I don't think the president will be calling."

Kurt largely avoided the pomp and parties that rung in this latest new era in Washington. I did go with him to a B-list reception honoring the 112th Congress at the L'Enfant Plaza Hotel a few weeks earlier, at which he rarely looked up from his BlackBerry. Representative Debbie Wasserman Schultz, a Florida Democrat, was addressing incoming members, reporters, lobbyists, and various party crashers. "I hate her," Kurt muttered into his BlackBerry, and then Wasserman Schultz shared that when she first came to Congress, "I was able to pass substantive legislation about Jewish-American heritage." (Kurt: "Substantial legislation about Jewish-American heritage. Give me a fucking break.") Wasserman Schultz concluded by urging everyone not to succumb to the "temptations" of Washington.

Bardella's BlackBerry trance was broken by Karin Tanabe, an

attractive reporter, who was then working for Politico and came over to introduce herself. Kurt's swoon was rather egregious. They spoke for several minutes. I heard Kurt tell Tanabe that he "worked in oversight," which sounded like a surefire Washington pickup line to me ("Is that a subpoena in your pocket?") until Tanabe broke the mood with "Oh, my boyfriend works in oversight," and the discussion ended soon after.

Issa had a full docket of interviews to ring in day one of the 112th Congress. He and Bardella headed down Pennsylvania Avenue for a scheduled appearance on Fox News with Neil Cavuto. The interview was held at the Newseum, halfway between the Capitol and the White House and fast becoming a seminal monument to The Club. Tim Russert's iconic *Meet the Press* set is displayed here.

Issa and Kurt headed up to the seventh floor of the Newseum to await their Cavuto hit. They were joined by a pastry tray of green room leftovers: Trent Lott, Dennis Kucinich, Ralph Nader, Republican congressman Paul Ryan of Wisconsin, and Republican congressman Mark Kirk of Illinois, who had just been elected to the Senate.

Kurt's eyes bugged, taking in the marquee scene of People on TV before him. Issa swept in and joined the green room Thanksgiving table, which instantly devolved into a bipartisan blur of back-slappy banter.

Trent Lott, walking up to Kucinich and Nader: "All right, which one of y'all is going to run for president this year?"

Laughter.

Kirk, to Kucinich, his now ex–House colleague: "You need some makeup, Dennis. Heavily need it."

Kucinich is unamused.

The downward spiral began for Bardella during a trip with Issa to Vegas, where the congressman was attending an electronics trade show. Bardella went ostensibly to babysit an interview Issa was doing with Ryan Lizza of the *New Yorker*, who was writing a profile of the congressman. Bardella spent much of his time unburdening himself to Lizza, showing him how smart he was. Lizza wrote a lot in the article about Bardella, whom Issa referred to as "my secret weapon."

"My goal is very simple," Kurt was quoted in the *New Yorker*. "I'm going to make Darrell Issa an actual political figure. I'm going to focus like a laser beam on the five hundred people here who care about this crap, and that's it. We've been catering more to that audience, so Darrell can expand his sphere of influence here among people who track who is up, who is down, who wins, who loses. Then we can broaden that to something more tangible afterward."

Representative Elijah Cummings of Maryland, the new top Democrat on the Committee on Oversight and Government Reform, sent a letter to Issa. "A profile of you posted yesterday by the *New Yorker* reports that you are using committee staff and taxpayer funds in an effort to transform your public image 'from an obscure congressman to a fixture of the Washington media-political establishment.' According to your aides, Issa Enterprises is 'a highly organized effort to manage his image,'" Cummings wrote.

"It is difficult to understand how any of this relates to the official activities of our committee," the Democrat continued.

"In addition to characterizing the committee's work as 'crap,'" Cummings continued, "your spokesman openly disparaged the media."

Yes, you could say that.

"Some people in the press, I think, are just lazy as hell," Bardella told Lizza. "There are times when I pitch a story and they do it word for word. That's just embarrassing. They're adjusting to a time that demands less quality and more quantity. And it works to my advantage most of the time, because I think most reporters have liked me packaging things for them. Most people will opt for what's easier, so they can move on to the next thing. Reporters are measured by how often their stuff gets on Drudge. It's a bad way to be, but it's reality."

Lizza also quoted Bardella as saying there was a new twist in his dealings with the media. Now that Issa had been elevated to chairman of the Oversight Committee, he said, "reporters e-mail me saying, 'Hey, I'm writing this story on this thing. Do you think you guys might want to investigate it? If so, if you get some documents, can you give them to me?' I'm, like, 'You guys are going to write that we're the ones wanting to do all the investigating, but you guys are literally the ones trying to egg us on to do that!'"

In the bland tundra of Talking Point Land, this was some radioactive stuff. And largely true, in many cases, but never mind that. Kurt was in big trouble. The Republican leadership team was furious over Kurt's bloviating. Top aides to House Speaker Boehner and Republican whip Kevin McCarthy wanted Kurt fired. They left the final decision to Issa. "I felt like I had disappointed my dad," Kurt told me.

Half of Issa's office wanted him gone, Issa told Kurt. Kurt had been called into a meeting with the congressman, the committee's staff director, and its communications director. It was agreed that Kurt, in his words, "came off like a pompous jackass" in the story. Issa told Kurt his job was in jeopardy. Issa told Kurt he would make a decision on his fate within twenty-four hours.

"I went back to my office, closed the door, and opened a Coke and thought, 'Holy shit,'" Kurt said. Clearly, he said, Darrell didn't want him to leave. The boss didn't even seem mad, Kurt thought, but he knew the "optics" might dictate that he whack Kurt. In truth, Issa was indeed not terribly mad. He knew Kurt could be immature and needlessly combative. He could be that way himself, especially when he was younger. He also knew that Bardella was an unusually vital member of his staff.

He decided to keep Kurt. Because, well, why not? Maybe he would catch some heat from colleagues for a few days, but Kurt was an ass kicker. His payoff was worth the trouble.

"Boss," Kurt told him, "I want to make this right. I am so sorry for putting you in this position."

Before the *New Yorker* fiasco, Bardella had been feeling a bit done with the Hill, he told me. He reached out to some big PR and government relations consultancies about possible jobs. He was making a base salary of $90,000 in Issa's office and ready to "monetize his government service" for an upgrade into the private sector.

He had conversations with David Marin, a former staffer on the Committee on Oversight and Government Reform who had gone to work at the Podesta Group, one of the top lobbying shops in town. After the *New Yorker* story, Marin called Larry Brady, the majority staff director on the committee—one of Kurt's bosses—to put in a good word.

"Thank you for your gracious and insightful comments to Larry," Kurt wrote Marin in an e-mail message. Marin assured him that it was "all true, man," and urged Kurt to keep his chin up. "Will do man," Kurt said. "I do want to get together to kind of talk about the future—1 yr, 2 yrs from now." They would keep in touch. Kurt also wrote a letter to the head of Creative Artists Agency, the Hollywood talent agency, about setting up a business to help movie stars deal with the media on their visits to Washington. He vowed to lie low and stay out of the press—even Playbook—for a while. Mike Allen took him to lunch, asked him how he was doing. He showed concern for Kurt "as a person, as a friend," which Kurt very much appreciated.

Kurt also received a reassuring e-mail from Juleanna Glover, a longtime Republican flack, lobbyist, and hostess best known for the People Worth Knowing parties she throws at her large Kalorama home.

In her note to Kurt, Juleanna assured Kurt that Lizza's full airing of Issa's past in the disastrous *New Yorker* profile would inoculate the congressman from future examinations of his sordid history—"especially," Glover wrote, "since Issa did such a sublime job in answering all of the questions." (Indeed, Issa was just *sublime* in explaining away the auto-theft raps.) "The piece turned out to be a real credit to your boss's intellect, insights and humanity," Glover wrote.

"Thanks for that Juleanna," Kurt replied. "Appreciate your insight."

Bardella said he was not angry at Ryan Lizza. It was Bardella himself who was stupid. He should have known much better. He even made a point of reaching out to Lizza and setting a lunch date, just to debrief. Everything was cool with Ryan.

But he was happy to bitch about Lizza when it was convenient. In many cases, fellow Republicans would approach him knowingly, assuming that the reporter was a biased liberal who had been out to get him. Matt Mackowiak, a GOP flack, sent a buck-up note to Kurt, with whom he often played basketball. "Yo dude . . . you ok?" Mackowiak wrote. "Thought Lizza excerpt might be problematic. . . . Did he screw you?"

Kurt replied, "Brother—talk about taken out of friggin context. I'll survive. More worried about Darrell than myself right now but thanks for checking on me."

For about a three-month period between December 2010 and February 2011, Kurt would forward me seven or eight e-mails a day, on average. Most of them were from reporters or television producer/booker types. They would ebb and flow, sometimes stopping for a few days and then picking up again. It was, sure enough, a window into how Kurt spent his days and a peek into how business is done on Capitol Hill. The vast majority of the e-mails were uninteresting and pro forma—requests to have Congressman Issa come on such-and-such a show, or Kurt reaching out to such-and-such a name brand to offer "guidance." Howie Kurtz sent Kurt a conciliatory note, saying that he regretted the episode in which he quoted "Issa" (after speaking to Kurt). He hoped they could move forward, and Bardella agreed.

I sensed that Kurt was sending me a lot of what he believed was his best work. These were the missives he felt most enamored of and that best projected himself as a real PR operator, not to be messed with.

For example, after receiving a request for Issa to appear on liberal commentator Ed Schultz's MSNBC show ("All best to you in the new congress," the booker signed off), Kurt was happy to bcc me in his reply: "Given that Ed has been lambasting Darrell for months every day, he has no interest in going on a show with a host who already has his mind made up."

In the vein of "This is how Congress really works," Kurt would forward me e-mails from counterparts in other Republican press shops. They would ask him to concoct quotes from Issa about their bosses that they could use in their own press releases. The press secretary for Representative Patrick McHenry of North Carolina, for instance, asked Kurt to contribute something (from Issa) for an announcement they were making about McHenry being named the chairman of an Oversight and Government Reform subcommittee. "Patrick will be at the heart of our Committee's effort to make the federal bureaucracy more accountable for how it spends the American people's money," Issa said/Kurt obliged, and the boilerplate went on for several more sentences.

Kurt also delighted in sending me an annoyed e-mail from the office of Maine senator Susan Collins, the ranking Republican on the Senate Committee on Homeland Security and Governmental Affairs. Collins was upset because Issa's office leaked out news that FEMA had improperly awarded a $450,000 grant to an affiliate of ACORN—the product of an investigation that Issa and Collins had worked on together. But only Issa was quoted in the story, which appeared in the *New York Times*.

"Hey Kurt," wrote Collins's spokesman Kevin Kelley, "needless to say, my boss really wishes she had a shot at including a quote, along with your boss, in the stories that have come out since your office decided to leak a report that was jointly requested."

Later that day, Kurt sent me a postscript to the exchange under the heading "You'll love this."

"Jen Burita, Sen. Collins' Deputy COS who was the Comm Dir when I worked for Olympia, just called my Chief of Staff to complain that I had not apologized for scooping them." What did the chief of staff say in response? "He hung up the phone and said, 'Did I sound indifferent enough?'"

One Friday night in late February 2011, I was at my office and my cell phone rang. It was Kurt, sounding shaky. "Jake Sherman at Politico is working on a story about me," he said. He explained that Sherman and his colleague Marin Cogan had heard Kurt had been copying me on e-mails. I had wondered when this would become an issue.

Kurt had been telling quite a few people of the e-mail forwarding. Boasting, it seemed. A few people had asked me about it in amused disbelief (never anger). It was only a matter of time before it got into the bloodstream. Bardella had told Ryan Lizza about it. Lizza asked me about it at one point when he was working on his twin killing of Issa–Bardella in the *New Yorker*. We joked—in the vein of me saying, "So, I guess you're having lunch with Bardella tomorrow at Bistro Bis, huh?" At one point I might have mentioned to Kurt that he should perhaps be a little less vocal about this. He claimed he had not told a soul about the e-mail forwarding. That was a lie but I didn't press it. The truth of it was I didn't think most of the e-mails were that interesting. The fact that he was forwarding the e-mails was more interesting—and apparently newsworthy. A random sampling:

- A producer at Fox Business wanted to know if Issa could go on David Asman's show, whoever David Asman was (apparently Issa used to go on but then stopped). "We felt spurned lately," the producer wrote.

- Newt Gingrich himself wrote, thanking Kurt for sending him unsolicited talking points before the former House speaker went on *Meet the Press* ("Very helpful thanks Newt").

- The Huffington Post's Sam Stein was pissed that Kurt would go to Politico with an exclusive about Issa attacking a mortgage program of some kind. "Brutal," Stein wrote. "This is huff posts wheelhouse. You should have come to us with this exclusive!"

On the phone, Kurt kept asking me what he should do. He was speaking hushed and out of breath, as if he were hiding under a stairwell. I told him he could always just say he was not at liberty to discuss his participation in my book—or some righteous stonewall like that. He told me that that's what he did. Except what he actually told Sherman was: "Am I bcc'ing him [me] on every e-mail I send out? Of course not." At which point it was clear Kurt was nailed. Any idiot knew what that meant: that he was bcc'ing me on some e-mails.

Jake Sherman called me a few minutes later. We had never met but I knew who he was: a good young reporter who had been covering the Committee on Oversight and Government Reform for about a year. I had been reading his stories (and, yes, a few of his e-mails) because of my interest in Kurt. We spoke mostly off the record. I confirmed nothing for him, which made me feel like an idiot, because he clearly had picked up the true rumor and my first instinct was just to tell him what was going on. But it was unclear if he had publishable goods and I was not going to be his confirming source on the e-mails. I was in no position to unless Kurt released me from our ground rules—that I would not reveal any details of our arrangement until after this book was published.

We went back and forth, Sherman and I. I reminded him that someone's career and reputation hung in the balance—which, in retrospect, must have sounded patronizing and manipulative.

To any normal population of news consumers, a Hill flack forwarding e-mails to a newspaper reporter writing a book would not be a "story" that anyone would care about. Few people—in places like Amarillo or Fort Collins or Macon—even know what flacks are or why they exist (much less that they account for billions of dollars in the economy of the nation's capital). But it—The Club—is no normal population. It is an exceptional population: Washington reporters and operatives and bystanders and time servers and coat holders. The people Politico writes for and about. What could be more interesting? Washington puts the "me" in "media."

At this point, my uh-oh bone was vibrating. This little Beltway amusement seemed primed for takeoff, with me in the middle of the story, not where a reporter wants to be.

The next day, Saturday, I received a call from John Harris, the founding editor of Politico and my former colleague at the *Washington Post*. He said he was particularly interested in this Bardella story and was trying to get to the bottom of it. Our conversation mimicked the one I had had the day before with Sherman: John wanted to know what was going on, and I told him nothing while trying to appear helpful.

The one difference in my conversation with Harris is that I had known and worked with him for years. Now we were on different sides of the field, theoretically, though united by our shared participation in the esoteric game: two socks tumbling in the same dryer, fellow patrons of the laundromat about to be staring at us.

The absurdity of it was magnified further by the fact that John and I would be together a few hours later at a fortieth-birthday party for Jim VandeHei, his fellow founding editor at Politico and our former colleague at the *Post*. "Couldn't this wait until VandeHei's party?" I joked to Harris at the beginning of our conversation, before we assumed our roles.

VandeHei's fortieth was held at the American Legion Hall on Capitol Hill and was its own festival of the D.C. prominent. There was a video tribute to Jim from rising-star Republican Paul Ryan and Obama economic guru Austan Goolsbee and Club royalty like Bob Woodward and Tom Brokaw. There was a classic garage rock band and a lot of Wisconsin things—Old Milwaukee beer, Green Bay Packers paraphernalia—in testament to Jim's home state. About 150 people showed up, including some of the Politico reporters and editors who were involved in this still-unpublished Bardella story. None of us discussed the in-the-works piece. I spent a portion of the evening wearing a cheesehead.

The next day, Harris wrote to Issa demanding that the congressman, the top investigator in the United States House of Representatives, look into the matter of whether his flack was forwarding e-mails from reporters to another reporter who was working on a book about people who found this kind of thing interesting.

If in fact this activity went on, Harris wrote, it would be "egregiously unprofessional" conduct. Harris was operating under the guise of an editor who was "raising concerns." It was also a smart reportorial gambit: an official complaint that would elicit some action from Issa that would propel a Politico-perfect story. Issa agreed that forwarding internal e-mails would be "improper."

(My personal view is that e-mails to public officials in a government office are a matter of legitimate public record. As Jack Shafer, the media writer at Slate, pointed out, "I don't see why a government official leaking to a reporter about a national security matter is kosher, but a government official leaking about what reporters are asking him about is 'egregiously unprofessional,' 'compromising,' or 'intolerable,' as Harris puts it.")

I t's the start of what I'm sure will be a memorable week," Bardella posted cryptically on his Facebook page on Monday, February 28.

Politico's Sherman and Cogan wrote their first story on the subject that evening. It began: "Rep. Darrell Issa, the Republican chairman of the powerful Oversight and Government Reform Committee, has launched an inquiry into whether spokesman Kurt Bardella improperly shared e-mails from other reporters with a New York Times reporter writing a book on Washington's political culture, Politico has learned." Politico is constantly telling its readers what Politico has learned. It continued: "Issa, Bardella and Leibovich were all given several opportunities by Politico to deny that the e-mails were improperly shared. Bardella and Leibovich declined comment. Issa says he simply does not know."

I particularly loved the sinister tone of that, as if all of us were caught together in an airport restroom or something.

Washington convention dictated that Issa must go through the all-important *Process* of *Investigating* this matter and then issue his *Findings*. Part of this would include him seeking me out for questioning. I would not cooperate in Issa's "investigation" because

(1) that would violate my ground rules with Bardella, (2) it would be partaking of a political exercise (which Issa's "investigation" clearly was), and (3) "refusing to cooperate" with the authority is the badass thing for a reporter do.

The next few days swirled. At least 150 stories were written about *l'affaire Bardella* in the seventy-two hours after the original "bombshell" was posted on Politico. (Politico would run seven stories on the subject in the first forty-eight hours.) VandeHei did a video clip on Politico.com declaring that this story would be "driving the day." Mike Allen devoted exactly half of Playbook to it on the Tuesday morning that it "drove the day." He and others sometimes referred to me in print as "Leibo," a nickname I acquired in about first grade that has persisted through every station of my life. As a general rule, I don't mind the nickname. It was always a good early-warning system in college of which women would never consider going out with me (if they called me by the infantalizing "Leibo," I had no chance). But I disliked being called "Leibo" in print because it suggested a level of coziness and clubbiness that, while pervasive, I'd rather not be so easily pegged with—especially since I'm writing a book on just that.

My employer, the *New York Times*, published a story on the Bardella matter, as did my last employer, the *Washington Post*. Many people I have known and worked and socialized with for years wrote essays and blog posts and columns about the saga. The stories were all comically larded with "full disclosures" about how the people writing them were friends with this person or that person or, in many cases, me.

I was in the middle of the mess yet feeling very popular. Shafer, the press critic at Slate, called out the grandstanding and overreaction of John Harris while adding: "FYI: Mark Leibovich is a friend of mine." (For good measure, he sent me an encouraging e-mail that day saying, "I worship your bald head.") Ryan Lizza wrote a long blog post for the *New Yorker* ("Full disclosure: both Cogan and Leibovich are friends of mine"). Jeffrey Goldberg, author of *Goldblog* in the *Atlantic*, weighed in with a short post in which he said I was a "friend of Goldblog," and so was Shafer ("except when he's yelling at me for something"), and that Lizza was his replacement when he worked at the *New Yorker* ("and also a friend—yes, it amazes me too, that I have friends, though mainly I have shifting alliances").

In his *Washington Post* column, Dana Milbank (a friend!) wrote that "if Washington's political culture gets any more incestuous, our children are going to be born with extra fingers."

The best thing written about the whole episode was on Twitter by John Dickerson, a political writer for Slate, talking head for CBS News, and you-know-what of mine: "Instead of writing a book about how self-involved Washington is," Dickerson wrote, "Mark Leibovich has gotten people to act it out in real time."

Issa called me on my cell phone Tuesday morning. "Hey, we're in the news," I said to him, maybe too glibly. "I've had better weeks," he said. And then, in boilerplate voice, I told him I would not help him in his investigation. My Tiananmen Square! Issa seemed to expect this and appeared to be just checking a box with his call anyway, buying the right to publicly say he had "talked to Leibovich" in his subsequent description of his inquiry. Our conversation lasted about two or three minutes. I told him that I did not think Kurt was a bad guy or that his intentions were malicious.

Later that day, Issa called Kurt into his office and fired him.

His actions reflected badly on Issa and the Committee on Oversight and Government Reform, Issa told Mini-Me. "The committee's deputy communications director, Kurt Bardella, did share reporter e-mail correspondence with New York Times journalist

Mark Leibovich for a book project," Issa said in a statement. "Though limited, these actions were highly inappropriate, a basic breach of trust with the reporters it was his job to assist, and inconsistent with established communications office policies. As a consequence, his employment has been terminated."

New stories popped online about Bardella's firing. A headline in the Huffington Post political tip sheet "HuffPost Hill" said the following: "A book about the incestuousness of Washington— written by a man everyone incestuously calls 'Leibo'—incestuously got someone fired."

It's not fun to be involved in something that gets someone fired. Plus, people were talking to/about me like I'd uncovered some amazing journalistic trove—as if getting a bunch of suck-uppy e-mails that reporters had sent to a Hill flack was like getting slipped the Pentagon Papers. Yes, reporters suck up, especially here, as Shafer pointed out in one of the endless analyses of this thing: "If sucking up to important sources were a crime, 95 percent of all Washington journalists would be doing time right now." Colleagues kept egging me on to publish as many of their peers' e-mails as I could possibly fit into this book. "A book that looks at the D.C. media nexus and doesn't offer someone a measure of embarrassment would be like a film on the desert showing no sand," wrote Clint Hendler in the *Columbia Journalism Review*. So here I was in the middle of the "Bardella incident" that FoxNews.com's Chad Pergram said "will reverberate for a while in the halls of Congress" and would "stand as an iconic tale of someone who rose and fell in one of the most unforgiving arenas on the planet."

If this "iconic tale" had happened a decade ago, maybe it would have merited a mention in Howie Kurtz's Media Notes column in the Monday *Washington Post* or be the subject of some longer thumbsucker in the *Columbia Journalism Review*. But because it happened in 2011, with all these new-media outlets and everyone eager to give their "take" on the matter, the story of the rogue flack came to "dominate" the Capitol during a week in which the majority party in Congress was otherwise threatening to shut the government down and a revolution had broken out in Cairo.

Kurtz even devoted part of his CNN show about the media, *Reliable Sources*, to the episode. In an interview with his former *Post* colleague John Harris, Kurtz reminded viewers of his own history with Bardella—the incident in which he quoted Issa in a story when he'd been speaking to Bardella. With Bardella now in full disgrace, Kurtz piled on with a new charge—saying that Bardella had "impersonated" Congressman Issa, which is why he had been confused.

In reality, any "scandal" in Washington that does not include elected officials, money, or nudity is not much of a scandal—except to the media, and only if it's about the media. "The break-up between Issa and Bardella . . . in Congressional terms is about as seismic as Brad Pitt and Jennifer Aniston hitting splitsville," wrote Pergram on FoxNews.com.

Salon's Alex Pareene produced one of the better "step-back pieces" on the whole affair: "The self-obsessed, navel-gazing Washington press corps is in a tizzy over the dismissal of a congressman's communications director (the guy whose job it was to befriend and spin and leak to members of the Washington press corps), who was fired for the crime of sharing journalists' e-mails with another journalist who is working on a book about the self-obsessed, navel-gazing Washington press corps."

Predictably, the "iconic tale" was a snowflake, dissolving after a few days. People assured me that this controversy had generated a whole bunch of "buzz" for my book, and what could be more important than that? True enough, I suppose, although my selfish writerly concern was that this seemed like a tidy endpoint for the Washington "narrative" of Kurt Bardella.

Kurt was laid low. All the career obituaries—the cautionary tales, the "boy who flew too close to the sun" invocations—catalogued the warning signs and "I told you so's."

Politico noted: "'It was only a matter of time,' said a reporter for one Capitol Hill publication who had worked with Bardella."

"Kurt has had danger signs," said a House Republican aide, granted anonymity by Politico. "If you had said, 'X press secretary did this,' Kurt would have been eight out of ten people's guess."

Bardella was deep in the barrel, which seemed to me the right place to leave him, story-wise. Silly me. That was premised on Bardella's being career-dead, never to be heard from again. Which defies the basic laws of nature for the giant Washington amoeba, the one that says you will always have lunch in this town again.

Bardella disappeared for a few weeks. I did not hear from him. He offered sporadic updates on his Facebook page about playing basketball and being on the Hill. He posted scripture: "'The LORD is my shepherd; there is nothing I lack.'" He had a bunch of new Facebook friends, which included George Deukmejian, the former Republican governor of California. He talked to friends about how he had lost his way and was returning to God. He was going through a period of self-reflection. I had never heard Kurt talk about religion other than to say he attended Catholic school, but now he was heavy into faith. Not to be cynical, but (oh, what the hell) public faith does tend to be the first step in any Washington rehab.

He e-mailed me at the beginning of April, apologizing for being out of touch. I was slightly surprised, figuring he might want nothing to do with me, the main accomplice in his downfall. I was also relieved that he was okay. No one I had spoken to in the previous weeks knew where Kurt was. A blogger reported that he had decamped to California, but it turned out he never strayed far from his home in Virginia, with occasional forays to Capitol Hill to visit friends. He told me he wanted to get together to fill me in on what he had been thinking and up to.

It was about this time that Bardella began submitting op-ed commentaries to Politico. Yes, Politico—the publication that made Bardella D.C.-famous, that published articles that mentioned his name two dozen times in two years, and that went into saturation mode over the e-mail sharing and covered every angle of his disgrace. Now, after just a few weeks in the barrel, Politico was serving as an engine of his rehabilitation. Writing as "Kurt Bardella, former congressional aide," Bardella wrote short essays for the website's "Arena" section, an open forum for people to "give their take" on some event.

"I needed to keep my name out there and stay sharp," Kurt would tell me a few weeks later about his Politico commentaries. He needed the oxygen of his name in print. When I mentioned to Kurt that maybe he had become addicted to the little crack hits of fame that a news-cycle player like himself had become accustomed to, he denied it strenuously. The commentaries, he said, "were just my way of getting a little bit back into the game."

Kurt asked me to meet him at a Sports Club/LA at the Ritz-Carlton downtown, where he said he had been playing basketball for three hours every day. I suspected he liked the cinematographic view of himself as a gym rat. He wanted me to see it—and ideally reflect it in print—as he had been relegated (for now) to the solitary consolation of his beloved hoops. He spoke to me while heaving up three-pointers and hit eight in a row at one point. Kobe Bryant can play. And the court was a perfect tableau for the sidelined operative—a perfect "visual" in the rehab narrative.

We had lunch at a snack-bar area just off the court. He ate a chicken teriyaki sandwich and spoke of his spirituality. "God has a path for all of us," he said somberly. He had been praying for patience and grace. He said he had spoken several times to Issa, who never seemed mad at him. "This is someone who would instinctively call me every time he got off an airplane for however many years," Kurt said. "You don't just lose that connection." I asked Kurt if he could see himself returning to Issa's office. Sure, he said, anything's possible. But he's going to wait a while, live on his savings, and see what's out there.

Bardella said he had lost fake friends in the saga—the anonymous bad-mouthers—which was fine. He had received affirmation too. Bill Burton, the Obama flack who was the first person to suggest that I write about Issa, sent Kurt a "Hang in there" note. Mikey checked in to see how he was holding up. Several reporters who suspected (rightly) that Kurt had shared their e-mails with me wrote to him, saying they were not mad. They offered to get together at his convenience. And if he was inclined to share his story, they would, no doubt, provide him a "fair hearing."

"I could sense the suck-up brigade coming back," he told me. Faux empaths make some of the best reporters in town, all promising "fair hearings." Kurt wound up "giving his story" to a reporter he had known for many years at the now defunct *North County Times*, the paper in his hometown, near San Diego. "I did lose my way a little bit," the 2001 graduate of Escondido High School told reporter Mark Walker. Bardella told me he knew that Walker would be friendly and that the story would be told in an unquestioning way, which it was. Kurt would then send the story to Mikey, who would excerpt from the "Bardella speaks" exclusive and his contrition would flow safely into the Playbook community.

A few weeks after Bardella was fired, I would run into people who said they'd been reading about me but did not remember why exactly. Kurt was finding the same thing. The life cycle of public disgrace has been condensed to where the actual offense gets washed away, leaving just a neutral sheen of notoriety.

Kurt received a call one day from a producer for CNN's Anderson Cooper. They were interested in Bardella's coming on air to talk as a "Republican strategist," or something, to discuss how some people were questioning if President Obama was actually born in the United States—the so-called Birthers. Kurt said the producer told him they were looking for "new voices" to put on the air. Kurt—who offered the bonus of being "diverse" (a rare Asian-American talking head)—said he would be interested. They did a pre-interview on the Birther show but the spot fell through. They agreed to keep in touch.

Kurt and I had another get-together at the end of May. He asked me to meet him at a cigar bar downtown called Shelly's Back Room. He had his own private humidor there. I hate cigar bars.

But I agreed to meet Kurt at Shelly's in the middle of the day. I was really trying to like him, even now, or at least find him interesting. He told me he had talked to some people about jobs: one with a conservative "super PAC"—an outside group whose primary purpose is to bankroll political advertising—backed by the billionaire Koch brothers, another with some public relations shop in town.

He had also talked to Jonathan Strong, a reporter at the Daily Caller, a start-up conservative website that was cofounded by the libertarian talking head Tucker Carlson. Strong had covered Congress, which is how he came to know Kurt. Kurt had forwarded me some of Strong's e-mails. One sequence in early February stuck out in my memory.

"Favor," Strong wrote in his subject line. He explained in his e-mail that the Daily Caller was compiling some promotional materials for advertisers. "I have been tasked with getting some quotes from Members about how they read and enjoy the Daily Caller," Strong wrote. "Is this something you could help me out with?" This struck me as cozy even by the standards of This Town: a congressional reporter asking a member of Congress to lend his name to his publication's promotional copy. Kurt was happy to be helpful. He asked Strong what he wanted Issa to say. "Just like, I enjoy reading the Daily Caller with some kind of mild variation on that theme," Strong wrote. "I read it daily, my staff stays updated by reading etc." Strong added that "my bosses are on my case about it." He had his response from Bardella in three minutes:

"Not only has the Daily Caller become one of Washington's must-reads of the day, but it has found its place in leading a daily news cycle that changes throughout the day. I can't tell you how many times my staff has sent me breaking news that originates with reporting from the Daily Caller—Rep. Darrell Issa."

"Epic," Strong wrote back to Bardella a minute later. "Thank you."

Now the Daily Caller was looking for a new promotions director, someone to circulate its stories and drum up excitement for the fledgling site. Strong asked Bardella if he could pass along Bardella's name to Tucker Carlson. Sure, he said. Carlson, who hoped to turn the Caller into a conservative version of the Huffington Post, had been intrigued by Bardella's energy and ambition. He had obviously won copious exposure for Issa, most of it good (until it turned bad).

Carlson has a special zest for goosing the self-righteous and condemning posture of The Club. "This is such a judgmental city when it comes to people like Kurt," said Carlson, who had appeared as a contestant on *Dancing with the Stars* several years ago. Tucker had called me in April for my opinion on whether he should hire Kurt. I was hesitant to get involved further in Kurt's fate, one way or another. But I figured it was the least I could do after getting the guy fired. I put in a good word.

I told Tucker what he already knew: that Bardella was high-risk and high-reward, driven and talented and immature. He had a desperate edge and would have to be watched closely. But it could be a smart, counterintuitive hire. Tucker invited Bardella in to talk about the job and hired him a week later.

Within a few weeks, Kurt was writing commentaries for the Daily Caller. His first involved Republican congresswoman Michele Bachmann's entry into the presidential race. "As long as her candidacy doesn't completely implode," Bardella opined, "her very presence in the Republican field creates dangers for the more established candidates regardless of whether she wins or loses." Bardella's op-ed was excerpted in the morning e-mail roundups, including ABC's "Note" and NBC's "First Read." People were reading what he had to say, sending him notes.

Bardella's time in the barrel lasted two months. Now he was back, just like Jack Abramoff was back, out of federal prison after three and a half years. His book (Abramoff's) would get plenty of buzz later that year and his book party, at Carlson's house, would include plenty of Washington journalists, waiting together in the valet parking line. Abramoff made a speech, did a lot of interviews, and stayed contrite. Every day was Yom Kippur. He pounded a tight message of atonement. Abramoff was also the subject of a video profile on Politico pegged to his book release. The host, Patrick Gavin, asked the friendly felon questions like "So, what's the take-away from jail?" and "Are you excited for this rollout?"

Kurt said his own "rollout" from the barrel was happening much faster than he ever expected. But he said he was having fun and trying to concentrate on being a better person, learn from his mistakes, and do right by God.

Meanwhile, the promotions director that Kurt replaced at the Daily Caller, Becca Glover Watkins, had taken a new job on Capitol Hill as deputy press secretary for a publicity-hungry Republican from California, Darrell Issa.

. . .

Less than four months after he was fired, Bardella was the subject of a 7,400-word profile by Luke Mullins in *Washingtonian* magazine, the glossy monthly that Club members pick up in the checkout line at Whole Foods. The story's headline, as surely it was: "Kurt Bardella: The Comeback."

Kurt felt the story painted him in a decent light and helped round out his profile. From reading the story, it was inevitable that Bardella would come full circle soon enough. Issa was quoted saying that Kurt "always has a home with us." Bardella and some of his coworkers had mentioned this to me as a possibility. On top of that, after Bardella disappeared in early March, so did Issa—from the media: the congressman was trying to keep a low profile after the e-mail unpleasantness. But it was also clear—and discussed on the Hill—that he missed Kurt. Without Mini-Me, he seemed to have reverted to being Congressman Nobody.

Bardella's return to Issa's office was announced August 24, 2011, a little less than six months after he was fired. It stood as the logical completion of the life-cycle: the snake eats itself.

In his new job, Bardella would not have any dealings with the press. He would work as a staff member, reporting to Issa's general counsel. The House Committee on Oversight and Government Reform released a statement saying that Issa believed Bardella deserved a second chance, even though he acted improperly.

9

Performing Arts

Richard Holbrooke stood at a White House urinal.

"Eric, I am very disappointed in you," he said to the startled White House aide peeing next to him. Holbrooke might have followed the young man in there. It's the kind of thing he would do.

The aide was Eric Lesser, a luggage handler on the 2008 Obama campaign plane who finessed that into a gig as David Axelrod's assistant at the White House. Like most assistants in D.C., Lesser was essentially a glorified secretary. But in a White House whose early months were devoured by the media like free food, even the former suitcase schlepper was hot property. He was the subject of two prominent stories in the *New York Times*: one on the subject of his *Odd Couple* yin-yang with Axelrod, and the other featuring Lesser as the de facto officiator of the White House Passover seder. Tammy Haddad honored Lesser at a party before he headed off to Harvard Law School. In his well-positioned Washington Way, Eric Lesser was "worth knowing."

Sweet-mannered and conscientious, Lesser sat two gates from

the Oval Office. Eric could get you to Axe, and Axe could get you to Obama. No one knew this better than Holbrooke, the inexorable diplomat who brokered a peace between warring factions in Bosnia during the 1990s. Other than possibly George F. Kennan, Holbrooke might have been the most accomplished American diplomat who never achieved cabinet rank. One reason for this was that he was irrepressible—the kind of guy who followed you into the men's room.

"The quintessential Washington know-it-all" was how Admiral Mike Mullen, the chairman of the Joint Chiefs of Staff, fondly described Holbrooke. But Holbrooke's credentials were relentless. He apprenticed under some of the last century's foreign policy royals such as Henry Cabot Lodge Jr., Dean Rusk, and Averell Harriman. He was the youngest Foreign Service officer tapped for the Paris peace talks, helped write the Pentagon Papers, served in the Peace Corps, ran *Foreign Policy* magazine, and was assistant secretary of state for East Asian and Pacific affairs and an ambassador to Germany and the United Nations. Obama appointed Holbrooke to be a special adviser on Pakistan and Afghanistan at the urging of Holbrooke's longtime friend, Secretary of State Hillary Clinton.

A connoisseur of power, Holbrooke studied the master moves of Clark Clifford, the city's signature power broker of the last century (Holbrooke cowrote Clifford's memoir). Holbrooke marveled over how Clifford worked it in Edward Bennett Williams's owner's box at Redskins games, positioning himself at the precise spot where important figures would see him upon entering the elite salon.

The men's room gamut was a favorite trick in Holbrooke's busybody arsenal. But he did not restrict his bathroom politicking to urinals. "Richard once followed me into a ladies' room to make a point," Hillary Clinton said. "In Pakistan!"

Now here was Dick Holbrooke standing next to Lesser, gatekeeper to one of the president's gatekeepers, announcing that he was disappointed in him. Why?

Because, Holbrooke said, "You haven't gotten me in to see David." Holbrooke had been trying to get in to see Axelrod for some time. Holbrooke figured Axelrod was his best hope for scoring his elusive one-on-one with Obama.

When I asked Lesser about the urinal episode, which I heard about secondhand, he declined to comment except to say, "I prefer to keep my urinal discussions private."

Washington is filled with self-appointed larger-than-lifers. Holbrooke represented its platonic ideal, both in its larger-than-life and self-appointed regards. "The Ego Has Landed," White House aides would tap out to each other on their BlackBerrys when Holbrooke entered meetings.

Convinced he was engaged in historic work at all times, Holbrooke's pestering, hectoring, and sucking up made him a bit of a Washington cartoon. "He would overdo all this flattery when you knew, basically, he didn't mean a word of it," Bill Clinton would say of Holbrooke.

But Holbrooke also attracted a deep following among his many protégés. He was both tolerated and revered within certain quadrants of the Democratic foreign policy establishment. He was an honorary pallbearer for Pamela Harriman, Averell's widow, when the Washington hostess was laid to rest in 1997 at the National Cathedral. He eulogized Les Aspin after the former defense secretary died in 1995, hailing Aspin's "triumphant but unfinished life." He dated Diane Sawyer—his third wife, the former ABC news correspondent Kati Marton, had been married to Peter Jennings—and was tight with a pantheon of big-name journalists (Tom Brokaw and Charlie Rose, among others). They hailed his intellect and big heart. They celebrated his quirky trips of ego. He employed a personal archivist. They spoke of "Richard being Richard," a favorite phrase of Hillary Clinton's to excuse Holbrooke's strenuous personality as worth the trouble, sometimes.

"What an asshole," one friend of Bill Clinton's once quipped to the former president about Holbrooke upon hearing him bloviate through an event at the Asia Society, a global nonprofit he had chaired.

"Yeah," Clinton said. "But he's *our* asshole."

Holbrooke was never Obama's asshole. The president tired of him quickly. In one oft-told story during the 2009 debate over troop levels in Afghanistan, a group of foreign policy advisers was meeting with the president in the Situation Room when Holbrooke melodramatically reminded the commander in chief that he faced a "momentous decision," comparable to what Lyndon Johnson confronted over Vietnam. To which the president coolly responded, "Do people really talk like that?"

Obama's national security team—namely National Security Adviser James Jones and his deputy, Denis McDonough—had little use for Holbrooke either. To many people in the White House, Holbrooke embodied the old guard of the Democratic foreign policy establishment. He was also just the ilk of drama queen the No Drama Obama culture could not brook. Vice President Biden described Holbrooke as "the most egotistical bastard I've ever met," according to Bob Woodward's *Obama's Wars*. Biden then conceded that Holbrooke's fanatical energy level and well of relationships in Afghanistan and Pakistan (known as "AfPak," as Holbrooke insisted on calling it) could make him just the man for the job. But things went south quickly, to a point where Jones suggested to Holbrooke twice in 2009 and early 2010 that he start looking for other jobs. One major sore point involved Holbrooke's participation in a

September 2009 *New Yorker* profile by George Packer that struck many as needlessly All About Dick. Titled "The Last Mission," the profile portrayed Holbrooke as heroically obsessed with avoiding the mistakes of Vietnam in Afghanistan. The president was not happy, and after the piece appeared, McDonough chewed out Holbrooke and insisted that he stay out of the media.

Another source of suspicion from the start was Holbrooke's deep allegiance to Hillary Clinton. Her 2008 presidential campaign, which he supported aggressively, represented Holbrooke's best hope of being named secretary of state, his dream job. When it was clear that Clinton was not going to win, Holbrooke moved to win favor with Clinton's former rival, writing memos for Obama and cultivating his foreign policy advisers. One of Holbrooke's top boosters inside the Obama camp was Samantha Power, who had gotten to know Holbrooke when she was working as a freelance journalist in Bosnia in the 1990s.

Power resigned from the Obama campaign during the 2008 primaries after referring to Hillary in an interview as a "monster," but she was brought back after the primaries and emerged as a key foreign policy adviser at the White House.

Hillary Clinton's surprise appointment as secretary of state was Holbrooke's ticket back into the game. Her first choice was to hire Holbrooke as her deputy, but the White House vetoed it. Then at Clinton's urging, Obama named Holbrooke to be AfPak czar. (Early on, Holbrooke decided to broker a détente between Power and Hillary—the aforementioned monster—as a wedding present to mark her marriage to fellow Obama campaign aide Cass Sunstein. When Power later told the president about this "wedding present," Obama quipped that "some people just get toasters.")

By November 2010, plugged-in observers of the situation assumed that Hillary was the only reason Holbrooke was still in his job. Sure enough, after one of the meetings—in March 2010—in which Jones urged Holbrooke to find other employment, Holbrooke called Clinton in Saudi Arabia to tell her. When she returned, according to an account in *Little America: The War Within the War in Afghanistan* by Rajiv Chandrasekeran, Clinton told Obama that he was free to fire Holbrooke "over the objection of your secretary of state."

Holbrooke's marginalization at the White House was sanctified in classic Washington form: the humiliating Woodward portrayal. Every few years, the Most Famous Reporter in Washington publishes a new tome on the doings of a particular White House that sets off a familiar sport over who came out best, who came out worst, and who Woodward's sources were. And in every book, it seems, one actor fares miserably above all others.

That distinction went indisputably to Holbrooke in Woodward's book *Obama's Wars*, published in September 2010, about the administration's debates over Iraq and Afghanistan. The book portrayed Holbrooke as a floundering figure in a shark tank. Among the indignities catalogued was an episode from January 22, 2009, the day Obama introduced Holbrooke at a ceremony at the State Department.

"Mr. President, I want to ask you a favor," Holbrooke said to Obama beforehand. He asked if the president could please refer to him as "Richard" during the announcement, not "Dick," which Obama had used previously but that Holbrooke's wife, Kati Marton, did not care for. Obama obliged, calling him "Richard." But the request struck Obama as odd. And we know this because Obama told many people about the episode. And Holbrooke was mortified upon learning that Obama had circulated it with such mocking glee.

To some at least, one of Holbrooke's more endearing qualities was that he wore his insecurities plainly. He was blatant in assessing his up-to-the-moment status. He unburdened himself constantly on the question of why the president disliked him, why the White

House was not listening to him, and why his talents were not appreciated. While nearly everyone in Washington is preoccupied with their place in the pecking order, few were as open about how they were "doing" at a given moment. On Saturday, December 4, 2010, my friends Peter Baker and Susan Glasser spotted Holbrooke at a nearby table of a Georgetown restaurant. Holbrooke's wife, Kati, had her arm draped around Holbrooke, who kept looking at his BlackBerry and showing it to his wife. Glasser wondered to Baker whether the rumor had finally proven true and Holbrooke had been fired. While he had not been, he had just been kicked again in the stomach: the day before, the president had made a secret trip to Afghanistan with a small delegation of staff and diplomats that did not include Holbrooke. It was the latest in what had become regular slights. Holbrooke's White House adversaries held AfPak briefings with Obama without telling Holbrooke. They nixed his requests for military aircraft to travel to the region. They tried to exclude him from an Oval Office confab during a visit by Afghan president Hamid Karzai (Secretary of State Clinton intervened and demanded that Holbrooke attend). Glasser, the editor in chief of *Foreign Policy* magazine, had just honored Holbrooke at a fortieth birthday party for the venerable publication that Holbrooke ran in the 1970s. He gave a long speech and stayed late, regaling guests—many of them young Foreign Service types—with stories. Anyone who knew Holbrooke's predicament would have perceived a man enjoying a salve of recognition.

Nearly everyone assumed Holbrooke would be gone from the administration sometime in 2010. But Obama did not initiate anything, largely out of deference to Hillary Clinton. One of Holbrooke's chief nemeses in the White House, National Security Adviser James Jones, resigned in October in part because he was suspected of being a prime source behind the trashing of Holbrooke via Woodward. Holbrooke, meanwhile, was still on the job in early December and determined to survive long enough to negotiate a workable peace in Afghanistan that would be the capstone of his fixated-upon "legacy." If only he could get through to the president before his time was up.

Holbrooke could not get his presidential meeting through the regular White House national security channels (McDonough and Jones's successor, Tom Donilon). The better bet was Axelrod, the president's mustachioed message maven, who was largely responsible for devising Obama's political rise.

The beleaguered diplomat felt he had rapport with Axe. Most people who came in contact with him did. Axelrod aptly described himself as a "kibitzer," not a "policy guy." He was difficult to dislike, although he had also amassed a share of enemies befitting his long and successful career as a Chicago political operative. Even as Hillary Clinton became an indispensable piece of the Obama team, the Clintons and their many loyalists still reserved a special place for Axe on their dead-to-us list for past sins. For starters, the Clintons were always supportive of CURE, David and Susan Axelrod's foundation to benefit epilepsy research and awareness. They appeared at CURE functions and Hillary was wonderful and generous upon meeting the Axelrods' daughter, Lauren. In turn, the Clintons felt betrayed that Axelrod would then campaign so aggressively against Hillary in 2008—his biggest sin coming shortly before the Iowa caucuses, when he seemed to indirectly blame the assassination of former Pakistani prime minister Benazir Bhutto on Clinton's support for the Iraq War.

While he complained often about what he called "the palace intrigue pathology of Washington," Axelrod clearly enjoyed his renown in This Town. He was seen a lot at restaurants and parties, and he was a good friend to political journalists—and had been one himself years ago at the *Chicago Tribune*. He was always gracious to the tourists who wanted to take his picture. Holbrooke himself was in many ways a creature of Washington—quintessential, actually, in his fascination with power, status, and day-to-day reminders of historic work under way. But it was a point of great pride for him that Manhattan is where he made his permanent home. He was never shy in running down "the parasitic culture" of the capital. "Washington is the only town where people feel big by wearing pictures of themselves around their necks," Holbrooke once told Samantha Power, referring to the familiar accoutrement around government buildings. People need these, Holbrooke joked, "to remember who they are." Removing his tags was the first thing he did every Friday when he got back to his Central Park West apartment. "Richard was an outlier in Washington," Marton told me. "He was too engaged in the world, and too big of a personality to be contained by Washington."

Like Holbrooke, Axelrod was being seriously worn down by the parasitic agents of the capital. For much of 2009 and 2010, the Washington genius set had determined that Obama's main deficiency was Axelrod's domain: a "communications problem." Obama had engineered passage of historic legislation, rescued the economy from collapse, and was killing terrorists like mosquitos, yet was apparently doing a lousy job selling his success. Thus, Axelrod—the communications overseer and revered protector of the Obama message—was blamed for having "lost the narrative." He took it hard and worried about his standing with the president.

Axelrod revered Obama, to a degree that he was sometimes teased as a lovestruck groupie. "I've heard him be called a 'Moonie,'" joked Axelrod's friend William Daley, the future Obama chief of staff. Some of the teasing would spill into ridicule and frustration, much of it disgorged behind Axelrod's back (the Obama White House in general could be quite passive-aggressive that way). One big Axe critic was Anita Dunn, a top aide on the 2008 campaign who did a brief stint as the White House communications director in 2009. Dunn derided Axelrod to colleagues for being disorganized, hard to persuade about anything message-related, and reluctant to "push back" on the president in meetings.

Senior adviser Valerie Jarrett, a close ally of Dunn's, and Axelrod's rival for first-among-equals status to Obama in the White House, would subtly undermine Axelrod by referring to him to the president as "one of the political guys." Jarrett, on the other hand, viewed herself—not Axelrod—as a personal custodian of the president's lofty motives and gifts. One high-level White House official dismissed Jarrett's role in the White House as "the voice of purity." Other detractors called her "the Night Stalker," in part for the regularity with which she would join the president and first lady at the residence after work. Just as the president was special, Jarrett believed that she, too, was special in her role. She was "mindful of being more than just an aide," said one high-level White House adviser. In an interview, Jarrett said her "first among equals" status with the president had been overstated and mischaracterized. "I think there is a mystique about our relationship that is not reality," she told me. "I do realize that this has become Washington lore, and I think it's perpetuated by people who may feel uncomfortable with the relationship we have." Still, coworkers believed Jarrett could be jealous and protective of her special status.

After a gunman opened fire at the United States Holocaust Memorial Museum in June of 2009, killing a security guard, the FBI found personal information about Axelrod on the shooter. Axelrod was then granted Secret Service protection. Jarrett was also given protection (being important enough to merit a Secret Service detail has been a source of intra-office envy through many administrations). While a high-profile White House official—especially an African-American woman, such as Jarrett—could legitimately be considered a more likely target than most, several West Wing officials I spoke to were dubious there had been any special threats against her. They suspected, rather, that Jarrett asked the president to authorize a detail out of "earpiece envy." "The person Valerie felt threatened by was Axe," quipped one top aide. Jarrett, who declined to discuss the Secret Service arrangement, has dismissed that notion as ridiculous and offensive. She has maintained that the decision was not hers, and that being accompanied by agents is more of an intrusion than a perk.

Regardless, Obama's allegedly close-knit team of advisers was very much a myth at this point. Dunn, who left the White House in late 2009 to run the strategic communications firm SKDKnickerbocker, was resented by some of her former West Wing colleagues over her willingness to represent clients whose agendas were at odds with that of the White House, which she was still advising and in close touch with (her husband, Bob Bauer, was President Obama's White House counsel). For instance, Dunn was instrumental in helping Michelle Obama set up her "Let's Move!" program to stop obesity in children. Then, as a consultant, she worked with food manufacturers and media firms to block restrictions on commercials for sugary foods targeting children. (In the two years after she left the administration, Dunn cleared every potential client with the White House deputy chief of staff's office for approval, according to a high-level White House source; if anyone objected, Dunn would not take on the account.) Obama's advisers, chief among them Axelrod, also believed that Dunn had fomented a great deal of internal division at the White House during her relatively brief time there. Many top aides also suspected Dunn of leaking anecdotes about internal doings that appeared in books published during the first term. Among those books were *Confidence Men: Wall Street, Washington, and the Education of a President* by former *Wall Street Journal* reporter Ron Suskind and *The Obamas* by *New York Times* reporter Jodi Kantor. Both books included accounts that were publicly disputed by the White House in an orchestrated push-back effort that, according to sources familiar with the operations, Dunn played a major role in.

As viciously political as the above-it-all Obama World could be, it was still considered an affront inside to be seen as "too political" or "an operator." Superior nonchalance, shrugging self-deprecation, and hardheaded wonkishness remained the preferred persona. To behave otherwise, "politically," was to be like a typical Washington hustler, a throwback to the Clinton era: someone like Richard Holbrooke.

Finally, Holbrooke succeeded in getting on Axelrod's calendar for the morning of December 10, 2010. The meeting was brief and to the point. He made his "ask" about seeing the president. Axelrod was noncommittal but not entirely discouraging. Before he departed, Holbrooke mentioned to Axe that it was noteworthy he was still in his job—and that Jim Jones was not.

Friends of Dick were becoming alarmed about his health.

He was pushing seventy, under crushing stress, barely sleeping, and getting fat. He had acquired that disconcerting "Could drop dead at any moment" look that comes over frantically driven and out-of-shape men of a certain age. Washington is filled with these. Bloated and beet-faced. Russert was like this at the end. Ted Kennedy wore the Death Look for much of his last three decades. "It's something you can't do forever," Axelrod said about the big Washington job. "Or it will kill you."

Holbrooke was sweating and out of breath in his morning meeting with Axelrod. He accepted Axelrod's offer of a cup of water, drank it, and then rushed off for a meeting with Secretary Clinton.

Clinton had also voiced particular worry about Holbrooke. She can become very maternal about personal health matters. As first lady, when young Chelsea was sick, Hillary always prepared for her a signature convalescent dish of applesauce and eggs. Numerous staffers over the years have stories about Hillary personally coordinating their medical care during health crises. Late in her husband's second term, she quietly turned over much of her life to caring for her best friend, Diane Blair, who was dying of cancer in Arkansas.

Soon after he left the White House on the morning of December 10, Holbrooke showed up in Secretary Clinton's seventh-floor suite at the State Department's Foggy Bottom offices. He threw his jacket off and sat down, and his face suddenly became pained and purple. His blue eyes went pale. Blood rushed to his head. "Richard, what's wrong?" the secretary asked. Holbrooke's chest heaved and he placed his hands over his eyes.

"I don't know," said Holbrooke. "I've never felt this way before."

Holbrooke walked on his own to the State Department's clinic downstairs. The in-house physician was not there, and the wait for an ambulance was interminable—about ten or fifteen minutes, to the frustration of everyone, especially Holbrooke, who remained conscious but agonized. At one point his legs gave out and he fell to the hallway floor. When the ambulance finally arrived, Holbrooke was taken to nearby George Washington University Hospital, where Secretary Clinton had called her personal physician to expect his arrival.

There, Holbrooke was diagnosed with a torn aorta, often a result of high blood pressure. It would require immediate, elaborate surgery. News of Holbrooke's collapse hit the wires and Twitter. As with every report of a famous person hospitalized, Holbrooke was said to be "in good spirits" (or, if unconscious, "resting comfortably"). Despite intense pain, he remained lucid, chatting with his doctors. One doctor urged him to try to relax, suggesting that he think about the beach or something. "I hate the beach," Holbrooke said, according to his deputy, Dan Feldman, who was with him. Besides, Holbrooke said, he could not relax because he was in charge of Afghanistan and Pakistan. "Ending the war in Afghanistan—that would relax me!" Holbrooke said. After the remark was reported, it became fodder for critics of U.S. policy in Afghanistan, including the Taliban. Either way, Holbrooke would be pleased that his fateful words would be a source of discussion and possibly imbued with historic weight. His archivist could sort it out later.

Holbrooke underwent twenty hours of surgery, an intricate last-resort procedure from which he would not awaken. Reports now characterized his condition as "grave," which is a surefire signal to get the obits ready (no one comes back from "grave"). Hillary Clinton spent hours at the hospital, silently holding Kati's hand. On the night of December 13, President Obama attended a holiday reception at the State Department—an annual event for the chiefs of diplomatic missions to the United States. Obama and Secretary Clinton both spoke and paid tribute to Holbrooke, and they also met privately with Holbrooke's family while Christmas carolers regaled the partygoers. Later that night, Holbrooke died.

The news, while expected, still sent Russert-esque shock through This Town. A hugely present figure was suddenly absent. It resonated through a book party for David Eisenhower (who had written something about his grandfather) at Al Hunt and Judy Woodruff's house, from which Andrea Mitchell would head immediately to cover the breaking news. Politico editor John Harris hailed Holbrooke as "a bucking stallion of ego" who did "not simply want to understand history, he wanted to gallop across its stage."

Packs of bucking-stallion senators, diplomats, journalists, and protégés galloped over to GW for a final homage. Hillary Clinton went into chief comforter mode, herding Holbrooke's staff down the street to the Ritz-Carlton bar for an impromptu "Irish wake." They took over a corner of the bar and shared hours of Richard stories,

Clinton staying until the end. Similar gatherings would break out in the next few days.

The big daddy of all Holbrooke send-offs took place, naturally, at This Town's secular church, the Kennedy Center, where Richard and Kati had just attended the Kennedy Center Honors a week before his death. The grand venue's full and proper name is: The John F. Kennedy Center for the Performing Arts. No mention of God here: the Performing Arts are deity at the red-walled opera house, down the hall from where Tim Russert was mourned and celebrated two and a half years earlier. Here, we would assess performances. The acclaimed American soprano Renée Fleming sang "Ave Maria" (beautifully) in tribute to Holbrooke, whose parents were Jewish but who was never observant himself. Fake palm trees adorned the stage, part of the set of *South Pacific*, Holbrooke's favorite musical, which happened to be in mid-run at the Kennedy Center. Instead of a cross at center stage, there loomed a massive screen flashing a photo montage of Richard.

This was just the Pan-Cake makeup cluster that he would have orchestrated with great care: the guest list, the eulogists, the seating (some reserved, some not), the parking of the Town Cars, and the blueberry scones and salmon at the rooftop reception. "A testament to the know-everything, know-everyone machine of a man who was Richard C. Holbrooke," said the next day's account in the *Washington Post*.

Holbrooke's Kennedy Center finale merited two presidents (Clinton and Obama), the VP, secretaries of state, foreign leaders, ambassadors, and network anchors. They were just the dignitaries Holbrooke would be looking for over your head if he happened to be stuck talking to you. The "D.C. scalp stare," as it is known.

As a military quartet in red-and-blue uniforms played somber tunes in the lobby, Colin Powell was pulled aside at the metal detectors. Extra wanding. Raised his arms, spread his feet, the whole rigmarole. Arriving late was Madeleine Albright, the second Clinton-era secretary of state (succeeding Warren Christopher). She was the one who was given Holbrooke's coveted State job in 1996 after Hillary lobbied her husband for a woman to get the position. Holbrooke held no grudge against Hillary, and fully expected that she would be the Democratic nominee in either 2004 or 2008. In the late nineties, Holbrooke began "honoring" Hillary at annual holiday parties at his and Kati's Manhattan apartment, a tradition that continued through her time in the Senate. Matt Damon and Glenn Close and Robert De Niro would sing carols with the Henry Kissinger types whom Holbrooke liked to be around.

Holbrooke offered lavish toasts to the guest of honor. It went without saying that still-in-government Hillary could be more helpful to Holbrooke than her postpresidential husband. She had a favorite story about Holbrooke's attempts to impress. She once made a passing remark to Holbrooke about her admiration for the Salvation Army—so passing that she did not remember saying it. But Holbrooke did, and at a future holiday party, to his great delight, the Salvation Army band came marching in to serenade her.

These stories were recounted after Richard's death in the endearing vein of someone who lacked a basic embarrassment gene— or shame gene. During night flights for diplomatic missions, Holbrooke would change out of his suit and into bright yellow pajamas—"my sleeping suit"—which he often wore while briefing the press. The stories were told in the spirit of "You can't help but love the guy," even if some people very much could.

Hillary Clinton told friends she felt badly that her loss to Obama in 2008 almost assuredly cost Holbrooke a chance at a bigger job (though appointing him secretary of state was hardly the sure thing some believed). She always had a weakness for Big Personality men—typically older, narcissistic, and often prone to self-destructiveness. Her late father, Hugh Rodham, a my-way-or-the-highway conservative with whom she would often clash in her youth, fit this category. And so did her husband, at least in key ways (narcissistic, prone to self-destructiveness). These were not No Drama men. And it was hardly surprising that Holbrooke was a bad fit with Obama and his staff. His "Richard being Richard" antics could be exhausting, even to Secretary Clinton, who confided in his final months that she was expending way too much time and energy dealing with Richard-related (or Richard-exclusive) matters.

The Obama team had much contempt for what they called the "I Told You So" crowd. These were Democrats—often Clintonites, if not Bill himself—who complained that people like Holbrooke were not being deployed properly. If only this administration was more savvy, they complained, like the Clintons were. In the foreign policy establishment, a chief annoyance to the Obama people was Leslie Gelb, a State Department official in the Carter years who went on to have a distinguished career as a national security correspondent and editor at the *New York Times*. Gelb had a knack for complaining on television or in the press that the Obama team was ignoring all the vast knowledge available to them. Whenever Gelb or one of his fellow I Told You So's went off, I would receive "There they go again" e-mails from someone in the White House like this one: "Remember how I told you that this guy Les Gelb craps on us and has told people that he does so because we don't call him? I would have thought he wouldn't say that on the record, but he basically did in this article. Nice window into the assholeishness of the foreign policy establishment in this city." Included in the e-mail was a clip from *National Journal* in which Gelb was quoted saying, "I don't get the sense that the Obama White House is reaching out. I rarely hear of them calling anybody on the outside." Or certain people on the inside, Gelb was also saying privately. Holbrooke was one of his closest friends.

As Obama's approvals sank in late 2010 and early 2011—and he had just been "shellacked" in the midterms—the I Told You So's were emboldened. Holbrooke's death became a flashpoint. "What in God's name would make you not make full use of Dick Holbrooke?" Gelb said in *Newsweek*.

Kati Marton herself had been a vocal critic of the Obama administration, especially over how she believed her husband had been treated. She viewed so many people in the White House as small-minded, easily threatened, and not mature enough to fully utilize the towering talent in their midst. "Richard knew his place in history was assured," Marton told me. "And when he came up against the likes of [Jim] Jones, he would say to me, 'Kati, this is all going to come out when history is written.'"

Fifteen eulogists performed (fifteen!) at the Kennedy Center, most of them no stranger to motorcades. They included Presidents Clinton and Obama, former UN secretary-general Kofi Annan, Chairman of the Joint Chiefs Mike Mullen, and of course Hillary. Gelb delivered a marquee performance, quite hilarious and without bitterness. Illustrating Holbrooke's competitiveness, he told a story of how Holbrooke would devote hours to mastering Donkey Kong, the old video game. He cursed the machine at one point, Gelb said, "accusing the Donkey Kong company of war crimes." The lineup offered a grand proxy for that particular moment in the Democratic power structure: the Obama administration was beaten down and the I Told You So's were engaging in a funereal end-zone dance on Richard's behalf.

"I loved the guy, because he could *do*," said Bill Clinton, the I Told You So in Chief, as Gelb nodded hard onstage behind him, and so did Hillary. Implicit in this statement was a question: What had the current president "done," peace-wise, in AfPak?

The service went on for nearly two hours. Obama was forced to sit through all of it. He sat to the left of Hillary, fidgeted, and stole "Get me out of here" glances backstage. Obama hated sitting through other people's speeches. Early in his presidency, he complained a great deal about having to hear Biden introduce every dignitary in the room while he waited behind him to speak. The president dispatched Jarrett to relay his displeasure to Biden's office, and from then on, Obama usually spoke first and left.

Even worse about this Holbrooke ordeal was Obama's lack of enthusiasm for the departed. He paid tribute to Holbrooke's career but didn't bother pretending he had any relationship with the guy. "We come together to celebrate an extraordinary life," Obama began, then launched into twelve boilerplate minutes of résumé recital and nods to someone who "made a difference," "spoke truth to power," and so forth.

After he was finished, Obama returned to his seat and was subjected to more verbiage, some of it veiled criticism of him. And some of it barely veiled at all. In this, no one topped the penultimate speaker, Bill Clinton.

"I could never understand the people who didn't appreciate him," Clinton said of Holbrooke. "Most of the people who didn't were not nearly as good at *doing*."

Clinton, like Holbrooke, was a ferociously social animal. Like Holbrooke, Clinton could also be desperately insecure and vulnerable. This had great drawbacks, but it also allowed him to identify with the neediness of others—recognizing, for instance, that late-night phone calls to Newt Gingrich, whose neediness rivaled his own, could go a long way.

Obama is impressively self-contained. That is a strength, but it can also exacerbate the isolation of his job and make him impatient with the fragile egos of the city. Larry Summers, a Treasury secretary under Clinton who later became one of Obama's top economic advisers, would express surprise to colleagues about Obama's tendency to eat lunch by himself in the Oval Office on many days. Marton said Henry Kissinger called to console her a few days after Holbrooke died. In the conversation, he compared Obama to Nixon. Both were loners, Kissinger said. "But the key difference is that Nixon liked to have big personalities around him," he said. "Obama does not."

The slumping president-of-the-moment never seemed more alone than when he sat on the crowded stage of eulogists. While Obama stared straight ahead, Bill Clinton finished by cuing up the final speaker, his wife.

"Hillary and I were asked to end the program, and we are appearing according to Holbrooke protocol," Bill Clinton said. "The one with the real power speaks last."

Though Barack Obama won the 2008 election, Hillary Clinton won Obama's first term.

As she rose to cap off the Holbrooke pageant, Clinton did so as the most popular political figure in Washington. She achieved this status by leaving town. As secretary of state, she could avoid the cesspool that Obama had vowed to purify in 2008. The Clinton campaign's big argument in 2008 was that Hillary knew the game. She knew Washington. How it worked. She was tough enough to play here and savvy enough to prevail. Obama's argument was that he would change the game. Voters opted for the game change. And Hillary, with a bright, tight smile, said, "Fine, I'm out of here," until Obama enticed her back to run the State Department.

Putting Clinton at State looked like a smart, even Machiavellian move, the kind of gritty political play that led skeptics to think maybe Obama did have the gonads to operate in This Town. (That skepticism was articulated by James Carville, who joked that "if Hillary gave up one of her balls and gave it to Obama, he'd have two." He had said this publicly a few times and Hillary asked him to please stop.)

While the president fidgeted and fumed onstage, the secretary of state strode with squared shoulders to the lectern. It had been thirty months since she and Bill had walked into the Kennedy Center for Tim Russert's memorial, laid low by the Obama dynamo. But the Big Dogs don't die. They can be disgraced, impeached, defeated. The Clintons come back, particularly Hillary, who frequently invokes a mantra she attributed to Eleanor Roosevelt: women in politics, she said, "need to develop skin as tough as a rhinoceros hide."

"I joke that I have the scars to show from my experiences," then candidate Clinton told me in an interview a few months before Russert died in 2008. "But you know, our scars are part of us, and they are a reminder of the experiences we've gone through, and our history. I am constantly making sure that the rhinoceros skin still breathes. And that's a challenge that all of us face. But again, not all of us have to live it out in public."

Hillary was, per trademark, the exemplar of that first political virtue: survival. She hung around, waited out the others, and stayed alive. Funerals and memorial services were crowning forums for her magnificent survival play. Like Bill, Hillary gave great eulogy. That's where she performed best, with perfectly maternal command and stoicism.

"I had a front-row seat for Richard being Richard," Hillary Clinton said, calling Holbrooke's sudden departure "a loss personally" and "a loss for our country." She hailed Holbrooke as "a genius at friendship," which was a classic construction of This Town, Clintonian vintage or otherwise. Friendship as craft, demanding "expertise," or "genius." The elite practitioners collected the biggest, shiniest friends and then exhibited them at grand pageants such as this. If Holbrooke was a genius at friendship, the Clintons were grand masters. "Friends of the Clintons'" (FOBs, FOHs) became their own subcommittees of the political class.

She is ever guarded, a fundamentally "private person" despite her global superfame. She has always been easier for people to follow than truly know. Her admirers speak of her in tones of distant awe, suggesting that they are more acolytes than real friends. "Hillary is a person who feels herself very vulnerable, and her response is to make herself bulletproof," said Nancy Pietrafesa, a classmate of Clinton's at Wellesley College and one of her closest friends in young adulthood.

But moments of grief offered her entrée into the rituals of mass comfort at which she and her husband thrived. They have honed public mourning to a raw perfection. Even semi-private mourning: a Democratic press aide I know was with Clinton in 2002 when the news broke that Paul Wellstone, then her Senate colleague, had been killed in a plane crash in his home state of Minnesota. Upon hearing the news, in a holding room in suburban Philadelphia where she was attending a campaign event for Representative Joe Hoeffel, Clinton burst into tears. Her personal assistant, Huma Abedin, asked my friend, the press aide, to leave the room. When she was allowed to return five minutes later, Hillary was again stoic and stone-faced, made no mention of anything being wrong, and gave her speech.

Hillary Clinton told friends she was "devastated" by Richard Holbrooke's death. "He lived enough for ten lives, so while we mourn, we have reason for joy," Clinton said of the man she called wholly unique in the world. She closed the marathon with a solemn "God bless you, my friend," and big applause from the home crowd.

Hillary was asking about possible replacements immediately. She called Kati periodically to check in, but This Town will always move on. That's the coldest part of any Washington ride, no matter how exhilarating. In March, Kati received a postcard in the mail addressed to "Richard C. Holbrooke" from the Democratic National Committee. "Your membership has expired."

Inevitably, people started asking Clinton if she was running for president again in 2016. No way, she said, and after she repeated this a few times, her husband and Terry McAuliffe urged her not to be so definitive. She laughed. In addition to everything else, there's no better point of seduction in politics than being reluctant, or acting it.

As 2011 hit spring, Washington was consumed by the head-slapping stalemate of debt-ceiling negotiations, threats of government shutdowns, and persistently high unemployment numbers. Hillary—off somewhere on the planet being Queen of the World—looked so much better than the small silliness of This Town. She told friends how little she missed the city when she was away. She expressed quiet relief that she did not have to worry about things like rehearsing a speech for the White House Correspondents' Association dinner, because, well, she didn't win the presidency, so she did not have to speak, let alone show up at all (and she did not).

I was sitting in the office of Robert Gibbs in the final days of his tenure as White House press secretary in early 2011. The officers of the White House Correspondents' Association were nervous because the British royal family had just announced that the wedding of Prince William would occur on April 29, the same weekend of the Correspondents' Association dinner. If the president traveled across the pond for the royal wedding, would he miss "the Prom"? Gibbs had to assure the president of the Correspondents' Association that the "other" president (Obama) would not be attending the royal wedding. And This Town exhaled.

As it turned out, the president's involvement was nearly messed up anyway by the U.S. raid on Bin Laden's compound in Pakistan. A few days before the mission, on April 28, the tiny group of high-level national security principals who knew about the operation was discussing the timing of it in the White House Situation Room. While the raid ultimately happened on Sunday night, Saturday night was first raised as a possibility. But someone pointed out that Obama was scheduled to be at the Correspondents' Association dinner that night and his absence (and that of other top administration officials) could tip off the journalist-filled room that something was up.

At which point, Hillary Clinton looked up and said simply, "Fuck the White House Correspondents' dinner."

Anarchy in the Quiet Car

B in Laden was killed on Sunday, which was good because it made the world safer and, more important, did not interfere with the Correspondents' Association dinner. The Big Get of the weekend was Sarah Palin, the former Alaska governor who showed up at Katharine Graham's old, uninhabited mansion for Tammy Haddad's brunch. *You go, Tamster!*

Palin, still considered an even bet at that point to run for president in 2012, was accompanied by her husband, Todd, her daughter Bristol, her Fox News pal Greta Van Susteren, and Van Susteren's lawyer husband, John Coale. Palin did her red-carpet duty and then descended into the mosh pit of "lamestream media" who, at the sight of her, became kids chasing the Good Humor truck.

Palin was a spectacle—exotic, even (from Alaska!)—and the crowds around her were three and four deep. Reporters snapped cell phone pictures and told her about their kids. In full revelation, I also chatted with Palin, though she came to me—or more like wound up next to where I was standing. Tammy snapped a picture and put it on some website somewhere. Jessica Yellin of CNN was standing between us in the photo. We (Jessica and I) both looked a tiny bit too enamored in the shot for our own good, but whatever. Palin could not have been nicer. We had met once before, for about five seconds on her campaign plane in 2008. At the brunch, I told her I had been in Alaska a few months earlier. And she opened her mouth wide in a look of genuine surprise, as if no one had ever gone to Alaska before. "Why didn't you look me up?" she said, again sounding sincere. I made a joke about not wanting to get shot. She made me promise to look her up in Wasilla next time. (How does one "look up" Sarah Palin in Alaska, anyway? Is she listed? Can we become texting buddies?)

A few weeks later, Palin was back in rogue mode, setting off on a bus tour of the Northeast that many thought to be a precursor to her getting into the 2012 race. She made a point of not releasing a public schedule to the press, which forced them to follow her bus on a wild-goose chase, from Virginia to New Hampshire (just missing a tornado in Western Massachusetts). Everyone bitched, Palin did not care, and all was back to normal.

"I don't think I owe anything to the mainstream media," Palin said in an interview aboard her bus—with Van Susteren. Coale, Van Susteren's husband, marveled at the media's nerve. "They have trashed her every which way," he said. "And they still expect to be kowtowed to?"

Well, yes!

But it was nice of Palin to show up and play nice on Prom Weekend. And it was a big win for the Tamster, who also "got" Rupert Murdoch to come to her megabrunch, among others. She—Tammy—was off on a great run. She seemed to be everywhere, even by her everywhere standards. At a time when Washington was getting nothing done and attracting massive scorn, Tammy was the prime mover behind the one thing This Town seemed to be doing right: celebrating itself.

A few months before, Tammy had cohosted a book party for first-time novelist Graham Moore, the twenty-nine-year-old son of Michelle Obama's chief of staff, Susan Sher. At one point, Tammy rushed over to me and the guy I was talking to and announced "ELIZABETH EDWARDS IS DYING! ELIZABETH ED-WARDS IS DYING! I JUST GOT OFF THE PHONE WITH HER DAUGHTER!

"Now c'mon, come meet the novelist," Tammy said, shifting midstream and pulling me away to meet Susan Sher's son. A woman intercepted Tammy and told her, "We're going to your party on Wednesday night."

"Oh, I'm just everywhere!" Tammy replied.

The Wednesday night party was put on by CURE, the Axelrod family's epilepsy research group, which was honoring Tammy as its Woman of the Year. The tribute included a video montage featuring several members of the news media (David Gregory, Joe, and Mika) all testifying to Tammy's power, stamina, and fabulousness.

That Saturday, Tammy did another bash, this one at the elegant Jefferson hotel to honor Gordon Brown, the former British prime minister. He had written an "important new book," *Beyond the Crash: Overcoming the First Crisis of Globalization*. Lots of dire talk in there about global poverty and income disparities, the kind of things you think of when you're eating salmon and caviar canapés under the chandeliers of the Jefferson.

The grand hotel, which opened in 1923, could not have sparkled brighter for the occasion. Festivities were webcast on Tammy's WHC Insider website. The actual in-person experience was a bit crowded and hot. I tried to slip out, but Terry McAuliffe insisted I join him in a private dining room to pay respects to Tammy's pal

Connie Milstein, the real estate maven who owned the hotel and who obviously set off the sensor in the Macker's brain stem that activates whenever he's within thirty feet of a rich campaign donor type. As I stood in the private room, waiting for Andrea Mitchell and Chairman Greenspan to finish talking to Milstein, Tammy bounded in with Gordon Brown himself. She introduced me to the former prime minister, who looked exhausted. "He's writing a book about how Washington works and trying to get me to participate," Tammy explained. "And I think he's crazy."

"I don't," Gordon Brown said, looking at me. "Just follow Tammy around. You could do worse."

Tammy blushed.

The evening's highlight came earlier, when Tammy gave her welcoming remarks praising Prime Minister Brown's book. She made several references to this being a "special night" and an "incredible night" and an "amazing night" even though "we are going through difficult times and tough times here in Washington and around the world." At which point, I surveyed the chandeliers, the high cream-colored ceilings, and McAuliffe standing a few feet away, raising a flute of champagne.

In July 2011, the Amtrak train I was riding broke down between New York and D.C., somewhere in godforsaken Delaware. All power was lost. We were without AC. It was hot. The bathrooms stank. People were cranky. The situation presented a philosophical/ethical dilemma. Do the rules of the Quiet Car apply aboard a grounded train? Some thought no, and spoke freely on their cell phones; others thought yes, glared at the alleged offenders, and in some cases yelled. A few yelled back. A third constituency urged peace. People kept talking on their phones. More stares, more yelling, back and forth. A passenger asked another if there was any news. "Shut up!" shouted a third passenger, a Quiet Car militant. "No, you shut up!" shot back a counterinsurgent. Another attempted a straight answer while another tried to be a comedian, saying they halted Amtrak service to pay down the deficit, and they should have sold off Delaware while they were at it. No one laughed.

It was anarchy in the Quiet Car. And also an apt reflection of the collaborative spirit back in Washington. The debate over the raising of the federal debt ceiling had been raging between the White House and Congress. It was one week from the August 2 deadline when the United States government would default on its credit obligations. Everyone was arguing, nothing was moving—like our train.

Eventually Congress and the White House struck a deal and, whaddaya know, the train started moving, too, and I got back to Washington in time to attend a going-away party for Joe Lockhart, Bill Clinton's White House press secretary during the darkest days of Monica. After leaving the White House, Lockhart joined with two top Gore aides—Mike Feldman and Carter Eskew—to start the Glover Park Group, a Democratic media firm that grew into a bipartisan "integrated services" colossus of lobbying and strategic communications that was bringing in $60 million in annual revenue. Lockhart was now heading to a new job as head of corporate communications at Facebook in Menlo Park.

The Glover Park Group's shiny downtown offices were crawling with regulars for the send-off. The gathering occurred in the midst of the News Corp. phone hacking scandal that was then roiling Great Britain and much of the media. It was a prevailing topic of seemingly every conversation at the party as we munched finger foods and sipped the cocktails courtesy of the Glover Park Group, which, by the way, was also a major lobbying and communications provider to News Corp.

Not far from the outdoor patio, I struck up a conversation with

Geoff Morrell, a former White House correspondent for ABC News who went on to be the chief spokesman for Defense Secretary Robert Gates under President Bush and then Obama. After four years in government, Morrell—one of Mike Allen's closest friends—was days away from leaving the Pentagon and would soon have several big job offers to consider. Morrell didn't say what companies he was talking to, but did mention he had retained Bob Barnett to help him navigate the process. No surprise there, and no sooner did Morrell tell me this than Barnett himself walked over to join the conversation. Barnett told me how "premium" a client Morrell was.

I later learned Morrell had been offered a leadership role at Hill & Knowlton Strategies, U.S., the public relations colossus run by Dan Bartlett, the former top White House aide to George W. Bush whom Morrell knew from when he covered the White House, as well as one from Tony Podesta, the Democratic mega-lobbyist whose firm, the Podesta Group, was having another stellar year despite the lagging economy.

On Labor Day, as the national unemployment rate stood at 9.1 percent, Morrell did his part to lower it, and Mike Allen broke the news in Playbook. Geoff had joined BP as its head of U.S. communications. "BP America, facing a spate of investigations and lawsuits stemming from the catastrophic Gulf oil spill, has chosen former Pentagon press secretary Geoff Morrell as its head of U.S. communications," Allen wrote in his lead item. This signaled "an aggressive new effort to recover from past communications debacles and improve its image in an essential market.

"Morrell, who starts Tuesday, will remain in Washington, with frequent travel to BP headquarters in Houston and London. . . . Morrell, forty-two, has worked both sides of the podium: He covered the White House for ABC News, then was Pentagon press secretary throughout the tenure of Defense Secretary Robert Gates, spanning two presidencies and consumed by two wars."

The Playbook item went on for 645 words and filled nearly 30 percent of that morning's edition. "You got more than Obama got for killing Bin Laden," Tony Podesta marveled to Geoff in a congratulatory e-mail. This is what is known in the political-corporate PR space as "a successful rollout."

When someone is leaving a government job to "pursue opportunities in the private sector," the successful rollout is critical. It is important that a big announcement accompany news of the new position—both as a means of reminding everyone how important you were while in government and to ensure that everyone knows where to find you now that you are out "monetizing government employment."

Morrell's big news illustrated the big tangle of interests that make up the D.C. self-perpetuation machine today: Old Media (ABC News), Republican administrations, Democratic administrations, corporate (BP), and New Media (Playbook) converging at the gold-plated revolving door, facilitated by Barnett.

Morrell was recruited into the BP fold in part by his friend Dick Keil, a former White House reporter for Bloomberg who had gone to work for Purple Strategies, the bipartisan media consultancy founded by Republican pundit Alex Castellanos (CNN) and Democratic talking head Steve McMahon (MSNBC). Keil, who had gotten to know Morrell on the White House beat back when Morrell worked for ABC, is a congenial and earnest operator whom I first met years ago when he was still a reporter. Like most people in Washington, Keil is always working. I once ran into him at the market and teased him about the work Purple had been doing to help BP "reposition" its image after its little problem on the Gulf Coast. Without missing a beat, Keil unleashed his own gusher—of flackery—calling BP the "the greatest corporate turnaround story in history," or some such, before moving on to the deli counter. Sure enough, BP was recovering quite well for itself, in part from the generosity of the United States

Defense Department. Bloomberg News would later report that BP's Pentagon contracts more than doubled in the two years after it caused the biggest spill in U.S. history (exploding to $2.51 billion, from $1.04 billion in fiscal 2010).

Morrell's hiring was part of an audacious trend of Obama big-wigs latching like newborns onto the teats of the administration's biggest nemeses. If BP wasn't the single biggest corporate villain of the first term, it certainly cracked the top three.

Other candidates? Perhaps no company had taken more blame (or revulsion) over the economic mess that the Obama administration inherited in 2009 than Goldman Sachs. They were at the center of the subprime mortgage crisis that started the whole thing. They took bushels of emergency loans from the government and subsequently paid out similarly huge bushels in executive bonuses. So it might look slightly odd, or even unseemly, to have a top Obama Treasury official helping Goldman to de-smudge their corporate image. But a few months later, the Treasury Department counselor, Jake Siewert, announced he was leaving the Obama administration; soon after, he would become the head of global communications for Goldman Sachs. Siewert, who served as White House press secretary at the end of Bill Clinton's second term, had de-camped to Alcoa for nine years before joining Obama. He was well-known and liked within operative and media circles, and his next trip through the revolving door had been speculated upon within The Club.

Mike Allen suggested in Playbook that Siewert could be the next head of the Center for American Progress, a progressive think tank that had been run by John Podesta, the former chief of staff in the Clinton White House and co-chair of the Obama transition team (and Tony Podesta's brother). Instead, Siewert landed at Gold-man. "We're lapsing into self-parody," one senior White House official told me on the subject of high-profile officials leaving the

Obama administration and then jumping to the corporate giants the White House had done battle with.

To complete the unholy triplet of Siewert going to Goldman and Morrell going to BP, Peter Orszag—the former director of the White House's Office of Management and Budget (OMB)—had previously gone to Citigroup, another prime avatar of the financial crisis, beneficiary of a government bailout, and bestower of numerous bonuses.

In his unique way, Orszag had represented a one-nerd case study in run-amok Obama-mania during his time at the White House. For starters—and this is weird—he became an unlikely sex symbol from the moment the then president-elect announced his appointment in November 2008. Never mind that speculation raged instantly over whether Casanova with a Calculator was wearing the World's Worst Toupee. Groupies announced themselves on a fan blog site, Orszagasm.com, devoted to the allegedly hunky brainiac who was "putting the OMG back in the OMB."

Rahm Emanuel declared to the *New York Times* that Orszag has "made nerdy sexy." Gossip columns reported on Orszag's dating life, while some Obama aides became worried that his profile might be getting a tad inflated and that he was getting a little big for his BlackBerry holsters (yes, plural).

And then things got complicated for Orszag. And not in the way that sustainable growth rates are complicated. Rather, in the way that it's complicated when a divorced father of two with a very important job gets very publicly engaged to a thirty-one-year-old financial correspondent for ABC News, Bianna Golodryga, just weeks after his ex-girlfriend gave birth to his daughter. Orszag had met Golodryga at the White House Correspondents' Association dinner, the same event at which President Obama had joked that the TLC network would be starting a new reality show called *Jon & Kate Plus Peter Orszag.*

But the real headlines were much worse. "White House Budget Director Ditched Pregnant Girlfriend for ABC News Gal," screamed the *New York Post* headline. Suddenly the "Orszag love-child story" became a full-term tabloid "distraction." *Inside Edition* started calling the Office of Management and Budget. MSNBC dubbed the story the "Budget Baby Mama Drama." Orszag asked for privacy, to which friends of the ex-girlfriend/baby mama noted that he wasn't exactly asking for privacy a few weeks earlier when Golodryga was showing off her engagement rock on *Good Morning America*.

As with any story of this nature in Washington, the Very Serious People who traffic in it are obliged to emphasize that such silliness is beneath them. Ken Baer, the OMB spokesman, told me that nearly every press inquiry he received on the matter was prefaced with the requisite faux sheepishness. "Everyone feels the need to say 'I'm really sorry I have to ask you about this' and 'I'm only carrying out orders from my boss,'" Baer said. And, of course, the Very Serious Media were not writing the Orszag love-child story per se; they were "stepping back," merely writing about the *phenomenon of the media frenzy* surrounding it.

As fun as the Budget Baby Mama Drama was to watch, Orszag himself appeared to be having little of it in the White House. Nor did many of his colleagues love dealing with him. Orszag managed to alienate a number of top White House and cabinet officials with his petty and turf-conscious tendencies. In 2009, I wrote a profile for the *Times* about Ray LaHood, the former Republican congressman who went on to become President Obama's secretary of transportation. In the story, LaHood problematically acknowledged that he did not think the White House "picked me because they thought I'd be that great a transportation person." In fact, he said, he was no expert on transportation issues and would have been just as happy to be named secretary of agriculture.

This was exactly the kind of refreshing candor that reporters loved about Ray LaHood. It was not always refreshing to the White House.

LaHood went on to speculate that he got the job only because he had good relations with Republicans on the Hill and because he was tight with Rahm Emanuel, his former House colleague. To illustrate how his friendship with Emanuel was useful, LaHood told me about a $36 million light-rail train project he had been set to announce in Arizona, only to have Orszag say there might not be federal money available for it. LaHood then called Rahm, who quickly took care of the problem. When Orszag read this, he became enraged that La-Hood would go around him and then talk about it in the press.

Orszag refused to accept LaHood's multiple apology calls. Emanuel tried to convene a peacemaking summit in his office, which did not work. LaHood eventually sent Orszag a case of wine, which he accepted grudgingly.

Regardless, all's well that ended well. Now comfortably tucked in at Citigroup, Orszag could afford all the wine he could ever drink, with plenty left over to support his families. He and Bianna would make a new baby of their own, Jake. Politico's chief economic correspondent, Ben White, tweeted: "Let the record reflect that @biannagolodryga and @porszag have one of the cutest babies I've ever seen."

Orszag remained a popular figure among reporters, to the surprise of no one, given his penchant for talking to them. (Reporters are suckers for the slightest of courtesies.) Personally, I think I've spoken only once to Orszag, although he recently friended me on Facebook. By the end of his tenure at the White House, Orszag was known around the building as the prime source of many of the leaks that kept dripping out of the place. One of the young wiseasses on the communications staff referred to him as "the leaky toupee with glasses."

If Obama had one major peeve, it was leakage. This hardly made him unique among presidents, but it seemed a particular sore point with him. Obama, who took immense pride in the rarity of leaks on his 2008 campaign, was incredulous over how so many people in D.C. needed to authenticate their importance by sharing privileged information with reporters. It drove him nuts that some of these people worked in his White House.

In the late summer of 2011, the White House was shifting into reelection mode after a brutal few weeks in which congressional Republicans were abusing them in negotiations over the debt ceiling. A parallel "narrative" was taking hold—both in the media and among certain Obama insiders—that the administration was not deftly coordinating strategy with its fledgling reelection operation in Chicago. To better synchronize their strategies, the president initiated a semi-regular Saturday meeting in the Roosevelt Room that included about fifteen top aides from the White House, the Vice President's office, the reelection campaign, and a network of outside consultants. At the first meeting, Obama voiced concern that the group was a bit large, but added that he trusted everyone and expected that everything discussed in these sessions would remain private. People who attended the meetings described them as dynamic and productive, a good forum for the president to hear views from people he did not speak to every day.

In about the fifth or sixth meeting, according to several people present, the president wrote down on a yellow legal pad a list of issues he believed that he had not been vocal enough about in his first term and hoped he could tackle if reelected. They included climate change, immigration, same-sex marriage, and the closing of the U.S. prison at Guantanamo Bay Naval Base, among others. A few days later, *Game Change* coauthors Mark Halperin and John Heilemann learned of the president's remarks and mentioned it to Obama's campaign manager, Jim Messina, who immediately told the president. Obama was furious—to a point that people who knew about the leak were dreading what he would say at the next Saturday meeting.

Obama addressed it immediately, in a tone more of disappointment than anger. "I trusted you guys," he said slowly. He told everyone that he believed the meetings had been helpful, and that he hoped they could continue in some form. But if they did, Obama said, they would not include him, and he walked out.

After Obama's departure, Biden told the group they had let the president down. The room fell silent. Eventually the remaining aides broke into an animated discussion about who would do such a thing and why the White House cooperates with books to begin with. Some lamented how impossible it had been to replicate the cohesive environment of their pre–White House endeavor in Chicago. Particularly vocal—and furious—was Robert Gibbs, Obama's longtime spokesman and adviser, who left the White House in early 2011 and was now doing consulting and surrogate work for the reelection campaign. Gibbs, known for his combative style and often fiery defenses of his boss, launched into a profane diatribe about how the 2008 campaign never had any problem with leaks at all. That ended as soon as they won and the shop moved to Washington. Now leaks had become a regular occurrence, to a point where they were met with an almost shrugging resignation. But this was a particularly bitter pill since Obama had ostensibly told everyone at the beginning of these gatherings how much he trusted them. "Someone in here decided that they were bigger than the president," Gibbs fumed. "Who the fuck would think that?"

When I later brought up the meeting with Gibbs, he confirmed my account and recalled the episode as an important marker for a group that had fought battles together over several years and was now confronting its own fractures as they approached their final campaign. This is of course a familiar evolution within successful political enterprises. Over time the idealism and focused drive of getting someone elected and surviving in the White House becomes diluted by the more selfish concerns of Washington nest-feathering:

winning chits with the press, raising one's own profile, and proving sufficiently important to maximize a post-government payoff. But the evolution seemed particularly jarring in this case. One high-level official on the reelection campaign said it felt like, at a certain point, people were thinking mostly about who would play them in the 2012 version of *Game Change*.

"Real life sort of became a political movie for a lot of us," he said. As if, suddenly, people started talking amongst themselves in sound bites, imagining their discussions as dramatic renderings or photo ops. In a broader sense, 2008 had the feel of an organic network of true-belief. The dos and don'ts were well understood, the rights and wrongs did not require spelling out. The "no ego, no glory" document that everyone on the Obama transition staff was asked to sign seemed unnecessary at the time, late 2008. Eventually that message was lost, or was at least weakened as the Obama change brigades became sucked up into the tentacles of Suck-up City.

Insomuch as this evolution had a cinematic crescendo, Obama's walk-out from the Roosevelt Room was it, followed by Biden's scolding and the reckoning session afterward. "It was the kind of discussion where we wondered, 'What happened to all of us?'" Gibbs told me. Even before he left the White House, Gibbs had asked that question many times, in various forums. He spoke often of being dispirited by all the small accommodations the Obama White House had been forced to make to the status quo that they had run against in 2008: the various exceptions to the no-lobbying rules; what he considered to be the excessive embrace of the Washington media echo-chamber; self-service winning out over public service, or at least loyalty to the president.

"I remember saying in that meeting, 'Somehow we have all changed.'" Gibbs said. "Or maybe Washington just changed us."

The Presidential Campaign:
This Movie Again

*In this election, the biggest risk we can take is to try
the same old politics with the same old players and
expect a different result.*

BARACK OBAMA,
Democratic National Convention, 2008

O f all the quaint maxims of Obama '08, the notion that the
"same old players" would be sidelined in his fresh-scrubbed
Washington was particularly rich. So was that pledge from
the candidate that lobbyists "will not run my White House." That
little keepsake from '08 popped up a lot whenever an exception
made its way through the revolving door.

One of the most decorated lobbyists in town, Steve Ricchetti,
became the latest exception when he joined Biden's office as a senior
adviser in early 2012. Ricchetti's lobbying clients had included Fan-
nie Mae, Eli Lilly, and the American Hospital Association, among
others. Loopholes, loopholes. It seemed Ricchetti had deregistered

as a lobbyist after Obama was elected, so it was all good, even though Ricchetti remained president of a lobbying firm.

"Ricchetti has been through the revolving door more often than a bellhop at the Mayflower Hotel," the *Washington Post*'s Dana Milbank wrote after Ricchetti was hired. Ricchetti supported Hillary in 2008, and Team Obama's aides attacked her campaign at the time for using him as a "bundler" of campaign contributions (while righteously adhering to their self-imposed lobbying ban). Ricchetti's appointment "shows just how flimsy Obama's ethical reforms have been—and how absurd the official standards are for who is a 'lobbyist' in the influence industry," Milbank wrote.

"We knew we were going to get hit for this," one top Obama adviser in the White House told me a week after the Ricchetti announcement. "But Biden really wanted him and fought for him. And we didn't think it would get much traction outside of the fake umbrage crowd anyway." Maybe, too, the reelection campaign hiring Broderick Johnson—a former lobbyist for AT&T, BellSouth, and Microsoft, among other companies—would get them spanked. For a day or two, tops. This had become the essential Team Obama MO whenever the cynical realities of Washington collided with its shiny ideals from 2008. Acknowledge the exception, wait out the indignant blog posts and press releases, and move on. That lobbying ban was so four years ago anyway.

Obama's recently promoted domestic policy adviser, Cecilia Muñoz, had also been a lobbyist: for the National Council of La Raza, a Hispanic advocacy group. To get her in, the president signed a waiver exempting Muñoz from his promise to "close the revolving door that lets lobbyists come into government freely."

Over four years, Obama World had accumulated an impressive collection of Never Minds. It began with the then senator's commitment in 2008 to not opt out of the public financing system for presidential campaigns. This would have limited the amount of money his campaign could spend. When it became clear that he could raise money at will—unlike John McCain, who remained in the system—Obama's commitment vaporized.

In February 2012, Obama ditched his long opposition to directing his campaign donors to "super PACs," which, the president had said, were a "threat to our democracy." But then he did a roundabout when Obama-friendly super PACs were getting outgunned by the other team. Bloomberg News reported that Obama's reelection campaign manager, Jim Messina, had met privately with a bunch of Democratic Wall Street titans and assured them the campaign would not demonize them (as Obama had spent the better part of the previous three years doing). While he was at it, Messina also begged them for cash to fund the campaign.

Obama's super PAC reversal brought a few days of predictable indignation from the right over his hypocrisy and hand-wringing from the left over his impurity. Overall, it was another notch in the argument that "change" was more a marketing slogan to Obama than a genuine ideal. The prevailing reaction from The Club was to step back and shrug off the outrage from their grizzled "It is what it is" perch. "Every modern president in the fourth year of his presidency resorts to the cheap political stunts, broken promises and truth-fudging it takes to win reelection . . . ," explained Jim Vande-Hei in Politico. "So much for the high road: Victory is more important than purity."

After everyone got over their shock and outrage, This Town celebrated the flip-flop. It was not only foreseen but great for business. Democratic media consultants and ad people and other barnacles would reap tens of millions in fresh business from the presidentially blessed super PACs. Republicans would continue the arms race, "which in turn means more money for their strategists, pollsters and ad-makers; and the media make more money as all of this is funneled into TV and Web ads," VandeHei wrote. "Incestuous, isn't it?"

Finally, the voting started. Thank goodness. Republicans had been playing front-runner roulette for too many months: first Michele Bachmann, then Herman Cain, then Newt. How many front-runners had to die?

Now it was time to get serious, for all of us in This Town to reacquaint with friends at the Des Moines Marriott or up at the Radisson in Manchester (the Granite State's Paris). And, of course, in "spin rooms," where everybody knows your name—or, if not, there's someone holding a sign over your head telling people your name, if you're important enough.

Hey, it's Bay Buchanan!

You never know who you'll run into in the spin room. Actually, Bay Buchanan is precisely the specimen you run into in the spin room. Like copies of *U.S. News* at the dentist's. Bay Buchanan belongs in spin rooms.

Spin rooms are hideous. They are where campaign aides and candidate surrogates gather after candidate debates to ritually humor a crush of media types. Their currency includes the lobotomizing talking points about how Candidate X "really hit it out of the park tonight" or how Candidate Y "was the only one on that stage who looked presidential"—candid insights. The rooms endure, for some reason, as routine appendages to the eight thousand or so debates that are inflicted during every presidential campaign.

Buchanan, who is not hideous, lives in that "political People on TV" nether ooze in which you lose track of whether she is a pundit or an operative or a surrogate or some hybrid squid (in the same way that you lose track of a lawyer for the SEC who takes a position at a

D.C. lobbying firm, or a Citigroup executive who takes a job at the SEC and is suddenly investigating his former and perhaps future colleagues). For all I can tell, Buchanan might have even entered the world in a spin room, after being conceived in the back of a satellite truck and gestated in a green room, to be hatched from a quivering egg incubated under warm TV lights into the welcoming obstetric hands of Wolf Blitzer.

It never changes. Presidents do, and elections come and go, and new technologies like Twitter come along and revolutionize. Paradigms shift, mistakes are made. It all moves along. And then here we all are again, making our way back to the spin room, with Bay B.

This particular spin room is about the size of a tennis court. It is housed in a convention center in North Charleston, South Carolina. January 19, 2012. The Republican primary race was sorta kinda threatening to get interesting again after default front-runner Mitt Romney—after winning big in the New Hampshire primary—suffered through a rough few days here in the political septic system of the Palmetto State. Newt Gingrich was getting a lot of attention. Key conservatives kept endorsing Newt and Rick Santorum, and Romney was being reduced to a well-coiffed mound of Jell-O every time someone asked him why he wasn't releasing his tax returns.

So Bay B was here to defend Mittens. She has been a well-worn part of the cable schmear for years: a Republican "activist" and, probably her biggest claim to fame, sister of Pat Buchanan. She ran brother Pat's three losing presidential campaigns and has achieved the mantle of "prominent conservative" over the years. Naturally she was a guest cohost of CNN's *Crossfire* for a time—like seemingly half the people in the room.

"Well, here we all are again," Buchanan said to me when I saw her in the spin room. Her greeting was a perfectly crystalline cliché to distill the unrelenting sameness of this exercise: lots of the same "people who are still kicking around." She had endorsed Romney a few days before the New Hampshire primary, which moved the Romney campaign to actually put out a press release touting her support. This was no doubt why Mittens won big in the Granite State—the Bay Buchanan Bounce! Okay, that's sarcasm; I do not mean to pick on Buchanan, who seems nice. Plus, you don't screw with Bay B, especially not in her house, the spin room.

She conveyed a workmanlike sincerity when she said that "Mitt Romney had an outstanding debate tonight, he truly did." The consensus, however, was that Romney did not have an outstanding debate tonight, he truly did not. His poll numbers cratered accordingly in South Carolina, where he was eventually crushed by Gingrich.

"There was cheering in our war room tonight," Buchanan told me. "It was a decisive victory!"

As with many things in politics, spin rooms mimic the social hierarchy of a junior high cafeteria. The big-ticket spinners attract the crowds and the smaller tickets attract fewer reporters—or, worse, members of the foreign press.

With all due deference, Buchanan is a puny ticket. She has much to say about why Romney "hit it out of the park tonight." But few are listening. And she was looking slightly lonely in the corner, especially compared with cool kids like Tim Pawlenty, the former Minnesota governor (spinning for Romney) and Santorum (spinning for self). Both Pawlenty and Santorum had multiple furry boom mikes in their faces at any given time, the ultimate spin-room status symbols.

If Buchanan had furry-boom-mike envy, she hid it. But as we spoke, she achieved a kind of spin-room rock bottom, suffering an indignity that triggered in me an emotion I never expected to feel on this great earth: genuine empathy for the likes of Bay Buchanan. Just as Bay started to get rolling—sharing with me how excited the Romney team was backstage during the debate—she was interrupted by a television reporter. From Iceland.

"Do you have a minute for Iceland?" the reporter asked her, at which point Buchanan drew a deep sigh and herniated a sense of physical deflation—literally closing her eyes, as if to contemplate the full degradation she was suffering in the middle of the cafeteria, with me bearing witness.

"This is what I've been reduced to," Buchanan said before rallying herself to the pursuit of Romney voters in Reykjavík. "Iceland."

Like Buchanan, spin rooms media-peaked in the nineties and are still here. They are evergreen habitats for the political class—like green rooms and war rooms and holding rooms. Spin-room dwellers typically hate the spaces, or at least make a show of it. They have from the beginning. "The spin thing is humiliating and degrading and the media insisted on it," the late GOP knife fighter Lee Atwater told the veteran political reporter Roger Simon for his book *Road Show: In America Anyone Can Become President. It's One of the Risks We Take.* "And when you did it the media ridiculed you for it," Atwater continued. "I was on the first spin patrol at the Reagan–Mondale debate [in 1984] and I'd be very happy to call it all off."

Sweaty, crowded, and depressing, spin rooms have become completely outmoded at a time when most real-time campaign propaganda has moved online. Many of the machinations that used to occur in spin rooms are now transacted—via e-mail, or blog posts, or Twitter—within seconds of the candidates speaking on stage.

The North Charleston spin room was located just off the media "filing center," where a few hundred journalists had just finished watching a beaut of a debate on cinema-size screens. We, the reporters, were arrayed along long tables like students taking standardized tests. It was all a familiar regimen but (like at a standardized test) not without its competitive tensions. *Did I miss something? Keep your eyes on your own laptops!*

The debate punctuated the most eventful day of the Republican campaign so far. Lots of stuff was happening within a few hours: Marianne Gingrich, Newt's second wife, had claimed in an interview with ABC News that her ex had asked her for an open marriage, a term that immediately started "trending" on Twitter, whatever that means. (Not since the seventies had open marriage trended like that.) Rick Perry, the governor of Texas, had quit the race and endorsed Gingrich; and Santorum learned he had won Iowa by a handful of votes, two and a half weeks after the state's caucuses were held and Romney was declared the winner by a handful.

Then came the debate donnybrook in which CNN's John King led off with an open-marriage pleasantry to Gingrich. Game on. Newty put on his best angry-teddy-bear face and smacked back at King with perfectly calibrated umbrage. He called the question "close to despicable," one of the many instances during the campaign in which the former speaker went bashing on the political media, a cohort that heaped endless free attention on him and with whom he privately enjoyed many friendships. Gingrich had favored us with his illustrious companionship in a Myrtle Beach spin room a few days earlier, where he and wife number three, Callista, were surrounded by about two hundred of their despicable media friends. And Newt frankly could not have looked more at home.

Gingrich also declared in the North Charleston debate, "I think grandiose thoughts," while Santorum contended that the former speaker's thoughts were "not cogent" and Mitt Romney awesomely used the pejorative term "Romneycare" without irony to refer to his health-care plan.

The whole North Charleston spectacle was an object lesson in how digital play-by-play has replaced the postgame rush of the spin-room ecosystem. In the course of the ninety-minute debate, I learned on Twitter that the Gingrich campaign was releasing the former speaker's tax returns at almost the very instant Romney was sputtering forth onstage about why he had not.

Meantime, the Romney campaign started in on a "grandiose Newt" offensive, ridiculing Gingrich with a flurry of Twitter messages (#grandiosenewt) citing examples of same. As the debate progressed, the Romney campaign issued a killer press release titled "I Think Grandiose Thoughts" with bullet-point examples of Newt declaring things like "I think I am a transformational figure" and "I am essentially a revolutionary."

For good measure, Romney spokesman Eric Fehrnstrom tweeted, "Is it me, or does Newt look like Pericles without the golden breast plate?"

And the *New Yorker*'s Ryan Lizza wondered (also via Twitter), "Why did Santorum start talking like Tow Mater from *Cars*?"

It would be hard to top that in a spin room. But the charge was on nonetheless within minutes of the debate's end. Reporters kept showing up by the swarm. "Like bees to honey," observed Ben Ginsberg, a longtime Republican lawyer, election-rules guru, and familiar Club member. He is here touting Romney, and, to be honest, his original metaphor featured flies instead of bees, and something less palatable than honey.

But this was not an entirely joyless and dutiful rush into the diseased kidneys. On some levels the operation was imbued with a familiar energy, the kind that attends practiced calisthenics (if inexplicable ones), like those first-day-of-holiday-shopping-blitz scenes that for some reason continue to receive gee-whiz coverage on TV news, as spin rooms do.

Probably the best way to answer the question "Why spin rooms?" is with the question "Why turkey on Thanksgiving?" It's tradition. The family convenes, and the crazy uncle gets a little crazier every year, and the offensive cousin gets drunk (again)—and there's Joe Klein (whom Newt name checked in a debate), and former congressman J. C. Watts, and former senator Bob Smith, and Frank Luntz, and other People on TV. *Hey, that guy on CNN—or is he on Fox News now? Is he still alive? And what did Howard Fineman do to his hair, anyway? It's gone from blackish to silvery.*

Really, Fineman's hair had become a BIG topic of discussion in our political-media fantasia since he stopped dyeing it in 2008. Stephen Colbert joked to him that watching the graying process on TV week by week was like "watching an army slowly march across an open field." For a time there was a whole website devoted to Howard's luminescent locks. He even attended a dinner where he met President Obama, who immediately addressed the matter. "The gray's looking good," the president said. Nothing about politics, journalism, or any of Howard's many talents. It was all so objectifying!

Regardless, Howard had new life at the Huffington Post, a youthful bounce in his step—if not his hair—that he'd lost at *Newsweek*. "Arianna," Fineman declared to me of his new boss, "is the Katharine Graham of online journalism." I knew this already, because Howard mentions it every time I run into him, which I inevitably do at a place like this.

As with many spin rooms, the one in North Charleston evokes the familiar circus time warp: people who've been around the business forever, who never go away and can't be killed. Newty is the paradigmatic example. But there were so many other familiar ghosts in this particular machine.

Oh my God, John Sununu. He served as governor of New Hampshire and chief of staff to President George H. W. Bush before hitting the pinnacle of his career, if not the pinnacle of all human achievement. This occurred in late 1991, when Sununu was named conservative cohost of *Crossfire* after the previous conservative cohost, Pat Buchanan, quit to run for president. Sununu came under fire while in the White House for, among other things, his prodigious use of military jets and government cars. He made the trip to South Carolina to spin for Mitt (maybe even flew commercial, who knows?) but he is not here to spin for the institution of the spin room itself. "I have no idea why we're here," Sununu says, too candidly for a spin room.

Wait, that *is* former Senator Bob Smith, the Republican from New Hampshire. He actually ran for president himself in 1999, you might recall (or might not). Same comb-over as you remember. He is working for Newt and eager to explain to me why spin rooms can indeed be worth one's time, even now.

"There's always the chance," Smith says, "that some poor bastard like me will put his foot in his mouth."

Next to Smith is Bob Livingston, the former Republican congressman from Louisiana who was in line to succeed Speaker Gingrich in 1998 until his ascent was thwarted by marital infidelity issues. He's here to vouch for Newt on the day the open-marriage story broke.

The irony of this seems lost on most of the bloggers, tweeters, and video embeds who are clustered around Livingston. By the looks of most of them, they were in junior high school during Livingston's late-nineties unpleasantness.

Like many pols whose public careers end badly, Livingston went on to become a rich lobbyist—another reason he is a curious choice to stand by Newt tonight. "I came here because I believe in the guy," Livingston says, and he is promptly asked by a reporter whether Gingrich's "affair issues" are going to dog him for the rest of the campaign. Livingston replies curiously.

"Bill Clinton is one of the most charismatic officials in American society today," Livingston says. "He's still very productive. He's got a lot of problems of that nature that if you guys wanted to talk about, you could talk about."

Bill Clinton? The question was about Gingrich. Here was another time-warp instant: back to when the Republican spin machine was essentially turning every question into a discussion of the forty-second president's "problems of that nature." Long live the nineties and the Clintons and the Livingstons. This was an audacious bit of spin, even for a spin room.

And especially rich given the popularity that Clinton enjoyed through that ordeal, and still does. Livingston was offering a sermon to familiarity, survival, and refusing to go away—ever so apt for a place like this.

Back in D.C., one of the major society events that winter was the bar mitzvah of Aaron Brooks, son of the *New York Times* op-ed columnist David Brooks, at the Adas Israel synagogue in Cleveland Park. The temple was packed with media *macher*s from across various spectrums (spiritual, ideological, dietary). Aaron was poised and precocious and described his travels on the campaign trail with Dad. Power kvelling ensued from gathered friends. That boy could be the Jewish Luke Russert!

Later, during the evening reception, celebrants were dancing the hora, the Jewish version of the traditional circle dance, which, in one sense, is a sanctified expression of what happens in Washington media every day. Amid the festivity, Andrew Ferguson, a conservative columnist for the *Weekly Standard*, approached Jeffrey Goldberg, the columnist for the Bloomberg View who writes *Goldblog* for the *Atlantic*. Ferguson, somewhat abashed—perhaps because of the setting, perhaps because he is naturally abashed—wanted to give Goldberg a "heads-up" that he would be attacking him in an upcoming column. It seems that Goldberg had, in his own column, recently called out Newt Gingrich for racial dog whistling—using coded language to appeal to white racists—in the Republican primary campaign. Ferguson, like many conservatives, believed that nonconservatives were simply hallucinating when they heard such dog whistles.

As "Hava Nagila" blared over the speakers, Goldberg processed the "heads-up," pausing to note to Ferguson that *PBS NewsHour* host Jim Lehrer was, to the collective surprise of just about every Jew in the synagogue, just then dancing counterclockwise in front of them. At which point Goldberg felt compelled to share with Ferguson his disbelief over his taste and timing. "I can't believe you're telling me this during the hora!" Goldberg said.

Goldberg, I should note, is a friend, a mensch, and something of a mayoral figure among Washington-area tribesmen. If in fifty years, for some reason, Jews decide to build their own airport in Bethesda, it will be named for Jeffrey Goldberg.

Fidel Castro apparently considers himself a friend of Jeff's as well. He had an intermediary call Jeff out of the blue a few months earlier to arrange an interview with Castro. And Jeff would soon score a forty-five-minute sit-down in the Oval Office with President Obama on the deadly serious subject of Iran's nuclear ambitions and Israel. After the interview, on the way out, Jeff reached into his bag for a gift for the commander in chief.

"I know this is cheesy . . . ," Goldberg said sheepishly. "What," the president interrupted, "you have a book?" Apparently a lot of journalists who interview the president give him copies of their books. And, yes, Jeff had a book. But not just any book. He handed Obama a copy of *New American Haggadah*, a revised version of the Passover service that included commentary by Goldberg (and was edited by Jonathan Safran Foer, the novelist and brother of the *New Republic*'s editor, Franklin Foer). Obama thumbed through the Haggadah, which Jeff wanted him to consider using for the White House seder.

"Does this mean we can't use the Maxwell House Haggadah

anymore?" asked the president, showing scary familiarity with a quirky Jewish tradition: the coffee company has famously printed Haggadahs for decades. As for a disproportionate number of residents of Boca Raton, Florida, and Shaker Heights, Ohio, Maxwell House has been the Haggadah of choice for Obama, who initiated the first-ever White House seder when he came into office in 2009. The president accepted Jeff's offering with a smile. But in the runup to the 2012 election, and eager to convince mainstream Jewish voters of his traditional pro-Semitic values, Obama opted to remain loyal to Maxwell House.

The first months of 2012 brought sleepy bustle to the nation's self-satisfied capital. Winter took another year off. Snow was as sparse on the ground as legislation was on the Hill. TV inquisitor Mike Wallace died at ninety-three, a not unsurprising but still momentous development that allowed everyone to trot out their "Such-and-such is happening in heaven" clichés, though Wallace was Jewish and did not believe in heaven. (NBC's Ann Curry spoke for all of us—yes, she did—when she imagined that "tough questions are being asked in Heaven today.")

In memoriam, members of The Club engaged in a Me Party of grief showmanship via Twitter. They shared stories about how Wallace touched *them*. "Mike Wallace once cursed me out over an unflattering story," Howie Kurtz tweeted. "I introduced Mike Wallace at an event a few years ago by saying he was so sharp it takes him ½ an hour 2 watch *60 Minutes*," former White House press secretary Ari Fleischer added. Kevin Madden, a Romney media aide, revealed in his own tweet that "I was fortunate enough to work w/ Mike Wallace & his team on a 60 Minutes profile of Gov. Romney during the '08 race." If he could read that, Mike Wallace would hate the "work with" construction that flacks like to use, implying collaboration. Wallace might even be spinning in his grave if he wasn't too busy in his afterlife asking tough questions.

As typically happens in election years, the real action was popping outside of town. The once orderly GOP had fractured into a schizophrenic mess in which its voters seemed to alternate between terrifying realizations: that they were on the verge of nominating Thurston Howell III (Romney) and should therefore consider alternatives, except that the alternatives (Santorum, Gingrich) were both destined to lose between thirty-five and forty states if placed before general-election voters. In the resulting picture, momentum kept flipping back and forth. The Club was puzzled by such a befuddling narrative. Whenever Romney would win a big primary (New Hampshire, Florida, Michigan) and seemed set to break into the clear, he would go on to lose big to Gingrich (in South Carolina) or Santorum (in Colorado, Alabama, and Mississippi).

Mittens could not go two days without reinforcing the notion that he lived in a rarefied quarter-billionaire's terrarium. His attempts to demonstrate a common touch proved inevitably butterfingered. He told a crowd in Michigan that his wife, Ann, drove "a couple of Cadillacs." He noted elsewhere that he knew the owners of NASCAR and NFL teams, and had previously challenged Rick Perry to a $10,000 wager during one of the Republican debates. This Town, especially those in the press, were aghast. What awful mistakes! Everyone marveled—between courses at The Palm—at how out of touch Mittens was. He just kept stutter-stepping along, unable to "close the sale" and act according to the wise men's conceit of his inevitability.

Alexander Burns, writing in Politico, said the campaign overall "has been more like a game of Marco Polo, as a hapless gang of Republican candidates and a damaged, frantic incumbent try to connect with a historically fickle and frustrated electorate."

Ah, the frustrated electorate—also known as the stupid voters.

Don't get us started. The primaries had moved into the heart of what much of the "permanents" of Washington think of as Deliverance Country: Mississippi and Alabama. Majorities of Republicans in these Deep South touchstones were too happy to play to regional type, telling pollsters that (among other things) they believed President Obama was a Muslim. Romney wound up losing badly to Santorum in both states, with many voters saying they would never support a Mormon candidate anyway, no matter how many times he (Romney) patronized them by dropping "y'alls" into his speeches or boasting that he ate cheesy grits and loved to watch college football "matches."

In terms of being a pure zeitgeist benchmark, Burns's story in Politico was one of the election cycle's seminal. It showed how voters often contradict themselves—and reality—when they express their views. They were angry at Obama for the rising price of gas even though there was really nothing he could do about it (experts of both parties agreed, Burns pointed out). They said they hated bailouts but also supported—after the fact—the government's propping up of the auto industry. Burns posited that voters believed in a "litany of contradictory, irrational or simply silly opinions." They were fickle.

"And 'fickle,'" he wrote, "is a nice way of describing the voters of 2012, who appear to be wandering, confused and Forrest Gump–like, through the experience of a presidential campaign. It isn't just unclear which party's vision they'd rather embrace; it's entirely questionable whether the great mass of voters has even the most basic grasp of the details—or for that matter, the most elementary factual components—of the national political debate."

Yes, "fickle" is being kind. The first quote in the story was from a Democratic pollster, Tom Jensen, who neatly distilled Burns's premise: "The first lesson you learn as a pollster is that people are stupid," he said.

Burns, a twenty-something graduate of Harvard, drew righteous flack for his story. Erik Wemple, the media critic of the *Washington Post*, said parts of it belonged in "the Beltway Snobbery Hall of Fame" and suggested it should have been titled "Why aren't voters as brilliant as Politico staffers?"

"An incredibly long and unbearably daft piece," is how Jason Linkins, a media writer for the Huffington Post, characterized it in a column headlined "Are Voters Really Stupid, or Are They Just Routinely Subjected to Terrible Political Reporting?" Linkins summed up the conceit of Burns's "turgid pile of condescension" this way: the electorate is "made up of a big shambling pack of helpless dumbasses, who would obviously be utterly adrift in their hopeless lives without Politico being around to occasionally mansplain things to them."

This is, admittedly, seizing on a fat vulnerability of the Politico story. It was nakedly condescending, elitist, self-consciously disdainful. The big centerpiece photo was of Forrest Gump himself sitting on a bench. That is precisely what I loved about the story. It offered one of the most revealing expressions of the dim view that so many residents of This Town have of the American voter. It is a belief held equally by Washington politicians, lobbyists, and certainly journalists. Inasmuch as Politico is a reflection of that local sensibility, it was a story that struck a perfect pitch for This Town.

The "stupid" story also seemed to strike an apt reflection of the White House's own view of the American electorate. It was an attitude that many suspected began with the president and first lady. "Barack will never allow you to go back to your lives as usual—uninvolved, uninformed," Michelle Obama said in a 2008 campaign speech that drew little notice at the time, but could work as an off-message proxy for the "Are voters stupid?" story.

Early in 2012, This Town was getting all lubed up about *The Obamas*, a new book by *Times* writer Jodi Kantor. Several scenes portrayed Team Obama as exasperated by the inability of the post-

2008 voter to fully appreciate the president's efforts. Kantor wrote about the first couple's trip to Norway in 2009 in which the president accepted his Nobel Peace Prize: "The trip spurred a thought the Obamas and their friends would voice to each other again and again as the president's popularity continued to decline: the American public just did not appreciate their exceptional leader." She quoted the president's best friend Marty Nesbitt, saying that Obama "could get 70 or 80 percent of the vote anywhere but the U.S."

Politicians, operatives, and journalists are no different from a lot of professionals in that they speak among themselves with repugnance for their customers. Goldman Sachs employees refer to ordinary investors as "muppets," we learned in a March 2012 op-ed in the *New York Times* by an outgoing Goldman executive. Flight attendants deride infrequent leisure flyers as "Clampetts," in reference to the *Beverly Hillbillies* family. Rail attendants dismiss excited train hobbyists as "foamers" (foaming at the mouth as they board their choo-choos). Barney Frank once said—to the late David Broder—something to the effect of "Everyone hates Congress, everyone hates the media, everyone hates Washington. But let me tell you something, the voters are no picnic either." The Massachusetts Democrat demonstrated just this a few summers earlier when he told a woman at a town meeting that "trying to have a conversation with you would be like trying to have an argument with a dining room table." Political consultants often refer to rich self-funded candidates as "checkbooks." Lobbyist Jack Abramoff referred (in e-mails) to a bilked Native American client as "the stupidest idiots in the land for sure."

Burns's piece served as a perfect thought bubble for so many of the Politico-reading actors whose livelihoods and industries relied on the dumbass clientele of American voters (and taxpayers, and media end users and customers). The story worked as a serviceable "talker"—a story that provoked discussion, or "buzz." But its real genius was that it was written at all. That Politico went there. That they dared go public with one of the great taboos of Fancy Washington life: voters are not bright. The basis of our democracy is Forrest Gump.

As soon as I saw the Burns story, I guessed immediately how it came about. A bunch of Politico types were shooting the breeze about something or other, and the topic turned to the dumbass electorate. This could have been happening in any newsroom in Washington or beyond. And typically, after a few minutes, this mingling of thought gas would dissipate and that would be that. But this being Politico, someone went ahead and actually commissioned a story that "asked the question" about whether voters are in fact stupid (one of the great self-soothes in journalism: we're not actually saying or endorsing an inflammatory sentiment, merely "asking the question"). Stupid voters have been around forever, but now Politico was here to explore the phenomenon explicitly.

Sure enough, a few days later, Politico's founding editor, John Harris, went on a new enterprise called "Politico TV" and revealed that that is exactly how the "stupid" story came about. "A lot of people's stories generate from people's rants," Harris explained. "Alex Burns wrote up one of my rants." Burns made some phone calls to prove—or "explore"—his boss's premise that voters were stupid. Lo and behold, the premise came back rock solid.

Alex "actually found a number of good voices from pollsters who say, 'Yeah, that's the first thing you learn as a pollster, that voters are stupid,'" Harris said. The pollsters did not mean that literally, Harris cautioned. Rather, they meant only that voters who respond to polls "are just expressing their opinion in a context of ignorance."

This was a deliciously transparent moment, courtesy of a rising media power unburdened by the traditional dictate that media arrogance must take place privately. This was an example of Politico's turning its obsession with Washington "process" on its own fascinating-to-us ecosystem. They put it on television.

Politico was on a nice roll through the 2012 campaign. They reported in late 2011 that then front-runner Herman Cain had some bad history with women (harassment charges, extramarital forays, etc.) that dated to his days as head of the National Restaurant Association. Their top campaign and White House reporters—Glenn Thrush, Maggie Haberman, and Jonathan Martin—were consistently turning out solid, authoritative, and often groundbreaking stories.

Some of the pieces were consistent with the smarty-pants parlor gaming for which Politico had become known. A prototype of this ilk occurred in March 2012 courtesy of Thrush, who wrote a classic about Biden possibly running for president in 2016.

From almost the day in August 2008 that Obama rescued Biden from the Senate by making him his running mate, the "Biden 2016" story has been kicking around town, thanks almost entirely to Biden and surrogates who are often begging reporters (deep background, of course) not to rule Biden out for the Big Seat down the road. Beyond the pro forma mention of how Biden "hasn't ruled out another run for president," no one took the prospect that seriously. He had run twice before (in 1988 and 2008) with disastrous results, would be seventy-four years old on Inauguration Day 2017, and was generally considered a lovable rodeo clown of the Obama administration, not a lot of people's idea of an heir apparent.

But Biden and his loyalists wanted to keep Joe "in play" to stave off the natural atrophy that sets in around a principal who is assumed to be drained of aspiration and possibility. And Politico cued up the notion perfectly with Thrush's "Joe Biden in 2016? Not So Crazy" story, which played big on the website and elicited the requisite snickers from the West Wing directed at Politico for running the story (insular, shortsighted, trivial, typical Politico, they said) and at the Biden jock sniffers who had quite obviously pushed it.

Biden himself was thrilled with the story, kept pointing it out to his friends, and even blew some sweet verbal perfume Politico's way from a podium in Coconut Creek, Florida, where he was talking to a bunch of seniors. "Go online to an outfit called Politico.com," Biden instructed the geezers, referring them to a story by Jake Sherman about the House Republican budget. "Extremely well-respected publication that all the major papers look to." Forget that the Obama circle supposedly hated Politico, at least when they weren't leaking self-serving items to its reporters. It was not the first or last time Biden would go off the reservation. "I guess he liked that Biden 2016 story," one senior White House official e-mailed me.

In the first months of 2012, President Obama and Veep Biden were spending more of their time on the road campaigning. Unemployment numbers were trending down, with Obama's approvals up. But then up shot gas prices, and down sank his approvals, and so it went.

Obama's reelect was exceedingly removed from the messianic enterprise of 2008. Hope and change were gathering dust like garaged yard signs. Obama kept using the phrase "grinding it out," while Biden trotted out a quote from Kevin White, the longtime mayor of Boston who had died a few weeks earlier: "Don't compare me to the Almighty," White had said, "compare me to the alternative."

By March it was clear the alternative would be Romney, perhaps the loosest, most everyday-guy-like presidential candidate from Massachusetts since John Kerry, if not Michael Dukakis. A particularly rich moment occurred in early February when Donald Trump endorsed Romney at his namesake hotel in Las Vegas. Not since Don King's last solo press conference had so much fabulous hair adorned a single Vegas venue. "There are some things that you can't imagine happening in your life," Romney said in a nod to the absurdity of the moment. "And this is one of them." By far the best part of the announcement—and maybe my favorite moment in this whole campaign—was watching Ann Romney standing off to the side, seemingly just one synapse away from an epic giggle fit.

Mrs. Romney stood with a slight smile, hands folded at her waist, while her face kept getting redder and her lips kept pursing tighter. Mittens whispered something to her at one point, some Mormon variant of "Can you fucking believe this?" I'd guess, and Ann jerked her neck slightly forward as if the spigots were about to open. She seemed to catch herself just in time. She then flashed a look of total terror, perhaps over how close she had come to losing it. She was fine the rest of the way—a winning character test for the prospective first lady.

Santorum quit the race in April. As losing candidates often do, he used his "concession" speech to claim victory. "We were winning," he said. "But we were winning in a very different way." In modern politics, "winning in a very different way" means increased speaking fees, greater demand for consulting services, and talk of a book and TV deal and return trip to Des Moines in 2016—all of which swirled around Santorum after his "victory."

After the media concluded its breathless narration of the "topsy-turvy GOP race," everyone acknowledged Romney had it in the bag all along. As it turned out, his nomination was as inevitable as the news (in January) that Haley Barbour would be coming home to K Street after serving out his second term as governor of Mississippi.

Romney was the son of the late Michigan governor George Romney, himself a onetime presidential candidate. George's White House hopes were dashed when he claimed to have been "brainwashed" into supporting the Vietnam War. (This made him the butt of one of the all-time great putdowns, courtesy of Senator Eugene McCarthy: With George, the senator said, "a light rinse would have been sufficient.")

The Obama team was banking heavily on their guy, the Great Man, coming off as much more accessible than the exotic Mittens. The president's image docs prescribed heavy doses of Obama-Just-Folks treatments. They do this every year or so, placing the various principals—POTUS, VPOTUS, and FLOTUS—in media settings where they can brandish their barstool bona fides. We were reminded, as we had been every March of his presidency, that the president knows tons about college basketball (and has devoted hours of ESPN interviews over four years to prove this). In this year's edition, he ate barbecue for the cameras and sang blues with B. B. King and showed off his literacy of contemporary sitcoms by mentioning that Malia likes *Parks and Recreation*. Regular Joe Biden, lover of muscle cars, was sent off to Rust Belt union halls to tell stories about his blue-collar dad, while Michelle went on the *Late Show with David Letterman* to remind everyone that she went shopping at Target the year before.

While pols are always straining for the proverbial "candidate you'd rather have a beer with" mantle—and such contests will never favor a milk-sipping Mormon like Romney—the president was laying it on as thick as the Guinness he drank at a barstool photo op on St. Patrick's Day in D.C.

"Yeah, it's all so natural and organic," sniffed Mike Murphy, a Republican media adviser on the topic of Obama's being such a photo-op everyman. "The President is making a big move, switching from Evian water to Dasani."

The subtext to this of-the-people competition is that both candidates are loath to be seen as Washington sorts. That Obama, who never loses a chance to say how much he hates it here, is so above the self-dealing and petty silliness and opportunism that never goes on in salt-of-the-earth places like Chicago (site of his campaign headquarters, a stone's throw from Michigan Avenue). That Romney, who had spent his primary campaign touting his nonconnections to

Washington, can present himself as a gust of fumigating air from the private sector. New approaches, new faces, all that.

And then, as soon as Romney had the nomination sewn up, he found himself surrounded by the same perennials who encrust party nominees every four years.

The campaign had entered its season of the "informal adviser." They regenerate in the local scenery like those repeating clumps of trees in the background of *The Flintstones*. It's always the same people, in the same movie, playing the same roles for this year's crop of self-fashioned "outsiders." Election Day as Groundhog Day.

Romney was swimming in "informal advisers." Start with the same old likes of Charlie Black, a prototypical "informal adviser" and familiar D.C. hybrid of campaign lifer, cable stalwart, and superlobbyist. Black, sixty-four, was among those counseling Romney. We know this because he was quoted and identified in lots of stories as an "informal adviser" to Mitt Romney. Black recycles every four years and makes himself available for old-pro advice, back-channel information, and whatever else the front-running campaign might need. That is what informal advisers do.

What they must not do is any harm, and this can be tricky, since they often embody the capital's permanent lobbying and money class that voters detest. And some of their past ties can be unsavory. Black's lobbying clients, for instance, have included strongmen like Ferdinand Marcos of the Philippines and Mobutu Sese Seko of Zaire.

It's a nice arrangement, though, the "informal adviser" gig. It helps both candidate and Usual Suspect. Being publicly linked to Romney can impress Black's clients—an important currency in This Town (informal advisers are almost never paid real currency by the campaigns, and usually don't need the money anyway). In return, they can vouch for the candidate within the embattled but still potent Republican establishment in Washington, providing a link to donors, endorsers, and various useful eggheads.

"I have the best job I've had in any election," Black told me of his latest role. He is an affable North Carolinian and veteran of nine presidential campaigns, dating back to Gerald Ford's in 1976. "I have no responsibilities. I am not accountable for anything."

Nice work if you can get it. And many, apparently, can.

They come out in spring, the informal advisers do, when the weather warms and the primary contests are winding down. The political calendar becomes safer for the likes of the congressman-turned-lobbyist Vin Weber, the senator-turned-high-priced-consultant Jim Talent, the former governor and White House aide John Sununu, and all-purpose insiders like Black, Wayne Berman, and (of course) Bay Buchanan—all of whom were advising the Romney campaign.

"I'm a big believer that campaigns are like a symphony orchestra," said Ron Kaufman, a former Republican lobbyist and operative who was a regular presence at Romney's side (and could be seen in many a hotel bar well after Mitt and Ann donned their pj's). "You have to add certain types of music at the right time. If you add it at the wrong time, it can destroy the whole piece. This is the right time."

Kaufman is in an elevated club of "unpaid advisers" in that he has known Romney for years and travels frequently with him, just as he did when Romney ran in 2008. He is thus a step up from being an "informal adviser," though that's the title that the campaign seems to prefer.

When Romney hit John McCain in 2008 for his ties to lobbyists—including the ubiquitous Black—Glen Johnson, then of the Associated Press, confronted Mittens about his own traveling buddy, Kaufman. Romney explained that he was just an informal adviser. "My campaign is not based on Washington lobbyists,"

Romney said then. "I haven't been in Washington. I don't have lobbyists at my elbows that are arguing for one industry or another industry."

Kaufman has since deregistered as a lobbyist. Black also gave the illusion of going straight in 2008, announcing his "retirement" from lobbying after he joined the McCain campaign. But here's an upset: Black's "retirement" ended shortly after the McCain campaign did.

Today, Black is chairman of Prime Policy Group, a bipartisan lobbying firm; clients include Walmart, Google, and financial firms. "After Obama won, I kiddingly told my Democratic partners, 'Great, now I don't have to go lobby the administration for four years,'" Black told me. "I can play more golf."

Overall, This Town spent a great deal of time in Campaign 2012 longing for its star-packed predecessor. The 2008 campaign loomed like an older sibling over the 2012 cast of motley inevitables (Romney), retreads (Gingrich, Santorum), and the Great Delustered (Obama).

As such, perhaps the marquee event of the late winter came in early March with the much-awaited opening of *Game Change*, the HBO adaptation of the bestseller about the 2008 "campaign of a lifetime." Written by veteran political reporters Mark Halperin and John Heilemann, the book came out in early 2010 to pretty good reviews, big sales, and buzzy bombshells. It packed lots of fresh meat (Elizabeth Edwards lifting her shirt to taunt her cuckolding and battered husband!) and was the picture of mass-market success in a category—political books—that almost never produces smashes outside of Woodward. It also favored Washington with a red-carpet night at the Newseum, and what could be better than that?

The stars paraded. The rug was not red but in fact blue, which was appropriate, since the filmmakers had contributed heavily to Democratic causes. Critics used this as a data point to prove leftist Hollywood bias in a film that focused on the train-wreck campaign of McCain and his Frankenstein running mate, Sarah Palin.

Co-producer Tom Hanks showed up at the Newseum opening, as did director Jay Roach, actor Julianne Moore (who played Palin), and the evening's Brangelina, authors Halperin and Heilemann. The much taller and oval-headed Heilemann resembled Bert from *Sesame Street* next to his shorter collaborator, Halperin (Ernie). Joe Scarborough and Mika Brzezinski stood together and posed for photos. Ben Bradlee looked spry and game at ninety, while White House officials, senators, congressmen, lobbyists, and journalists nibbled from a buffet of marinated hanger steak with Maui onions. Everyone congratulated Heilemann and Halperin and hugged Tammy, who of course helped put this all together—part of her work for HBO.

It was a fun film, filled with billboard lines that resonated on many levels. "I am not going to ignore the people of Alaska anymore," said an indignant Palin, just a few months before she bolted the governor's office.

"You don't get to go back in time to do do-overs in life," campaign chief Steve Schmidt said at one point, referring to the need to make bold decisions. No do-overs indeed, but you can still shape events retroactively and get paid more and enhance your brand in the long run.

Looking nervous, Schmidt greeted old friends in the lobby. He is the bullet-headed Republican operative who ran the McCain campaign and is credited/blamed for convincing the trailing nominee-to-be to pick Palin. Schmidt was played by Woody Harrelson. Reliving the Palin nightmare on the screen was surreal, Schmidt said, although he had presumably gotten used to reliving the Palin nightmare while serving as a source for the book, adviser to the film, and dogged after-the-fact critic of the rogue running mate.

True to the entrenched Washington precedent of cooperative sources getting more favorable treatment, Schmidt came off in the film as a tortured hero. He was portrayed as torn between his loyalty to McCain (played nobly by Ed Harris), his revulsion for Palin, his desire to win, and—not reflected in the film but obvious in real life—his instinct for self-preservation. His *Game Change* parlay honored the finest Washington tradition of strategic ass-covering.

Around the time of the *Game Change* premiere, Politico's Maggie Haberman reported that Schmidt's business partner, Brian Jones, had written a memo ten days before the 2008 election about how best to shield Schmidt from blame for the campaign's inevitable loss. "A well organized and coordinated effort is needed to defend Steve's good reputation," Jones wrote in the memo to two other associates, Adam Mendelsohn and Kirill Goncharenko. (Schmidt says he did not know about the memo.)

Before signing on with the McCain campaign, Schmidt worked in a variety of media strategist roles in the Bush reelection campaign of 2004 and in the White House. He took on special assignments like shepherding Supreme Court nominees through their confirmation processes. He served for a time as a special counselor to Vice President Dick Cheney. He enjoyed a reputation as a decisive and hard-charging operative, and stuck it out with McCain even when many had left his campaign for dead in 2007. He had effectively taken over the day-to-day management of the campaign by the summer of 2008.

But fair or not, Schmidt will always be known as the guy who advocated for Palin, and then revealed countless details about the whole ordeal to the authors of *Game Change*, among others. He besmirched Palin (and by extension McCain) in the most humiliating of ways.

It did not matter that both Palin and McCain maintained that the book and movie were fiction. Everyone loves a crack-up. And that's what Schmidt was selling, the Palin crack-up. That's what the filmmakers focused on: Palin (no room for the Hillary crack-up, or the Edwards crack-up, or the history-making winner, what's-his-name). It was a riveting crack-up. And for that, readers and viewers owe a debt to Steve Schmidt.

To hear Schmidt speak, promoting *Game Change* on television and reflecting on the campaign, it seems his conscience really nagged at him. He did seem sincere in his pain, and was so, his friends attest. He was also speaking out, in part, as a lucrative catharsis. He spoke of how terrified he was at the prospect of Palin's being just one seventy-two-year-old heartbeat away from the Oval Office. Schmidt was retroactively scared for his country. But not so terrified that he blew any whistles before 130 million people voted—60 million for McCain and Palin. America is a glorious land, to be sure, but self-preservation is sacred ground in This Town. Would Schmidt ever have lunch in This Town again? After being linked to this debacle? After making it impossible for John McCain to do the one thing he truly craved after 2008: to move on with his life?

Are you kidding?

Schmidt would have the run of the buffet table at the Newseum. Starstruck moviegoers kept rushing up to him with congratulations. Schmidt was a star there, as he was at the *Game Change* opening in New York the night before. He started showing up often on TV, got a pundit gig on MSNBC. He started going on *Meet the Press*. He scored a cameo (playing himself) in an indie campaign film called *Knife Fight* about a maverick political strategist. He purchased a lovely new place on Lake Tahoe, which the cable network outfitted with an in-home TV studio so he could pontificate without walking out his front door. He did paid speeches. His whole contrition rap, the ostentatious guilt, had natural appeal.

"I've been involved in a lot of victories and a lot of defeats," Schmidt told Adam Nagourney in a *Times* Sunday Styles cover story about how tortured Schmidt still was over the McCain campaign— and how much of a celebrity he had become after *Game Change*. "And the ending of that particular campaign felt like being in a car crash."

Few genres are more media marketable than the car crash. It explains, in large part, the left's ongoing fascination with Palin. In his public agony, Schmidt deftly cut himself into the Palin buffet line. Left-leaning operators from the Hollywood and Washington–New York media fell deeply for him. It was another instance of the media swooning over Republicans with self-flagellating tendencies, especially when they defy conservative orthodoxy and move left (McCain being the object lesson in this with his maverick campaign of 2000, when he was the "refreshingly candid" McCain, as opposed to when he later moved right in 2008 and became the "bitter" McCain).

Schmidt was making a seven-figure income when McCain lured him to join his presidential campaign in 2007—and was doing even better after the car crash. He was now the vice chairman of public affairs at one of the world's biggest public relations outfits, Edelman. He became an early Republican proponent of same-sex marriage (the media LOVES Republican same-sex marriage boosters). He was recognized at airports, ate lunch in the White House mess with top Obama adviser David Plouffe, and was photographed with the president himself. He was celebrity fodder at the White House Correspondents' Association dinner and assorted after-parties a few weeks later. His "date" for the evening was the real Woody Harrelson, his new BFF.

You couldn't script a better comeback story for the tortured public figure. Nor could you have provided a better test case in the political tradition of spinning glory from a fiasco, an art form whose Picasso was, of course, Sarah Palin.

Many people around This Town snickered at *Game Change*. Claimed it was too gossipy. And no one here cares about gossip, no way. They are way too high-minded for that. Some critics scoffed. They said the book focused too much on the titillating tensions while ignoring the substantive policy debate. How dare they?!

Quite a few people felt aggrieved. Burned. For instance, Jim Manley, the longtime spokesman for Ted Kennedy and Harry Reid. Manley arranged a deep-background interview for Reid with the authors. In the interview, Reid fell into his bumpkin default mode and carelessly referred to Obama as a "light-skinned" African-American who didn't have a "Negro dialect, unless he wanted to have one."

Uh, Senator Reid shouldn't have said that. Not good. Luckily, this was on deep background, as Manley reminded Heilemann and Halperin, just to be triple safe, after the interview ended. Sure, sure, they said.

And then the words wound up in *Game Change*. Manley raised Holy Hell. Heilemann and Halperin had their justifications— then said something about how they would not talk about how they conducted their research for the book. There was some misunderstanding over ground rules, or something, that I never quite understood. Really, you could ask a hundred different reporters and flacks what "deep background" meant, and get a hundred different answers.

Everyone agreed that Reid's remarks were "unfortunate." Republicans called for Reid's resignation. The majority leader called Obama immediately to apologize. Manley called Heilemann and Halperin "liars."

Whatever. *Game Change* was coated in the pixelated dust of a commercial sensation. So were the authors. Everybody loves a winner.

Or, more to the point, is jealous of a winner. Halperin and Heilemann elicited complicated reactions to their commercial success: writing a mega-bestseller, getting a sweet HBO deal and speaking paydays all over the country and a reported $5 million advance to write another version of *Game Change* after 2012.

The ambivalence was borne of more than jealousy. This was particularly true in the case of Halperin, a former political director for ABC News who in 2002 founded the Note, the online political tip sheet that was a precursor to Mike Allen's Playbook. He was something of a kingmaker within "the Gang of 500," a term he coined and a role he seemed to enjoy.

Halperin got the regular TV gig that had eluded him at ABC when MSNBC hired him as its senior political analyst on *Morning Joe*. He screwed up in 2011 when he referred to President Obama as "kind of a dick" on the air and was suspended by the network indefinitely—"indefinitely" being a most ominous word in these contexts. There was some unseemly rejoicing within the twin seats of schadenfreude America (politics and media). Halperin waited it out. He was back on the air in a few weeks. And then, here everyone was at the Newseum, applauding him and Heilemann when they were introduced before the screening.

In many cases, revelers at the *Game Change* opening were participating in a curious show of their own journalistic failure. Dozens (maybe hundreds) of participants in allegedly the most intensely covered presidential campaign in history were in fact there to celebrate a monument to just how little key information they had uncovered at the time. Maybe "Heileperin" enjoyed an advantage in that they were writing after the election. Still, if all of these juicy details and unwritten front-page stories were so plainly obvious, you'd think some blogger or embed would have stumbled onto something. Mostly, *Game Change* itself had become a franchise and a spectacle and a new institution for This Town, something to celebrate and be there for. And it was a great party!

Outside the Newseum, a small group of protesters—Palin loyalists—were handing out white and yellow fliers (designed to look like a Broadway-style *Playbill*). They reiterated the former Alaska governor's oft-quoted charge that *Game Change* was based on a "false narrative." Whether it was or not, much of Washington ceased being about true narratives long ago, anyway. It is about virtual reality: the video game in which we are all characters and try to be players. It brought to mind a line that I had underlined years ago, in 1993, from the late great Michael Kelly, in a *New York Times Magazine* profile of David Gergen ("Master of the Game," it was titled). "What happens in the political world is divorced from the real world," he wrote. "It exists for only the fleeting historical moment, in a magical movie of sorts, a never-ending and infinitely revisable docudrama. Strangely, the faithful understand that the movie is not true—yet also maintain that it is the only truth that really matters."

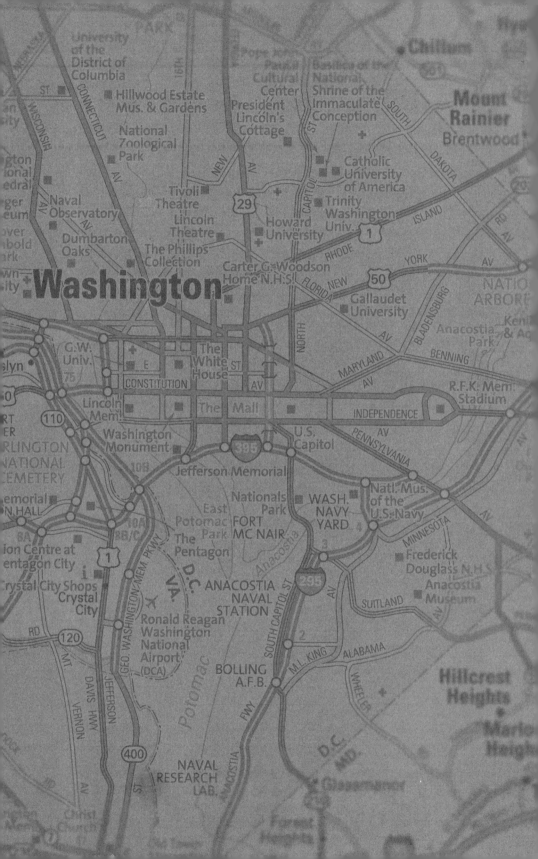

....

The Presidential Campaign: Saddened, Troubled

April–November 2012

The Exalted Gods of the Narrative had rendered a swift and furious judgment upon the president's reelection campaign: It had stumbled out of the gate.

Surrogates kept skidding off message on *Meet the Press*. First, regular Joe Biden took the stand and said he was "comfortable" with gay people marrying each other. He was not supposed to "make news on that," as the politicians like to say these days (an odd meta-term of demurral). The president—who had said his views on the subject were "evolving"—was. Supposedly the White House and re-elect team had a big ROLLOUT STRATEGY planned for the president's coming out, so to speak. It would be the culminating phase of his evolution. And yes, the evolution would be televised.

But then Biden went and ruined the rollout by blurting out the true and obvious thing—the thing that other cool Obama followers like Axe or Plouffe would be too righteously disciplined to ever say out of turn. It is for this reason hard to dislike Biden, a joyful campaigner who—unlike the introverted Obamneys—was not someone you imagined reaching for the Purell as soon as he escaped the ropeline.

It was around this time that I accompanied Biden on a trip to a union hall in Toledo, billed by the White House as an "unofficial kickoff of the campaign" (there were, like, fifty of these supposed "unofficial kickoffs" before Labor Day). En route, the VP strolled to the back of *Air Force Two* to say hello to the traveling press. One reporter asked the VP how it felt to be doing his first "legitimate campaign event." "Legitimate?" Biden said. "Is anything I do legitimate?" He laughed, as everyone did for several seconds before his communications director, former *Washington Post* and *Wall Street Journal* reporter Shailagh Murray, ushered Biden back behind the protective curtain in the front of the plane and another press aide, Liz Allen, swept through the press cabin and tried to declare—retroactively—that Biden had been speaking off the record.

While Obama had come to like Biden, he often talked about him with a patronizing overfondness—as if the VP were the beloved family dog that kept peeing on the carpet. Obama was also protective. For the president's comedy routine at the 2012 Correspondents' Association dinner at the end of April, his speechwriters composed a riff on how things had changed in four years. The bit was supposed to include the line "Four years ago, I chose Joe Biden as my running mate. Four years later, I am *almost* positive I'm going with Joe again." The president would then affect an exaggerated wink for the audience. But he told his speechwriters to kill the line, figuring it would only reactivate the "Dump Biden" chorus. More to the point, it might hurt his feelings. (Obama seemed to expend many mental calories worrying about the VP's feelings.)

In a private meeting in the Oval Office, Biden apologized to Obama for his candor malfunction on gay marriage. Then the president went on ABC to affirm that, yes, he also thought same-sexers should be able to marry. His VP had gotten "a little bit over his skis," POTUS said. Instead of Obama making history with his announcement, his lame sloppy seconds to Biden only called attention to the fact that he had been withholding his true convictions from voters on a momentous cultural matter, maybe for years.

Nonetheless, *Newsweek* slapped Obama on its cover over the headline "The First Gay President." (This was only fair, since Bill Clinton had already been dubbed "The First Black President" years ago.)

The next Sunday, another Obama surrogate, Newark mayor Cory Booker, went on *Meet the Press* and said that the Obama campaign's attack on Romney's work in the private equity sector was "nauseating to the American public." (This would be the industry that Booker had relied on for a great deal of cash, so apparently it was nauseating to Booker too.) Booker's remarks made for instant pundit catnip. Here was another talking-points failure, the second in as many *MTP*s that a hoped-for partisan robot had come unwired. Suddenly, Booker morphed into an elusive superdarling of TV talk-show bookers. The Obama people got to the mayor and his nausea cleared promptly. But not before he had created a "distraction" that contributed to a rough week for the reelection campaign.

"Obama Stumbles out of the Gate," declareth the big Politico headline a few days later. The story, by Mike Allen and Jim VandeHei, catalogued the Biden and Booker boners, the reelection team's "muddled message," and the dismay among "some Democrats" about the flailing reelection effort. Suddenly, the reelection campaign found itself, yes, *on the defensive.*

The story included an unforgettable caveat in paragraph six, one that could rightly appear in 99 percent of all campaign stories.

"Surely," went the caveat, "all of this could prove to be ephemeral and meaningless in the arc of a long presidential contest."

. . .

Another Regrettable Remark (RR) for the reelection enterprise came in April, courtesy of Hilary Rosen, the Tammy BFF, CNN pundit, gay activist, and corporate communications hybrid who spent years as the top lobbyist for the music industry. Hilary got a little out over her skis herself when she said on CNN that Ann Romney had "never worked a day in her life." She apologized for this, sort of, the next day.

But the Romney campaign sensed an umbrage opportunity. The victim was so exorcised that Ann Romney herself called the Rosen crack an "early birthday present." The Romney-bots were in full whirl-up-the-crap mode. They kept describing Rosen as a "confidante" to the president. This was a reach, although she had visited the White House thirty-five times since Obama took office, according to public logs. And Rosen had, just one month earlier, attended a state dinner at the White House to honor the British prime minister, David Cameron. She brought with her as her guest a corporate client, John Kelly, an executive at Microsoft. "An abuse of access" is how one high-level White House official described it to me—making sure to add that Hilary was a friend.

The Obama people tried to bury Hilary R.'s Regrettable Remark by doing the smart and sensible thing: overreacting. The White House, from the president and vice president on down, condemned the slur. Press secretary Jay Carney ran from Rosen as if she were a lesbian version of John Edwards. His initial response when asked about her was "I know three, personally, women named Hilary Rosen." At this point my mind went to a memory from a few years earlier of Carney and Hilary Rosen—the Hilary Rosen who, wouldn't you know it, looked a lot like that one on CNN—dancing at a party for *Meet the Press* gatekeeper Betsy Fischer at lobbyist Jack Quinn's house. (I recall a chain of guests being enjoined in a conga line, though Carney disputes being part of this, so we'll leave it at "dancing.")

This Hilary Rosen is another classic Washington survivor. As the former head of the Recording Industry Association of America lobby, she was lashed as an outspoken defender of the industry's right to intellectual property at a time when online file sharing was becoming habitual. A 2003 profile of Rosen in *Wired* noted that "on a scale of odiousness, devotees of the website Whatsbetter.com rated Rosen just below Illinois Nazis but better than Michael Bolton (and way above pedophile priests)." She was subjected to death threats that led her to travel with security guards. Protesters at her speeches urged other "Hilary Haters" to send her poop in the mail.

Compared with such nastiness, the Ann Romney thing was a small tummy ache. Still, Rosen realized it would be an issue as soon as she returned home from the CNN studios and her babysitter told her about a constant beeping from a computer upstairs. That's what Rosen's TweetDeck page did to signal each mention of @HilaryR on Twitter. She also received a call that night from Stephanie Cutter, Obama's deputy campaign manager, with a heads-up that the campaign would have to condemn her remark. Okay, sure, Hilary said. She knew the game, she understood. Anita Dunn, her business partner at the consulting firm SKDKnickerbocker, had been the president's communications director in the White House—and remained an adviser to Team Obama. Hilary received similar consolation calls and e-mails over the next few days from friends at the campaign and in the White House as they did their public "distancing" acts. The White House wanted to kill this gaffe fast, even if their friend was collateral damage for a few days. Yes, do what you have to do, Rosen replied, though she did become annoyed at the total pile-on from so many top officials (Biden, Axelrod, Messina, etc.). Everyone assured her that she would be fine, if not enhanced, by the little dustup.

And of course she was. *Meet the Press* invited her on the following Sunday—a first-class upgrade from her usual coach seat on CNN. She declined the offer, at the request of the White House, which preferred she lie low for a while. Then she appeared on ABC's *This Week* for the first time a few Sundays later with a bunch of green room buddies that included Ralph Reed, the conservative Christian activist and former BFF to Jack Abramoff. @RalphReed tweeted out an adorable photo of himself and Hilary grinning together backstage, both of them good sports and great patriots.

Rosen's only real sin with the Ann Romney crack was to "provide an opening" for the other side to take up their umbrage guns. She also made a nice foil—outspoken lefty with Hollywood ties—and the Romney-bots knew they had Swing Voter Poison on their hands. They played the opening, won the cycle.

And then it was over, like a brief bout of chicken pox. Everyone stopped "distancing themselves" from Hilary R. She was back being her hot-ticket persona at the White House Correspondents' Association dinner festivities the following week, someone who could get you into parties. At a party at the White House a few months later, Michelle Obama pulled Hilary aside in a receiving line, looked her in the eye, and said, "I've been thinking about you. Are you okay? Are WE okay?" Of course they were okay. It was never a question.

A few weeks after the Ann Romney slip, on the Sunday of Memorial Day weekend, Rosen joined other guests for the nuptials of NBC's Betsy Fischer to Jonathan Martin of Politico—known as "JMart" within the Playbook community. Mike Allen himself officiated the wedding, held at an estate in Warrenton, Virginia, about an hour outside of Washington. In his toast to Jonathan and Betsy, Tom Brokaw, who had flown down from New York, dubbed theirs a union of the "two most powerful organizations in American political journalism," Politico and NBC. "It's . . . as if a member of the Gotti family married a member of the Gambino family," Brokaw said, according to Allen, the wedding presider, who quoted extensively from the toast in the next day's Playbook. "This is what our life, our culture, our country is all about," Brokaw continued. "We're awakened every day, these days, and reminded about what divides us. But this is what unites us: the idea that two people who care passionately about their country and about the political system that drives it, finding each other."

Brokaw wore his special TJR (Timothy J. Russert) tie to honor Jonathan and Betsy. The garments were made special by Vineyard Vines for a select few friends of Tim after he died nearly four years earlier. Has it really been a full cycle in the life of This Town without him?

The TJR tie was adorned with little footballs and Nantuckets and Capitols—things Tim loved. Another thing Tim loved: Betsy. He was her patron, for whom she had worked for nearly two decades. "I remember the first time Tim began to tell me about Betsy and what a genius she was," Brokaw said, "and how much she meant to him. And then we went through the emotional trauma of losing Tim, and Betsy and I formed our own bond."

Brokaw was good at events like this. Tribal speeches are a key medium. Now seventy-two, Brokaw had become the de facto absentee mayor of The Club after Tim's death. He was the interim host of *Meet the Press* for a few months in 2008 until David Gregory prevailed in the beauty contest to succeed if never replace Russert.

The show suffered a ratings slump through much of 2012, and rumors were flying about Gregory's being removed. In fairness, it took years for Russert to become Russert, and Gregory—despite sometimes seeming as full of himself as many say he is—also has a reputation for wanting to improve, as a host and a person. Still, "the show's in trouble and nobody likes Gregory," one person identified as an "insider" told the iPad news service The Daily in an item that circulated fast through This Town after the Huffington Post played it big and linked to the story. Another insider provided the requisite "Tim Russert would be spinning in his grave" quote. (NBC slammed the story as "recklessly reported" and "categorically untrue," and Gregory would eventually re-up as host of *Meet the Press* in early 2013.)

Brokaw is one of the few people left who drew a Russert-level reverence in Washington. He actually did work on behalf of veterans, not just tweet about them on holidays. His mega-bestseller on World War II vets, *The Greatest Generation*, made Brokaw the go-to celebrant of vets in the same way Tim, via *Big Russ and Me*, became self-appointed ambassador to the glories of fatherhood.

Brokaw spent most of his time at his ranch in Montana, with occasional cameos at big political to-dos, like the Iowa caucuses, political conventions, and debates. He tended to walk around with a wry, happy smile that indicated that he got a lot of inside jokes, not just the ones that everyone else did. He floated above at a venerable, self-amused reserve. He wore a hearing aide, though he claims it's "a Viagra drip."

After the 2012 Correspondents' Association dinner a month earlier, Brokaw did an interview with Howie Kurtz in which he bemoaned what the political-media culture had become. Americans, he said, had come to view the political system as a "closed game." In addition, the media is now less concerned with being in tune with America than they are with promoting their own brands and worshipping celebrities. "It's all 'Look at Me,' 'Look at Me,' 'Look at Me,'" he said.

The Correspondents' Association dinner was the perfect symbol of all that the Washington media had become, Brokaw said: a towering exercise in hedonism and manufactured celebrity. It sent the message that nothing was more important than the people inside the ballroom—which is why tens of millions of dollars were being spent on their enjoyment over several days. Who would celebrate Washington if it didn't celebrate itself? "I do feel strongly that it's gone way too far," Brokaw told Kurtz about the Correspondents' Association dinner.

At which point, Kurtz—rather remarkably—said to Brokaw, "Well, you're a celebrity, I hope you'll be my guest next year." He laughed nervously.

"I don't go anymore," Brokaw said, flashing the wry smile and then putting an even finer point on it. "If you go, it will steal your soul."

After the Kurtz interview, Brokaw said he received dozens of e-mails and notes praising his critique. Bob Schieffer, for his part, sent over a photo of himself with his date for the evening, the actress Claire Danes.

At the end of his remarks for Betsy and Jonathan, Brokaw invoked the Other Almighty: Russert. Brokaw said he had some "religious artifacts" to share with the newlyweds. Brokaw's wife, Meredith, a former Miss South Dakota, brought the artifacts up and held Tom's mike while he presented them: his and her Buffalo Bills jerseys.

The unemployment rate still languished at 8.2 percent a few days later. It stoked fears that the short-lived appearance of an economic recovery was an illusory blip. The *Times-Picayune*, in New Orleans, announced that it would cease daily print publication, making New Orleans the first major city in America without a daily paper.

But This Town's particular political-media boom was in the midst of another abundant harvest. It was reported the day after Memorial Day that independent super PACs loyal to Romney would spend more than a billion dollars on ads depicting Obama in the most hideous of ways. The "mega-donors" behind the anti-Obama ads would be matched by comparable efforts on the other side. Between the independent groups and the Romney and Obama fundraising machines, upwards of $2 billion was expected to pour into the empty-calorie economy of two men destroying each other. In this gluttonous contest, casino magnates and campaign hobbyists like Sheldon Adelson would blithely send more than $20 million in pocket change to prop up Newt Gingrich against Romney during the Republican primaries—and tens of millions more to help Romney beat Obama in the general. Meanwhile, back in the United States, the median net worth of an American family dropped to $77,300, which is about where it was in the early 1990s.

Pundits and candidates of all stripes would bemoan this on TV, the influx of so much money into politics and the cynical messages both sides would fashion. But really, This Town loved the trickle-down payday of it all. Millions more poured to the ad makers, "strategists," and networks. The Huffington Post reported that week that during the 2012 campaign the top 150 consulting companies had already grossed more than $465 million, a great deal of which had come from outside groups. One candidate would win, one would lose, and millions of political consumers would be freshly dispirited. But once again, this year more than ever, This Town would prevail in this peculiar battle of ideas.

That week, the end of May, Romney would win enough delegates to secure the Republican nomination. This was treated as a classic breaking news–free event by the media. It marked, once again, the end of the "bruising primary battle" and the unofficial start of the general election campaign.

President Obama made the customary I-wish-you-and-your-family-well phone call to Romney—"cordial," no doubt—before the two men embarked on five more months of character assassination.

. . .

made a determination sometime in the summer of 2012: I would hate to be one of those people who on his deathbed wished he had spent more time speculating about potential running mates. So I decided to throw myself into just that for several weeks, studying the possibilities of whom Mitt Romney might pick to be his vice president in the event he was elected in November.

I had guessed Joe Biden correctly as the Democratic running mate last time, though I don't think I ever made the prediction on cable, so it was not really official or boastworthy. A friend of Biden's once told me that the eventual VP was wary of Barack Obama's picking him to be his running mate because, as Biden said, "the minute you agree to be someone's running mate, you get your balls cut off." (The Biden pal who relayed this wished to remain anonymous for fear that Biden would cut *his* balls off.)

Biden apparently has some manhood insecurities. It set him apart from pretty much zero male politicians in Washington, but he had a pronounced case of it. He loves to remind people that he did not have a boss for thirty-six years in the Senate. There he prided himself on being "my own man." If he ever felt pressured to do something, he would tell aides and Senate colleagues that "my manhood is not negotiable."

I remember interviewing Biden around October 2008, after he had spoken to a rally in Maumee, Ohio. He was telling me the story of how he had been trying to reach John McCain, his longtime colleague in the Senate and now his general-election opponent. Biden was ticked off because he'd heard the McCain campaign, or some affiliate thereof, had been peddling some dirt on Biden's grown daughter. McCain wasn't taking his calls, so Biden tried to go see him backstage at a Clinton Global Initiative event they were both attending in New York. Biden told me that an aide tried to stop him at the entrance to McCain's holding area. "But I said I'm going back anyway." Biden added that he "expected to be treated with more respect" than that.

I wrote a story about Biden in the spring of 2012, right around the time he got in trouble with the president for truthfully saying that he supported gay marriage. His people arranged for Secretary of State Clinton to speak to me on the phone to vouch for Biden. I expected the predictable few minutes of happy talk about how "Joe is great" this and "I love Joe" that. Both of us, the secretary and I, knew the drill.

But then, to my surprise, Hillary slipped me this undercutting nugget on Uncle Joe: "Being a vice president is a little like being a first lady," Clinton said. "You are there to support and serve the president." Whoa. How deliciously, unexpectedly emasculating! And so completely on point to Biden's bridesmaid insecurities. I quoted the line. I knew it would kick up some wise-guy intrigue: Was the Almighty trying to put the understudy in his place? Was she undermining Biden with an eye to running against him in the 2016 Democratic primaries? This would be all over Twitter, the blogs, instantly. This would be viral gold. For about twelve hours. And then This Town would be on to something else, embarked on a summer of masturbatory guesswork on whose balls Mittens would be excising if he got elected.

After a while, I became bored with Veepstakes and decided to instead devote my energies to getting invited to Walter Isaacson's annual Aspen Ideas Festival. Aspen—or "Walter's Bar Mitzvah," as it is known—is a nourishing group bath of Club members frolicking in the Rocky Mountain resort town. Held every summer, all the mob families—journalists, corporates, pols, operatives, formers, and hybrid squid—are stoutly represented. To my great shame, I have never been invited.

But thanks to the ubiquity and diligence of Mike Allen, it was easy to get a vicarious taste of Aspen via Playbook. "Good Monday morning from the Aspen Ideas Festival—summer camp for D.C. and the Upper East Side," Allen dispatched in early July. He called the ideas festival "an intellectual utopia where David Brooks is God, smoothies are free and 'overparenting' is a problem. Actual panel: 'Why We Don't Want Everyone to Go to Harvard.'"

It has become quite easy to experience the magic of Aspen via the political media, which of course treats this high-minded spittle swap as an event of great national consequence. Andrea Mitchell did her show from there. "When we come back," Andrea reported, "we are live in Aspen with the MAN HIMSELF, Mike Allen!"

Allen, in turn, shared via Playbook his "ASPEN PICS," which included one of "Alan Greenspan [hanging] out, waiting to take his bride to a long-delayed breakfast, as she broadcasts MSNBC's 'Andrea Mitchell Reports' live from the DLA Piper Terrace at Aspen Meadows Resort, home of the Aspen Institute. That's Charlie Cook kneeling to kibitz with Chairman Greenspan, Peter Orszag waiting for his hit." Aside: Jeffrey Goldberg had the privilege this year of introducing former Pakistani president Pervez Musharraf to Barbra Streisand. "Ms. Streisand, I would like to have you come to Pakistan when I return to the country," the retired general told Streisand. "Pakistan," Barbra said to Goldberg as she walked away, "is that safe?"

Not much was going on back in D.C. anyway, other than record heat—July was the hottest month ever recorded in the lower forty-eight states, beating a mark set during the Dust Bowl. The local Washington economy hummed right along as the country's continued to sputter. It "uncomfortably calls to mind the rapacious Capitol in Suzanne Collins's 'Hunger Games' series," wrote David Leonhardt in the *Times*. He reported that the District of Columbia had sucked in more stimulus cash per capita than any state in the country. Its unemployment rate checked in at 5.7 percent in June, which compared with 9.3 percent in Chicago, 9.6 percent in New York, and 10.3 percent in Los Angeles. Gallup released a poll that rated Washington the most economically confident region of the United States.

This economic abundance was a product of, among other things, the continued growth of government, the boom in lobbying, the tidal wave of money pouring into the campaigns and super PACs—not to mention the continued and sweaty orgy raging between corporate and political enterprise.

The most maddening beneficiary was the ever-widening "failing upward" sector. Mark Penn, the Democratic pollster who ran the public relations giant Burson-Marsteller, was hired as a top executive at Microsoft—his longtime consulting client—in the summer of 2012. Penn had been best known recently as the chief strategist on Hillary's 2008 presidential campaign. He was marked there as a singularly divisive figure and considered by many inside the campaign to be the main captain of that *Hindenburg*. He was also an exemplar of a familiar Washington success profile that contrasted with the more popular archetype of the class president smoothie. Penn was more of a social misfit type, probably teased as a youngster and picked last in gym. But he nonetheless forged a workable, or thriving, brand as a data-mad genius type—a parlay that was also common among revenge-of-the-nerds technology entrepreneurs, like Bill Gates.

No one doubted that Penn, despite his failings, would retain his permanent meal ticket in Washington. After the Hillary fiasco, he returned to his CEO gig at one of the world's biggest PR firms and somehow managed to retain guru status in the eyes of Bill and Hill. It helped that he was a first-class suck-up, which the Clintons were particularly susceptible to, especially in memo form. In a document that Penn wrote to Boss Hillary in 2006 (obtained by writer Joshua

Green, published in the *Atlantic*), Penn flattered her with a comparison to Margaret Thatcher and warned against excessive efforts by her other advisers to soften her persona. "A word about being human," Penn wrote. "Bill Gates once asked me, 'Could you make me more human?' I said, 'Being human is overrated.'"

In homage to Penn on the occasion of his heady flight to Microsoft, his Burson colleague Karen Hughes—the former top aide to George W. Bush—said this to Politico: "Mark brought great strategic insights and a strong focus on communications grounded in data that raised the bar for Burson's work on behalf of our clients."

A better summation of the D.C. reaction to Penn's hiring by Microsoft was provided in a tweet by Politico's Alexander Burns, channeling the company's shareholders: "Sell!"

As Penn switched allegiances over to his new trough, other developments stirred through the poli-media pigpen.

- Ann Curry was dumped as a host of the *Today* show and replaced by Savannah Guthrie, NBC's former White House correspondent and a favorite among so many of us in This Town. NBC billed Curry's firing as a promotion into the hazy transitional role of "special correspondent." She would "produce network specials"—typically a precursor to a formal, lucrative divorce settlement within the next year or so.

- Andy Griffith died at eighty-six in early July, "saddening" the president and first lady, needless to say, and Paul Begala tweeted something about how Heaven had just become "more neighborly."

- Likewise, everyone was "saddened" and "deeply troubled" by the presidential campaign. It kept sucking worse and worse through the summer. The 2012 edition of the Democracy Show was the "worst I've ever seen," according to whoever was writing John McCain's tweets in the middle of August. "About as ugly as I've seen it get," Brit Hume added on Fox News. Saddened, troubled.

Both the president's reelection operation and Romney's Boston-based wizards had reached twenty-seven declared "new lows" in the six weeks leading up to the two conventions (sources: each other). Neither candidate appeared to take any pleasure in campaigning for president. One exception on the periphery was Biden, who was the only thing resembling a happy warrior in this trench—though the Obama campaign was tempted to lock him in a basement at certain points.

Biden had one of his episodic accidents on the rug in August when he told a predominantly black audience that a President Romney would "put y'all back in chains." This was an unfortunate metaphor that came in the context of a discussion about Romney "unshackling" the restraints that the Obama administration had placed on Wall Street. Biden was accused, of course, of "playing the race card" (because political rhetoric is merely one big card game, and the fraught purview of race relations is merely one card to be "played").

But "put y'all back in chains" was one of Biden's stupider remarks. Even his steadiest protector, Obama, just kind of shook his head over it and said, "What can you do?"

As in 2008, the Obama campaign was a young, grass-roots-oriented and data-driven machine that, it is now clear, ran circles around the opposition. But in contrast to 2008, the grind-it-out reelection campaign was rife was internal dramas and ego clashes that became public. A series of e-books by Politico—namely *Obama's*

Last Stand by Glenn Thrush—provided an in-progress repository for leaks about internal conflicts, like the heated one between Axelrod and Stephanie Cutter over who would get a high-profile TV appearance.

In the early summer of 2012, one of the campaign's celebrated computer whiz kids was forced to apologize to the senior staff after being caught leaking proprietary technology information to a reporter in Europe. And a young aide volunteering for Obama's Convention team was fired after leaking the campaign's convention plan to Mike Allen.

Obama did his best to stir the old magic on the stump. He talked a lot about how his hair was really gray now—which was about as interesting the two thousandth time he said it as his interminable "I have big ears" line was four years earlier. (Physical self-depreciation, check.) The president's stump speeches could carry the forced air of a Van Halen reunion tour with Sammy Hagar in for David Lee Roth. It was as if the Big O were just checking days off a calendar. I saw him speak at an event in Mansfield, Ohio, in July—and in Akron later that day, and Loudoun County, Virginia, in early August, when he annoyingly kept droppin' his g's, talkin' real to the hardworkin' voters of the middle class about how the Republicans wanted to go back to that whole trickle-down economics that we keep hearin' so much about. That's POTUS, playin' the folksy card.

Obama still had his moments, often suffused in nostalgia for the last go-round. In the middle of August, he partook of a beer-soaked bus tour of Iowa that harked back to his cornfield halcyons of '08. There were chants of "Four more beers!" Michelle came too. "Our family has so many wonderful memories of our time here in Iowa," the first lady said. She asked Barack what he had eaten at the state fair. "Pork chop and beer," he said to laughter, his beaming manner suggesting ample volumes of the latter. "He's so pleased with himself," Michelle said. Yes, he was.

At a certain point in the summer, Obama and his top brass became convinced that Romney was hitting the "too much of a douche bag to be elected" threshold. This seemed to coincide, conveniently, with Senate Democratic leader Harry Reid hitting a new "I RE-ALLY don't give a damn what I say" threshold, much of which was directed at his fellow Mormon, Romney. Reid, whose wife had just completed a brutal course of chemotherapy to treat an advanced case of breast cancer, seized on Romney's refusal to release his past tax returns, which he kept mentioning over and over. Reid noted that if Romney were up for a cabinet position, the tax-return issue would make it impossible for him to win Senate confirmation. "He not only couldn't be confirmed as a Cabinet secretary," Reid said, "he couldn't be confirmed as a dog catcher, because a dog catcher—you're at least going to want to look at his income tax returns." (It's unclear exactly when the Senate started confirming dog catchers.) The majority leader also noted that George Romney had been happy to release twelve years of tax returns in 1967 when he was running for president. "His poor father must be so embarrassed about his son," Reid told the Huffington Post of George Romney, who, embarrassed or not, had been dead for seventeen years. And, citing a friend at Bain Capital, Reid claimed that "the word is out" that Mitt had not paid taxes for ten years.

I later asked Reid if he had something personal against Romney, which very much seemed to be the case. "He and I come from different worlds," Reid said after a long pause. "So at the very beginning, there was kind of a friction there, no matter how hard I try. I have a hard time thinking someone like that understands what I've been through in my life." Reid said he kept giving his "information" about Romney's not paying taxes to people in the White House and campaign, but no one ever did anything with it. "So I said the heck with it, I'll do it," Reid said. "If I hadn't done it, it probably never would have been done." When I asked Reid if anyone at the White House or the campaign ever asked him to tone it down a little, he just smiled.

The wise guys settled on Tim Pawlenty, the former governor of Minnesota known as "T-Paw," as Romney's most likely running mate. He was, for a time, at the head of a so-called "short list" of possible choices that circulated in the genius ether in the pre-announcement dog days. Pawlenty, who had been a short-time candidate for the GOP nomination in 2011 and a VP short-lister in 2008, seemed to badly want the job. He endorsed Romney shortly after he gave up his race, did endless spin-room duty, and served as a national co-chairman of Romney's campaign. Pawlenty was the prevailing guess in Chicago, where the T-Paw–Mittens fit was seen as potentially formidable. One of his chief assets was that he was a Republican luminary who did not instantly evince the starched-shirt zillionaire's aura of a Mitt Romney or a Donald Trump.

The son of a milk truck driver, Pawlenty talked constantly of his stint as a hockey player, his upbringing in a Minnesota "meat-packing town," and his penchant for Sam's Club, the discount retail warehouse. He portrayed himself as a little-guy poster child of the American Dream and was even the rare Republican who dared to criticize Wall Street. Before his presidential campaign ended in 2011, Pawlenty vowed in a TV interview that his "truth message to Wall Street was going to be, 'Get your snout out of the trough.'"

Unfortunately for Pawlenty, Romney's truth message to him on the running-mate gig was that he was "going in another direction." T-Paw was disappointed at being passed over—again—but pro forma gracious in defeat, and vowed to keep campaigning for Romney.

And then, in a predictable twist on his American Dream, Pawlenty swerved into the trough himself. He was named CEO of the Financial Services Roundtable, a lobbying group representing the elite Wall Street banks.

Romney ultimately settled on U.S. Representative Paul Ryan of Wisconsin to be his running mate, ending our quadrennial season of fun.

Ryan, a forty-two-year-old Wisconsinite with an excellent physique, was well received by the Republican base and hailed by many in the media as the kind of "bold pick" they had assumed the cautious Romney would never make. Over the years, Ryan had also acquired a coveted Washington reputation as a Man of Substance. He had, after all, studied the federal budget. He also talked a lot about his "love of ideas."

Ryan read the works of the conservative philosopher Ayn Rand as a teen—and there's nothing like a dog-eared copy of *Atlas Shrugged* to get a guy laid in high school. In Congress, he was the author of a stripped-down budget plan that was viewed as a fiscal Magna Carta by House Republicans in 2010. Many of the intellectual conservatives who bemoaned the ascendance of Sarah Palin in 2008 celebrated Ryan. He wore the Halo of the Wonk.

Romney's selection of Ryan salved two of the nagging insecurities on the right: one was that their standard-bearer, Romney, was a closet moderate; the other was that Tea Party conservatism had acquired a dangerously anti-intellectual strain, embodied by the likes of Michele Bachmann, Herman Cain, and especially the last Republican running mate, Sarah Palin. Palin's name was verboten inside the Romney bubble. One person close to Romney's running-mate search told me that "No Palins" was a working imperative throughout the selection process. Meaning, Mittens wanted no vetting surprises, no prima donnas, no lightweights. At a town hall meeting I attended in Orlando not long after Ryan was chosen, the running mate took a question from a man about "the death panels we are going to have" as a result of the Obama health-care bill. "Well, that's not the word I'd choose to use to describe it," Ryan said, fleeing immediately from the term—"death panels"—that Palin popularized in 2009 during the health-care donnybrook.

Ryan looked even younger and more angular in person than he did on television. Capitol police officers would routinely mistake him for an intern or a young Hill staffer. He had a general appearance that seemed to conjure other familiar figures. He told me he was teased as a child for looking like Eddie Munster because of his black widow's peak; I also heard people liken him to Greg Brady; Will Schuester, the music club director in *Glee*; Kyle MacLachlan, who played Special Agent Dale Cooper on *Twin Peaks*; a bat; an owl; an eagle; and Boner from *Growing Pains*.

Unlike Romney, Ryan did not convey any sense that a chandelier was about to fall on his head at any moment. He did not emit a pre-traumatic gaffe anxiety at all times. He could talk football, fishing, or bow hunting. In an interview aboard the new Romney–Ryan campaign bus, Ryan told me that the first firearm he owned was a squirrel gun. At which point I was compelled to mention "varmints," referring to Romney's ridiculed claim in 2007 that he was a hunter of "small varmints, if you will." Ryan chuckled. "Tastes like chicken," he said, and then asked his press secretary, Michael Steel, "Did I just say that on the record?"

Ryan was especially strong on popular culture awareness, with a Generation X bent that counterbalanced the Lawrence Welkish Romney, who was twenty-three years older. In Orlando, a woman raised her hand and signaled her desperation to ask a question with a cry of "OH, OH, OH" until Ryan called on her. "I feel like Horshack," the woman said, referring to Sweathog Arnold Horshack from *Welcome Back, Kotter*, who was known for a similar gesture. One could imagine at this moment Romney being baffled, perhaps thinking that "Horshack" referred to a small home that one of Ann's dressage horses could live in. Ryan missed nothing.

"I'm old enough to know that Horshack joke, actually," he said. I asked Ryan later if he was aware that the actor who played Horshack, Ron Palillo, had died earlier in 2012, as did Robert Hegyes, who played the character of Juan Epstein (bad year for the Sweathogs). "Yes, I thought about that," Ryan told me. "I almost said something. But then I thought, huh, maybe I shouldn't say that, it might ruin the moment."

Romney seemed to acquire an instant lightness after his Ryan selection—like a shy eight-year-old transformed by a new pet turtle. At a rally in Norfolk, Virginia, in which Romney unveiled his selection of Private Ryan, "the Gov" (as his staff called him) was actually seen bouncing in his shoes. It looked as if he was actually enjoying himself, not playing "enjoying himself" according to stage direction.

It became clear to the Romney-bots that Mittens really wanted his running mate around. His mood was much improved. (They used to say the same thing about Michael Dukakis when his wife, Kitty, was around.) They decided after a few days that they would unite the ticket on the stump whenever possible. Bottom line, the Mittens–Ryan bromance was worth celebrating. Ryan described for me a personal e-mail that Romney had sent him after he had successfully completed his first solo campaign events. "He said, 'I basically picked you because I thought you could help me govern,'" Ryan said. "'I never knew you'd be decent at campaigning and you turned out to be pretty good at that, too. So thanks.'" It was a curious thing for Ryan to volunteer, showing Ryan to be more transparently insecure than he usually betrayed. Message: Mittens approved!

Political reporters also approved. They tend to love the "these guys have real rapport" story, anyway. They're easy to do. You can read body language from joint appearances. Plus, campaign aides love sharing the easy feel-good tales about how close the two candidates are—at least until the campaign ends and they start dishing out all the stories about rogue running mates and unease between the families and whatnot.

In general, the political media loved Ryan's selection, in large part because he met another key requirement: he was nice to the political media. This was an exotic practice on the Romney bus, which had endured a series of clashes between its overwhelmed flacks and the media zoo animals tired of being fed the daily lint of the Mittens all year. The low point occurred in July, during Romney's junior week abroad, in which the press became increasingly frustrated over Romney's refusal to talk to them. It came to a head in Warsaw during a visit by Romney to the Tomb of the Unknown Soldier there. As the former governor walked to his car, reporters shouted questions at him about his earlier mishaps. "Kiss my ass," admonished Romney's traveling press aide, Rick Gorka. "Show some respect. This is a holy site for the Polish people." Channeling Fonzie, Gorka also instructed Jonathan Martin of Politico to "shove it." Some in the political echosystem treated this as a major international incident, a skirmish between weary but still potent superpowers—the press, the Romney campaign—that conjured Cold War–like tensions. After Gorka's unsacred words raced around the world, the jackals rechristened the Polish holy site "Gorka Park."

Ryan, on the other hand, actually inquired into the well-being of the jackals when he saw them on the plane (Romney and Obama typically never did). He joined the reporters assigned to his campaign for two off-the-record dinners, one in Roanoke, Virginia, and the other in Cincinnati. The campaign reporters, most of them in their twenties, bought Ryan and his top aides doughnuts during a stop at Voodoo Doughnut in Portland, Oregon, for which Ryan dutifully walked back on the plane to say thanks. (He then tossed out most of the blueberry cake doughnut, which offended his health consciousness and which he later conceded that he found disgusting.)

Ryan's anointment led wise guys on both sides to declare that his selection would lead to a more high-minded and ideas-based debate. And again, this had to be true because William Kristol said so. "The selection has changed the nature of the 2012 presidential contest," the conservative oracle wrote in the *Weekly Standard*. "It means we now have a big campaign, about big issues and big choices." He called Ryan "the Republican party's intellectual leader."

Biden called Ryan to "welcome" him to the race, and Obama praised Ryan's "beautiful family."

And then, within a few days, the two campaigns were back to volleying about how many old people the other guy's Medicare plan would kill.

For some reason, Ryan agreed to talk to me for a profile I started shortly after he was named. Romney's campaign people in Boston were not happy about this. They feared any perception that Ryan was overshadowing the nominee, an insecurity that became more acute, as it was clear Ryan was generating more excitement with the base. Ryan allowed me in anyway and even let me eat barbecue and drink beer with him while he watched his Green Bay Packers play on *Monday Night Football*.

"Is this the guy who's writing that hit piece on me?" Ryan said as his press guy, Michael Steel, led me into the candidate's suite at the Cincinnatian Hotel (located, surprisingly, in Cincinnati). Ryan is adept at wielding sarcasm in a way that can both disarm and manipulate—signaling a mock fatalistic awareness of how the game is played while issuing a tacit invitation to like him anyway.

Ryan's suite included a small roster of name-brand Republicans that included Rob Portman, a Republican senator from Ohio; the

Republican National Committee chairman, Reince Priebus; and Dan Senor, one of Ryan's top campaign lieutenants, who was a top flack for the U.S. operation in Iraq under President Bush. Ryan kept swigging from his bottle of Miller Lite and sniffling. He had a cold. A bad head cold. He kept mentioning this. He had had it for weeks. "I should not be drinking," he said. "But c'mon, it's ribs, it's football, so I gotta have beer." He started coughing (Atlas Coughed!). Ryan's eyes were tearing up and he had an early wake-up the next morning.

After about forty-five minutes and several more coughs, Ryan announced that he would be watching the second half of the game in bed. I assured him that I would leave at that point.

The following week, Steel led me onto Ryan's campaign bus in Iowa. It was a cushy vehicle with deep vinyl seats emblazoned with the Romney–Ryan insignia, a wood-paneled kitchen, a living room in back, and many flavors of laptops, iPads, TVs, and other gadgets. The bus contained about a dozen members of the extended Ryan family: his two sons, Charlie, eight, and Sam, seven; and daughter, Liza, ten. His wife, Janna, was also here, along with her younger sisters, Dana and Molly; the three sisters come from a prominent Democratic family in Oklahoma and all attended Wellesley College (as did their late mother, Prudence). As I walked onto the bus, Steel loudly announced me as "the guy from the *New York Times* who is writing a profile of Paul." He said this each time I entered a restricted area around the candidate. Watch what you say, in other words. It is the press secretary's variant on an arresting cop saying, "You have the right to remain silent" (or, more aptly, an admitting nurse in a psych ward who is obliged to ask a patient if he is feeling suicidal).

Steel then clarified that I would be writing a "hit piece" on Ryan. I corrected him, saying that I had more of a "hatchet job" in mind. "It's more of a 'hit-hatchet piece,'" summarized Ryan, the consensus finder. He offered me a midday Miller Lite. Still fighting the head cold, he opted for a plastic bottle of purple Vitamin Water.

Ryan's body and nutrition freakishness was by now common knowledge—central to Brand Ryan, a study in discipline and exactitude in his approach to physical as well as fiscal fitness. He partook five days a week of P90X, a DVD-based workout that was advertised on late-night TV. Within days of his selection, an online photo of Ryan in a bathing suit made his the most-discussed abs in the history of running mates, other than possibly Joe Lieberman's.

Ryan fashions himself a small-town middle-American dude, "not a D.C. guy." This is usually the first tip-off in Washington of a Beltway insider. And in fact Ryan had spent half his life in This Town, arriving right out of college to work in a series of staff jobs before getting elected to Congress in 1998, at age twenty-eight.

People in both parties who know Ryan personally say he is pleasant, thoughtful, and one of the easier members of Congress to get along with. But he can also give off a smug and off-putting air, emblematic of a particular type. He was in his high school yearbook recognized as his class's "biggest brown-noser." During the fall campaign, Manhattan Mini Storage ran an ad on a New York billboard asking, "Doesn't Paul Ryan Remind You of Every Frat Guy You Regret Sleeping With?"

Like most members of Congress with half a brain, Ryan had a pretty low opinion of many of his colleagues and had been thinking of how to escape. He thought about running for president himself, in early 2011. "A lot of people were encouraging me to run," he mentioned to me, deploying the humble-brag construction preferred by politicians. In early August, when Romney tapped him, Ryan's life got predictably insane: he coined a new phrase, "to get Wienermobiled." It referred to a summer he once spent working for Oscar Mayer in northern Minnesota. A reporter asked him if he ever drove the Wienermobile. "I did actually, as a promotion for turkey bacon at a grocery store," he said. "Then Wikipedia or something wrote that I was the guy who drove the Wienermobile." That was its own job. Ryan only drove it once. But the story spread and he gets accused of lying. "So now, whenever something like that happens, we say, 'Oh, I'm getting Wienermobiled again.'"

One of the fun things about watching a supernova rise is to see how people in Washington react to him. They are suddenly falling over themselves to say how well they know the Paul Ryans of the world, how they have been mentors. "We are VERY good friends," said Representative James Sensenbrenner, a Wisconsin Republican. "I was definitely a mentor to him."

A few weeks after he was announced, Ryan returned to the House floor for the first time as a running mate. In a private reception with his fellow Republicans, he was swarmed. People he had served with for years, almost twice his age, were reduced to fanboys. They asked for his autograph. They asked him to pose for pictures. Biggest Brownnoser grows up to be the Biggest Brownnosee—another winner in the Suck-up City pageant of This Town. I asked Ryan how many colleagues wanted pictures.

"I don't know, fifty?" he said. "I thought that was very strange."

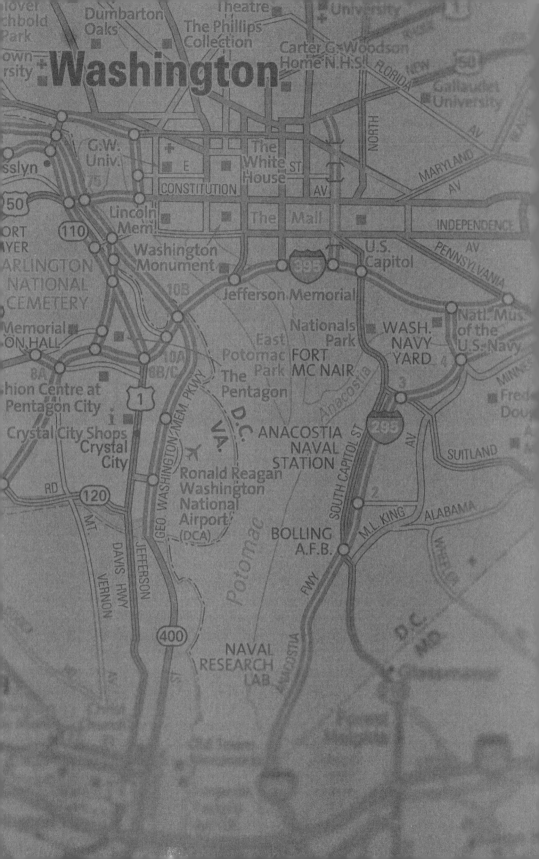

The Presidential Campaign: Belly Flops, Bourbon Chocolate Truffles, and Wonderful Ruins

n midsummer, the keepers of heaven's green room stole from us Gore Vidal, the acerbic titan of letters and author of one of the few great literary works about this city, *Washington, D.C.* Dick Cavett said that after spending time with Vidal, "you felt you had just had a lovely bath in the elegant and witty use of our sadly declining English language." Vidal also produced two of my favorite This Town–applicable statements ever: (1) In response to Cavett's asking him his philosophy of how to conduct your life: "Never turn down an opportunity for sex or being on TV." And (2) "Success is not enough. One's friends must fail."

Vidal, who was eighty-six when he expired July 31, was the grandson of a U.S. senator from Oklahoma who himself was the author of one of my favorite all-time quotations about the D. of C.: With its architectural grandness, Senator Thomas Gore said, Washington "will make wonderful ruins."

As Obama–Romney death-marched to its end, it was clear that

ruins could wait. The Political Class was doing just fine. Both conventions—the Republicans in Tampa in late August, the Dems in Charlotte in early September—were transformed into the Fattest of Cities in these leanest of times. The partygoers were swimming in corporate cash and feeling so very good about themselves—pretty much the opposite of where the recession-drained citizenry was and how many were feeling generally about the two major political parties. Festivity was breaking out everywhere. Anyone with rudimentary door-talking skills could finagle his way up to the troughs. There were lines of idling limos, ice sculptures, free media-sponsored food centers (the Huffington Post's "Oasis" also offered free massages, aromatherapy, and yoga classes in both cities), and so many politicians to honor for their service. Tony Bennett performed to fete Nancy Pelosi's twenty-fifth year in Congress with eight hundred others in Charlotte.

Also, lots of panel discussions to remind us that this is all about issues.

The unquestioned Big Man on Campus in Tampa, at least for the first part of GOP-looza, was Chris Christie, the rotund Republican governor of New Jersey. Romney awarded the coveted keynote speaker's slot to Christie, who had acquired (thanks largely to You-Tube) a reputation for colorfully beating down the hecklers, reporters, and teachers' union types who annoyed him. These tantrums had become as basic to the Christie persona as perma-tan was to Snooki's. (Angering Christie, David Letterman said, was "like crossing a rhino.") They also imprinted Christie with the reputation of a no-nonsense purveyor of hard political truths and granted him a status as the cathartic id of impatient conservatism and counterbalance to the superego Romney.

Likewise, the press had granted Christie one of those coveted political badges of being "someone who tells it like it is," who "gives it to you straight," and all that. They come along periodically—Ross Perot wore it in the early nineties, John McCain during his "straight-talk express" days. Smitten observers reliably treat them with a holy-shit reverence befitting their stature as the *first person in political history who actually tells the truth.* And just as reliably, their acts wear thin.

Christie came in with great pockets of goodwill. He was huge with the key *Morning Joe* demographic. Joe and Mika were big fans and hosted him regularly (it always helps Club cred to be based in or around New York). Bill Kristol was a booster, Brokaw was his pal, and Springsteen his idol—loving Springsteen being a popular pose among many politicians, but Christie was the real deal (he had gone to more than a hundred of the Boss's concerts and everything).

The governor had nailed for himself a killer persona of charismatic crankiness. He also made a big show of almost running for president through much of 2011. He engaged in the familiar dance of public indecision, speaking endlessly about how *flattered and humbled* he was that people kept asking him about running for president. Never do public figures appear less humble than when they are telling you how humbled they are. (A case in point occurred roughly fifteen minutes ago, as I was writing this, via tweet from Howard Fineman of the Huffington Post. "@howardfineman: Just hit 45K followers, a big sum by my humble standards. I'll do my best to merit your continuing attention to what I write and say Best, H.")

Christie's rolling ego trip through Tampa resembled a dress rehearsal for 2016. The week began with an article in the *New York Post* saying that Christie did not want Mittens to pick him to be his running mate because he would then have to leave his governor's job (and he loves his job, which they always have to say). Christie denied the article's claims, but at least two Romney advisers I talked to had no doubt that the notion had come from Team Christie, if not directly from Governor Powder Keg himself.

He hit three or four delegation breakfasts a day, meeting key activists in important primary states (South Carolina) and fund-raising ATMs (California). "This is not about me," Christie said, often. "It's about Mitt Romney." Christie only expended 1,800 words and 16 minutes in his keynote address talking about New Jersey before spitting out the name of the nominee. Christie's speech was dubbed the "Me Note Address." "A prime-time belly-flop," Politico called it. By week's end, the whale had jumped the shark.

My defining image of Christie that week occurred on the Tuesday morning of his Me Note. He was speaking to a breakfast assembly of Michigan delegates and comparing himself to an agitated racehorse. "You know, the horse that's at the starting gate of the Kentucky Derby," he explained. "Just banging up against that gate, you know?" Christie kept rolling his broad shoulders back and forth so the delegates could appreciate the full effect of his impatience and excitement. Then he bolted the breakfast, threw off his navy suit coat, and barreled his way through the lobby of the Embassy Suites in Tampa.

"No questions today!" Christie shouted back to the group of about fifteen trailing reporters and cameramen before plopping himself into the passenger seat of a waiting SUV that would transport him two blocks to the convention floor for his walk-through.

Christie checked out the convention stage while the rock band 3 Doors Down rehearsed nearby. Playing the Republican Convention these days is usually a signal that a band has become totally lame. Exhibits A (3 Doors Down), B (Journey), and C (Jack Blades of Night Ranger) were all scheduled to play Tampa this week. So were the predictables (Kid Rock and what's left of Lynyrd Skynyrd) and the proverbial "country legends" that are GOP standbys. Ron

Kaufman, the longtime lobbyist and Republican state committee man from Massachusetts, was parading around with the Oak Ridge Boys. Kaufman, who has a hideously fabulous little moustache and talks with a mumbling Boston accent, introduced me to the Oak Ridge Boy with the long ZZ Top beard. I kept running into the bearded Oak Ridge Boy all over Tampa, including during Christie's walk-through. "Hey, you here with that Christie fellow?" he asked me. "I'm a big fan," he declared. I'm guessing Christie would rather be caught naked than at an Oak Ridge Boys show.

After about a fifteen-minute walk-through, Christie headed off the floor as 3 Doors Down kept blaring away. As he stomped through narrow hallways and tunnels in the concourse, the pulsing music nourished a decidedly WWE aura around Christie. I kept following him through the concourse because no one was telling me not to. You can go a long way at a convention by just walking with a sense of purpose and looking like you belong in the entourage. Finally, I walked up alongside Christie—who was "only doing TV interviews this week," his people said—and fearlessly asked him if he had a special pre-speech meal planned.

"Something light," he told me. "Maybe a salad, with chicken or something." At which point, one of Christie's security henchman—who resembled an extra from *The Sopranos*, needless to say—noticed me and told me to stop asking questions. It was just as well, because Christie had already hoisted himself into the passenger seat of his SUV and slammed the door behind him. His bright white dress shirt rose a few feet in the air to where it almost touched the glove compartment, making it appear as if the airbag had deployed.

cannot believe so many Americans are currently on food stamps," the Democratic lobbyist Heather Podesta was telling me. None of these food stamp recipients appeared to be in this room: a sunlit function hall of the Mint Museum, in Charlotte, where Heather and her superlobbyist husband Tony were hosting their daily brunch salon during the Democratic Convention.

The Podestas care deeply about food, not only people on food stamps. They had made a special preconvention "tasting trip" to Charlotte to ensure the best chow at the elite functions they hosted for the many senators, congressmen, and candidates they gave money to. Heather and Tony sampled from thirty local eateries to yield this day's decadent smorgasbord of bourbon chocolate truffles, cucumber slices topped with chicken salad, and crab cakes slathered with peach chowchow.

"The situation is still spinning out of control," Heather continued, shaking her head. She was apparently still trying to make her point about food stamps. Yes, whatever. Where'd the lady with the crab cakes go?

Heather, who is forty-two—or nearly a quarter century younger than superlobbyist Tony—cut a much more stylish and, yes, much prettier version of Cruella De Vil. She has gray and black hair, a big smile, and slightly devious eyes. She wore a multicolored silk suit that looked as if it were spray-painted on. "Graffiti-inspired," Heather called the outfit.

Heather was trying to stay on her best behavior after landing in a bit of hot water with the locals. She had been quoted in a Reuters article that described Charlotte as a "second-tier city." "It's grim," she said in the article. "Going to the NASCAR Hall of Fame isn't reason enough to be in Charlotte." People noticed that—local people, and not happy ones. "Now I'm being good," she vowed.

She did not seem terribly broken up about things, one way or another. Maybe the food stamp epidemic was troubling to Heather—and she said she had some ideas on how to get people off them—but Charlotte was a No Guilt Zone, liberal or otherwise.

Democrats have become quite good at justifying their lavish detours. They are, after all, the party of the little guy and must therefore make big, extravagant shows of principle. Party chair Debbie Wasserman Schultz, for instance, vowed that Charlotte would be "the first convention in history that does not accept any funds from lobbyists, corporations, or political action committees." Besides, no one would learn about that $5 million in corporate donations until much later.

Nor, for that matter, had the quaint vilification of lobbyists that accompanied the rise of Barack Obama stopped any of them from celebrating themselves. Four years earlier, at the Dems' convention in Denver, the Podestas even made up scarlet L's—for "lobbyist"—as badges of defiance. Even sweeter defiance? Business is fabulous these days, and so are the Bloody Marys.

Tony Podesta's firm, the Podesta Group, was in line to have its best year ever, Tony told me. He added that he or the lobbyists he employed had not struggled at all to get face time in the White House despite the administration's repeated boasts about how little use they had for lobbyists. As of the end of May 2012, Tony's name had shown up twenty-seven times on White House visitor logs. It didn't hurt, no doubt, that he shared a last name with John Podesta, the former White House chief of staff for Bill Clinton and co-chair of the Obama transition team in 2008 and 2009. People assumed that John and Tony were brothers (because they were) and that they talked all the time (they did) and that it gave Tony a big inroad to the administration (they swore not, but clients could assume all they wanted).

As his brunch wore down, Tony took a seat in the corner of the lemony-sunned function room. John walked over and said hi, and so did a circle jerk of Democratic senators and congressmen—Senators Sheldon Whitehouse of Rhode Island and Ben Cardin of Maryland,

Representatives Ed Markey of Massachusetts and Jerrold Nadler of New York—who all were paying respects. They were longtime friends, beneficiaries of Tony and Heather's, er, "wi$dom." And maybe future employees, too, who knew? The *Atlantic* had just reported that in 1974, 3 percent of retiring members became lobbyists. Now 50 percent of senators and 42 percent of congressmen do.

"You were great on TV this morning, sweetie," Tony said to Senator Kay Hagan as he kissed her sweetly on the cheek. He reminded the first-term senator from North Carolina that she had a "permanent invitation" to his and Heather's vacation home in Italy.

As for these lavish outpourings at the conventions, Tony admitted that perhaps they were a bit much. "Do too many shrimp die on a week like this? Yes, probably," said Tony, who was wearing a tan suit and laceless red sneakers. He was more shrugging than sheepish about the shrimp. And, as the head of a firm that lobbied for BP, whose crude had poisoned many a defenseless shrimp, his crustacean-friendly bona fides were suspect anyway.

Heather said the antilobbying trash talk of the Obamans did bother her for a time. "It felt like I was in a cage," she said, as she had before. "But the food was good."

Oh my God, Bob Rubin's fallen in the pool!"

Bob Rubin's trademark hooded eyes were droopier than I remembered them. But presiding over billions in investor losses can take a toll.

He was still moving with that aura of a Big Deal through the lobby of the Ritz-Carlton in Charlotte. He was the undisputed king of the Ritz-Carlton Democrats: the primest of movers in the modern marriage of politics and wealth creation. When Bill Clinton hired the longtime domo at Goldman Sachs to be his secretary of the Treasury, it represented the contemporary consummation of a simmering romance between Washington and Wall Street. The experiment was hailed a success: to wit, the late-nineties economic boom, perhaps the sweetest second-term triumph for Clinton to enjoy when he wasn't getting impeached.

When Rubin "retired," Clinton called him the "greatest secretary of the Treasury since Alexander Hamilton." The former president seemed to hedge on that a decade later in an interview on ABC's *This Week*, saying that he should have done more—against Rubin's advice—to regulate the derivatives market, which subsequently helped tank the economy.

But never mind that. Rubin spent his "retirement" as a major sovereign at Citigroup, where he earned a total compensation of about $126 million between 1999 and 2009—a time when many of Citigroup's investors lost everything.

"Hey, that's Bob Rubin," said one of the many gawkers stationed in the lobby of the Ritz to watch this festival of pin-striped populism unfold. "This is our temporary Gucci Gulch," gushed Rick Williams, a Democratic lobbyist who was in from Nashville, christening the one-percent scene.

Rubin's leathery brown skin and stunned eyes made him look like the kind of really old lizard that you can only see on those eco-tourism tours of Costa Rica (the kind of hyper-expensive expeditions loved by Ritz-Carlton Democrats). Looking tired, Rubin seemed not to notice Senator John Kerry, another paragon of the Ritz-Carlton Democrats, who was walking right past him while reporting for duty in the lobby, cell phone to ear (not to be bothered). Rubin was apparently headed up to a reception for big donors and White House officials on the eighteenth floor.

Later, in what passed for news during a convention week, Rubin fell into the pool.

He was pulled out by other guests and reported to be "in good spirits." Politics might be swimming in money—but in this case, money was just swimming.

Back in the lobby, William Bennett, the former education secretary and drug czar, was laboring through the lobby en route to dinner next door at BLT Steak. Passing outside was Karl Rove, oblivious to the odd shouts of "Rove, you suck!" emanating from passing cars. Yes, Bennett and Rove were Republicans. But they were men of diverse affiliations and allegiances: to the media, to celebrity, and to the millionaire classes that dominate conventions. They fit.

Heather Podesta had hit the lobby, too, and collapsed into a chair. "I am exhausted," she revealed to me while picking from a bowl of sesame-crusted almonds. After a few minutes, she hauled herself to another reception, this one at the palatial home of Erskine Bowles, the former chief of staff in the Clinton White House. Suddenly, the dull power roar of the Ritz lobby was interrupted by shrieks. Protesters—about a dozen of them, all in pink—nuisanced their way through the lobby. They were singing something (hard to make out the words) to the tune of "Hit the Road Jack" before breaking into a chant of "Get money out of politics!" They were led out by security.

By far, the star of the week—of the summer, and of maybe the whole election—was William Jefferson Clinton. His rehabilitation was total after his fiasco of 2008: his pathetic performance on the Hillary campaign, the accusations of subtle racism, whispers that he was one of those heart bypass surgery survivors who had subsequently lost his mind. Bubba was back.

He gave what was by far the best speech of either convention, rocking a strong endorsement of the president while managing to convey the reelection rationale far better than Obama or his campaign had. Obama, who wrapped his former rival in a full-on stage hug following Clinton's Wednesday night speech, said he should name Clinton to a new position of "secretary for explaining stuff."

Charlotte at times resembled a Clinton reunion and staging area for the Clintonites gearing up for what seemed like the inevitable: Hillary in 2016. Doug Band, Bill's top post–White House gatekeeper, held court in the Ritz lobby. "Hey, can you get me with him?" Representative Steve Cohen of Tennessee asked me, pointing to Band. Cohen, who represented a mostly black district of Memphis, had tried to join the Congressional Black Caucus a few years earlier but was denied (maybe because he's white). Now he just wanted to meet Band, whom he dubbed "someone who is definitely worth knowing."

As you'd expect, Terry McAuliffe was a Ritz stalwart all week. The Democratic moneyman was as natural to this habitat as the milk chocolate fondue, mini lobster rolls, and $420 bottles of Louis Roederer champagne.

"You can always tell by the way they move, that sense of purpose," said Jeff Smith, a former Missouri state senator who taught political science at Washington University. I used to quote Smith from time to time in the early 2000s. He then ran for Dick Gephardt's old seat (after the former House Democratic leader "retired" to work on i$$ues he was pa$$ionate about). Smith lost narrowly and then I lost track of him. It turns out that he had run afoul of campaign finance laws and wound up in jail for a year. Mr. Smith never got to Washington, in other words.

But he did get to Charlotte. After he got out of jail in November 2010, Smith began teaching public policy at the New School in New York and contributing to Politico. He was sitting in the lobby of the Ritz, studying that walk of the powerful. "It's just that walk," Smith continued. "You recognize it when you see it. It screams, 'I'm someone, I'm rich, and I belong here!'"

As Jeff spoke, McAuliffe, who presumably had emerged from his mother doing That Walk, was blitzing his way through in the lobby, waving to everyone. "Hey, Terry!" someone yelled at him, and he detoured past the table-hopping former congressman from Tennessee, Harold Ford, whose district is now represented by Steve Cohen.

Smith was introduced to McAuliffe. An ex-girlfriend of Smith's, Lis Smith, used to be Terry's press secretary. "I used to date one of your biggest fans," Jeff Smith told the former DNC chairman, "and I'm pretty sure the feeling is mutual."

"Who is that?" Mr. McAuliffe asked. "Hillary?"

Big white men are awesome!

I had seen the Macker and BFF Bill Clinton together earlier that summer in Horn Lake, Mississippi. The occasion was the grand opening of a plant that would build little electronic cars for McAuliffe's new company, GreenTech Automotive. Haley Barbour, McAuliffe's old green room friend and the former governor of Mississippi, was also there. It was Barbour who had helped McAuliffe secure a good deal on land and tax incentives for the plant back when he was governor. He left office in January and returned to his namesake lobbying firm. McAuliffe and Barbour were planning some paid speeches together, too—at fifty grand a pop. (Macker had done one with Rove in Texas not long before.)

Clinton, McAuliffe, and Barbour were goofing around backstage before the ceremony, getting pictures taken with a bunch of Chinese employees and investors. As the former president prepared to go onstage, I asked if he would ever consider buying a car from McAuliffe, whom he had once marveled could "talk an owl out of a tree." "Absolutely, I would buy a new car from Terry," Clinton told me. "But a used car? I am not so sure about a used car." He laughed and wheeled around and repeated the line to Barbour, slapping his fleshy back. "Listen to what I just told him. . . ."

By the last weeks of the campaign, Bill Clinton owned the country again—the citizenry that had twice elected him, the Republicans who had impeached him, and the Democrats who had disowned him, for a time, four years earlier. He even owned the president, Obama, whom he previously couldn't stand, and who was now in his debt to a point that he was compelled to make Clinton one of the first people he called when the campaign came to a merciful close.

Clinton had lost considerable weight, which had been clear from photographs ("Big Dog" was now more "Vegan Dog"). But it was jarring still to see the svelte Clinton up close, especially since his head was as big as ever—a fact accentuated by the ruddy brightness of his face and pronounced cheekbones. Encountering Clinton these days is like meeting a skinny older guy wearing an oversize rubber Bill Clinton head.

The GreenTech opening was set up like a campaign event: big flags, balloons, bused-in guests, and a band. Everything was geared to the appearance of the politicians—McAuliffe, Barbour, and of course Clinton. The actual car-making process had thus far yielded just a few Crayola-colored cars, displayed behind a security fence, and the event had a slightly frantic feel. It was as if someone (like the Macker, maybe) had told his employees, "Hey, we have Bill Clinton down here July sixth and we need to build a crowd and start making some cars!" The car makers looked harried as guests designated as VIPs kept streaming through, many of them in from China. They arrived, dozens of them, via a Harrah's shuttle bus with a big "Fun in Store for Those Who Ride" painted on the side. McAuliffe was later seen cruising the Mississippi River on a party boat with a bunch of his Chinese friends.

In his speech, McAuliffe said that during the nineties "President Clinton created more millionaires and billionaires than any other president in the history of this country." At which point Barbour, who had been chatting onstage with Clinton, gave the former president a special nudge.

After the event, Barbour made his exit and McAuliffe and Clinton stayed behind to pose for a group photo with assorted staff and stragglers. "Hey, get in here," someone called out to a young African-American aide to McAuliffe. "We need some diversity in this photo."

"Yeah, we only got one Jewish guy in this picture," Clinton said. "That's not enough." With that, Clinton headed out a back door and into his motorcade, while the Macker bounded back down the hallway like he owned the place.

In late October, I ran into Bob Barnett on a flight from Fort Lauderdale to Reagan National Airport in D.C. Barnett told me (immediately) that he would be heading to Camp David to help the president prepare for his last debate with Mitt Romney. After limited success in 2008, Barnett had finally managed to crack the Obama debate-prep circle. It helped that he continued to serve as the singular point man in helping top administration and campaign luminaries—POTUS and Hillary, Michelle and Bill—cash in. He remained perhaps the single most powerful lawyer in the world of politics, publishing, and broadcast media. Yet more remarkable was Bob's seeming neediness, his hunger for recognition as a wise counselor to Great Men and Women—ALL OF THEM—a modern sage in the Clark Clifford and James Baker and Edward Bennett Williams tradition. So the debate-prep identification remained paramount. It put Bob in a room with the real players and principals in a non–hired gun context. Naturally, Bob's small role in the Obama debate sessions was already known to everyone, well before he dropped Camp David to me on the plane. Playbook had previously "SPOTTED" the "super-lawyer" at an earlier "Obama debate camp" near Las Vegas. That mention brought smirks from many members of Obama's team, who suspected that Barnett had in fact "spotted" himself to Mikey.

During the sessions, the president would go around the room and encourage input. When he was called upon, Bob's view usually parroted what the Obama team called "the Politico view" or "what D.C. insiders and people in the media were talking about." Barnett prefaced one of his remarks to the president that "the conventional wisdom is" such and such, to which Obama joked, "Bob, you ARE the conventional wisdom," and everyone laughed, including Bob.

In the closing days of the campaign, the conventional wisdom suggested a close Election Night, although both campaigns were predicting easy victories. Before an Obama rally in Columbus, Valerie Jarrett was even wondering aloud to a group of fellow aides backstage, "I don't know why we're not getting 80 percent of the vote here," she said. David Plouffe, who the question was directed to, felt compelled to give her a straight answer. Meanwhile, the Romney campaign had filed permits to celebrate Mittens's big victory with an eight-minute fireworks display over Boston Harbor.

By ten p.m. on November 6, the results were sealed for POTUS and the $2 billion cacophony was officially in the books and e-books. Mittens's Secret Service detail vanished like unused fireworks. Suddenly no one was tweeting anymore about his Chipotle orders.

The campaign's end brought the requisite calls for unity. "After Tuesday, one thing is certain: Everyone needs a break from politics,"

Terry McAuliffe said in a statement he issued a few days after the election. After breaking for a full two and a half sentences, the Macker announced he would be running for governor of Virginia in 2013.

He boasted of his "proven record of working across the aisle." He had every reason to, evidenced by his paid bipartisan "debates" with the likes of Eddie Gillespie, who had spent the previous few months on the Romney campaign, and Karl Rove, who had spent them blowing through $300 million in super PAC cash on behalf of underperforming Republicans. Rove then threw an Election Night hissy fit on Fox News over the network's call of Ohio for Obama. Nonetheless, Fox renewed his big contract that summer, while Rove auctioned off dinner with himself to benefit victims of Hurricane Sandy. And, apropos of nothing, someone in D.C. went on Craigslist to advertise a recliner that was "once owned by Senator Max Baucus of Montana." Another Macker debate partner, Barbour, joined GOP eminences in calling for a tough self-assessment of the party—or, as Haley delightfully put it, "a very serious proctology exam."

David Petraeus was, at that moment, enduring something worse. NBC's Andrea Mitchell broke the story that the decorated general would quit as head of the CIA over an affair with his "official biographer." "I don't take any pleasure in this in the sense that this is really a personal tragedy," reported Mitchell. "Having covered Gen. Petraeus myself here and overseas, I am absolutely convinced from all the communications I have had from people directly involved that this was a matter of honor." Not long after, Mitchell and Greenspan would attend a dinner party for David and Holly Petraeus at the home of David Bradley, publisher of the *Atlantic*.

Figuratively speaking, Petraeus had been in bed with the press for years. He was unfailingly generous with chatty backgrounders and cultivated "friendships" in the fourth estate. Just as unfailingly, he was portrayed as a fearless and scholarly hero, maybe even a future president. Roger Ailes, the head of Fox, reportedly kept urging him to run, and a lot of operative-media types were floating his name for VP. Not surprisingly, "official biographer" Paula Broadwell produced a gushy tome on the studly soldier. *All In*, it was titled, hilariously, but not as hilariously as the blurb from Tom Brokaw: "Petraeus is one of the most important Americans of our time," he wrote. "In or out of uniform."

The Petraeus tragedy left many people in The Club deeply saddened and gravely concerned for the well-being of their four-star friend. What an awful way for his decorated career to end.

By the next week, however, concern had abated, as Mike Allen reported in Playbook that the disgraced adulterer was in good hands. "**EXCLUSIVE**: Gen. David Petraeus has retained super-lawyer Robert Barnett of Williams & Connolly for advice on post-governmental issues, and to assist him in planning his future." Playbook reported three days later that Broadwell, the "official biographer," was also in expert care: "**EXCLUSIVE**: Glover Park Group's Dee Dee Myers and Joel Johnson are working with Paula Broadwell . . . The two quietly began providing communications counsel." This Town loves running to Playbook about all the "quiet" work they do.

Beyond such trivial titillations—and I feel dirty just writing about them, yes, I do—everyone agreed it was time for both parties to get serious about fiscal responsibility. The so-called "fiscal cliff" deadline was just ahead, which could mean massive spending cuts and tax increases by the end of December unless Congress acted on cutting the deficit. Simpson–Bowles, the bipartisan deficit reduction plan named for commission chairs Alan Simpson and Erskine Bowles, was suddenly being widely pined for in This Town. It was held up as a totem of compromise, tough love, and statesmanship that had been so lacking during Obama's first term. As proof of how lacking it had been, the Simpson–Bowles report was roundly rejected by both sides when it was issued in 2010.

But now that everyone had achieved patriotic clarity, the folksy octogenarian former senator from Wyoming (Simpson) and his Democratic straight man (Bowles) had become public paragons of fiscal purity. Their elevated status was sanctified in classic Washington fashion by the $40,000 speaking fees they were now commanding for joint appearances. An even better example of the earning power behind a fiscally pure reputation was revealed in late November: former representative Dick Armey, a Tea Party leader who led the group FreedomWorks, left the organization in a dispute with its management—walking away with an $8 million buyout. You can buy a lot of pitchforks with $8 million. And tea.

A few days later, This Town was again abuzz over the news that South Carolina's Jim DeMint, the Senate's most celebrated spending hard-liner, had bolted for a $1 million-plus-a-year gig at the Heritage Foundation. The following week, my colleague Carl Hulse ran into former Democratic senator Christopher Dodd at a movie screening at the I Street offices of the Motion Picture Association of America, the powerful film lobby Dodd now runs. "Boy, DeMint really cashed in," Carl said to the former Peace Corps volunteer. "He might be making more than you."

"No, he's not," Dodd replied, laughing. "I checked."

@howardfineman: Happy Thanksgiving. Much to be thankful for: family, friends and freedom in a country that, tho flawed, remains the best hope of mankind.

After everyone was done giving thanks, a troupe of Club members field-tripped to Cambridge, Massachusetts, to attend a quadrennial postelection debrief at Harvard's Institute of Politics. The exercise, which had taken place after every presidential election since 1972, featured the masterminds of all the presidential campaigns and dozens of well-credentialed journalists.

Both the Obama and Romney teams fielded eight presenters, lined up along two tables facing each other. It was a weird scene: the winning team trying (not perfectly) to hide their smugness, while the losers tried to conceal their unhappiness at having to do this not even three weeks from a bitter defeat. Matt Rhoades, Romney's campaign manager, kept flexing his cheeks and mouth into what looked like grins but were in fact full-faced grimaces. On the same day, Obama hosted Romney at the White House for the traditional "Let's everyone be gracious" ritual.

The entire Kennedy School exercise seemed wholly forced and somewhat superfluous. Many of the self-preserving insiders had already unburdened themselves in real time via Twitter and to the various e-book authors. Late in the afternoon of one of the final sessions, much of Cambridge—including the building where the event was held—lost power. The participants kept right on talking in the dark until the sun went down outside and the event organizers canceled the rest of the program. Everyone then repaired to various taverns.

I headed to Charlie's Kitchen, a dive across the street in Harvard Square, and walked in right behind David Axelrod, who promptly received a standing ovation from the packed college bar. A mob scene of congratulations, free beers, and photo requests ensued. He got this everywhere, apparently, as did the other Obama derivatives. But not like Axelrod did. He was the most recognizable folk hero of the Obama juggernaut. Since the political class began treating recognizable consultants as demigods, every winning campaign had one or two—Karl Rove for Bush, Begala and Carville for Clinton. But Axelrod's über-aide status in the media was a source of some resentment among certain campaign and White House insiders. He was no longer the sacred cow inside the Obama orbit that he was when the magical ride to the White House began. Some colleagues—many of them loyal to Valerie Jarrett—believed he had become increasingly mindful of cultivating his public profile with an eye to his post-Obama celebrity life.

In the final days of the campaign, Axelrod went on *Morning Joe* and vowed to shave off his moustache of forty years if Obama happened to lose Michigan, Minnesota, or Pennsylvania, as the Romney campaign was suggesting he might. Such public wagers were once the province of the principals themselves—think Super Bowl bets between opposing mayors. Now, in the age of the celebrity operatives, the aides themselves had become central to the antic action. Even a duo of lower-wattage aides—DNC spokesman Brad Woodhouse and his RNC counterpart, Sean Spicer—bet that the losing flack would have to shave his head, and the denouement was deemed sufficiently interesting for ABC's esteemed Sunday show *This Week* to broadcast it live. Both Spicer and Woodhouse wound up getting buzz-cut together, for charity—vowing to raise $12,000 for a cancer group.

Even though Obama won all of the appointed states, Axelrod agreed to get his moustache shaved on *Morning Joe* anyway, provided Joe and Mika could help raise $1 million for David and his wife Susan's foundation for epilepsy research, CURE. And they did, with help from celebrity donors like George Clooney, Tom Hanks, and billionaire Donald Trump, who in the course of the campaign had fully devolved from being merely a garish curiosity to a nativist laughingstock.

But through his generous contribution, the Donald could enjoy a sweet morsel of image rehab on national TV, and he called in to *Morning Joe* to share a telephonic hug with Axelrod as the latter got his 'stache slashed for a good cause. I cannot emphasize enough that this *was* a good cause. David and Susan Axelrod, who have been through hell with their daughter Lauren's disability, have done heroic work. "I will pull every lever I can to get people to contribute to this cause," Axelrod told me. "I don't apologize for it. And I'm not going to spend any energy trying to get into Donald Trump's head and wonder about his motives. It was a generous gesture, and I appreciated it."

The ongoing spectacle, however, was beginning to draw some "Enough already" whispers around This Town, especially as many worthy causes and charities were struggling to raise five figures at their end-of-year benefits. To go even remotely public with this skepticism was asking for trouble, as Greg Sargent, a blogger for the *Washington Post* learned. On the day of the *Morning Joe* thing, Sargent tweeted, "Am I alone in not caring at all about @davidaxelrod's 'stache'?" Apparently he WAS alone, based on the hostile return-fire, and Sargent reversed course immediately.

With its enviable position on the political-celebrity-media axis, CURE continued to reap a symbiotic bounty. On the night after Axelrod's *Morning Joe* shave, Tammy hosted another big party in Washington for CURE. I spent a good portion of it talking college basketball with Luke Russert, who, in the four years since his father died, had become a fixture on the Hill as MSNBC's chief congressional correspondent. He had taken a fair amount of grief, too, for the obvious reasons—"the Nepotist Prince," Salon called him—and I'll cop to my share of aspersion initially too. But Luke won me over by keeping his head down and working hard to surmount a doubly tough circumstance: losing his best friend/dad and then grinding through a prematurely big job while half the city snarked over his hiring. He had a good sense of humor for his situation and for the parasitic environment he grew up in, not to mention for the swarming opportunists on the Hill who would try to get all sincere with him by invoking his dad.

Otherwise, Tammy's epilepsy gig was a thoroughly familiar scene in an era now extended four more years: Georgetown manse, valet parking, buffet table, and a whole lot of Tammy. Joe Biden showed up and spoke for twenty minutes in that hushed and intimate way he does. There were many jokes, as one might imagine, about Axelrod's moustache being gone. Democratic superlobbyist Heather Podesta and Republican media consultant/CNN contributor Alex Castellanos co-chaired the event.

Castellanos revealed that night that he, too, would shave his moustache if CURE could recruit an additional 500 donors in December—another reminder that there is no shame in Washington, only charity.

It also, to be sure, did not hurt Brand Alex to be so publicly involved with such a beyond-reproach pursuit, or that of Purple Strategies, his "full-service public affairs firm," which itself had performed heroic image-buffing work on behalf of many companies in need—like BP after the Gulf spill.

On December 10, I received a blast e-mail from Castellanos in which he announced his offer. It appeared under the bizarre subject heading "David Axelrod Nude," which grabbed my attention, and also that of my spam filter. "Everyone comes to Washington to change the world," Castellanos wrote. "We all want to do something that matters." He urged all of us to donate to CURE, not just for the great cause, but also for the sweetener of getting to see a marquee Republican pundit/consultant get his moustache shaved live on CNN's *Situation Room*. In conjunction, Axelrod sent out an e-mail appeal directly to eighty-eight political reporter friends seeking donations. (There might have been more, though the e-mail was sent to eighty-eight addresses—not mine, but I received a forwarded copy.)

"Thanks for what you're doing," host Wolf Blitzer told Axelrod and Castellanos during a joint appearance on the show that night, a link to which was featured on the website for Purple Strategies.

Now safely victorious in the election, many top Obama officials were preparing to move on from the campaign and White House and were eager to unburden themselves of more lingering grievances. A prime target was Jarrett, the enduring confidante to the president and first lady, whom many members of Obama's inner circle never had much use for. Her clashes with Robert Gibbs and Rahm Emanuel were well documented in the various book and magazine treatments of the first team.

My *Times* colleague Jo Becker wrote a profile of Jarrett that was published in September 2012. It included such tidbits as Jarrett ordering a drink from a four-star general she believed was a waiter. The anecdotes followed the theme of Jarrett becoming too enamored of the trappings of power, such as her full Secret Service detail. Jarrett was exercised over the story, she told colleagues, and was particularly galled over a quotation from Axelrod that addressed the management complications of having a senior adviser in the White House who is essentially part of the First Family. "There is an inherent challenge in managing anyone, this is not particular to Valerie, who is a senior adviser and part of a structure, and also close personally with the family," said Axelrod. "Obviously it's cleaner and less complicated if everyone is discussing things at the same meetings. But it's a manageable problem."

After Becker's story ran—and a few weeks after the election— a top Obama aide forwarded me a set of confidential talking points that were circulated through the West Wing when Becker was reporting her story. The memo, written by deputy press secretary

Jamie Smith, was titled "The Magic of Valerie." It included an un-relenting thirty-three talking points, none of which contained the term "manageable problem."

- The magic of Valerie is her intellect and her heart. She is an incredibly kind, caring and thoughtful person with a unique ability to pinpoint the voiceless and shine a light on them and the issues they and the President care about with the ultimate goal of making a real difference in people's lives.

- Valerie is the perfect combination of smart, savvy and in-novative.

- Valerie has an enormous capacity for both empathy and sympathy. She balances the need to be patient and ju-dicious with the desire to get things done and work as hard as possible for the American people from the White House.

- To know what both drives Valerie Jarrett and why the President values her opinion so much, you benefit greatly from really getting to know the woman.

- Valerie is very tapped in to people's experiences, their good times and bad. She knows from her own life what it is like to believe and strive for your dreams.

- Valerie expects people to work their hearts out for the Pres-ident and never forget where you work and the magnitude.

- Single mother, woman working to the top in a competitive male dominated world, African American, working for change from grassroots to big business.

(My personal favorite "Magic of Valerie" bullet point is the one where we learn that "Valerie is someone here who other people inside the building know they can trust. (need examples.")

Jarrett was viewed by many inside as the true custodian of the president's interest, and brand, or as someone who wanted to be viewed that way. "The voice of purity" rap against her from some colleagues reflected the self-righteousness she could project. But Jarrett's defenders inside, and she had many, said that her effectiveness was based largely on her indifference to cultivating the press or concern about how she was viewed outside of the president's orbit. "I've lived in Washington a long time," said Cecilia Muñoz, the White House domestic policy adviser and a close ally of Jarrett's. "You can spot, especially in this building, somebody who has one eye on their work and one eye on their next career move. Valerie is not one of those people. She is not trying to construct a next big thing for herself."

Another Jarrett loyalist pointed out that during the reelection campaign, many Obama advisers seemed to be auditioning for post-election broadcast jobs. It created a dynamic in which aides would be competing with one another to get on TV—ostensibly vying for better positions in the same pundit class they made such a show of running against four years earlier. Jarrett never partook of this, said the aide, who also noted that Axelrod and Gibbs both signed substantial deals as contributors with MSNBC within a few months of the election; Plouffe, who railed against the "jackals" in the media in 2008, joined Bloomberg Television as a contributor and strategic adviser; and Politico's Dylan Byers reported that Stephanie Cutter was talking to CNN about cohosting a relaunched version of *Crossfire*, the high-decibel debate show. Her conservative counterpart would be Newt Gingrich.

In early 2013 I visited Jarrett in her White House office to discuss some of the palace intrigue of the first term. She seemed completely bored by the proposition. She betrayed no defensiveness and a hint of smugness at having outlasted her detractors. The president was ensconced in the White House for another four years and many people expected Jarrett would stay at his side right through to January 2017. She kept steering the conversation about internal dynamics into the present tense, which of course carried a slap at some former colleagues. "If you talk to people who are here now, I think you'd hear people say that we have a great team, that it's collaborative," Jarrett said. Her overriding message seemed to be that she *was* still here, had learned to rise above "the parlor games," and had outlasted her riff-raff. She spoke in an even, high-pitched voice and kept shrugging her shoulders. "This town will break your heart," Jarrett said. "But you can't let it." And she shrugged her shoulders again for emphasis, or non-emphasis.

14

The Last Party

December 2012

Early on the Thursday night before Christmas, traffic was stacked up in a honking mess at the valet station on N Street, in front of Ben Bradlee and Sally Quinn's. There, in the rain, was another reminder, if one was again needed, that the movie-set streets of Georgetown were designed for bygone vehicles.

Across town on Capitol Hill, dignitaries had just finished paying respects to another bygone vehicle, Senator Daniel Inouye, the eighty-eight-year-old Democrat of Hawaii, who died a few days earlier. Colleagues praised their war-hero friend in the usual "quiet dignity," "respect for the institution," "disagreed without being disagreeable" ways. As mourners filed past the casket perched atop the Lincoln catafalque, everyone marked another somber recollection of the proverbial "bipartisan era that once was."

A week earlier, a gunman had slaughtered twenty-six people—twenty of them kids—at a Newtown, Connecticut, elementary school. Even by our uncomfortably numb routine of mass slaying aftermaths, this one stole your breath. Obama delivered what might have been the best speech of his presidency in Connecticut. He read the first names of the kids and made me cry.

Yet everyone knew this would all default soon enough into the familiar Kabuki. And a few days later, Wayne LaPierre, the head of the National Rifle Association, gave a rambling press conference that was ridiculed by solemn commentators, gun-control Democrats, and a growing class of hand-wringing/self-hating Republicans. It made everyone feel better to ridicule, to feel superior to, the gun nut at the podium, never mind that his NRA still had at least half of Washington by the gonads, and that Obama was conceding privately that there was probably nothing he could do to change gun laws in any major way—as was eventually borne out.

But the outrage Obama channeled was powerful, or felt powerful. As often happens here, much of the outrage turned inward. This Town was having one of its periodic "We're not worthy of this historical moment" moments. It happens every few months, usually when some predictable circus greets a legitimate crisis. Another was unfolding simultaneously on Capitol Hill as Republicans were blowing up a proposal that Speaker Boehner had floated to stop the "looming fiscal cliff" fiasco. By eight p.m. on the rainy Thursday night before Christmas, news came down that Boehner had adjourned the House for the holidays, and the city's center of gridlock shifted to the clogged streets of Georgetown, in front of Ben and Sally's Federal-style Laird-Dunlop House.

This was not just any party. It was "The Last Party," as Sally Quinn had billed the much-anticipated get-together. The evite landed a few weeks earlier. Nearly everyone who'd received one thought initially that The Last Party referred to some special parting hurrah for the great Benjamin Crowninshield Bradlee, Sally's husband, the *Washington Post*'s balls-out editor during the Watergate era and beyond. At ninety-one, Ben finally seemed to be reaching his last legs. He had been forgetting names and faces, appeared confused much of the time, and was less than his spit-brass self. "Not doing well" was the phrase. "Dementia" was the word, whispered. Sad. Could Ben's be This Town's next mega-funeral? Could this tribal assembly be a kind of "pre-game," as Politico might call it?

Like so many in This Town, I revered Ben, whom it was of course always fashionable to revere, but I really did. I fell in love with the Jason Robards version, the dashing fire-breather he presented in his memoir, *A Good Life*, in which he told of his unbridled newspaper adventures with no hint of the preening insecurity that defines so much of the business today. A lot of Ben was bravado, maybe exaggerated and sprinkled in the potent mythmaking powder of Hollywood and history. But he embodied a spirit and a newspaper that wanted, more than anything, to have impact—and that actually did have impact: a White House brought down, history diverted. Who had impact now, really? Who even remembered who won last year's Pulitzers, or last month's ratings, or last week's top Sunday morning "gets"? It all can feel so fleeting and entangled, and often at the same time.

I hesitate to suggest excessive nostalgia here, or certainly to imply some "Well, wasn't it all better here in Nixon's day" lament. Nor would it be right to say Bradlee was a paragon of journalistic mission, independence, and subversion. His career was suffused with ample coziness with the powerful that many would condemn today. There's virtually no way that any journalist could carry on the close friendship that Bradlee did with John F. Kennedy while he was covering the president as *Newsweek*'s Washington bureau chief (a time when, by many accounts, Kennedy was sleeping with Bradlee's then wife's sister). In other words, to impose some false modern standard of purity on Ben would illicit from him a trademark "Fuck it."

Still, one of the glories of Watergate was that it ended in a clean kill. The *Post* prevailed, Nixon was exposed. There were spoils and consequences. "For the first time, really, I felt in my guts that we were going to win," Bradlee wrote of a period in 1973 in which a vindicating groundswell of revelations laid bare the scope of the White House's wrongdoing. "I had no idea still how it would all come out. But I no longer believed that Watergate would end in a tie."

Journalists often debate whether the Watergate story could have been broken today, or would at least have the legs that it did four decades ago. Forget the question of whether Woodward and Bernstein would have been given the time, space, and editorial backing to pursue such an endeavor. Even if they did, the Nixon White House would now have a massive Fox/Rush/Drudge apparatus at its back. A complicated story would devolve into the familiar left-right rock 'em, sock 'em. "Okay, the liberal media is at it again," the first defense would be, and then everyone would assume their places in the noise machine.

Soon enough, Watergate would be over, eclipsed by the next shiny object, and no one would remember who won or lost, and even what "winning" and "losing" meant beyond the ESPN-style scoring: To wit, a modern analog to that unfolded a few days later. After the fiscal cliff battle was finally resolved on Capitol Hill, Mike Allen included in Playbook an "e-mail du jour" from a Democratic aide. In it, the aide distilled—with perfectly of-the-moment, of-the-medium simplicity—the current state of play in the complicated economic debate that has dominated This Town through the Obama years:

> *So we have a split decision as of now: GOP won 2010 elections, then got the Budget Control Act deal with all cuts, no tax hikes. Obama won 2012 elections, and scores this deal with all tax hikes, hardly any spending cuts. So each side has one victory each.*

You can't decide who wins overall until the rubber match happens in March. That side will be the winner—best two out of three.

Ben Bradlee used to throw around a favorite phrase, "The caravan moves on." This was his way of always moving forward, not dwelling. It was a quality familiar in powerful WASP types—and, even more, to combat vets of a certain era, like him, who fought a good war in the Pacific and lived to "move on."

At a time when journalism was becoming a hot profession—in large part thanks to Watergate and *All the President's Men*—Ben became the object of the biggest personality cult in This Town. I spent much of the first half of my career imagining what it would be like to work at the *Washington Post* under Bradlee.

By the time I reached the paper in 1997, Ben had been retired for six years and was working out of the *Post*'s emeritus wing on the seventh floor. He was well removed from the newsroom, though he strolled through it frequently and ate lunch most days in the cafeteria. "I'm a stop on the tour," he said then, and still does. He would sometimes send me fan mail after a worthy piece. "Your story today makes our newspaper so good," he wrote once after I'd been at the *Post* a year or so. To this day, if someone forced me to relinquish everything I owned except what could fit into a single box, I would make room for that note.

We had lunch a few times, Ben and I, usually some nice place in the neighborhood where he would speak French to the maître d'. Once, when I was weighing another job offer, he said to me, "You're working for the best fucking newspaper in the world. Don't be an asshole." He was a *Post* exceptionalist, even when he knew better (and he did). "You're a fucking traitor," he scolded me in 2006, when

I finally did leave—for the *Times*. "And now you're working for a bunch of assholes." He knew that the *Post* had "lost a lot of its horsepower" and that I was probably making the right move. On the way out, he reminded me to "keep your pecker up," a common Ben-ism.

As it turned out, The Last Party was not meant as any special tribute to Ben, at least officially. Rather, it was meant as a play on the end of the world—which, according to the Mayan calendar, was scheduled for the next day or so. A lot of people had been making end-of-the-world jokes, and this was Sally's offering—although she later told me that she was fully aware of the double meaning here. Whatever the occasion, it's always a thrill to score the invite to Ben and Sally's: a landmark house, once owned by Robert Todd Lincoln (Abe's son), whose grounds occupy nearly an entire block. Portraits of Bradlee's ancestors, Josiah and Lucy Bradlee, hang in the foyer, while a mingling local royalty mosey through, sipping drinks. (Is "ColinPowellJimLehrerAndreaMitchell" one word?)

My first entrée into a Ben and Sally soiree had come exactly four years earlier, at the end of 2008, a few weeks after Obama was elected. Bill Burton, the former campaign press secretary, was there, along with a host of hot new Obama arrivals. Burton was a big "destination" that night, as was David Gregory, who had just prevailed in the competition to replace Russert as host of *Meet the Press*.

The 2008 gala was ostensibly to welcome the new editor of the *Washington Post*, Marcus Brauchli, to town after a long career at the *Wall Street Journal*. My major recollection was being confronted at the buffet table by Chris Matthews, who was mad about a profile I had written about him earlier that year. Matthews blamed that story, he said, for "costing me a job that I really wanted." It was not clear what he meant exactly, although I wondered if it was the Senate seat in his native Pennsylvania that he had been making noises about running for—just noises, as it turned out. Anyway, he stormed away before I could ascertain more. Ben, who was standing nearby and apparently heard the exchange, met my eyes and shrugged. "Fuck 'im," he said, patting my back. And then, as he walked away, he said, "Keep your pecker up."

Four years later, there was Ben again, now parked in the front hall, greeting guests as they arrived. He looked typically stellar—silvery white hair, barrel chest out, grinning handshakes and ever the impresario in full command of his charisma, if not his memory.

A few feet from Ben, Brauchli was taking condolences on his removal from Ben's old job as executive editor. He had been canned a few weeks earlier ("invited to resign," if you prefer) after an extended spiral of the diminished print subscriptions, ad revenues, and headcounts that have hit the entire business, but the *Post* especially. Brauchli had in fact just been "caked" in the *Post* newsroom that afternoon—"caking" being a term coined for the sugary farewell rituals that had been breaking out repeatedly at the paper in recent years. It is not clear if anyone could have weathered those declines better than Brauchli had. But regardless, he was now fully deposed to the emeritus wing and not happy about it (and neither was his wife, who was uncomfortably open about her feelings via Facebook). On the upside, Brauchli had plenty of time now for lunch, as he told people who were consoling him at The Last Party.

In the back of the foyer schmoozed Susan Rice, the U.S. ambassador to the United Nations, who made for a timely destination herself tonight because she was "in the news." Earlier that week, Rice's prospective nomination to be the next secretary of state had been harpooned, mostly by Republicans. John McCain, who had picked Sarah Palin to be his running mate four and a half years earlier, said Rice was "not very bright" and "not qualified" for the job. In truth, Rice rubbed a select bipartisan contingent the wrong way. She was often called a "brusque" and "doesn't suffer fools gladly" type, which can be big trouble in This Town, especially for a woman. Richard Holbrooke, too, was the epitome of brusque and doesn't-suffer-fools-gladly, yet he was a particular darling among the same set of Thought Leaders he spent much of his life cultivating. Rice did not, and one member of the White House national security team noted that her ultimate kiss of death was inflicted by the supreme Thought Leader himself, *Times* columnist Thomas Friedman: "I don't know Rice at all," he wrote, "so I have no opinion on her fitness for the job."

In the vein of too-little-too-late, it was ironic that Rice would show up at The Last Party. It was also precisely the kind of shindig Richard Holbrooke would never have missed. He had so many great friends here, starting with Ben and Sally, and his name had also been invoked a fair amount of late—two years after his death—for an incident that took place during the Clinton years in which Rice gave him the finger during a senior staff meeting at the State Department. Not classy! Less remarked upon was the condescending diatribe from Richard that allegedly incited Rice.

Walter Isaacson had Rice corralled while Colin Powell walked a few feet away. This was notable because Walter Isaacson is someone who absolutely *lives* to be in the same room as people like Colin Powell. Not so much the likes of me, whom Walter always blows right past en route to the Colin Powells—and if he greets me at all, he calls me "Matthew," which I've never bothered to correct because Walter is so smart, for all I know my name IS Matthew and I've been going by the wrong name all these years. Anyway, the fact that Walter was staying fixed on Susan Rice and letting the gravy train pass was testimony to her timeliness in This Town, at least for another day or so. Isaacson eventually proceeded into the living room, which was adorned with plush couches, fresh flowers, and Vernon Jordan. Whenever I see Jordan, the perennial This Town insider, I think of a story told by Jeff Connaughton, a former top aide to Joe

Biden and superlobbying partner of Ed Gillespie and Jack Quinn. Connaughton, who made plenty of money as a lobbyist, then became disgusted with This Town and moved to Savannah, Georgia, recalled an encounter he and Quinn had with Jordan back in the 1990s.

"Let's have lunch someday," Quinn told Jordan. "Give me a call."

"You call me," Jordan replied. "You're the junior partner in this friendship."

Rice was still a junior partner in the Obama cabinet. But by dint of her status now—in the news, a useful destination—she was a senior attraction at The Last Party. Even Vernon Jordan himself sidled up to her. As Rice navigated the masquerade, people staring at her like a zoo animal, it struck me that she was the only top Obama administration official that I recognized here. Few journalists under the age of forty attended, either, let alone any of the new political superbloggers like the *Washington Post*'s Ezra Klein, just dubbed by the *Atlantic* to be "the presumptive dean of Washington Journalism."

Senator Amy Klobuchar of Minnesota and Representative Debbie Wasserman Schultz of Florida were the only actual elected officials I saw. Wasserman Schultz said she felt like she had "walked into a novel." In general, the party was conspicuously devoid of "earpieces," denoting the presence of sufficiently high-value targets. One of the few guests meriting a security detail was Michael Oren, the Israeli ambassador, who hovered dangerously over the buffet table, eyeing a massive Christmas ham (his detail was trained to protect him only from terrorists, not *treif*).

This Town parties fall into three basic categories: the parties for young, hyper-ambitious operators, who are critical—even sneering—about the people currently in power; the parties for has-beens, who spend their time being critical of the people currently in power, because they know they once did a better job; and the parties heavy with current officials, who fear the young, because they know they are circling their jobs, and who fear the old, because the ex-officials remind them of what their futures will be like. The Last Party was mostly old, with a little bit of current Washington sprinkled in.

Later in the evening, Colin Powell was seen holding court in the kitchen with a small group of journalists that included Isaacson and Jeffrey Goldberg. Powell appeared to be explaining to everyone *how things really should get done* in This Town, based, of course, on his experience.

I encountered Chris Matthews at the buffet table, the same place he had stormed away from me four years ago. Whenever I see him now, Matthews always mentions "that hatchet job" but says he is no longer mad at me. He does not hold grudges, which he says "proves that I am not really Irish." Good for him. We'll likely never have lunch in This Town, but the shepherd's pie at Sally's buffet was superb.

In the corner, Alan Greenspan and Andrea Mitchell were huddled around a small table with Barbara Walters, Alan's former girlfriend. I overheard Barbara saying something about Jake Tapper, ABC's handsome White House correspondent who that day had announced that he was leaving for CNN, where he would have his own show. Tapper was, at that moment, back in the living room taking congratulations—performing his gracious duty as a destination—while the Alan-Andrea-Barbara trio remained parked in place, nursing their drinks.

I t was around this time that I read a biography of Bradlee written by Jeff Himmelman, a former research assistant for Bob Woodward who had also collaborated on a memoir by Ben and Sally's son, Quinn Bradlee. Published earlier in 2012, the biography, *Yours in*

Truth: A Personal Portrait of Ben Bradlee, had kicked up some major dust inside This Town, mostly because Himmelman included quotations from a 1990 interview that Bradlee gave when writing *A Good Life* in which he seemed to suggest that Woodward might have embellished certain cinematic details about his dealings with Deep Throat. The revelation did not strike anyone as that big of a deal—good editors are supposed to have doubts, and the substantive core of the Watergate stories has certainly held up. But Woodward reacted to the Himmelman book with guns blazing and accused his former protégé of ignoring a 2010 interview Himmelman had conducted with Bradlee in which the editor said he did not think Woodward embellished anything. Sally backed Woodward and said she was speaking for Ben. Himmelman was, needless to say, no longer invited to dinner, let alone The Last Party.

I liked *Yours in Truth*, mostly for its primary-source mine and the window it afforded to Ben at the peak of his powers (via old letters, speeches, and interviews). It portrayed a world, especially after Watergate, in which journalists had entered the cultural spotlight as they never had. Even while this ink-stained Camelot did not last, celebrity sheen lingers on the profession in This Town, with or without the wins. And here we all were.

Bottom line, The Last Party was a good party: comfort food heaped at the buffet, shelter from the elements, and plenty of folk heroes. It barely mattered that the ornate theater held a slight mustiness, that it was a few stages removed from the prime dramas being performed that night on the business ends of Pennsylvania Avenue. Or, for that matter, that it felt worlds removed, more than usual, from the solid ground of the Real America.

It still felt good to be invited—to be part of The Club, at least for now. I watched Bob Schieffer greeting Mike Allen, who would be on CBS's *Face the Nation* that Sunday. There, in the green room,

Allen would take a photo of the red and green Christmas bagels with his iPhone, which we all know because CBS's Major Garrett took a photo of Mikey taking the photo of the bagels, which Garrett then put out on Twitter.

In the course of the night, I twice overheard Susan Rice telling people about her "out-of-body experience," while the historian Michael Beschloss was getting praise for his "awesome Twitter feed" and Woodward and Bernstein walked out together into the rain. Ben disappeared for a while in the middle, but was back in the foyer by the end of The Last Party, bidding farewell to the invited as the caravan moved on.

Epilogue

At the beginning of January, Mike Allen, God bless him, mentioned in Playbook that this tome would be coming out a few months later. He included a blurb from the publisher's catalogue and a link to its Amazon page. He also mentioned the title, *This Town*, a play on the two-word refrain that people (in This Town) put into so many sentences—a cliché of belonging, knowingness, and self-mocking civic disdain. "Well, I guess that's the way it is in *This Town*."

This Town was first suggested to me as a title several months ago by my publisher, David Rosenthal. It has been the working name of the book since, the last in a series of them that has also included "Suck-up City," "You'll Always Have Lunch in This Town Again," and "The Club."

The power of Playbook continues to amaze: After Allen's mention, e-mails flooded in immediately from friends around town, real friends and fake. They congratulated me on being finished with the book (I wasn't) and many of them said they had preordered it (thank you for your service!). In the coming days, I was inundated with queries from people, some through intermediaries, about how they or their clients would be portrayed. Others were worried that they would not be in the book at all. Still others wanted to make sure I would be "taking down" so-and-so in some way, because he/she deserved it. And, by the way, if I took out that tiny thing about them, they would give me something better about one of their "friends."

This pre-release freak-out was itself a corroborating data point: not the most flattering study of This Town doing its vainglorious bidding, in other words. Everyone was so convinced of their outsize place in the grimy ecosystem that, surely, this book had to be about *them*. They feared narcissistic injury, whether by inclusion or omission. At the very least, this desperate hustle reinforced the not-terribly-new assumption that This Town imposes on its actors a reflex toward devious and opportunistic behavior, and also a tendency to care more about public relations than any other aspect of their professional lives—and maybe even personal lives. Several people had warned me this would happen.

I had gotten a taste of the self-loving paranoia a few times as I reported this monster. It was especially pronounced during the Kurt Bardella–Darrell Issa affair. That was when many people first learned that I was writing the book. When Allen wrote of the Bardella saga, he referred to it as my "D.C. takedown book," which is essentially how he described it this time too.

The most stunning by-product to the Playbook mention in January was an e-mail received by at least two of my editors at the *Times* and maybe to others (not to me). It was from Sidney Blumenthal, the former journalist for the *New Republic*, the *New Yorker*, and other places, who became fully intoxicated with the Clintons and joined the White House as a senior adviser in 1997. Caught up in the Lewinsky matter, he was called before Kenneth Starr's grand jury and was also one of three witnesses called to testify at the Senate impeachment trial. Blumenthal was renowned in the Clinton orbit for his egotistical bent, bare-knuckled loyalty, and robust imagination. Coworkers referred to him as "GK," for "Grassy Knoll." He joined Hillary Clinton's presidential campaign in 2007, and Clinton wanted to bring him with her to the State Department until a small White House revolt ensued. When Blumenthal's name came up as a job candidate, Axelrod said he would quit first. Gibbs, sitting next to Axelrod, seconded this. Kibosh.

Last anyone heard, Sid was doing some writing, a book or something.

Back in the 1990s, Blumenthal had apparently written a play called *This Town* about the Washington press corps. I was not aware of this. In the course of my telling my title to dozens of the city's political-media insiders, not a single one mentioned that *This Town* had also been the name of a play. I doubt more than a handful had a clue.

Finally, in late December, as I was leaving The Last Party, Sally Quinn mentioned to me that she liked the title *This Town* and that, by the way, it had also once been the name of a play in the 1990s by Sidney Blumenthal. Who knew? But I was not surprised. It is a good title. Elvis Costello had a song called "This Town," I remembered, and Frank Sinatra, too, I think. It goes without saying that titles cannot be copyrighted.

But Sid was nonetheless aggrieved. His e-mail to my editors—again, not to me—included the subject line "Re: Mark Leibovich: Potential Plagiarism Problem." Yikes.

Blumenthal, whom I think I have met once, began the e-mail by demanding that I acknowledge that he "wrote a widely produced and reviewed satirical play, entitled 'This Town,' on the Washington press corps . . . and that is the origin of the phrase and concept." He boasted that his play had been "prominently staged at the Washington Press Club." He concluded that "of course, titles, unlike trademarks, can't be copyrighted, but they shouldn't be plagiarized.

Perhaps Leibovich is unaware of the problem. Perhaps he was born yesterday. But he should not open himself up to a silly plagiarism problem."

The key word here is "silly," though admittedly my credentials are suspect because I have never had anything "prominently staged at the Washington Press Club." Still, I feel bad to have inflicted hurt unto Blumenthal by overlooking a play that's been forgotten by nearly everyone, in "this" or any town. And by Sidney's own Wikipedia page too. So, in good faith, I will acknowledge that Blumenthal apparently wrote a play in the nineties called *This Town*, and future editions of this book will hereby be known as the New Testament.

As Obama's sequel inauguration approached, dreariness overhung This Town (formal citation: Sidney's play). No one seemed that excited about the quadrennial pageant, especially compared with the historic hopefest of four years earlier. The "peaceful transfer of power" felt more obligatory, especially since no power was being transferred, but even more so because another massive corporate-funded celebration of the political class seemed completely unnecessary and undeserved. Not that this ever stopped anyone before, or that Obama and his helpers didn't deserve a party; but no one's heart seemed really in it.

Plus, everyone seemed to be getting sick with the flu, or worse, or double-worse. Hillary Clinton suffered a nasty concussion and was not heard from for weeks, except when she was checked into the hospital after being diagnosed with a blood clot near her brain. Whoa. Hillary! This Town had big plans for her, had already written her fully into the 2016 narrative. She can't leave yet. (Luckily, she recovered nicely.) George Herbert Walker Bush, the last gentleman, was in and out of intensive care. As is routine these days, at least one outlet—Dallas radio station WBAP, in this case—had to report him prematurely dead. They were first with the news.

The great Richard Ben Cramer died January 7 of a lung cancer that few knew he had. Cramer's exhaustive portraits of presidential candidates in *What It Takes* was the kind of immersive and access-driven blowout that no politician would tolerate today, and probably no writer would have the guts and genius (and indulgent publisher) to pull off. Cramer inspired me in big and small ways. When people ask me why this book has no index, I will point to what Cramer told the *New York Times* in 1992. "For years I watched all these Washington jerks, all these Capitol Hill, executive-branch, agency wise-guys and reporters go into, say, Trover bookstore, take a political book off the shelf, look up their names, glance at the page and put the book back," he said. "Washington reads by index, and I wanted those people to read the damn thing." But Cramer won me over for life in the late nineties when I saw him declare, at a conference in Seattle, that journalism had been "overtaken by a biblical plague of dickheads."

Even Tammy Haddad seemed not her usual Tam-o-sonic self. Her husband, Ted, had been sick with lymphoma, and you could tell the whole thing was taking a toll on the Force of Nature. I saw her a few days before the inauguration, after she returned from her annual hop to Las Vegas for the Miss America Pageant. She was also getting ready to attend the World Economic Forum in Davos, which she does every year—and mentions this a few times. Just as I've never been to Aspen, I've never been to Davos, which makes me sad, though I was able to experience the magic through things like the Twitter feed of my *Times* colleague Andrew Ross Sorkin: "Nice to meet you @johnlegend," @andrewrsorkin wrote. "I've been to good parties @davos before but your performance @sparker's blowout tops them."

In between Vegas and Davos, Tammy would also be producing two big shindigs on inaugural weekend, one for the Daily Beast on Sunday and the other for Third Way at the Old Ebbitt Grill on Monday. She said she convinced the Huffington Post to sign on to the Ebbitt Grill party, which Tammy arranged to be simulcast on her WHC Insider website. But then, on the eve of the festivities, Tammy's mother died and she had to rush to Pittsburgh, leaving This Town to carry on without her.

It wasn't the same. The Sunday thing, at Cafe Milano in Georgetown, offered a high-end diplomatic spread of John Kerry and Colin Powell, a Hollywood sprinkling of Eva Longoria and Harvey Weinstein, and lots of fresh shellfish and cannoli and not-so-fresh moustache-related jokes for David Axelrod, who is always gracious but seemed a bit done with all this. Chris Dodd worked the room, eating a brownie, laughing at everything.

Someone introduced me to Powell, whom I was careful to address as "General," not "Secretary," because he supposedly notices this stuff. (Several Bush White House officials believed this was an attempt by Powell to distance himself from an administration he was at odds with. Matt Latimer, a former Bush speechwriter, suggested this in his memoir, *Speech-less: Tales of a White House Survivor*, which received little notice. But Powell noticed. He fired off an e-mail to Latimer that read, in part: "Someone told you or your speech writers that I preferred the title 'General' after I left the State Department. That is true. In typical paranoid White House fashion, it was thought I was not using the Secretary title in order to distance myself from the President and you guys wrote in 'Secretary' in the President's remarks. At least, that was what you thought. The reality is that 'General' is proper. I was no longer Secretary Powell, but 'former Secretary Powell.' I am never 'former General Powell.'" The e-mail, which Latimer forwarded to me, went on from there.)

Now fully ensconced in his campaign for governor of Virginia,

Washington outsider Terry McAuliffe walked the Cafe Milano red carpet, just like they do in Roanoke. The superlobbyist couple of Heather and Tony Podesta were leaving as I arrived. They had, a few days earlier, announced their separation, "as best friends," and everyone tried to respect their privacy during this difficult time. They said they were off to a Google party.

"Welcome to the land of no eye contact," said Mike Barnicle, the former *Boston Globe* columnist, now fully reinvented as a regular on *Morning Joe*. People kept rushing up to him, excited, because he's on TV now, *a presence*, which is everything. "The fucking pope could be here," Barnicle said between well-wishers, "and if people think you're a fucking weatherman on TV, they're more excited to meet you."

The Huffington Post joint was more of the same. Arianna couldn't make it because she, too, was in Davos, where she sat on a "Will Washington Work?" panel with the likes of Darrell Issa, David Gergen, and a few others for whom Washington has in fact worked quite well. In Arianna's absence, ample star power shined in her stead at the Old Ebbitt Grill. Paula Abdul was leaving a unisex bathroom as I waited to use it. We were introduced by an upstart D.C. publicist, Susan Toffler, and I went to shake Paula's hand but she demanded a hug. Why? "Because I'm a hugger," she shouted, and so Paula and I hugged.

Susan the publicist told me that she and a few others were trying somehow to fill Tammy's unfillable void as the party's prime orchestrators. "We keep asking ourselves, 'What would Tammy do?'" she said, invoking the Force of Nature as one might Jesus. And one day, like Jesus, Tammy will return. But then Susan the upstart publicist was gone, before I could even wish her well and thank her for her service.

The Inauguration itself moved me. This was surprising but shouldn't have been, because I'm moved every time no matter who's taking the oath. I spent much of the day wandering the streets: orderly frozen crowds, more diverse than usual in D.C., filing toward the Mall and parade route. Kids sat on parents' shoulders waving little flags, a street-corner chorus sang "God Bless America." These were good moments on one of those stately occasions that transcend the serial battering that This Town inflicts. The monuments were scrubbed clean and the Metro was mobbed but festive and on time. I ducked into a bar to watch the president's speech on TV. It was crisp and short, and then I started reading tweets until I was jarred from my handheld trance by David Gregory on TV, distilling for America the momentous proceedings before her.

"I think what we've learned from this president," he said, restoring the narrative to its pundit lingua franca, "is that his outside game is much better than his inside game." Well, yes, if we've learned anything.

And the future was officially under way again in This Town.

Acknowledgments

Infinite thanks to Arthur Sulzberger, Jill Abramson, Dean Baquet, Bill Keller, and everyone at the *New York Times* for your support professionally and, even more so, personally. You run the best newspaper in the world, but more important, you know what matters.

Thanks to Rick Berke for bringing me to the *Times* and looking after me, and to Janet Elder for being an angel. In the Washington bureau, to David Leonhardt, Carl Hulse, Bill Hamilton, Paul Volpe, and researcher supreme Kitty Bennett (!). Dick Stevenson, a fantastic journalist, has been a great mentor and friend. Rebecca Corbett, the editor here whom everyone wants, was mine for five years, and she made everything about coming to work better, especially the finished product. She is, foremost, a wonderful pal.

I'm in daily awe of my fellow reporters here. I'll exclude some if I start throwing out names (Zeleny, Rutenberg, Nagourney), but as my real-time co-masochists in this book-work-dad juggle, Peter Baker and Mark Mazzetti get special exemptions. Columnists Maureen Dowd and David Brooks are menschen across the spectrum, and I think about Robin Toner all the time.

Since I joined the *Times Magazine* last year, Hugo Lindgren's distinctive genius has been a boon. He has also been a patient, indulgent, and wickedly fun boss, especially as I've finished this project. It'll be good to have him as a friend when we're both run out of our respective towns. Joel Lovell is a rock-solid, whimsical, and risk-encouraging editor who is also skilled at saving me from myself. Thanks, too, to Gerald Marzorati and Megan Liberman for letting me write for the magazine as a novice and for teaching me the joys of it. Stuart Emmrich and Laura Marmor in "Styles" are a pleasure to write for when the spheres align. I feel an enduring affection and gratitude for Don Graham and everyone at the *Washington Post*, a great newspaper where I spent nine familial years.

So many people—in This Town and beyond—have nurtured these pages. They include a special cabinet of wise men (and "Weisman," i.e., Steve), Frank Foer, Dan Balz, Rajiv Chandrasekaran, Anne Kornblut, Hank Stuever, Susan Glasser, Ned Zeman, and Matt Brune, and a bipartisan council of friends/readers/sources whom I can't acknowledge by name, for obvious reasons and sensitivities. We'll all have lunch again after an appropriate interlude.

Elyse Cheney is the best agent! Exclamation point! (Special thanks to Alex Jacobs at Cheney Literary.)

David Rosenthal at Blue Rider/Penguin is the real father of this book. I don't know what that makes me (the bastard son?), but David was its first inspiration at Simon & Schuster, and I was lucky to follow him to Penguin. He has handled me with humanity, hilarity, and guts. He is everything a writer would want in an editor and publisher. Associate publisher Aileen Boyle is a total pro, and I'll be thrilled to have her at my side in the next phase of the adventure. Thanks also to Linda Cowen, Linda Rosenberg, Phoebe Pickering, Eliza Rosenberry, Gregg Kulick, David Chesanow, Janice Kurzius, and Anna Jardine.

Grateful to all at the Wilson Center for their hospitality in 2011; props to the awesome researcher Molly Corbett, daughter of the awesome Rebecca, and to Lindsay Crouse, my researcher/fact-checker extraordinaire during the nervous-breakdown phase.

This book is dedicated to my family, which encompasses a far-flung brood of non-blood members: my oldest pal, Josh King, and the King family; Paul Farhi and all the Farhim; endless affection for my Michigan and Boston friends, and also the Oyster-Adams *comunidad*. Greatly cherish the family's kibbutzian life-merge with Hanna Rosin, David Plotz, and all the Markey-Daveys, with whom we share the most sacred of occasions and ordinary of minivans.

Big and eternal love to my parents, Joan and Miguel Leibovich, whose grace, survival skills, and unconditional support have sustained and inspired me; and to my amazing sister, Lori Leibovich, whose love and friendship I will hold dear forever. Parents 2.0 Ted Sutton and Betty Grossman are godsends, as are in-laws Jack and Barbara Kolbrener, *hermanos* Bill and Michael Kolbrener, and Larry Kanter (of Resistor!), and kids 2.0 Carlos and Clara Kanter. I am guided every day by the memory of my brother, Phil Leibovich, but mostly I just miss him.

Best for last: To my daughters, Nell, Lizey, and Franny, who make my heart grow about a million sizes every day. I could never put this crazy love for you into words. Likewise, my wife, Meri Kolbrener, who has always been too grounded—not of This Town—to care about public shout-outs. "Just don't make me seem long-suffering," she told me. So I'll skip the part about Meri's sacrifices for this damn thing over three years—solo parenting, etc.—and just say that she makes it all possible and joyful, and me the luckiest.

Notes

This book is the product of more than three hundred interviews, some of which were conducted in the course of reporting stories for the *New York Times* and *New York Times Magazine*. Portions of this text have appeared previously in those publications and, for any material gathered before 2006, in the *Washington Post*. I rely additionally on quotations and information that have appeared in other media outlets, including books and, in many cases, memoirs. When the source is not noted directly in the text, the citation appears below.

Prologue

Page 1   *Gibbs is the son of librarians:* Mark Leibovich, "Between Obama and the Press," *New York Times*, December 17, 2008.

Page 2   *Gibbs once called Axe "the guy who walks":* Mark Leibovich, "Message Maven Finds Fingers Pointing at Him," *New York Times*, March 6, 2010.

Page 4   *"Your Majesty, this is one of our premier American journalists":* Andrea Mitchell, *Talking Back* (New York: Penguin, 2006), 177.

Page 6   *Duberstein made inquiries about running his theoretical transition team:* Jake Tapper, "McCain Camp: Duberstein Lobbied to Be Our Transition Chief; Duberstein Calls That 'Bulls***,'" ABC News, October 21, 2008.

Page 6   *"All of the most important people in politics and media are in the same room":* Anne Schroeder Mullins, "The Russert Memorial," Politico, June 19, 2008.

Page 9   *Washington has defied the national economic slump:* Derek Thompson,

"Report: Washington, D.C., Is Now the Richest U.S. City," *The Atlantic*, October 19, 2011.

Page 13   *"Did he use me? Of course he used me":* Jeff Himmelman, *Yours in Truth: A Personal Portrait of Ben Bradlee* (New York: Random House, 2012), 78.

Page 14   *some of them (18.7 percent) even below the poverty line:* Mike DeBonis, "Census: D.C. Poverty Rates Stay Level as Incomes Rise," *Washington Post*, September 20, 2012.

Chapter 1. Heaven's Green Room

Page 21   *"that handful of insiders who invent":* Joan Didion, *Political Fictions* (New York: Vintage, 2002), 22.

Page 23   *In an interview with* Playboy *years earlier, Matthews volunteered:* Mark Leibovich, "The Aria of Chris Matthews," *New York Times*, April 13, 2008.

Page 24   *Sally Quinn, an avowed atheist for much of her life:* Sally Quinn, "The Faith and Joy of Russert," *Washington Post*, June 23, 2008.

Page 24   *"Senator Kennedy on the left!":* Dana Milbank, "Russert's Grand Goodbye," *Washington Post*, June 19, 2008.

Page 25   *"If he's dead or alive, it doesn't matter":* Mark Leibovich, "Fall from the Top Lands McCain in a Scaled-Back Comfort Zone," *New York Times*, October 7, 2007.

Page 26   *"To whom much is given, much is expected":* Dana Milbank, "Russert's Grand Goodbye," *Washington Post*, June 19, 2008.

Page 27   *"In a Washington way":* Jason Horowitz, "Before Meeting the Press, They Met Green Room Attendant 'Mr. Aly,'" *Washington Post*, January 26, 2011.

Page 31   *"A man's either trying to make up for his father's mistakes":* Jon Meacham, "On His Own," *Newsweek*, August 22, 2008.

Page 32   *"Is anyone still an atheist now?":* Tammy Haddad, "The Russert Miracles," Daily Beast, June 19, 2008.

Page 32   *"No benign deity plucks television news show hosts":* Christopher Hitchens, "Mourning Glory," Slate, June 23, 2008.

Chapter 2. Suck-up City

Page 35   *"The founding fathers, whose infinite wisdom gave us a Constitution":* Jack Lait and Lee Mortimer, *Washington Confidential* (New York: Kessinger, 2009), 14.

Page 35   *His image had been "tarnished":* Greg Ip, "His Legacy Tarnished, Greenspan Goes on Defensive," *Wall Street Journal*, April 8, 2008.

Page 37   *"She knows where to draw the line":* Brian Stelter, "For Greenspan's Wife, Covering the Financial Crisis Is on a Case-by-Case Basis," *New York Times*, October 12, 2008.

Page 37   *like Laura Bush covering the federal government's reaction to Katrina:* Megan Garber, "The Elephant in the Control Room," *Columbia Journalism Review*, September 24, 2008.

Page 37   *"We see a distinction between pure analysis of the bailout":* Don Kaplan, "Near Mrs.," *New York Post*, September 29, 2008.

Page 40   *"back to school and get a postgraduate degree":* John Harwood and Gerald F. Seib, *Pennsylvania Avenue* (New York: Random House, 2008), 134.

Page 41   *People who worked on the Obama transition staff received:* Jonathan Alter, *The Promise: Obama Year One* (New York: Simon & Schuster, 2010), 16.

Page 44   *"No one who has ever passed through American public high school":* Joan Didion, *Political Fictions* (New York: Vintage, 2002), 215.

Page 44   *"Loners may be able to sell themselves electorally":* Meg Greenfield, *Washington* (New York: PublicAffairs, 2009), 36.

Page 45   *"One thing our founding fathers could not foresee":* Ronald Reagan, "Meet the Students" taping for television, Sacramento, California, September 17, 1973.

Page 47   *Speaking of Teddy, it was Mike Allen:* Mike Allen, "In Buffalo, President to Make Aggressive Case on Economy," Politico, May 13, 2010.

Page 47   *"In a world in which we all tend to pay not enough attention":* Erik Wemple, "Why Is Politico's Cash Cow Asking Readers to 'Support Our Journalism'?" *Washington Post*, November 29, 2011.

Page 47   *Allen even included the name "Washington Superlawyer Robert Barnett":* Mike Allen, "Dems Sketch Obama Staff, Cabinet," Politico, October 31, 2008.

Page 48   *"If God were writing the Bible again":* Ellen Gamerman, "He Makes Deals for D.C. Elite," *Baltimore Sun*, July 6, 2004.

Page 49   *"To list Barnett as a signifier of Washington connectedness":* David Montgomery, "Washington Lawyer Bob Barnett Is the Force Behind Many Political Book Deals," *Washington Post*, March 7, 2010.

Page 50   *Barnett is bipartisan:* Peter Lattman, "Washington Law Firm

Finds Niche in Sports and Entertainment," *New York Times*, June 21, 2012.

Page 52   *"Robert Barnett, who also represents the president-elect":* Mike Allen, "Publishers Jump at Plouffe Book," Politico, December 5, 2008.

Page 54   *"felt this thrill going up my leg":* "Chris Matthews: 'I Felt This Thrill Going Up My Leg' As Obama Spoke," Huffington Post, May 25, 2011.

Page 54   *a reported nineteen would join the administration:* Michael Hastings, *Panic 2012: The Sublime and Terrifying Inside Story of Obama's Final Campaign* (New York: Blue Rider Press, 2013), 65.

Page 54   *"As Barack Obama stacks his staff with studs":* "Hotties of the Obama Cabinet," New York *Daily News*, January 9, 2009.

Page 55   *"honor Robert and Mary Catherine Gibbs with drinks, laughs":* Mark Leibovich, "Between Obama and the Press," *New York Times*, December 17, 2008.

Page 55   *Obama ate portobello mushroom salad:* Mark Leibovich, "The Making of a New Washington Insider," *New York Times*, January 16, 2009.

Page 58   *"the best brand on earth: the Obama brand":* Amy Chozick, "Desirée Rogers' Brand Obama," *Wall Street Journal*, April 30, 2009.

Page 58   *"Obama's People":* Nadav Kander, "Obama's People," *New York Times*, 2009.

Page 58   *The appetite was insatiable:* Mark Leibovich, "Minutiae? In This White House, Call It News," *New York Times*, March 13, 2009.

Page 60   *the new president's hair was going gray:* Helene Cooper, "For Young President, Flecks of Gray," *New York Times*, March 4, 2009.

Page 60   *a withering profile of Arianna:* Maureen Orth, "Arianna's Virtual Candidate," *Vanity Fair*, November 1994.

Page 64   *"The social question is, Who are the closest people to the Obamas personally?"* Julie Bosman, "The Pleasure of His Company," *New York Times*, January 2, 2009.

Page 65   *None of these donors have been disclosed:* John Cook, "White House Refuses to Release Donors to David Axelrod's Charity," Gawker, November 29, 2010.

Chapter 3. Three Senators for Our Times

Page 69   *"A man never stands taller than when he is down":* Jonathan Alter, *The Promise: Obama Year One* (New York: Simon & Schuster, 2010), 166.

Page 71   *"So I say to John Kerry": Congressional Record*, vol. 153, pt. 2, January 18–February 1, 2007.

Page 74   *He once drew a favorable parallel between his press secretary:* Mark Leibovich, "Between Obama and the Press," *New York Times*, December 17, 2008.

Page 80   *Reid writes about how his father was never as happy:* Harry Reid with Mark Warren, *The Good Fight: Hard Lessons from Searchlight to Washington* (New York: Berkley, 2009), 36.

Page 81   *Reid's unfavorable rating in Nevada had risen to 52 percent:* Laura Myers, "Reid Hits New Low in Poll," *Las Vegas Review-Journal*, January 9, 2010.

Page 81   *"Reid fatigue," diagnosed Ralston:* "Reid's Public Option Push Comes amid Tough Re-election Bid," CNN, November 2, 2009.

Page 81   *"in the event that he could not carry out his duties":* Mark Leibovich, "Despite Fragile Health, Byrd Is Present for Votes," *New York Times*, December 24, 2009.

Page 83   *I wrote a profile of the brash Pennsylvania Republican:* Mark Leibovich, "Father First, Senator Second," *Washington Post*, April 18, 2005.

Page 85   *"The sensation of stepping inside the Inner Ring of Congress":* Tom A. Coburn with John Hart, *Breach of Trust: How Washington Turns Outsiders into Insiders* (Nashville: WND Books, 2003), 32.

Page 86   *"spiritual godfather":* Peter Boyer, "Budget Debate's 'Dr. Maybe,'" *Newsweek*, July 25, 2011.

Page 87   *his vote could not be bought but "could be rented":* Jacob S. Hacker and Paul Pierson, *Winner-Take-All Politics: How Washington Made the Rich Richer—And Turned Its Back on the Middle Class* (New York: Simon & Schuster, 2011), 6.

Page 90   *"waterboarding" his five grandchildren:* Mark Leibovich, "A Senate Naysayer, Spoiling for Health Care Fight," *New York Times*, October 29, 2009.

Page 91   *"one of the most influential and conservative members":* Steve Kroft, "Is the U.S. Senate Broken?" *60 Minutes*, CBS News, November 4, 2012.

Chapter 4. The Entourage

Page 93   *the unemployment rate was approaching 10 percent:* National Conference of State Legislatures, "Unemployment Drops to 7.6 Percent for March 2013," April 8, 2013.

Page 98   *special interests collectively spent $3.47 billion:* Communications, "Federal Lobbying Climbs in 2009 as Lawmakers Execute Aggressive Congressional Agenda," Open Secrets, February 12, 2010.

Page 98   *"This agenda has been great for OUR economy":* Arthur Delaney, "It's Official: 2009 Was Record Year for Lobbying, Despite Recession," Huffington Post, April 14, 2010.

Page 100   *"No single development has altered the workings of American democracy":* Jill Lepore, "The Lie Factory," *The New Yorker,* September 24, 2012.

Page 101   *"Those inside the process had congealed into a permanent political class":* Joan Didion, *Political Fictions* (New York: Vintage, 2002), 9.

Page 101   *"this wild self-congratulatory ski-jump":* Jeff Himmelman, *Yours in Truth: A Personal Portrait of Ben Bradlee* (New York: Random House, 2012), 323.

Page 103   *By the time he left to run for Congress:* Michael Luo, "In Banking, Emanuel Made Money and Connections," *New York Times,* December 3, 2008.

Page 103   *The dinner has sold out every table since 1993:* Todd Purdum, "The Evolution of D.C.'s Premier Event," *Vanity Fair,* April 30, 2010.

Page 104   *"If either of them had been in love with a tree surgeon":* Walter Shapiro, "Star-Crossed Politicos," *Time,* June 24, 2001.

Page 109   *It was suddenly news in the capital:* Mark Leibovich, "Titillating or Not, Washington Gossip Blossoms," *New York Times,* February 3, 2007.

Page 109   *I authored a story on the proliferation of flies:* Mark Leibovich, "What Has 132 Rooms and Flies?" *New York Times,* June 17, 2009.

Chapter 5. Embedding

Page 113   *a New York Times Magazine story about Mike Allen:* Mark Leibovich, "The Man the White House Wakes Up To," *New York Times Magazine,* April 21, 2010.

Chapter 6. "Thank You for Your Service"

Page 129   *June profile of General Stanley McChrystal:* Michael Hastings, "The Runaway General," *Rolling Stone,* July 8–22, 2010.

Page 130 *$60,000 a pop for speaking gigs:* David Gura, "Gen. Stanley McChrystal Reportedly Earns $60,000 per Speaking Engagement," NPR, August 30, 2010.

Pages 130–31 *Some members of McChrystal's staff said as much:* Sean D. Naylor, "Sources: *Rolling Stone* Quotes Made by Jr. Staff," *Army Times*, July 7, 2010. Howard Kurtz, "Rolling Stone's McChrystal Interview Shows the Magazine's Nonmusical Side," *Washington Post*, June 24, 2010.

Page 131 *Hastings was quizzed:* CNN *Reliable Sources* transcript, interviews with Michael Hastings and Lara Logan, June 27, 2010.

Page 132 *"If there's a lower form of life":* Matt Taibbi, "Lara Logan, You Suck," *Rolling Stone*, June 28, 2010.

Page 136 *"too many d-bags":* Kiki Ryan, "Tammy Haddad's Brunch 'Fun, Personal,'" Politico, April 30, 2010.

Page 139 *"There's just something about her that pisses people off":* Henry Louis Gates, Jr., "Hating Hillary," *The New Yorker*, February 26, 1996.

Page 139 *"Anyone who sleeps with that bitch deserves a medal":* John F. Harris, *The Survivor: Bill Clinton in the White House* (New York: Random House, 2006), 357.

Page 139 *"outraged by the president's behavior":* Sally Quinn, "In Washington, That Letdown Feeling," *Washington Post*, November 2, 1998.

Page 140 *"24/7 echo-chamber":* Remarks by the President at the University of Michigan Spring Commencement, The White House, May 1, 2010.

Page 140 *"Japan Surrenders—Where's the Bounce?":* Remarks by the President at the White House Correspondents' Association dinner, The White House, May 2, 2010.

Page 141 *"You know, Alsop":* Purdum, "The Evolution of D.C.'s Premier Event," *Vanity Fair*, April 30, 2010.

Page 142 *spearheaded a $50 million television campaign:* Aaron Smith, "BP's Television Ad Blitz," CNN, June 4, 2010.

Page 143 *Governor Haley Barbour of Mississippi had to stay home:* Mark Leibovich, "Terry McAuliffe and the Other Green Party," *New York Times*, July 18, 2012.

Page 151 *"One of the reasons they wanted to hire me":* "First Mover: Ed Henry," *Adweek*, September 12, 2011.

Page 152 Chronology of events: Frank Rich, "They Report, You Don't Have to Decide," *New York Times*, May 8, 2010.

Page 153 Rachel Sklar, "From 'Lone Wolf' to Taliban: The Disconnect in the Developing Times Square Bombing Story," Mediaite, May 6, 2010.

Page 154 *The guy memorizes four words":* Bill Sammon, "Bush Mocks and Dismisses NBC White House Correspondent," *Washington Times*, May 27, 2002.

Chapter 7. The Roach Motel of Power

Page 158 *He is the five-term senator:* Mark Leibovich, "Dodd Prepares to Depart in Triumph," *New York Times*, May 24, 2010.

Page 158 *He worked as a Senate page:* David Halbfinger, "Citing Tough Race, Dodd Steps Aside," *New York Times*, January 6, 2010.

Page 161 *"Tip O'Neill once came down here":* Mark Leibovich, " 'Top-Tier' Candidate? Maybe Not, but Dodd Is Still Enjoying the Ride," *New York Times*, April 28, 2007.

Page 166 *David Obey . . . joined the lobbying shop run by former colleague Richard Gephardt:* Thomas Edsall, "The Trouble with That Revolving Door," *New York Times*, December 18, 2011.

Page 166 *a lobbyist who was being paid about $70,000 a month:* Dan Eggen, "Armenia–Turkey Dispute over Genocide Label Sets off Lobbying Frenzy," *Washington Post*, March 4, 2010.

Page 167 *Susan Bayh as a "professional board member":* Sylvia Smith, "Across the Boards," Fort Wayne *Journal Gazette*, December 16, 2007.

Page 167 *"perfectly representative face for the rotted Washington establishment":* Glenn Greenwald, "The Face of Rotted Washington," Salon, November 30, 2009.

Page 168 *"acting to entrench the culture of narcissism and hypocrisy":* Matthew Yglesias, "Evan Bayh's Narcissism," ThinkProgress, December 16, 2009.

Page 168 *Evan Bayh wrote a much-discussed op-ed:* Evan Bayh, "Why I'm Leaving the Senate," *New York Times*, February 20, 2010.

Page 169 *"They look at us like we're worse than used-car salesmen":* Ezra Klein, "In Congress, Fundraising's Steep Price," *Washington Post*, October 31, 2010.

Page 169 *"practically a caricature of what a sell-out looks like":* Steve Benen, "Evan Bayh and a Never-Ending Series of Disappointments," *Washington Monthly*, June 7, 2011.

Page 169 *congressman-turned-lobbyist Billy Tauzin:* Alex Wayne and Drew Armstrong, "Tauzin's $11.6 Million Made Him Highest-Paid Health-Law Lobbyist," Bloomberg, November 29, 2011.

Page 170 *Their company would bring in $11 million:* Silla Brush, "Patton Boggs Acquires Lobbying Firm of Former Sens. Lott, Breaux," *The Hill*, July 1, 2010.

Chapter 8. How It Works

Page 183 *story that explored whether excessive BlackBerry use:* Erika Lovley, "BlackBerry, Forbidden Fruit?" Politico, October 28, 2009.

Page 183 *"I haven't sent a press release":* Ben White, "Bernanke Gives Highly-Anticipated Speech at 10 a.m.," Politico, August 27, 2010.

Page 184 *"It is only 11:30 a.m. but Kurt Bardella is on his third Red Bull":* Andie Coller, "Blasting Politicos," Politico, July 20, 2009.

Page 184 *"I don't ever stop":* Erika Lovley, "Is Congress a Health Threat?" Politico, January 15, 2010.

Page 184 *"It rubbed a lot of folks the wrong way":* Luke Mullins, "The Comeback," *Washingtonian*, July 2011.

Page 188 Los Angeles Times *exposé that was published:* Erik Lichtblau, "Issa's Rags-to-Riches Tale Has Some Ugly Chapters," *Los Angeles Times*, May 23, 1998.

Page 189 *felony charges related to car thefts in 1972 and 1980:* Mark Leibovich, "Republican Emerges as Obama's Annoyer-in-Chief," *New York Times*, July 6, 2010.

Page 189 *"notorious hatchet man":* Erik Wemple, *"New York Times* and Rep. Issa: A Spat to Remember," *Washington Post*, September 8, 2011.

Page 192 *Howard Kurtz conducted a phone interview with Issa:* Howard Kurtz, "The GOP's New Top Cop," Daily Beast, November 27, 2010.

Page 193 *Ryan Lizza, who was profiling Issa for the* New Yorker: Ryan Lizza, "Don't Look Back," *The New Yorker*, January 24, 2011.

Page 194 *Barbara Walters herself, the queen of the "get":* Bill Carter, "Barbara Walters Apologizes for Helping Aide to Assad of Syria," *New York Times*, June 5, 2012.

Page 195 *It was assumed that the job would go to Edolphus Towns:* Betsy Woodruff, "Elijah Cummings, Party Man," *National Review*, October 23, 2012.

Page 218 *"I did lose my way a little bit"*: Mark Walker, "Exclusive: Former Issa Spokesman Breaks Silence," *North County Times*, March 18, 2011.

Page 221 *"As long as her candidacy does not completely implode"*: Kurt Bardella, "Bachmann Can Win by Losing," Daily Caller, May 16, 2011.

Chapter 9. Performing Arts

Page 225 *"The Ego Has Landed"*: Al Kamen, "In the Loop," *Washington Post*, April 27, 2009.

Page 225 *"He would overdo all this flattery"*: Bill Clinton, eulogy delivered at Richard Holbrooke's funeral, Kennedy Center, January 14, 2011.

Page 226 *"Do people really talk like that?"*: Rajiv Chandrasekaran, *Little America: The War Within the War for Afghanistan* (New York: Alfred A. Knopf, 2012), 230.

Page 226 *"the most egotistical bastard I've ever met"*: Peter Baker, "Woodward Book Says Afghanistan Divided White House," *New York Times*, September 21, 2010.

Page 228 *free to fire Holbrooke "over the objection of your secretary of state"*: Chandrasekaran, *Little America*, 229.

Page 229 *They tried to exclude him from an Oval Office confab:* Ibid., 230.

Page 226 *One major sore point:* James Mann, *The Obamians: The Struggle Inside the White House to Redefine American Power* (New York: Viking, 2012), 234.

Page 244 *In March, Kati received a postcard:* Kati Marton, *Paris: A Love Story* (New York: Simon & Schuster, 2012), 32.

Chapter 10. Anarchy in the Quiet Car

Page 252 *"BP America, facing a spate of investigations"*: Mike Allen, "BP America Hires Geoff Morrell," Politico, September 5, 2011.

Page 254 *exploding to $2.51 billion:* Danielle Ivory, "BP's U.S. Defense Contracts Doubled Since Year of Gulf Oil Spill," Bloomberg, February 6, 2013.

Page 255 *"made nerdy sexy"*: Jodi Kantor, "Obama's Man on the Budget: Just 40 and Going Like 60," *New York Times*, March 27, 2009.

Page 255 *a divorced father of two with a very important job gets very publicly engaged:* Mark Leibovich, "If Peter Orszag Is So Smart, What Will He Do Now?" *New York Times*, January 8, 2010.

Page 256 *I wrote a profile . . . about Ray LaHood:* Mark Leibovich, "G.O.P. Résumé, Cabinet Post, Knack for Odd Jobs," *New York Times*, May 4, 2009.

Chapter 11. The Presidential Campaign: This Movie Again

Page 262 *"Ricchetti has been through the revolving door":* Dana Milbank, "Settling In to Washington's Ways," *Washington Post*, March 6, 2012.

Page 263 *"threat to our democracy":* Sam Stein, "President Obama Softens Super PAC Opposition," Huffington Post, February 6, 2012.

Page 263 *Bloomberg News reported that . . . Jim Messina:* Hans Nichols, "Obama Campaign Chief Messina Seeks to Assure Wall Street Donors," Bloomberg, February 8, 2012.

Page 273 *forty-five-minute sit-down in the Oval Office:* Jeffrey Goldberg, "Obama to Iran and Israel: 'As President of the United States, I Don't Bluff,'" *The Atlantic*, March 2, 2012.

Page 276 *Burns's story in Politico was one of the election cycle's seminal:* Alexander Burns, "How Much Do Voters Know?" Politico, March 13, 2012.

Page 277 *"Are voters stupid?" story:* Jason Linkins, "Are Voters Stupid, or Are They Just Routinely Subjected to Terrible Political Reporting?" Huffington Post, March 15, 2012.

Page 278 *"The trip spurred a thought":* Jodi Kantor, *The Obamas* (New York: Little, Brown, 2013), 161.

Page 292 *a reported $5 million advance:* Matthew Flamm, "Penguin Press Pays Mega Bucks for Political Book," *Crain's New York Business*, March 25, 2010.

Chapter 12. The Presidential Campaign: Saddened, Troubled

Page 297 *"The First Gay President":* Andrew Sullivan, "Obama: The First Gay President," *Newsweek*, May 13, 2012.

Page 297 *"Obama Stumbles out of the Gate":* Mike Allen and Jim VandeHei, "Obama Stumbles out of the Gate," Politico, May 25, 2012.

Page 298 *"I know three, personally":* Mary Bruce, "White House Distances Itself from Hilary Rosen," ABC News, April 12, 2012.

Page 299 *A 2003 profile of Rosen:* Matt Bai, "Hating Hilary," *Wired*, February 2003.

Page 302 *political system as a "closed game":* Jack Mirkinson, "Tom Brokaw Doubles Down on WHCD: 'If You Go, It'll Steal Your Soul,'" Huffington Post, May 8, 2012.

Page 303 *The unemployment rate still languished at 8.2 percent:* Bureau of Labor Statistics, "The Employment Situation in May 2012," June 4, 2012.

Page 304 *the median net worth of an American family dropped:* Binyamin Appelbaum, "Family Net Worth Drops to Level of Early '90s, Fed Says," *New York Times*, June 11, 2012.

Page 304 *the top 150 consulting companies had already grossed:* Howard Fineman, "Political Consultants Rake It In, $466 Million and Counting in 2012 Cycle," Huffington Post, June 5, 2012.

Page 306 *"Being a vice president is a little":* Mark Leibovich, "For a Blunt Biden, an Uneasy Supporting Role," *New York Times*, May 7, 2012.

Page 307 *July was the hottest month ever recorded:* Joanna Foster, "What Cornfields Show, Data Now Confirm: July Set Mark as U.S.'s Hottest Month," *New York Times*, August 8, 2012.

Page 308 *It "uncomfortably calls to mind the rapacious Capitol":* David Leonhardt, "Why D.C. Is Doing So Well," *New York Times*, August 4, 2012.

Page 309 *a comparison to Margaret Thatcher:* Joshua Green, "The Hillary Clinton Memos," *The Atlantic*, August 11, 2008.

Page 312 *The majority leader also noted that George Romney:* Jonathan Capehart, "On Tax Returns, Mitt Won't Follow the Leader— His Dad," *Washington Post*, July 11, 2012.

Page 312 *Mitt had not paid taxes for ten years:* Sam Stein and Ryan Grim, "Harry Reid: Bain Investor Told Me That Mitt Romney 'Didn't Pay Any Taxes for 10 Years,'" Huffington Post, July 31, 2012.

Chapter 13. The Presidential Campaign: Belly Flops, Bourbon Chocolate Truffles, and Wonderful Ruins

Page 326 *"A prime-time belly-flop":* John F. Harris and Tim Mak, "Chris Christie's Flop at the GOP Convention," Politico, August 29, 2012.

Page 328 *"second-tier city":* Mark Leibovich, "In a Swirl of Excess, No Guilt Included," *New York Times*, September 7, 2012.

Page 329 *$5 million in corporate donations:* "Democratic Convention Used Corporate Cash, Despite Pledge to Only Use Funds from Individuals," Associated Press, October 18, 2012.

Page 329 *Tony's name had shown up twenty-seven times:* T. W. Farnam, "White House Visitor Logs Provide Window into the Lobbying Industry," *Washington Post*, May 20, 2012.

Page 330 *The* Atlantic *had just reported:* Elliot Gerson, "To Make America Great Again, We Need to Leave the Country," *The Atlantic*, July 10, 2012.

Page 331 *a total compensation of about $126 million between 1999 and 2009:* Eric Dash and Louise Story, "Rubin Leaving Citigroup; Smith Barney for Sale," *New York Times*, January 9, 2009.

Page 333 *had tried to join the Congressional Black Caucus:* Josephine Hearn, "Black Caucus: Whites Not Allowed," Politico, January 22, 2007.

Page 334 *"Absolutely, I would buy a new car from Terry":* Mark Leibovich, "Terry McAuliffe and the Other Green Party," *New York Times*, July 18, 2012.

Page 337 *"After Tuesday, one thing is certain":* Benjamin Freed, "Terry McAuliffe Is Running for Governor, Again," DCist, November 9, 2012.

Page 338 *"a very serious proctology exam":* Elyse Siegel, "Haley Barbour Recommends 'Proctology Exam' for Republicans Following Election," Huffington Post, November 16, 2012.

Page 340 *Jim DeMint, the Senate's most celebrated spending hard-liner:* Jennifer Steinhauer, "Tea Party Hero Is Leaving the Senate for a New Pulpit," *New York Times*, December 7, 2012.

Page 343 *"the Nepotist Prince":* Alex Pareene, "Luke Russert, Nepotist Prince," Salon, May 24, 2012.

Page 345 *Jarrett ordering a drink from a four-star general:* Jo Becker, "The Other Power in the West Wing," *New York Times*, September 1, 2012.

Chapter 14. The Last Party

Page 352 *"For the first time, really, I felt":* Ben Bradlee, *A Good Life: News-papering and Other Adventures* (New York: Simon & Schuster, 1996), 350.

Page 352 *"So we have a split decision":* Mike Allen, "Fiscal Patch: GOP Leaders Split . . . ," Politico, January 2, 2013.

Page 355 *"not very bright" and "not qualified":* Kevin Robillard, "John McCain: Susan Rice 'Not Qualified' for State," Politico, November 14, 2012.

Page 356 *"I don't know Rice at all":* Thomas Friedman, "My Secretary of State," *New York Times*, November 27, 2012.

Page 356 *Rice gave him the finger:* Lloyd Grove, "Susan Rice's Personality 'Disorder,'" Daily Beast, December 12, 2012.

Page 357 *"the presumptive dean of Washington journalism":* Conor Friedersdorf, "The Right's Jennifer Rubin Problem: A Case Study in Info Disadvantage," *The Atlantic*, November 8, 2012.

Page 358 *Published earlier in 2012, the biography:* Jeff Himmelman, *Yours in Truth: A Personal Portrait of Ben Bradlee* (New York: Random House, 2012).

Page 359 *Woodward reacted to the Himmelman book with guns blazing:* Dylan Byers, "Jeff Himmelman Calls Out Bob Woodward," Politico, April 30, 2012.

Epilogue

Page 363 *Clinton wanted to bring him with her to the State Department:* Peter Baker and Jeff Zeleny, "Emanuel Wields Power Freely, and Faces the Risks," *New York Times*, August 15, 2009.

Pages 364–65 *at least one outlet . . . WBAP . . . had to report him prematurely dead:* Eric Nicholson, "WBAP Announces Death of George H. W. Bush, Quickly Realizes He's Not Actually Dead," *Dallas Observer*, December 28, 2012.

Page 365 *"For years I watched all these Washington jerks":* Margalit Fox, "Richard Ben Cramer, Writer of Big Ambitions, Dies at 62," *New York Times*, January 8, 2013.

About the Author

Mark Leibovich is chief national correspondent for the *New York Times Magazine*, based in Washington, D.C. In 2011, he received a National Magazine Award for his story on Politico's Mike Allen and the new media culture of D.C. Before working at the *Times Magazine*, Leibovich was a national political correspondent in the paper's Washington bureau. He previously worked for the *Washington Post* and the *San Jose Mercury News*. He is the author of *The New Imperialists: How Five Restless Kids Grew Up to Virtually Rule Your World*. Leibovich lives with his family in Washington.